THE WISDOM OF THE LIMINAL

The Wisdom of the Liminal

Evolution and Other Animals
in Human Becoming

Celia Deane-Drummond

William B. Eerdmans Publishing Company
Grand Rapids, Michigan / Cambridge, U.K.

Published 2014 by
Wm. B. Eerdmans Publishing Co.
2140 Oak Industrial Drive N.E., Grand Rapids, Michigan 49505 /
P.O. Box 163, Cambridge CB3 9PU U.K.

Printed in the United States of America

19 18 17 16 15 14 7 6 5 4 3 2 1

Library of Congress Cataloging-in-Publication Data

Deane-Drummond, Celia.
The wisdom of the liminal: evolution and other animals in human becoming /
Celia Deane-Drummond.
pages cm
Includes bibliographical references and index.
ISBN 978-0-8028-6867-1 (pbk.: alk. paper)
1. Theological anthropology — Christianity.
2. Animals — Religious aspects — Christianity.
I. Title.

BT701.3.D45 2014
233'.5 — dc23

2014012171

www.eerdmans.com

In memoriam

Anthony John Deane-Drummond

June 23rd 1917–December 4th 2012

RIP

Contents

Acknowledgments

This book has taken over four years to complete, and, as a consequence, I owe a debt of gratitude to many colleagues and friends who have inspired me along the way. At least up until the summer of 2011, I benefited from the input of my colleagues at the University of Chester, especially David Clough, whom I collaborated with on several projects related to other animals, beginning with the conference "Animal Matters" at the University of Chester in 2006, prior to his appointment as a full-time member of staff. Gladstone's Library, located in Hawarden near Chester, proved a particularly congenial and stimulating place to work and think, and I am especially grateful to the warden Peter Francis and all the staff of the library. Many a summer holiday was spent in the quiet recesses of the library, and during the academic year I also had the opportunity to use the library as a nonresident Friend of the Library and honorary Fellow when my teaching and other commitments permitted it.

I have presented some of the material that appears in this book at various conference venues, colloquia, and public lectures; a number of these pieces have been published in works relating to these events. Steven Shakespeare invited me to deliver a keynote paper, "Degrees of Freedom: Humans as Primates in Dialogue with Hans Urs von Balthasar," at the conference entitled "Animality: Revolutions to Come" at Liverpool Hope University, April 23-24, 2009, which was subsequently published as "Degrees of Freedom: Humans as Primates in Dialogue with Hans Urs von Balthsar," in *Beyond Human: From Animality to Transhumanism,* edited by Charlie Blake, Claire Molloy, and Steven Shakespeare. On the invitation of Dr. Lieven Boeve, Yves De Maeseneer, and Ellen Van Stichel, I took part in the "Anthropos" project at the Catholic University of Louvain, Belgium, and presented "The Nature of Freedom in a Post-Darwinian World" for the colloquium entitled "Anthropos: Developing a Theological Anthropology for the 21st Century," April 13-16, 2011. This paper was developed into a chapter entitled "In God's Image and Likeness: From Reason to Revelation in Humans and Other Animals," in *Questioning the Human: Perspectives on Theological Anthropology for the 21st Century,* edited by Lieven Boeve, Yves De Maeseneer, and Ellen Van Stichel. Paul Wason and Michael Murray invited me to take part in the colloquium "Human Becoming," funded by the John Templeton Foundation, and I presented a paper entitled "In God's Image and Likeness"; the event was held in celebration of Owen Gingerich's eightieth birthday and held at Omni Island Resort, Florida, February 26-29, 2012. This paper became "God's Image and Likeness in Humans and Other Animals: Performative Soul-Making and Graced Nature," published in *Zygon* (2012). I am grateful to the Templeton Foundation and to all the other participants for feedback during and after this colloquium. I would like to thank Carl Helrich for the invitation to deliver the Goshen Lectures in Science and Religion at Goshen College, March 23-25, 2012, entitled "Reimaging the Image of God," which will be published as *Re-imaging the Image of God, Goshen Lectures, 2012.* Elisabeth Jeep invited me to deliver the Albertus Magnus Society Lecture at the Dominican University, Chicago, entitled "Human Uniqueness Reconsidered: Human Evolution and the Image of God," on November 15, 2012. I am grateful to the audience for their helpful feedback, as well as the discussion at a lunchtime seminar entitled "Are Animals Moral?" on November 16, 2012. I would like to thank John Berkman (Regis College, University of Toronto) and Charles Camosy (Fordham University) for the invitation to join them for the panel discussion, held at the meeting of the Society for the Study of Christian Ethics, Chicago, January 4, 2013, entitled "Ascending to the Margins: Speciesism as a Concern in Catholic Thought," at which I presented "Is 'Human Nature' Also 'Speciesist'? Evolutionary Perspectives on *H. sapiens* and Other Hominids." Finally, I would like to thank William Storrar for the invitation to deliver the endowed William Witherspoon public lecture on May 8, 2013, under the title "Re-imaging the Image of God: Human Nature, Evolution, and Other Animals," and for the helpful questions from the floor.

My colleagues in the theology department at the University of Notre Dame, especially Jean Porter and Gerry McKenny, have been a source of great encouragement as I have worked on different aspects of this book. In addition, colleagues at the Association of Teachers in Moral Theology provided helpful comments on the chapters on reason and cooperation at conferences held at Hinsley Hall, Leeds, May 11-13, 2012, and May 17-19, 2013. I owe a special thanks to Nick Austin, S.J., who read and commented on six chapters of the book, as well as responding formally to chapter 6.

This book took on its final shape, which was significantly different from the way I had originally envisaged it, at the Center of Theological Inquiry, Princeton, between September 2012 and May 2013. During this academic year, a team of researchers from across different disciplines worked alongside one another on a special project focusing on human nature and evolution, in what one of its members has described as coming close to academic heaven. This was made possible by the generous contribution of the John Templeton Foundation. I would particularly like to thank warmly the Director of CTI, Will Storrar, and his Senior Research Fellow, Robin Lovin, for their generosity in service; without their hard work, this project would not have been possible. It goes without saying that I owe a great debt of gratitude to all my colleagues with whom I interacted over the year on this special project. I wish to name them all, as they all in different ways contributed to the final shape of this book. The coleader of this team with me was Dominic Johnson, but alongside him were the other Fellows, Jan-Olav Henriksen, Nicola Hoggard-Cregan, Hilary Lenfesty, Conor Cunningham, Aku Visala, Lee Cronk, Gene Rogers, Agustín Fuentes, Robert Song, Marcus Mueling, Jeff Schloss, and Rich Sosis.

In particular, I should perhaps single out CTI Fellow Agustín Fuentes, now head of the department of anthropology at the University of Notre Dame, whose insights into the need to rethink a secular anthropology through a deeper acknowledgment of the lives of other animals in some senses parallels my own project in theology. Furthermore, his argument for the importance of niche construction is analogous in some ways to my own theological approach to theo-drama. But inasmuch as we all influenced one another in our writing and working, the benefits accrued are more than simply the sum of the parts. In addition to this, we were privileged to have special visits from highly distinguished scholars who all served to contribute to the way this book finally took shape; Sarah Coakley, Melvin Konner, Denis Edwards, David Sloan Wilson, Holmes Rolston III, Niels Gregersen, Angela Creager, Simon Conway Morris, and Wentzel van Huyssteen all contributed in an outstanding way to our group seminars, and in some cases through public lectures.

I also need to acknowledge my special debt to Rebecca Artinian-Kaiser, my research student, who meticulously went through the book prior to submission and assisted with the fine details of references, format, and compilation of the index. I am also very grateful to the chair of the department of theology at Notre Dame, Matthew Ashley, for providing the grant to allow Rebecca to act as a part-time research assistant for 2012-2013 when the most intensive work on this book took place. I would particularly like to thank Matthew Ashley and the deans and officers of the University of Notre Dame for giving me permission to take a year's sabbatical leave so soon after taking up my appointment in 2011, and Ken Garcia of the Institute for Study in the Liberal Arts for encouraging such a research venture in science and theology.

I am also grateful to my husband, Henry Curtis, and my children, Sara, age thirteen, and Mair, age eight, for their tolerance in allowing me the time and energy necessary to bring this book to completion, and for accepting the dislocation to their lives in moving to the University of Notre Dame in Indiana in 2011 and then to CTI in Princeton for the 2012-2013 academic year. Without their support, this book could never have been done. Finally, I am grateful to Jon Pott from Eerdmans for agreeing to publish this work and for his energetic enthusiasm for it, even at the outline stage.

Preface

It would be remiss of me not to acknowledge at the start of this book that in the course of its composition over the last five years, culminating in an intense research period in conversation with evolutionary biologists, evolutionary anthropologists, theologians, and philosophers at the Center of Theological Inquiry in 2012-2013, I have become ever more aware of both what I am presupposing in developing my arguments and what I have not yet been able to accomplish. The genesis of this book took its orientation from two apparently unrelated research projects that I was undertaking at the time. The first was on the development of a Christology that aimed to take sufficient account of the Western, scientific, and cultural influence in contemporary society, epitomized through the evolutionary paradigm and marked by the influence of Charles Darwin and his successors.[1] At about the same time that I became interested in a newly conceived Christology, I also became more interested in theological discussions about other animals, and believed, along with others, that attention to them had been unreasonably marginalized in theological discourse.[2]

For the Christology text, I drew on current debates in evolutionary theory but also argued for a way of thinking through Christology that was decidedly theological, drawing on the theo-dramatic approach of Hans

1. Celia Deane-Drummond, *Christ and Evolution: Wonder and Wisdom* (Minneapolis: Fortress; London: SCM, 2009).

2. I collaborated with David Clough in Celia Deane-Drummond and David Clough, *Creaturely Theology: On God, Humans, and Other Animals* (London: SCM, 2009). Clough has since developed a significant work in systematic theology on animals that pays close attention to the way they have been dealt with in traditional and contemporary literature. David Clough, *On Animals: Systematic Theology* (London: T. & T. Clark/Continuum, 2012).

Urs von Balthasar. I did not absorb his approach uncritically, however, but sought to correct what might be perceived as the gap between what he intended theo-dramatic theory to achieve and his own, at times, dogmatic theological stance mixed in with attention to more mystical, existential experience. Furthermore, as far as I was concerned, he did not take sufficient account of evolutionary science or indeed biological science in general, so the overall position that I ended up with was considerably different from his, even if in some senses it was inspired by it. Yet my investigations into developing what was intended to be a more adequate Christology for contemporary society, like that in Balthasar, opened up further questions about what it means to be human.[3] Balthasar's understanding of human holiness, if anything, encouraged a separation from the world, but that trajectory was mollified by his Ignatian spirituality and admission that the created world as such showed intimations of the divine. Yet his overall view of the human ended up being far too distant from practical lived reality.[4] His perception that we, as human beings, can never be abstracted from our contexts and are active participants in a theo-drama can still be used to reconstruct a new way of thinking about image bearing that is deeply in tune with the recognition in biological and evolutionary terms of the importance of the lives of other creatures, not just for their own worlds, but for the human world as well.

This book on theological anthropology has emerged as something of a dialogue between what it means to be a perfected human person in Christ, as reflected through an investigation of Christology, and what it means to be a human animal, as reflected through consideration of other animals. As in the book on Christology, I use the basic paradigm of theo-drama as a way of orientating what I think is significant in terms of a theological contribution to human becoming and meaning. I am interested to

3. Balthasar's interpretation of the human through a christological lens has been noted by others, such as Victoria Harrison, *The Apologetic Value of Human Holiness: Von Balthasar's Christocentric Philosophical Anthropology* (Dordrecht: Kluwer Academic, 2000).

4. This is illustrated by his own explicit work on theological anthropology, where the majority of his discussion is on historical aspects of the church, and the humanity and divinity of Christ. While I agree with Balthasar that Christology needs to inform the background of reflection on humanity, his theological anthropology seems like an internal conversation that is remarkably distanced from the secular world. His starting point, then, is the possibility of human perfection that is grounded in the life of the church. It seems to me that this is more suitably discussed in a work in pneumatology or ecclesiology. See Hans Urs von Balthasar, *A Theological Anthropology* (Eugene, Ore.: Wipf and Stock, 2010 [1967]).

show in this book not explicit ethics as such, but how far and to what extent other animals could be thought of as displaying morality in their own worlds. I also want to convince the reader that theological interpretations of humanity to date have generally been far too narrow in their interpretation of what it means to be human. Instead of viewing humanity and the image of God in particular in a narrowly individualistic way as merely conducting human affairs in isolated cultures, I am arguing for a much richer and embedded understanding of the human rooted through millennia of evolutionary living in a common creaturely world. So while, like many theological anthropologists, I am ready to admit distinctive features as well as commonality with other creaturely kinds, I do so to end up with a communitarian understanding of human becoming and being, at least in an eschatological sense. Furthermore, I make the case that shared sociality is the means through which we become more fully what we are divinely intended to be, and when orientated to a theological goal, it reflects more fully what it means to be perfected in the image of God. Such a re-visioning of the image of God does not need to be thought of as totally alien to the tradition; rather, the particular way that tradition is commonly interpreted needs to be challenged and reviewed in the light of classical sources. I therefore draw heavily in this text on the work of Thomas Aquinas, whose Aristotelian approach lends itself to a dialogue with contemporary biology, even if his knowledge of empirical studies has been superseded.[5]

I want to lay out as clearly as possible my own intentions. The title I am using for this book, *The Wisdom of the Liminal,* is deliberately intended to intrigue the reader by being somewhat cryptic and suggestive. It carries with it some profound insights that have begun to emerge in working through different aspects of what it means to be human. "Wisdom" as a term escapes analytical definition theologically, and has been used in various ways by different scholars of different strands of the tradition. David Ford, for example, equates wisdom with the task of theology as such; theology *is* Christian wisdom.[6] Biblical scholars, on the other hand, associate

5. I for the most part followed the English translation offered by the Blackfriars edition of *Summa Theologiae,* which includes a parallel Latin text. However, I have also checked sections of this text against the more literal English translation that is currently available in its complete version online, in *The Summa Theologica,* Benziger Bros. ed., 1947, trans. Fathers of the English Dominican Province: http://dhspriory.org/thomas/summa/index.html (different sections of which were accessed at intervals from June 2009 to May 2013).

6. David Ford, *Christian Wisdom: Desiring God and Learning in Love* (Cambridge: Cambridge University Press, 2007).

wisdom with a particular genre, namely, a specific wisdom literature that appealed to a wider cultural set of values than that defined by Hebrew salvation history. Wisdom was also linked with the natural world; close observation of other creatures pointed to what "natural" wisdom was like.[7] Wisdom treated broad issues such as education in right living, character development, and eventually the search for divine Wisdom personified through the figure of Lady Wisdom.[8] I intend "wisdom" as used in the title of this book to signify the particular kind of *creaturely wisdom* that is integral to what it means to be human.

Traditional understandings of human divine image-bearing have habitually focused on one particular characteristic of the human, most notably human reason, human language, human freedom, or human creativity. The seemingly unique capacities of human beings have then been used to separate humans from other animals (in some cases men from women also) and provided an excuse for their oppression and further domination.[9] But wisdom in relation to the liminal suggests something else about human beings, namely, that we have become ourselves and importantly become ourselves in evolutionary terms through navigating *boundary relationships* with each other, in both a temporal and a spatial sense, including relationships with other species. Further, these liminal space/time boundaries do not have hard-and-fast edges but are fuzzy, certainly showing up highly distinctive marks of the human, but only through association with other beings in a community, including other animals. The liminal boundary is not so much a hierarchical *gradation between beings,* but more a mark of *becoming through associations.* The liminal also points to another relational facet of the human, namely, the *human capacity for a spiritual life,* the associated boundary with the divine. Working out how and in what sense such boundaries came to be expressed is of interest not just to theologians, but to anthropologists and evolutionary biologists as well.

7. There is no developed natural theology here, that is, an argument for God from the experience of the natural world, since God, understood as a Creator of all that is, was presupposed.

8. Biblical treatment of the wisdom literature is legion, but a good summary text is John Day, Robert P. Gordon, and H. G. M. Williamson, eds., *Wisdom in Ancient Israel* (Cambridge: Cambridge University Press, 1995).

9. The default position in this literature is anthropocentric, as discussed in C. Deane-Drummond and A. Fuentes, "Human Being and Becoming: Situating Theological Anthropology in Interspecies Relationships in an Evolutionary Context," *Philosophy, Theology and the Sciences* 1, no. 2 (2014): in press.

I am conscious, also, that I could have investigated in more detail the scope to develop here what some have regarded as fundamental aspects of human nature. I do not, for example, have a separate chapter on human ensoulment or on human sinfulness, since the book uses the interpretation of the image of God as an orientating strategy, exploring both common and distinctive marks of the human relative to other animals. What it means to have a human "soul" is therefore implicit throughout this account as joined to the bodily reality of living, rather than isolated or separated from the natural world. I am arguing, then, that just as, theologically speaking, human beings become themselves through their encounter with God, after the pattern of Christ, so, equally theologically speaking, humanity's encounter with other animals illuminates the human condition in a way that is a reminder of our creaturely roots of becoming and human distinctiveness. In tracing different facets of what has often been used as a way of defining human distinctiveness according to the image of God, I have had to engage with a range of scientific disciplines, including, for example, animal behavior, ethology, and cognitive psychology, but I have done so insofar as they are influenced by evolutionary theory. Secular anthropology has also become increasingly important to this work insofar as it is able to think both in the manner of evolutionary science and through methodologies presupposed in the humanities; so in this sense it offers a fitting companion discipline to the kind of work I am attempting to forge here.

But I draw back somewhat from the thought of Karl Rahner, who believed, rather like his thesis of anonymous Christianity, that the relationship between secular anthropology and theological anthropology should be seen necessarily as one of hidden and explicit theology. For him, "what are apparently merely secular anthropological assertions prove to be secretly theological assertions, if they are only taken seriously in the radical form which is implicit in them." Theological anthropology statements, in reverse, "are really only the radical form of secular anthropological statements."[10] Of course, there is an element of truth in such a view, in that aspects of secular evolutionary theory or other strong anthropological theories may imitate aspects of theological theses, and theological statements may show some analogies with what is found in common across different religious traditions. However, it is condescending to assume that secular

10. Karl Rahner, *Theological Investigations,* vol. 17, *Jesus, Man, and the Church,* trans. Margaret Kohl (New York: Crossroad, 1981), p. 64.

anthropology necessarily points in a direct way to Christian aspects of revelation; the most that may be hoped for are analogies between them, rather than direct correspondences. In addition, insights may surface in the anthropological and scientific literature that challenge theology to reinterpret its traditions; Rahner's thesis does not seem to allow sufficiently for such a movement, for one seems to be a mirror of the other.

I do need to acknowledge, nonetheless, that both Karl Rahner (1904-1984) and Pierre Teilhard de Chardin (1881-1955), a generation prior to Rahner, contributed considerably to the discussion about human evolution and hominization in a way that has impinged on present debates. I do not treat either of these authors in any detail in this book, however, since there is already sufficient primary and secondary literature available on this topic.[11] Teilhard de Chardin was a pioneer in that he was both a practicing scientist working in paleontology and a theologian, even if his theology was somewhat loosely constructed. In this respect, his approach differs sharply from the more rationalistic approach of Rahner, who, despite having a significant place for mystery, drew heavily on philosoph-

11. For primary literature, see Rahner, *Theological Investigations,* vol. 17; Karl Rahner, *Hominisation: The Evolutionary Origin of Man as a Theological Problem,* trans. W. T. O'Hara (New York: Herder and Herder, 1965 [1958]); Karl Rahner, "Man (Anthropology): Theological," in *Sacramentum Mundi III,* ed. Karl Rahner (New York: Herder and Herder, 1969), pp. 365-70; Karl Rahner, "Man (Anthropology) III. Theological," in *Encyclopedia of Theology: A Concise Sacramentum Mundi,* ed. Karl Rahner (London: Burns and Oates, 1975), pp. 887-93; and Pierre Teilhard de Chardin, *The Human Phenomenon,* trans. Sarah Appleton-Weber (Brighton: Sussex Academic Press, 1999 [1955]); Teilhard de Chardin, *Man's Place in Nature: The Human Zoological Group,* trans. René Hague (New York: Harper and Row, 1966 [1956]). For secondary literature, see Josef Speck, *Karl Rahners Theologische Anthropologie. Eine Einführung* (Munich: Køsel, 1967); George Vass, *The Mystery of Man and the Foundations of a Theological System* (London: Sheed and Ward, 1985); and Anton Losinger, *The Anthropological Turn: The Human Orientation of the Theology of Karl Rahner* (New York: Fordham University Press, 2000). Although I agree with Denis Edwards that aspects of Rahner's thought are useful in dialogue with contemporary science, my own reading of Rahner is that it requires considerable modification in order to be situated in a contemporary ecological context, and the reliance of Rahner's Christology on his anthropology is problematic, even if, unlike Balthasar, he was at least far more open to the insights emerging from modern science. See Denis Edwards, *Jesus and the Cosmos* (Mahwah, N.J.: Paulist, 1991), and a discussion of Rahner's view of the deification of matter in Denis Edwards, *How God Acts: Creation, Redemption, and Special Divine Action* (Minneapolis: Fortress, 2010), pp. 152-59. For secondary literature on Teilhard's perspective on humanity, see David Grumett, *Teilhard de Chardin: Theology, Humanity, and Cosmos* (Leuven: Peeters, 2005); Thierry Meynard, ed., *Teilhard and the Future of Humanity* (New York: Fordham University Press, 2006).

ical concepts in a way that Teilhard did not. Teilhard was influential in inserting his portrait of human beings into a wider history of the cosmos as such and other hominins in particular, but his understanding of human evolution still bears the marks of one who assumed a somewhat linear evolutionary trajectory to *Homo sapiens.*[12] He is, in this respect, decidedly anthropocentric in his views, even though he was knowledgeable about the evolutionary biology that prevailed at the time he was writing. He also joined that knowledge with a mystical approach to God and the human that points to a pantheism and, on some occasions, almost a somewhat surprising lean toward viewing a special force in nature, a vitalism, sitting somewhat uneasily alongside a strong Christomonism, where Christ appears as detached from the natural world.

Insofar as Teilhard was determined to integrate the wider cosmological narrative of science with that of a theological interpretation of human becoming and being, he anticipated process thought and narrative approaches to theology and the work of influential scholars such as Thomas Berry and Brian Swimme. I do not deal with Teilhard in this book because to do so would have made it a historical study of anthropology and its relationship with evolution, and my concern is to gain a theological anthropological perspective in the light of contemporary evolutionary debates. His particular discussion of evolution, and human evolution in particular, is therefore outdated in scientific terms. Teilhard was, nonetheless, ahead of his time in thinking through why, in a relatively short time, humanity has outcompeted all other rivals and come to dominate planet earth. He attributed such a change to an explosion of consciousness, a shift from what he called "direct psychism to reflective psychism."[13] This change in consciousness was an evolutionary breakthrough that he dubbed "convolution," in what he termed a radically new phase in evolutionary history, namely, the appearance of the "noosphere."[14] In naming self-reflective cognitive powers of human beings as crucial in their evolutionary significance, he was anticipating contemporary discussions of the distinctive cognitive

12. The terminology used in the literature to describe human ancestors is somewhat confusing, but I am defining "hominin" to mean all modern humans and extinct humans, including members of the genera *Homo, Australopithecus, Paranthropus,* and *Ardipithecus.* "Hominid," on the other hand, is used where the ancestry goes even further back from modern humans, including chimpanzees, gorillas, and orangutans, plus all their immediate ancestors.

13. Teilhard de Chardin, *Man's Place in Nature,* p. 62.

14. Teilhard de Chardin, *Man's Place in Nature,* p. 79.

capacities of humans and questions as to why *Homo sapiens sapiens,* among all the now extant hominins and *Homo* species and subspecies, were so successful. He also recognized, more than many others, the importance of socialization, named in contemporary discourse as "supercooperation," as well as the importance of entanglement and interrelationships between living things, including symbiotic relationships, in a way that anticipates contemporary discussions on the importance of cooperation and interrelationships in evolutionary history.[15] He also applied that evolutionary cooperative trajectory to the way human groups form political alliances, in a way that would warm the hearts of those supporting group selection and similarly inclined evolutionary psychologists, though, of course, with virtually no evidence to substantiate his claims. But because his work is either highly speculative or informed by scientific work that has since been superseded, it lacks an explicit reference to what I am attempting to do in this book, and so has historical rather than direct relevance to the particular way I am developing this discussion. My acknowledgment of his work in this preface is by way of an apology for omission given the limitations of space of a work of this length.

Rahner was similarly ahead of his time in noting the difficulties associated with the whole question of hominization, the tension between the evolutionary origins of human beings and the official Roman Catholic position on ensoulment.[16] He rejects, therefore, what he terms a "lazy compromise" between theology and science, where theology and science are simply different subjects that have little to do with each other.[17] Instead, he is concerned to discover in "prehistory" important aspects of not just the biological aspects of humanity, but the spiritual aspects as well. He rejects, therefore, any notion that God becomes a cause among other causes by the "insertion" of a human soul in matter; such a dualistic approach is unacceptable not least because it seems to deny the basic transcendental ground of all reality, that is, belief in God as Creator of all that is, alongside a belief in secondary causes. So, an interpretation of the traditional view of ensoulment as "an exceptional extraordinary occurrence whose special features contradict everything that is otherwise understood regarding the relation of first cause to second causes" no longer seems to make sense.[18]

15. Teilhard de Chardin, *Man's Place in Nature,* pp. 79-82.

16. Rahner, *Hominisation.*

17. Rahner, *Hominisation,* p. 63.

18. Rahner, *Hominisation,* p. 68.

Instead, Rahner holds that in the ensoulment of the first human, and indeed of every human person, God actively enables finite beings to transcend themselves. Such self-transcendence, inasmuch as it is related to *self,* comes from that person, but, at the same time, as *transcendence,* involves God so that personal becoming moves beyond and above itself. Of course, here Rahner encounters some difficulty, in that the involvement of absolute Being, or God, cannot be a reality inserted alongside finite reality; however, it is not simply a finite efficient cause either, but a factor "linked to the finite agent and belonging to it, though transcending it."[19] In dialogue with scholastic thought, he is attempting, therefore, to envisage infinite reality as constituting finite reality without becoming an intrinsic constituent of finite reality as such. So, on the one hand, infinite reality is free and detached from the act of becoming, but it also provides the ground for self-transcendence. But he is also a clear enough thinker to recognize the paradoxical elements in making such a statement. Accordingly, he takes up a different slant in his argument and presses for a new way of thinking about human cognition, namely, that human beings are cognitively ordered toward a horizon of transcendence, rather than toward a specified object as such.[20] He believes, furthermore, that such an orientation toward transcendence is an essential factor in all intellectual knowledge and a *precondition* of its possibility. In this way, he claims that "The orientating term of transcendence moves the movement of the mind; it is the originating cause, the fundamental ground and reason for the mind's transcendental dynamism."[21] At the same time, Rahner still holds to the idea that the absolute Being is the cause and ground of self-transcendence, even if intrinsically immanent in the finite, and even if not, therefore, considerable as a movement within absolute Being as such. He is able, therefore, to claim that in self-transcendence the person "attains its own proper nature." In other words, humans become themselves.[22] Hence, Rahner argues for a measure of continuity in different beings, but also for discontinuity.

Rahner anticipates, then, contemporary discussion of human nature and ensoulment and the evolutionary development of matter toward spirit, without reducing the latter to an evolutionary account.[23] I believe he is at

19. Rahner, *Hominisation,* p. 75.

20. Rahner, *Hominisation,* p. 83.

21. Rahner, *Hominisation,* p. 86.

22. Rahner, *Hominisation,* p. 89.

23. See, for example, Malcolm Jeeves, ed., *Re-thinking Human Nature: A Multidis-*

least partially successful in his thesis in that he has found a way of involving God in the evolutionary history of the human without falling into the dilemma of introducing the human as a special miracle of divine intervention in disjunction from the rest of evolutionary history. His solution is through a metaphysical reading of that history in terms of a theory about the possibility for human transcendence. At the same time, he acknowledges the difference between what might be termed human biological history and revealed salvation history, where the encounter between God and humanity is one of address and response. Yet overall his position remains heavily anthropocentric in orientation. Other animals are given some credit for informing the biological basis of the human soul, but generally are forgotten about as the backdrop for the working of absolute Being in engendering human self-transcendence. His view of the evolutionary history of the human, therefore, has a Kantian, rationalist flavor in a way that is different from Balthasar's concentration on organic being as such.[24] Balthasar took evolution even less seriously than Rahner in his theological works, but arguably for different reasons.[25] But Balthasar's interpretation of Christology in a manner that leans more toward that of Karl Barth means that it is not as heavily dependent on anthropology as is Rahner's Christology.[26]

Instead of viewing Christology in the light of anthropology in Rahnerian fashion, I believe that the ultimate orientation of anthropology should be the other way round, even if Christology finds its way into the discussion as a second step. Christology, and theo-drama in particular, therefore introduces a new and, I would argue, crucial *theological* element into an understanding of theological anthropology, one that views the becoming and being of the human through being and act, rather than simply

---

ciplinary Approach (Grand Rapids: Eerdmans, 2011). Scientific and theological accounts exist side by side, so while they are certainly in conversation with one another, the agenda in each disciplinary approach is not challenged, as the term "multidisciplinary" accurately acknowledges.

24. Edward Oakes argues that Goethe's resistance to philosophical aspects of Newtonianism shapes Balthasar's methodology. Edward T. Oakes, *Pattern of Redemption: The Theology of Hans Urs von Balthasar* (New York: Continuum, 1994), p. 83.

25. Rowan Williams discusses the differences between Rahner and Balthasar in "Balthasar and Rahner," in *The Analogy of Beauty: The Theology of Hans Urs von Balthasar*, ed. John Riches (Edinburgh: T. & T. Clark, 1986), pp. 11-34. Balthasar presupposes God's existence, while Rahner seeks to argue for the existence of God through a consideration of human subjectivity. In this respect, I am following Balthasar in that my presupposition is Christology.

26. See discussion in Deane-Drummond, *Christ and Evolution*, pp. 40-43.

in either ontological *or* functional *or* relational terms. Of course, it is possible to interpret ontology through relational categories rather than through specific capacities such as reason or freedom, but I consider it helpful to have an expansive version of image bearing, rather than limit it to one or another categorization. Such inclusivity is possible through an understanding of performance, since this includes particular capacities, such as freedom, reason, and so on, but it also elevates relational and functional aspects. Theo-performance is relation and function in a certain direction, namely, that given by God. I prefer, then, to understand a re-visioning of human image bearing in terms of *performance,* but it is a performance caught up in a shared drama with other species and orientated toward God's purposes for history. The elementary bases for that performance and acknowledgment of the distinctive role of human beings alongside other creaturely kinds necessitate paying attention to different facets of the human and other animals in terms of reason, freedom, language, and community. I also point to the way that performance might be played out in practice in terms of justice making and the forging of caring relationships.

The kind of theological approach that I develop here is, therefore, both a re-envisioning of what has been traditionally counted as important in theological anthropology and one that is aware of the pressing practical basis for such a reassessment. In considering what it means to be human, or in developing a theological anthropology, theologians generally take into account experience, reason/philosophy, Christian tradition, and a biblical account. Theologians have usually started with the biblical record shaped by the Genesis account of God's creation of human beings in the image of God: Genesis 1:27 speaks of God creating humankind in the image of God and as male and female, and 1:28 of having dominion over other creatures. But centuries of textual debate have not really resolved what image bearing means. Is it primarily the human capacity for reason, or freedom, or perhaps language, or even religion as such, which all point to a different kind of mentalizing and to specific abilities that no other creature seems to have? Or is image bearing more about how human beings *act* in the world, namely, the specific task that is given to them by God in the Genesis text to have "dominion over the fish . . . and the earth"? Or maybe image bearing is a reflection of the *relationships* that are possible in human societies, including relationships with God, and that mirror faith in God understood as Trinity.

All these possibilities assume that there is something different about human beings and so place them on a pedestal above other creatures, with

God seeming to give permission for human dominance of the world, even if qualified through arguments about the meaning of dominion. I suggest that in practice dominance cannot be denied and has been endorsed by contemporary science. We are living in a new era, the era of the Anthropocene, understood as the permeation of *Homo sapiens* into virtually every aspect of the earth's systems.[27] The Anthropocene is understood as a new geological era, one that marks a new period in the history of the earth. While some scholars put the start date at the industrial revolution, others place it at the rise of modern agriculture some 10,000 years ago. Regardless, it is clear that we are in such an epoch now, and that if the Anthropocene is not going to lead to disastrous results, due to the limited carrying capacity of the earth, we need to find new and imaginative ways of telling the human story.[28] I believe that just as theology was part of the problem, so ancient theological wisdoms may give us some clues that help us construct alternative narratives and face the particular responsibilities that we have as human agents.

There are two crucial areas of tension that pose some difficulties to the argument that theology may have something to contribute to a transformed view of the human as appropriate to the era in which all creatures now live, the Anthropocene.

The *first difficulty* is that the philosophical presupposition of the dominant contemporary Western culture is *anthropocentric,* that is, one that perceives the human as important to the virtual exclusion of everything else. Theology seems in many interpretations to reinforce such a position, even if perhaps a little more qualified in the work of pioneers such as Teilhard, Rahner, and Balthasar, all of whom, in different ways, acknowledged cosmological or scientific elements in their discussion. The *second difficulty* is that while evolutionary biology, by putting emphasis on

27. Deborah Bird Rose, "Introduction: Writing in the Anthropocene," *Australian Humanities Review* 49 (2009): 87. For further discussion of the significance of the Anthropocene for work at the human-alloprimate interface, see Agustín Fuentes, "Social Minds and Social Selves: Redefining the Human-Alloprimate Interface," in *The Politics of Species: Reshaping Our Relationships with Other Animals,* ed. Raymond Corby and Annette Lanjouw (Cambridge: Cambridge University Press, 2014). I am grateful to Agustín Fuentes for giving me access to this chapter prior to final publication.

28. For a fascinating commentary on the social significance of the Anthropocene, see Bronislaw Szerszynski, "The End of the End of Nature: The Anthropocene and the Fate of the Human," *Oxford Literary Review* 34, no. 2 (2012): 165-84.

the millennia of evolution of other creatures, could challenge this anthropocentrism in its more aggressive form, it tries to *explain away* religious beliefs, and thereby undercuts the possible significance of theology for anthropology. While I am concentrating in this book on the first difficulty, the second problem comes into view as well.

While theology will sometimes claim to resist the charge of anthropocentrism by naming itself *theocentric,* or God-centered, human beings are still cast, wrongly in my view, in terms of a *separation from* other creatures, rather than in consideration of what *links them* with other creatures as named in ecology, for example, or evolutionary history. Thus, the popular understanding that science is inevitably *at war* with religion is not really true; rather, it is much more common in my view that one summarily *ignores* the other. Like a once-close married couple who are now estranged, science and religion coexist but no longer communicate with each other. Theologians therefore do their theology without considering what science has to say, and vice versa.

I am acutely conscious, nonetheless, of the limitations of this study both in the scope of what I could have addressed and with respect to its intersection with other aspects of human experience of the divine. I have only hinted at, therefore, the experience of a graced life, rather than dealing rigorously with pneumatological aspects of human experience. That will need to wait for a further monograph. I also have not begun to spell out how the theological anthropology that I am arguing for will become enfleshed, as it were, in theological ethics, especially in relation to creatures other than human beings. That I intend to attempt in a work on a theology of sustainability. I am also conscious that far more could have been said on the virtuous life, and not only the theological virtues of faith, hope, and charity, but also the gifts of the spirit. I have woven in a discussion of the opposite of virtue (vice) rather than dealing explicitly with theological accounts of the Fall of humanity; in my view, a detailed discussion of the Fall of humanity and its aftermath is more about soteriology than anthropology, even if anthropology bears a relationship to virtually every systematic category that theologians have constructed, namely, creation, ecclesiology, pneumatology, soteriology, Christology, theodicy, eschatology, and so on. I have also not dealt with the huge volume of literature on religion and other animals as much as I wanted to, but I view this work in some respects not just as a work in theological anthropology, but also as a contribution to that literature. I do not view this book as a work in natural theology, if that means a way of interrogating what is in the natural world and thereby pointing to the divine. Rather, it is more ambitious in that it is a reworking of constructive theological anthropology through close engagement with those biological and anthropological disciplines that are relevant, a bio-theological anthropology, rather than a fully comprehensive account of all aspects of theological anthropology. My hope, at least, is that in spite of these limitations, aspects of this work will inspire others to consider and reflect on new ways of thinking about human becoming and being through a theological lens.

This book is dedicated to the memory of my father, Major General Tony Deane-Drummond, whose last years spanned the composition of this text and who died on December 4, 2012. His courage, modesty, generosity of heart, idealism in service of his country, and devoted love for his wife, Evie, and care for his children are rare virtues today. His companion dogs were also part of our family when I was growing up, namely, a black Labrador, Lady Zena, and a Jack Russell, Vino. He was also something of a gentleman farmer, and for some of my formative years we had a smallholding of about fifty acres, as well as various ponies. My father, therefore, showed me an example of what a remarkable species *Homo sapiens sapiens* can become, what one individual member of that species can achieve in a lifetime, along with the importance of affiliation with other creatures and deep affection for the land. I owe him a debt of gratitude not just for my physical life, but also for inspiration on how to live that life to the full. RIP.

Finally, this book goes to the publisher on the feast day of one of the best-loved dramas in the Christian narrative, namely, the visit of Elizabeth by her cousin the Virgin Mary. In that encounter, both Mary and Elizabeth recognized more fully the significance and mystery of their divine callings. I too believe that it is in encountering God, each other, and other creaturely kinds that we are able to recognize more fully the persons that we are intended to become.

Friday, May 31, 2013.
Feast of the Visitation of the Blessed Virgin Mary

CHAPTER ONE

Human Becoming and Being: Theological Starting Points

What might be the possible starting points for a theological discussion of humanity? Given the plethora of possible approaches, and to clarify what this book is about, I will set forth the parameters limiting my discussion. In attempting a theological account of the human, it would be relatively easy to restrict attention to a purely religious or ecclesial context in which human beings are situated and work to flesh out what the particular vocation of humanity might be as those called to live in obedient relationship with God. Certainly, when understood in terms of Christian discipleship, a rich account of what human identity might mean cannot be situated apart from reflection on the Eucharist and the dynamic involvement of the Holy Spirit in the Christian community, and more specifically apart from an ecclesial setting. While I recognize the importance of such reflections, I prefer to consider such a development as an aspect of *pneumatology,* rather than a *theological anthropology,* simply because the former pneumatological account, it seems to me, depends on a prior consideration of the creaturely context in which human beings are situated.

Similarly, when reflecting on the significance of evolution for understanding humanity, one possible methodological approach would be to narrow attention to accounts of *religious origins* in evolutionary terms, rather than attempt a broader framework of creaturely becoming and being. In this chapter, I will set out the broad epistemological premise that I will assume in this book, while also situating the discussion in the context of current debates on the evolution of religion. I will argue that we need to be rather more self-aware in acknowledging that theological anthropology depends on an analysis of those features that make up the human condition in a way that takes account of the particular cultural aspects that shape human self-perception. Further, once cultural aspects of that condition permit inclusivity with respect to other animals, this raises questions about the exclusivity of an anthropological focus in theological terms.

Throughout this book, my working assumption is that theologians need to go beyond a rather stale appropriation of human evolution as simply "post-neo-Darwinian," conceived in narrowly genetic terms, and engage more rigorously with some of the lively current debates and emerging paradigms in evolutionary anthropology. Such debates explore the fuzzy biological *and* social boundary in human becoming, thus resisting either extremes of social constructivist or genetic determinist models.[1] But this also means that instead of viewing human becoming in terms of one trajectory related to the sociocultural or biological paradigms, characterized loosely as the nurture/nature divide, it is viewed in terms of "a myriad of entangled agents in the processes of human becoming."[2] This makes the interrogative task with evolutionary theory far more difficult than if one or another aspect was isolated to the exclusion of other factors. Such a technique of oversimplification has characteristically prevailed in those evolutionary psychological approaches that aim for an "optimal end point" in order to explain human becoming in evolutionary terms.[3] Traditional evolutionary theories that focus, then, on "design" features that are crafted by natural selection are rapidly becoming outdated. Modern human bipedalism as an end point in identifying what "kind" human beings might be, for example, is being challenged by a recognition of a much slower process of change in upper- and lower-body morphology in Miocene apes that spent considerable time in the trees.[4] Optimal models assume "cultural" information as input and behavior as output, rather than taking proper account of the way behavior both shapes and is shaped by the ecological and social context, the *bio-sociocultural niche*. Hence, in the first place, there are more evolutionary factors involved than genetic evolution alone; rather, what might be called *multiple systems of inheritance* are important,

1. As clearly represented in Agustín Fuentes, "Blurring the Biological and Social in Human Becomings," in *Biosocial Becomings: Integrating Social and Biological Anthropology*, ed. Tim Ingold and Gisli Palsson (Cambridge: Cambridge University Press, 2013), pp. 42-58.

2. Fuentes, "Blurring the Biological," p. 42.

3. An optimal end point is the premise that natural selection works to produce individuals that are best suited to the prevailing environmental conditions. The fact that many organisms do not show optimality is interpreted in terms of constraints in the system, rather than a problem with the model as such.

4. Fuentes, "Blurring the Biological," p. 48.

so that genetic, behavioral, epigenetic, and what might be termed symbolic inheritance pathways all contribute to evolutionary change.[5] In the second place, bio-sociocultural approaches stress the *dynamic* processes of becoming human in a way that is still ongoing, rather than assuming a static, universally evolved end point at some time in evolutionary history. These factors, I suggest, open the door for a more positive way to interpret the kind of symbolic becoming that is characteristic of theological interpretations of human beings in a way that does not require a genetic correlate. Moreover, this new way of perceiving human becoming places considerable significance on the importance of human agency.

So far, I have deliberately avoided use of the term "human nature," not least because of the considerable philosophical confusion such terminology commonly elicits.[6] As indicated above, most biologists, inasmuch as the species boundaries are becoming more fluid, especially in an evolutionary perspective, are reluctant to view "natures" in a hard or essentialist manner. This shift, combined with a closer recognition of human beings sharing in facets of animality, and even perhaps vice versa, means that the sharp boundaries between humans and other animals that have been constructed for theological and/or cultural reasons seem less necessary to maintain. Philosopher Mary Midgley recognized the importance of this boundary and the need to stress human continuities with other animals in her pioneer work first published over thirty-five years ago in 1978, *Beast and Man: The Roots of Human Nature.*[7] In this book she makes a strong case for stressing continuities between humans and other animals rather than differences. The denial of the existence of human nature from social scien-

5. Kevin Laland and Gillian Brown, *Sense and Nonsense: Evolutionary Perspectives on Human Behavior* (Oxford: Oxford University Press, 2011).

6. For a useful mapping of different philosophical uses of the term "human nature" in terms of human uniqueness, universal and innate human nature, see Jonathan Jong and Aku Visala, "Three Quests for Human Nature: Some Philosophical Reflections," *Philosophy, Theology and the Sciences,* in preparation. Some scholars resist using the term entirely in the name of semantic hygiene, preferring an alternative such as "human personhood." I believe, however, that a fixation on personhood creates as many problems as it solves, not least as it implies at the outset a separation from the natural world in a way that is not all that desirable. For discussion in the context of neurobiological studies, see Fernando Vidal, "Human Persons and Human Brains: A Historical Perspective within the Christian Tradition," in *Rethinking Human Nature: A Multidisciplinary Approach,* ed. Malcolm Jeeves (Grand Rapids: Eerdmans, 2011), pp. 30-60.

7. Mary Midgley, *Beast and Man: The Roots of Human Nature,* 2nd ed. (London: Routledge, 1995; original 1978).

tists and empiricist philosophers alongside equally vocal advocates from a biological perspective gave way to sociobiological forms that are still influential in current evolutionary theory. Midgley found it surprising that it was necessary to reissue her book nearly twenty years later in 1995. What would surprise her even further is that another twenty years later such debates continue. The difference, however, is that the environmental wave that stressed cooperation is now becoming integrated into evolutionary biology as such, and thus changing the shape of evolutionary biology. The sociobiological narrative of selfishness is not the only evolutionary narrative in contemporary discussion. The temptation for theologians might be to choose to ignore the complexity of evolutionary biology entirely and insist on a purely theological view of the human person in detachment from any scientific knowledge. Yet, while this solves one problem, it introduces another one, a bigger elephant in the room: it is in our ability to detach from our cultural context that one facet of human distinctiveness shows up, but we cannot deny our creaturely evolutionary origins and current shared interspecific dependencies because to do so would be to deny our God-given creatureliness as such.

But all these questions focus on human uniqueness vis-à-vis other creatures, on the question, what is special and different about human beings? Another common trend among those interested in "human nature" is the search to find universal human social, behavioral, and physiological characteristics across different cultures and societies. As I indicated above, the attempt to find such human universals in terms of "design" features is becoming rapidly outdated; the complexity of variation within groups and individual variation as part of the matrix of natural selection means that even talk of "universal" characteristics among evolutionary scientific positivists is less convincing now than even a decade ago. In addition, characteristics that are distinctive for humans do not necessarily have to be expressed universally; so while discussions on uniqueness and universality meld into one another, the questions are somewhat distinct. This is an important point, since the claim that human beings are *uniquely* religious is not equivalent to saying that they are *universally* religious. Such a quest for universality is common among the more strident and arguably outdated theories of evolutionary psychologists who still tend to represent a troubling essentialist position on human nature. Unfortunately, such a perspective has the habit of persisting in the public sphere since it is relatively easy to understand. While for many theologians a stress on human universals is important in order to maintain a concrete basis for human rights, the way it is parsed out in strident versions of evolutionary psychology is highly ambiguous, since the explanation for human behavior in such evolutionary terms weakens belief in the possibility of genuine freedom and human responsibility. Of course, if the claim is made for finding such universals, it is then possible to ask ourselves how far and to what extent such characteristics are learned or not, and how this learning is related to their social or biological origin. The latter is often associated with the idea of "innateness," but, rather like human "nature," the term is loosely applied and not used very precisely.[8]

More positively, and as an exercise in constructive theology, overall this book should be viewed through the lens of an unfolding theo-drama, one that pays careful attention to different facets of the human condition that are important to consider in allowing us to be active agents in that drama. Here I presuppose the existence of God and God's active presence in the world that makes the language of theology possible at all. Yet, as *theo*-drama, the most profound drama of all on the human, earthly stage is the incarnation of God in Christ, his passion narrative, and his dramatic resurrection.[9] For Christians, therefore, humanity makes no sense apart

8. Biologists are beginning to object to the use of the terms, as in, for example, Patrick Bateson and Peter Gluckman, *Plasticity, Robustness, Development, and Evolution* (Cambridge: Cambridge University Press, 2011), pp. 12-13.

9. I take the basic idea of theo-drama from Hans Urs von Balthasar and his five-volume work, *Theo-Drama,* on theological dramatic theory. Significantly, his discussion of humanity in volume 2 comes first after the prolegomena in volume 1, and it also comes prior to his developed discussion of Christology in volume 3, Trinity in volume 4, and eschatology in volume 5. But this ordering should not obscure the fact that Christ's dramatic struggle informs his perception of what human freedom means, which forms a weighty section in his discussion of anthropology, or that reflection on human nature is integral to reflection on Christology, hence the subtitles to the second and third volumes, *Man* in *God* and *The Person* in Christ. The present book draws on Balthasar in that it picks up the idea of theo-dramatics, especially his key discussion of human and divine freedom that I discuss further in chapter 3, and theo-dramatic theory that I discuss in chapter 6, but the intent behind his use of theo-drama leans much more to literary analysis, rather than engagement with scientific understanding of life-forms. I am also aware of critics of Balthasar who press against his more speculative theology in favor of apophatic modesty, as in Karen Kilby, *Balthasar: A (Very) Critical Introduction* (Grand Rapids: Eerdmans, 2012). The way I am using Balthasar here escapes such criticism entirely in that it takes up one of his key concepts but transforms it. Kilby criticizes Balthasar for advocating a dramatic theology, but then failing to deliver, or more problematically, failing by dogmatic assertion to allow the possibility of alternative points of view and argument (pp. 63-65). To some extent, the approach I am using that deliberately seeks to ground theological discussion in current debates and

from some reference to the God-man, Jesus Christ, in acknowledgment of the God who is not simply Creator of all that is but also redeemer of humanity and the earth. However, as animals able to physically and symbolically construct our own worlds, we need to take particular care to recognize the ways in which we might be using not just evocative religious symbols, but powerful evolutionary metaphors as well. The difference that *theology* makes to such meaning construction is that it brings a vivid and existential sense of the active but often hidden and silent presence of God, understood as permeating the natural world, and yet points to a transcendent, mysterious, transformative Other in whom our deepest longings are met. To put this more succinctly, the human soul cannot be reduced to the mind or brain. Theological anthropology, therefore, straddles not simply a constructive theology of creation, but also key theological premises, including Christology, Trinitarian theology, and eschatology.

I am aware, too, that other writers have ventured into the territory of placing a theological discussion of the human in engagement with evolutionary accounts, not least J. Wentzel van Huyssteen in his monumental volume *Alone in the World?*[10] I place this volume high on the list of works that have inspired me to enter into this highly complex and challenging area of theological inquiry. Much of what van Huyssteen's great work has achieved forms a background to and basis for arguments that I am attempting to develop here. However, his emphasis is somewhat different. His book concentrates on the discernment, as far as is possible from paleontology, of those evolved qualities that stress human uniqueness, weaving into that expression theological notions of *imago Dei* alongside the fascinating capacity for cave painting and symbolization in the earliest human civilizations. He is also concerned to see how such discussion intersects with interdisciplinary models for working more generally, including a reference to wider religious contexts such as the Jewish tradition. There are aspects of his work that resonate with my own approach developed here. In the first place, it is "postfoundationalist" in seeking to move beyond

---

engagement with human evolutionary and biological discourse already avoids that criticism. The five volumes of Hans Urs von Balthasar, *Theo-Drama: Theological Dramatic Theory,* are all translated by George Harrison and published by Ignatius Press in San Francisco; following are the titles of the five volumes and their dates of publication: vol. 1, *Prolegomena* (1988); vol. 2, *The Dramatis Personae: Man in God* (1990); vol. 3, *The Dramatis Personae: The Person in Christ* (1992); vol. 4, *The Action* (1994); vol. 5, *The Last Act* (1998).

10. J. Wentzel van Huyssteen, *Alone in the World? Human Uniqueness in Science and Theology* (Grand Rapids: Eerdmans, 2006).

the modernist metanarrative of universalism and the postmodern stress on contextuality and personal judgment.[11] More specifically, he argues for transversality, meaning that in the course of dialogue there are promising liminalities that emerge between disciplines.[12] He also, following Wolfgang Welsch, argues for a philosophical approach to human reason that views it as "a dynamic faculty of performative transitions that interconnects the various forms of human rationality."[13] Inasmuch as I am seeking a way of considering the human in performative terms, this perspective on a convergence of rationalities is coincident with my own.

While I am deeply appreciative of van Huyssteen's efforts in this domain and acutely aware of the dangers of an uncritical fideism that he has correctly identified, the purpose of the present book is deliberately more self-consciously theologically focused. It is an expression of the kind of hermeneutic of the relationship between science and theology that is best characterized by an informed faith seeking understanding. Kenneth Reynhout argues brilliantly for the cogency of such a position on the interdisciplinary dialogue between theology and science in the light of reflection on Paul Ricoeur's hermeneutics.[14] In other words, I find distinct ways of drawing on that liminal space that van Huyssteen has correctly identified, but in this case for explicitly theological purposes. I also, however, want to give sufficient space to what might be termed the voice of scientific debates, as well as their critical interpretation and interrogation, rather than simply absorbing those theories that happen to be conducive to my theological intentions. Given that my particular focus is human relationships with other animals as well as evolutionary theory, the scientific literature I engage in will also overlap with but be distinct from that in van Huyssteen's work.

I am attempting to reexamine each of the dimensions that have become important in classical theological constructions of *imago Dei* and reshape them in the light of what we know about the intersectionality of human evolution and other animal lives understood in theo-dramatic terms. The concept of the "image of God" draws from an account of the creation of humanity as recalled in the first chapters of the first book of

11. See, for example, van Huyssteen, *Alone in the World?* p. 12.

12. Van Huyssteen, *Alone in the World?* p. 9.

13. Van Huyssteen, *Alone in the World?* p. 19.

14. Kenneth Reynhout, *Interdisciplinary Interpretation: Paul Ricoeur and the Hermeneutics of Theology and Science* (Lanham, Md.: Lexington Books/Rowman and Littlefield, 2013). Reynhout argues for faith seeking understanding through explanation as a way of appropriating science into the task of theology.

the Bible, Genesis, and in this respect Christian traditions have sought to interpret and reinterpret the word of God for contemporary culture. I do not, however, engage in textual exegesis of the meaning of divine image bearing except to acknowledge difficulties in interpretation.[15] I also presuppose that image bearing is *inclusive* in gender terms — that is, it is certainly not confined to the male gender — and inasmuch as I will argue for a theological anthropology that is *performative* in relation to other creatures, it reflects a shared and inclusive task for men and women.[16] In other words, this is a deliberately constructive theological proposal, but one that aims to be open-ended inasmuch as this is an imaginative exploration in theological anthropology, but also one that seeks to find its reference points in classic traditions, drawing inspiration from Thomas Aquinas or those who have been influenced by him. The notion of theo-drama itself draws from the work of Hans Urs von Balthasar, but as in the constructive Christology proposal developed earlier, I widen out Balthasar's discussion so that both evolution and other animals come to the front of the stage, rather than just forming the backdrop on which human action is played out.[17] Through this articulation, I offer a different way to consider human distinctiveness, one founded as much on performance in the theo-drama as on specific capabilities. Further, that performance puts emphasis on identity understood through relational community development, though now humans have the capacity to widen out that identity in relationship with other animals and include in that self-identity a sense of ecologically

15. I am aware that some scholars may find this disappointing, but it seems to me that many scholars have already devoted attention to this matter, including biblical scholars engaging with contemporary science. See, for example, discussion of image bearing and humanity more generally in William Brown, *The Seven Pillars of Creation: The Bible, Science, and the Ecology of Wonder* (Oxford: Oxford University Press, 2010), pp. 47-49, 230-40. Brown argues that the term "dominion" is best interpreted as a noble constructive enterprise, lacking any sense of exploitation. Of course, historically, the interpretation of this term in this positive sense is often not as benign, but Brown's idea of humanity as positive constructors of their environment and the work of wisdom in fostering a wider kinship toward other creatures converges in a significant way with the approach I am developing. See also Joel Green, "Humanity — Created, Restored, Transformed, Embodied," in *Rethinking Human Nature,* pp. 271-94.

16. Janet Martin Soskice raises the feminist question about the particular role of women and sexual difference in shaping accounts of the image of God. See Janet Soskice, "Imago Dei and Sexual Difference: Towards an Eschatological Anthropology," in *Rethinking Human Nature,* pp. 295-306.

17. Celia Deane-Drummond, *Christ and Evolution: Wonder and Wisdom* (Minneapolis: Fortress; London: SCM, 2009).

entangled lives. But before we get to this point, it is important to lay out some basic premises for such a discussion.

Epistemological and Theological Starting Points

Even if van Huyssteen makes bold steps in the direction of convergence, it is worth identifying at the outset where difficulties in communication are likely to arise in the development of what he terms transversal rationality. Alasdair MacIntyre perhaps sets the stage for understanding more clearly *why* there are likely to be difficulties when communicating across seemingly incommensurable and untranslatable systems of thought. While MacIntyre is referring to three rival versions of *moral* inquiry within the humanities, his insights bear on interdisciplinary thought in general in arguing that even such systems could be viewed as standpoints formulated within common norms of intelligibility and evaluation. In such a view, it would be possible, at least in theory, to exclude one or the other on the basis of rational superiority. But the continued incommensurability within the humanities was also used within the university to exclude theological reflection as worthy of serious academic consideration.[18] The nineteenth-century view that rationality is unitary, and that science is about the application of such a unitary method to a bald collection of data (facts) that would be obvious to any attentive observer, leads to what MacIntyre describes as an encyclopedic mind-set "whose supreme achievement is an account of the progress of mankind."[19] MacIntyre believes that no such authoritative pronouncements are remotely possible in contemporary culture, where each alternative position is more like an episode in an ongoing narrative of conflicting positions.

Yet, the popular rendition of evolutionary science remains locked into what might be termed naïve optimism about its own truth claims.[20]

18. Alasdair MacIntyre, *Three Rival Versions of Moral Inquiry* (Notre Dame, Ind.: University of Notre Dame Press, 1990), p. 7.

19. MacIntyre, *Three Rival Versions,* p. 32.

20. Richard Dawkins's pronouncements in *The God Delusion* are a case in point, and do not satisfy more discerning scientists or humanities scholars. Dawkins is one of a number of new atheists who view religious belief as not just fictional, but also as having negative social consequences. Richard Dawkins, *The God Delusion* (London: Houghton Mifflin, 2006). For a sharp critique, see Conor Cunningham, *Darwin's Pious Idea: Why the Ultra-Darwinists and Creationists Both Get It Wrong* (Grand Rapids: Eerdmans, 2010).

MacIntyre's portrayal of counterreaction to such fixity in Nietzsche's stress on the construction of truth as "illusions" that are "worn-out metaphors," like "coins which have lost their faces,"[21] bears striking resemblance to the way contemporary scientists, collectively known as the "new atheists," portray religious claims as once-useful (or, in some cases, useless or even positively damaging) myths. However, rather like Nietzsche, such authors are also generally unwilling to view their own perspective as culturally situated, and, like Nietzsche, their perspective on the world as a whole, and human life in particular, tends toward a sense of depressing meaninglessness. Furthermore, Nietzsche and postmodern genealogical deconstructivists after him recognized that all truths were culturally constructed, including those of science, and thus provided some ammunition for its deconstruction that in itself provided a kind of universalism that Nietzsche failed to acknowledge. The irony is that those adopting what I would term "strident new atheism" tend to be explicit in their scientific claims for factual authority, and that places such views hovering uneasily between an encyclopedic assertion of "factual" truth claims in science and its associated political ramifications in what Nietzsche described as a "will to power," but now set up in uneasy rational combination with the perceived constructive, illusionary standpoints of religion. MacIntyre ends up arguing for tradition-constituted enquiry, drawing inspiration from Thomas Aquinas as one who was able to integrate two very different traditions, namely, the philosophical tradition of Aristotle and the theological tradition of Augustine.[22] Yet, while it seems to me that MacIntyre is correct to assert that Aquinas drew respectfully from both traditions, Aquinas still resisted placing philosophical reflection over and above his theological commitments.[23]

How did Aquinas achieve this synthesis that also allowed theological

21. MacIntyre, *Three Rival Versions,* p. 35.

22. MacIntyre, *Three Rival Versions,* p. 81.

23. This is a point that has certainly been noted by others, as in, for example, Eugene Rogers, *Thomas Aquinas and Karl Barth: Sacred Doctrine and the Natural Knowledge of God* (Notre Dame, Ind.: University of Notre Dame Press, 1999). I depart from Rogers, however, in interpreting Aquinas as not so much absorbing Aristotle into his theology, which is in direct contradiction to those who claim that he is merely Aristotelian. Rather, I believe Aquinas gives voice to the science and intent of Aristotle, but then gathers up his interpretation into a theological treatise. This does not diminish the science in the way that Rogers seems to imply, but corrects it by viewing it through a theological lens. Further, hints at this interpretation are throughout the *Summa,* and so there is no need necessarily to rely on Aquinas's *Commentary on the Romans* to bring his theological premises into view.

reflection a voice? One important way he did this was through his own prior commitment to developing what might be termed a "wisdom" perspective. For him, wisdom found in theology, which he names "holy teaching," is "higher" than human wisdoms as it reflects on "ultimate" causal relations in God, but not in such a way as to swamp human wisdoms as found in science, for example. Theology is therefore to some extent set apart from other human sciences, assuming its principles from "divine science, by which as by supreme wisdom, all our knowledge is governed."[24] Other sciences derive from natural evidence, but the truths in theology are derived from revelation, so it is in a position to stand in judgment over the conclusions of sciences that are incompatible with its teaching. For Aquinas, wisdom can take the form of a gift, given by what he believes draws on a natural bent from a habit of virtue, or through a self-conscious cognitive process in study. This way of adjudicating theology as queen of the sciences is very different from contemporary theology's diminished position in the academy. Yet, at the same time, Aquinas set out possible objections to his view that theology is also a kind of wisdom since it takes its premises from different principles compared with science, or that it could not really be wisdom since it is received by gift from the Holy Spirit. He is aware, therefore, that theology and the natural sciences are not working on the same "flat plane," but he nevertheless argues that they still have something to say to each other — in his case, weaving possible objections into his argument and still insisting that revelation be placed in an ascendant position relative to human sciences, which still share in wisdom but not in the same way as theology. In other words, he holds to a metaphysical priority of revelation in naming theological truths.

The monumental contribution to theological anthropology from a wisdom perspective in David Kelsey's *Eccentric Existence* is worth discussing in this context, not least because it attempts to counter what he sees as negative aspects of traditional theological anthropology's claim for human superiority over other creatures, a view that Aquinas largely assumed, but whose own ontological position on human beings in relation to other animals was also much more complex through his encounter with Aristotle.[25] To be clear, "eccentric" as used by Kelsey stresses that the real value of

24. Thomas Aquinas, *Summa Theologiae, Christian Theology, Vol. 1 (1a. 1),* trans. Thomas Gilby (London: Blackfriars, 1964), 1a, qu. 1.6.

25. I will return to this issue below in relation to how Aquinas navigated what were traditional accounts of the human seen through the lens of reason and freedom.

human beings and their identities are "grounded outside themselves in the concrete ways in which the triune God relates to all that is not God, including humankind."[26] Eccentricity bears some resemblance to Wolfhart Pannenberg's historical discussion of anthropology.[27] Pannenberg argues that human beings' understanding of this world is shaped not so much by the innate characteristics that define responses in other animals, but by the cultural world in which human beings are placed. This then leads once more to a gap between human beings and other animals, where the "instinctive" drive in human beings is thought to be suppressed or deficient, and is such that Arnold Gehlen, Max Scheler, and Helmeth Plesser all developed anthropological theories based on the particularly human "openness to the world" in Scheler or Gehlen, or "exocentricity" in Plessner. Kelsey is critical of a negative form of anthropocentrism cast in terms of human superiority over other creatures that he believes stems from a traditional premodern account of theological anthropology drawn from the early chapters of Genesis.[28] He is also sharply critical of attempts to frame what a human being might be in relation to other creatures on a continuum of degrees of value, which ends up, in his view, with a "conflation of human stewardship with human self-interested exploitation and devastation of fellow creatures."[29] He is, therefore, similarly critical of the use of "soul" and "body" to house discussion of image bearing, believing that such categorization inevitably undermines and disparages the body. He rejects theological anthropologies that set up comparisons with other creatures, considered to be lesser, and comparisons between mental and bodily processes (1:31). In particular, he resists the idea that human dignity comes from the distinctive array of powers and capacities by which we are

26. David Kelsey, *Eccentric Existence: A Theological Anthropology,* vol. 2 (Louisville: Westminster John Knox, 2009), p. 1008.

27. Wolfhart Pannenberg, *Anthropology in Theological Perspective,* trans. Matthew J. O'Connell (Philadelphia: Westminster, 1985), pp. 32-33. Pannenberg ends up focusing his discussion on image bearing in relation to the church, thus leaving behind any discussion of creaturely being as such.

28. David Kelsey, *Eccentric Existence: A Theological Anthropology,* vol. 1 (Louisville: Westminster John Knox, 2009), p. 29. Kelsey argues that a theological anthropology can be conceptually "housed" in different systematic frameworks, including creation, redemption, eschatology, and revelation. He weaves creation, redemption, and eschatology together in three interwoven aspects. I will focus here on his engagement with creation theologies, as this is most pertinent to the discussion.

29. Kelsey, *Eccentric Existence,* 1:30. References to Kelsey's two-volume work are placed in the text in the following paragraphs.

able to respond to God, or even in their exercise in acts of response to God. Rather, for him, human dignity "is inherent in the sheer gift-character of creation" (1:278). One reason he is so reluctant to use the term *imago Dei* is because it is somehow tainted from its history of use in terms of capacities or even functions; he refrains from using this term explicitly until the coda, at the very end of this monumental, two-volume book. The conventional way of using *imago Dei* to structure theological claims for him "systematically will not do" for other reasons, for it relies on what he perceives is a "single narrative logic," and he wants to replace this with a threefold triple helical approach that weaves together creation and eschatological and redemptive themes (2:896-98). For him, only Jesus is normative as the genuine image of God, and humans are imagers of the image of God. He also seems reluctant to give human beings the credit in relation to that imaging, so human beings in their relationships with each other cannot aspire to reflect directly the relations between the Trinitarian persons, yet are still ultimately mysterious (see, e.g., 2:1009-10).

His theological approach begins with an account of creation that, given his resistance to the Genesis texts, has to begin elsewhere, namely, from wisdom literature. While I am broadly supportive of his overall intention to think through a theology of creation from the perspective of biblical wisdom,[30] thus situating human persons in such a context, the particular privilege he affords wisdom in his theological anthropology leads to a particular framing of the questions he seeks to address. In particular, he deals with the bodily aspects of human existence rather oddly in terms of networks of energy systems, which he connects with physical, biological, and social existence (Kelsey, 1:160). He seems to prefer the multifaceted wisdom accounts in Scripture, as they are in one sense distinct from eschatological formulations, thus keeping this strand of the helix free, as it were, from the other strands. This creates its own problems in that it effectively houses a discussion of creation in the category of "proximate" contexts in relationship with the "ultimate" creativity of God (1:162). His engagement with wisdom literature leads to the conclusion that God relates to creation in hospitable generosity, free delight, and self-determining commitment (1:163). In this, he rejects the idea that God is somehow "within" creation as one entity among many, or "between" creatures. This may be one reason

30. I have attempted as much myself in my work on a theology of creation, but more explicitly in the light of the challenges of contemporary science. Celia Deane-Drummond, *Creation through Wisdom: Theology and the New Biology* (Edinburgh: T. & T. Clark, 2000).

why he is resistant to the classical terms to describe God's action in the world, such as "immanence" and "transcendence," terms that he suggests create opposing concepts (1:175). He also believes wisdom literature implicitly rejects the idea that God was somehow constrained by chaos, as implied in Genesis. If the "quotidian," as he defines it, is the lived world in which human beings are situated, along with everyday finite reality of all kinds, including animal, vegetable, and mineral, then "that network of realities defines the spaces and times of our everyday lives and provides us with fellow agents sharing those spaces and times. All taken together they (we!) are a society of everyday being. For convenience, in this theology of creation I shall call it the 'quotidian'" (1:190).

In his rejection of the way anthropocentrism seems to have crept into discussions of image bearing in a negative, exploitative sense toward other creatures, and in his view of the quotidian as inclusive of other creaturely agency, Kelsey is affirming of the significance of the lives of other creatures in shaping human identity from a theological perspective. He is also insistent on the loving generosity of God as engaged and present to creation in a manner that affirms creaturely life. Further, he seems to want to take into account the discoveries of science when exploring the anthropological significance of the book of Job, so he suggests that the two ways of telling the story of our birth are important. First, as living human bodies: this stresses human givenness that implies the importance of "law governed physical processes into which the natural sciences analyze a living human body," but this should not imply that it gives "an exhaustive account of its reality." Rather, a second strand, which corrects the first, is one where we are given that creatureliness by God; so a human being is not just given, it is also a project and one that is central to existential anthropology (1:284-85). But then we are left with this question: Has Kelsey, in developing the notion of the quotidian as shorthand to describe human situatedness, not muted the significance of other creaturely lives for theological anthropology? For he takes the scientific account to be summarized thinly in physical sciences of human bodily existence, preferring to use terms like "energy systems" to describe the way in which humans are situated in this world.

The above also raises a further challenge. Kelsey is keen to reject classical notions of humans as *imago Dei* as he believes that they inevitably lead to distancing and negative comparison between human beings and other creatures. He also rejects the idea of the soul and body as adequate. But he seems to bring back the same ideas indirectly:

> By God's gracious hospitality, she or he is still, in company with other creatures, God's genuine "other" partner in a community of discourse, called by God to be wise, and capable of responding in some manner to God, even if only, like many living creatures, by its sheer mute presence before God. This is because creaturely ontological integrity of human creatures lies not in their physical, psychological or moral centeredness but in their ex-centeredness. It is rooted in the peculiar ways in which God actively relates to them as their creator, the ground of their reality and value. (1:282)

But if that is the case, then it is also profoundly the case that the relationship between God and human beings is unique, and that the vocation of human beings is completely distinctive from that of other creatures. The question that arises, then, is whether all comparative projects necessarily lead to the kind of negative connotations that Kelsey assumes to be the case. For I would argue strongly that paying attention to other creatures in their genuine creaturely capacity need not lead to their diminishment relative to human beings. Part of the issue here seems to be the failure of Kelsey to take into account biological, anthropological, and evolutionary realities, preferring scientific discourses such as energy systems, physical realities, etc., but in a rather loose, generalized way, and avoiding specific engagement with actual scientific debates. I am also less convinced that image bearing in and of itself is destructive to the human in terms of relationships with other creatures; given its preeminence in the anthropological traditions, its avoidance borders on eccentric in a sense that Kelsey certainly does not intend. Nonetheless, highly evocative and creative themes come to the surface in his discussion that are useful in developing a theological anthropology, not least the idea that the fundamental relationship between human beings and God needs to be grounded in the first instance in a wisdom tradition that Kelsey characterizes as living on "borrowed breath." If only Kelsey had taken the universal cultural reach of that wisdom tradition more seriously and applied it to his discussion of theological anthropology! For in his second and third strands, dealing with eschatological completion and reconciliation, the relationship between human beings and other creatures seems to have been all but forgotten, left behind in the first narrative strand as the anonymous quotidian in which human beings are situated. If all three strands are woven together in a helical arrangement, why are only human beings considered worthy of discussion in two of these strands? Has Kelsey really avoided the anthropocentrism that he avers as emerging in his critical treatment of image bearing?

Hence, I take Kelsey's call to situate a theological anthropology within the context of creation with absolute seriousness, but I weave strands of the discussion that deal with reconciliation and future hope into the account. I also, like Kelsey, believe that a theological anthropology necessarily borders on ethical reflection, but I formulate this more explicitly around a discussion of human intersocial relationships with other animals. My focus, then, throughout the present work is to reexamine what might be described as traditional ways of exploring image bearing, but I refocus the discussion in the light of critical engagement with evolutionary and cultural anthropological understandings of the human in relationship with other animals. I prefer, too, to construct a theological anthropology that seeks not so much a grand narrative, be it of a single unitive or rather more sophisticated tri-apartheid reality, as in the case of Kelsey, but to invite consideration of humans in relation to God as perceived in the light of theo-drama, as outlined in more detail below. For the moment, I merely want to show how this theo-dramatic approach might compare with Kelsey's position.

In the first instance, theo-drama takes its cue from historical Christology, informing human relationships with each other and with God, but in my own interpretation of the term, it widens out so that other creatures are not simply the stage, or in Kelsey's case, the "quotidian" in which human beings act. Like Kelsey, theo-drama places the incarnation as central to understanding the human, so the present volume could be seen as in some sense a companion volume to my earlier work on Christology,[31] where I deal with incarnation, reconciliation, and future hope, seen in the light of evolutionary interpretations of the human condition. I end up arguing that human identity needs to be thought through in relationship to who Christ is, that he is the model, as it were, of what human beings need to become. I do not repeat this material here, but it can be presupposed as a starting point of this discussion on theological anthropology. Furthermore, I am also aware that I can do only so much in a compressed volume to take account of the role of the Holy Spirit in the life of the human community and in the community of creation.[32]

My methodological starting point is unashamedly metaphysical, so that I presuppose not only that God exists but *also* that considering a theological interpretation of the human does not favor an exemption from

31. Deane-Drummond, *Christ and Evolution.*

32. I intend to develop this in more detail in a future monograph.

at least a working awareness of current debates in evolutionary biology, evolutionary anthropology, and animal behavior as relevant for that discussion. Such an interrogation, therefore, attempts to develop a theology that is in conversation with biological sciences, but not as if the premises of each were exactly the same, as in the naïve encyclopedic approach identified by MacIntyre, noted above. Rather, my starting point acknowledges the importance of tradition, especially that inspired by reflection on facets of Thomistic theology, but interpreted in the light of new scientific theories and approaches. Further, acknowledgment that we are creaturely kinds like other animals does not mean that our distinctive characteristics become hidden from view, but I suggest that the porosity of the human/animal boundary illuminates a distinctive ontology and a distinctive ethic. Such an unfolding ontology of the human is not to be thought of as existing in isolation, but through relationships, not just with God, but with other creaturely kinds as well.

Other theologians have also started to notice this negative trajectory of human beings defined by separation from animals in philosophical, cultural, and theological discourse. David Clough, for example, has been vociferous in his protest against theological and philosophical views of the human that seem to define that humanity by difference from other animals, going back to Descartes's philosophy.[33] He approves, too, of David Kelsey's theological anthropology that deliberately avoids using categories such as *imago Dei* and soul in order to construct his theological anthropology. Importantly, Clough insists on stressing common creaturehood as a basis for resisting humanity defined by separation and difference. The human vocation is to recognize that common creatureliness. Of course, inasmuch as ancient cosmology presupposed a fixed Chain of Being, the separation narratives seemed set in stone, buoyed by a view of the natural world that took hierarchical arrangements for granted.[34] Clough is also understandably hesitant to endorse more traditional works, including that of Aquinas, because his stress on human reason reinforced the separation narratives.

While having some sympathy with Clough's focus on creatureliness, I am less convinced that image bearing is as barren as he claims it to be for

33. David Clough, "Not a Not-Animal: The Vocation to Be a Human Animal Creature," *Studies in Christian Ethics* 26, no. 1 (2013): 4-17.

34. Clough has also commented on this aspect in David Clough, "Putting Animals in Their Place: On the Theological Classification of Animals," in *Animals as Religious Subjects: Transdisciplinary Perspectives,* ed. Celia Deane-Drummond, Rebecca Artinian-Kaiser, and David Clough (London: Bloomsbury/T. & T. Clark, 2013), pp. 209-24.

theological anthropology. My presupposition is this: rather like the early feminist movements that insisted on sameness in relation to men, those pioneers on behalf of other animals are bound to stress sameness rather than difference. But over time feminists have begun to recognize that there are important distinctions between men and women that should not be threatening to a basic stance of common equality, and further, those distinctions can be worked out in what is sometimes called the third wave, ecofeminism, which now also includes discussion of other animals.[35] My approach in this work is therefore one that is not afraid to acknowledge distinctions, but at the same time interrogate those facets of the human condition that have characterized Western debates. In other words, approaching those areas of reason, freedom, language, and morality that have been associated with separation narratives actually is illuminating, both because of degrees to which other animals could be said to possess such qualities, and because of what makes human beings distinctive. How we might work out the relationships between humans and other animal kinds is a task for humanity, and in theological terms it is eschatological in that it is ongoing. I therefore do not just keep to a critical appraisal of image bearing, but take it in a new direction in the light of what could be called a performative perspective on human distinctiveness. But other creatures, as creatures, also play a part in the performance, but not in the same way as human beings.

Finally, as I mentioned earlier, important philosophical issues need to be touched on when defining what "human nature" means when viewed in the light of evolutionary processes. Does "human nature" mean simply characteristics that I share with other animals but which are expressed in a different way? Or does it mean that which distinguishes me from other animals, or even that which characterizes my particular sense of being a person, as worked out in particular human roles and relationships? Mikael Stenmark sets up what he calls the minimal characteristics required for having a "human nature," resisting the idea that a functional approach to human beings gets round the problem of having to name specific ontological characteristics.[36] He deals with antiessentialist objections to the idea of having a "nature" at all from postmodern deconstructive writers who claim that it provides a political means through which to control human popu-

35. The literature on this is vast, but for a basic survey see C. Deane-Drummond, "Creation," in *Cambridge Companion to Feminist Theology,* ed. Susan Parsons (Cambridge: Cambridge University Press, 2002), pp. 190-207.

36. Mikael Stenmark, "Is There a Human Nature?" *Zygon* 47, no. 4 (2012): 890-902.

lations. Some biologists, on the one hand, including philosophers such as John Dupré, are prepared to join this discussion by arguing against such an idea based on a supposed common genetic ground with other creatures.[37] On the other hand, some evolutionary psychologists are busy searching for core characteristics of a supposed universal "human nature" that can be mapped through psychological testing. Stenmark calls this "species specific" or "kind" nature. Nature can also mean a "type" nature according to which someone belongs to a specific gender, race, social, or cultural type. A typifying view of "human nature" is presupposed in evolutionary discussions of sex selection, which models human behavior according to particular patterns of "pair bonding." Finally, there is individual "nature" that is those personal characteristics that make up individually characterized human uniqueness. Stenmark does not comment on this characteristic in evolutionary terms, but rather more attention is beginning to be paid to individual differences as sources of variation, along with the wide range of plasticity in response to different conditions. The biological characteristics that Stenmark names as that which mark out human uniqueness relative to other species are a bipedal walk, erect posture, and a large brain.[38] Such characteristics are those that are *typical,* in answer to the antiessentialist objection that not all humans share such characteristics. Furthermore, just because evolutionary biology shows changes in biological characteristics of the human, these changes coexist with those characteristics that are more conserved in evolu-

37. John Dupré, *Humans and Other Animals* (Oxford: Oxford University Press, 2002), p. 109; see also John Dupré, "On Human Nature," *Human Affairs* 2 (2003): 109-22. Dupré argues not just against essentialist notions of human nature as incorrect given the great cultural, geographical, and historical diversity, but also against evolutionary psychologists who claim to have found human universals based on what seem to him to be *statistical* measurements of behavior. To claim to have found some sort of fundamental "essence" of human nature is, for him, deeply mistaken. Inasmuch as Dupré argues against some of the strident claims of evolutionary psychology and for a view of human nature combining individual development with location in a society, I have some sympathy with his views. However, to argue that *nothing* can be usefully said about human nature in a collective sense of species characteristics goes too far, for denying that there is such a possibility opens up an argument for the justification of all kinds of manipulative transgenomic practices. There are ethical dangers with extreme essentialism that locates innate tendencies in deep biological roots, and such a view would tend, therefore, to deny the possibility of genuine human freedom and responsibility.

38. Stenmark, "Is There a Human Nature?" p. 890. Of course, this categorization applies to hominids in general rather than *Homo sapiens* in particular, so such a view would mean that human beings share a human nature across all hominids. See above for comment on bipedality.

tionary terms. Of course, in defining the human, Stenmark has to add to his biological list rational and moral thinking along with artistic and linguistic expression. Stenmark believes that Christian theological notions of image bearing most naturally lean toward an essentialist understanding of human nature. To try and avoid speaking of capacities in favor of image bearing, understood in terms of relationships, does not, for Stenmark, avoid the issue, since human relationships presuppose certain capabilities.

In the present book, I am working on the assumption that although we need to be cautious, for reasons given above, we *can* speak meaningfully about human "nature," but working out when and how and why such a "nature" appeared in evolutionary terms is hotly contested. As hinted at already, I am also extremely cautious about some of the universalizing tendencies in evolutionary psychology inasmuch as they can imply that human behavior is built into who we are as persons. The social worlds in which different branches and debates within evolutionary biology are constructed need to be taken into account, alongside the particular, in some cases, exaggerated claims made for particular genetic roots of particular behavior, such as violence, for example. Overall, genetic essentialism is to be avoided especially where it becomes too all-embracing and takes the form of metaphysical naturalism; rather, as noted above, evolution needs to be viewed as taking place in four dimensions:[39] the genetic, the epigenetic, the behavioral, and the symbolic. Once we do this, the plasticity present in "human nature" comes to the surface and discussion of what that nature entails becomes rather less threatening from the perspective of essentialist critics. On the other hand, I agree with Stenmark that to lose *all* ideas about "human nature" in an ontological sense would be mistaken in thinking through a theological anthropology. That does not need to imply fixity or flexibility in what that nature might entail, but implies boundaries within which to rethink the human.

The Evolution of Religion

One of the core characteristics of a universal approach to human species nature that has been flagged up in recent years is the idea of human beings as a symbolic species. According to this argument, human beings gener-

39. Eva Jablonka and Marion Lamb, *Evolution in Four Dimensions: Genetic, Epigenetic, Behavioral, and Symbolic Variation in the History of Life* (Cambridge: MIT Press, 2005).

ated complex symbol systems at about the same time that they developed capacities for language.[40] And following from such a view is the idea that human beings evolved to be religious. Of course, precisely why religiosity appeared in the map of human history is a topic of intense debate, even within the scientific community. Possibly the most extreme view in terms of a tight connection between evolution by natural selection and religious belief is that religious beliefs have evolved, either due to a selective advantage of a belief or due to an associated trait that is advantageous, such as the ability to cooperate. One might ask: How can belief in God carry a selective advantage in biological terms, especially if that belief leads to practices such as celibacy that seem to show a lack of advantage? Answers here include somewhat convoluted explanations. If such a trait or collection of traits showed no obvious selective benefit in the past and no obvious benefit today, it is known as a spandrel, whereas if it showed no benefit in the past and some benefit today, it is known as an exaptation. It is possible to make the case for entirely opposite conclusions on whether religion is selectively advantageous or not. For example, belief in God is a different expression of a capacity that proved useful in the past, such as agent detection that evolved to take account of presumably threatening agents. Pascal Boyer, for example, views religion as parasitic on other mental capacities that were useful in evolutionary terms.[41] Others suggest that religion provides reassurance in the face of uncertainties.[42] Michael Ruse concludes that "Discussions are simply all over the place" and "Everyone seems to have their own angle," so "one is repelled by bad or casual or hopeful (or hopeless) attempts at doing science."[43]

How can some clarity be brought to bear on this seeming mess? One way is to distinguish among those who argue for evolutionary origins of religious belief, between those who argue for the beneficial impact of religion through social and cultural means and those who argue for that impact through cognitive science. In the former case, religion is either

40. Terence W. Deacon, *The Symbolic Species: The Co-evolution of Language and the Brain* (New York and London: Norton, 1997).

41. Pascal Boyer, *Religion Explained: The Evolutionary Origins of Religious Thought* (New York: Basic Books, 2002), p. 311.

42. Scott Atran, *In Gods We Trust: The Evolutionary Landscape of Religion* (New York: Oxford University Press, 2004).

43. Michael Ruse, *The Philosophy of Human Evolution* (Cambridge: Cambridge University Press, 2012), p. 97. Ruse does not help that confusion by seeming to simplify the evolutionary problem associated with religion as restricted to neo-Darwinian inheritance.

selected for as a way to strengthen cooperative practices in groups, which invokes natural selection working at the level of groups, or is operative as part of a symbolic inheritance system in a way that is in some sense distinct from specific neo-Darwinian evolutionary processes through natural selection. An unanswered question is why specifically religious ideas have dominated over other alternatives. In this case, cognitive science seeks to try and explain why some religious ideas take hold in the human mind in the way they do. Justin Barrett takes this approach, and he argues that scientific explanations of why our brains are "hard-wired" in some sense to be religious do not threaten the theological truth claims of that belief.[44] The "mental modules" required for religious belief rely on an intuitive psychology that includes a hypersensitive agency detection device (HADD) that, apparently, is able to detect the particular movement of a body as entailing agency, and the theory of mind (TOM) as that which attributes particular beliefs and other states to that agent. The concept of god or gods is labeled counterintuitive inasmuch as such a belief either violates expected behavior, or an ontological property is transferred from one category to another. But, the reasoning goes, such counterintuitive elements need to be sufficiently minimal to be successful culturally. There are scientific problems with this discussion in that it is very hard to prove that such agency detection modules exist in the brain as a discrete unit, even if there might be evidence for parts of the brain becoming specialized for certain activities, such as language, for example. If we go further and map every behavior according to computerized mental "modules" in the way that some evolutionary psychologists have been inclined to do, then one suspects that the information technology of our own culture is serving to shape the metaphors being used and adapted in scientific investigations. It would also be more accurate to say religion is *constrained* by such mental categories, rather than *explained* by them. But even if we say that religious belief is constrained by the particular way human cognition works, what does that tell us explicitly about the evolution of religion? Furthermore, is the characterization of religious belief in terms of "agency" really correct as a universal, given the vast range of religious beliefs and the differences in manner of believing?

44. Justin Barrett, "The Naturalness of Religion and the Unnaturalness of Theology," in *Is Religion Natural?* ed. Dirk Evers et al. (London: T. & T. Clark/Continuum, 2012), pp. 3-23. See also Justin Barrett, *Why Would Anyone Believe in God?* (Lanham, Md.: Alta Mira Press, 2004).

Evolutionary biologists are, of course, remarkably imaginative when it comes to thinking through why religious belief might have appeared in evolutionary history. One theory, for example, is that religious belief was a selective advantage for group cooperation where the "defector" in that cooperation is difficult to detect, to punish, or to regulate. According to this theory, belief in a punitive god was an advantage in encouraging individual conformity to group norms.[45] While belief in a punitive god may be relatively common in some cultures, is this necessarily an essential element of all religious beliefs, which it would need to be to argue that this counts as an adequate explanation of religions?[46] Furthermore, if we allow for the fact that religious beliefs are passed down from one generation to the next, it would make more sense to think of mental capacities for religion as only very loosely, if at all, connected with neo-Darwinian genetic mechanisms, and more likely to be affiliated with behavioral inheritance and symbolic inheritance systems. A narrowly conceived focus on particular beliefs is not sufficient in the exploration of the dynamics of religious belief, for it is the *practices* of religion that arguably cement communities together and serve as a powerful means to justify those beliefs.

If practices are important, and we attend to a more flexible understanding of evolution compared with that narrowly constricted to evolution by natural selection, then how might the evolution of religion have come about? One possible clue is provided by play among mammals, where play is viewed as a way of being that expresses what might be called a "relaxed field" and "repeated performance" and a freedom from striving necessary to meet everyday demands.[47] Furthermore, religions engage in

45. Dominic Johnson, "Why God Is the Best Punisher," *Religion, Brain and Behavior* 1, no. 1 (2011): 77-84. For a fuller version, see Dominic Johnson, *Payback: God's Punishment and the Evolution of Cooperation* (Oxford: Oxford University Press, 2013). Chris Boehm seems to endorse this possibility in his account of the evolution of morality, naming this as a form of "otherworldly sanctioning"; see Chris Boehm, *Moral Origins: The Evolution of Virtue, Altruism, and Shame* (New York: Basic Books, 2012), pp. 202-3.

46. Criticism of this theory is also found in Jeffrey Schloss and Michael Murray, "How Might Evolution Lead to Hell?" *Religion, Brain and Behavior* 1, no. 1 (2011): 93-99.

47. Gordon Burghardt, *The Genesis of Animal Play: Testing the Limits* (Cambridge: MIT Press, 2005), pp. 71-81. He mentions five indicators of animal play: (a) limited immediate function in that it does not contribute to immediate survival needs (note, this is different from saying it has indirect survival value, which is necessary to affirm if such behavior has evolved through neo-Darwinian means); (b) an endogenous quality, or done for its own sake; (c) structural or temporal difference, that is, using behavior that may be taken from ordinary life, including fighting, mating, etc., but without that aim; (d) repeated performance,

narrative thinking that, arguably, is at the heart of our individual and collective psychological identity.[48] Robert Bellah situates his own discussion of religion within a scientific account of cosmological and evolutionary origins that he is honest enough to admit functions like a metanarrative and gives rise to feelings that are pre-Copernican, even religious in orientation, even if their content is post-Copernican.[49] Parental care is the prerequisite of mammalian play, and play may have a maintenance role in terms of providing a "training ground" for stock behaviors, or a more active role in enhancing that behavior in novel directions. In human beings, once we align ritual to a highly developed type of play, then "ritual is the primordial form of serious play in human evolutionary history . . . religion . . . grows out of the implications of ritual in a variety of ways that never leave ritual entirely behind."[50] Bellah believes that some kinds of rituals began prior to complex language acquisition in humans. Bellah's comparison between chimpanzee celebrations and human rituals may not be all that helpful in delineating human evolutionary processes,[51] given that the recent common ancestor is not like either the *Pan* or *Homo* lineages.[52] However, there is some scope to Bellah's comment that early ritual has very little to do with so-called supernatural beings that are often used in the definition of religion.[53] Once narrative took hold, then other animals that have human-like characteristics appear in religious rituals regularly,

---

but not in a stereotypical manner; and (e) a relaxed field, that is, it can only take place when the animal is relatively free from stress.

48. Robert Bellah argues as much in his *Religion in Human Evolution: From the Paleolithic to the Axial Age* (Cambridge: Harvard University Press, Belknap Press, 2011), p. 34.

49. Bellah, *Religion in Human Evolution,* p. 45 He also admits that when it comes to the religious implications of scientific stories, "it is better to face this fact head on rather than try to deny it" (p. 46).

50. Bellah, *Religion in Human Evolution,* p. 92.

51. Bellah, *Religion in Human Evolution,* p. 93.

52. For a comment on the difference between *Pan* and *Homo,* see the excellent discussion in Agustín Fuentes, "Cooperation, Conflict and Niche Construction in the Genus *Homo,*" in *War, Peace, and Human Nature,* ed. Douglas Fry (Oxford: Oxford University Press, 2013), pp. 78-94, where he claims that "Chimpanzee analogies in human evolutions are only partial at best, as the genus *Homo* and the genus *Pan* (consisting of the two species *P. paniscus,* or bonobos, and *P. troglodytes,* or chimpanzees) are extremely different in a wide array of behavioral, ecological and physiological arenas. Considering the available fossil, physiological and morphological evidence . . . the recent common ancestor was largely unlike the present forms. This means that behavioral analogies need to be used with extreme care" (p. 85).

53. Bellah, *Religion in Human Evolution,* p. 95.

but it is hard to conceive of "supernatural" as a concept when such cultures did not have a conception of "nature," let alone something that was somehow distinguished from it. This brings up another point, namely, how far is any study of anthropology inevitably going to be culturally laden, bound by the traditions in which we find ourselves?

The Human Condition

The anthropologist Tim Ingold is perhaps one of the clearest writers on the way those who have imbibed Western traditions characterize humans vis-à-vis other animals.[54] Since classical times, the way to think about humanity has been in relation to and often in opposition to animality; humans are thought of as in some sense making up for the deficiencies that we find in other animals, be it through reflection on reason, language, intellect, moral consciousness, or, though he does not mention it, the topic I have just alluded to above, namely, religion. And writers of every generation, including the classic writers, emphasize, "as though it were some startling new discovery," that we are animals as well, so that what makes us human is founded in comparisons with other animal kinds.[55] Ingold argues that there are two ways of thinking about a human being: as an *animal* among other species of animal, and as a *condition* of being human revealed in the many and varied cultures in which human society is placed. However, if these two are conflated, then we arrive at an odd view of human uniqueness that depends less on recognizing different species in their uniqueness and more on what sets human beings apart from other animals.

Ingold is insistent that we should not seek some fixed, essential biological ingredients in defining human beings; rather, "humanity presents itself as a continuous field of variation," so any divisions are "artificial products of our penchant for classification and stereotyping."[56] Biological species are not "natural kinds" in the sense of fixity in the manner of inorganic substance; rather, biological species are structured according to *genealogical* relationships. He also seems bent on stressing the highly *contingent* aspects in human evolution, so that "Humans did not *have* to

54. Tim Ingold, "Humanity and Animality," in *Companion Encyclopedia of Anthropology,* ed. Tim Ingold (London: Routledge, 1994), pp. 14-32. See also Tim Ingold, introduction to *What Is an Animal?* ed. Tim Ingold (London: Routledge, 1994), pp. 1-16.

55. Ingold, "Humanity and Animality," p. 15.

56. Ingold, "Humanity and Animality," p. 17.

evolve."[57] While he is correct, in my view, to affirm different creatures in the genealogical trajectory to the human, so that other apes, for example, are not considered a "botched" attempt at humanity, there are arguments for constraint in evolutionary processes that suggest that in some respects human evolution is teleonomic or, to use Simon Conway Morris's term, "inevitable."[58]

It is the manner in which the philosophical debate about human beings has been set up that is the most interesting aspect of Ingold's thesis. For he argues that if we pose the question, "What makes humans *different* in kind from animals?" then this radically changes the inquiry from "What makes humans animals of a particular kind?"[59] The former question changes the inquiry from one about the human being as a member of an animal species, to one about "the state or condition of being human, one radically opposed to the condition of animality" (p. 19), shifting the human-animal relation from an inclusive to an exclusive relationship. Here, humanity and animality are viewed in dualistic relationship with each other, along with other dichotomies such as nature/culture, body/mind, emotion/reason, instinct/art, and even further to the division of the natural sciences/humanities and so on. So where does "human nature" reside? Is nature simply the "lowest common denominator" or a universal for each kind, as many sociobiologists would have us believe? Or does "nature" mean the material world somehow in opposition to culture? A common view is to pitch "human nature" as that which is distinctive in terms of mind, leaving the *biological* aspects of what it is to be human to the "brutish" state of humankind, its animality. Ingold is, therefore, just as critical of anthropologists who stress the unique capacity for multiple human cultures as he is of those religious writers who stressed the ancient idea of a unique spirit. He still seems to want to keep cultural aspects in some sense apart from those of other animals, so that "culture underwrites the identity of a human being, not as a biological organism, but as a moral subject. In this latter capacity, we regard every man or woman as a person" (p. 23). Thus, the tension between human as *Homo sapiens* and human as a moral condition excludes certain questions being asked, such as how far are other animals endowed with language, or how far, in other

57. Ingold, "Humanity and Animality," p. 19.

58. Simon Conway Morris, *Life's Solution: Inevitable Humans in a Lonely Universe* (Cambridge: Cambridge University Press, 2003).

59. Ingold, "Humanity and Animality," p. 19. References to this essay have been placed in the text in the next few paragraphs.

words, might there be animal humanity and not just human animality? Significantly, therefore, this "suggests that the boundary between human and other animal species does not run alongside, but actually crosscuts the boundary between humanity and animality as states of being" (p. 24). Ingold offers the example of the Ojibwa, who believe that personhood is not necessarily confined to human beings, but can exist in other animals as well. Is this fanciful? Certainly, argues Ingold, but no less so than the imperialistic notion of humanity as lord of nature in Kantian philosophy.

When Ingold then turns to address human uniqueness, he lists those characteristics that have come to the fore as candidates for human distinction, including reason; language; religion; capacity to design, or make symbols, often attributing such distinctions to the male members of the human species. Against such a view, gradualists argue that other species share in some of these capacities. Ingold presses his criticism more sharply by suggesting that such characteristics are not so much about human beings alongside other species, but about the introspective establishment of the *human condition* (p. 27). He objects to such a comparison as it assumes humans are not different from other animals in the way that animals are different from each other; instead, it is a way of placing humans beyond the bounds of animality entirely. More specifically, he accuses the gradualist thesis of being loaded with "a strong bias of ethnocentrism," so the comparisons made between humans and other animals represent only a fraction of the human population as a whole, namely, the "Western civilized man" who is intelligent, scientifically enlightened, self-consciously liberated, and male (p. 28). But once we recognize that this is culturally laden, this separates humans from other animals as the stress is on human cultural variety in distinction from animality. Hence, for Ingold, we are left with a dilemma: for while human cultural diversity stressed in anthropology displays a form of anthropocentrism, a gradualist view displays a form of ethnocentrism based on the conflation of the human condition with the biological species (p. 29).

Ingold's proposal is to find ways of crossing the divide between anthropocentrism and ethnocentrism and to avoid limiting study to the evolution of the human species, *Homo sapiens,* or the human condition as shown in culture or history. Therefore, "we have to comprehend the relation between the species and the condition, between human beings and being human" (p. 30). The question, of course, is how precisely to do this, given that we are all inevitably situated in particular cultural traditions ourselves. Certainly, aspects of the human condition such as freedom, language, morality, and so on can be interpreted in terms of the specific characteristics of different creatures, that is, their species kinds, rather than just being used as a way of making unfavorable comparisons with human beings. So, once the evolutionary biological literature and the anthropological literature start to be mixed up in a way that both speak to each other, this will begin to break down the established dualisms between nature and culture. Furthermore, I suggest that this enables at least a start to formulating in the midst of this dynamic interchange a *new kind* of theological anthropology, one that draws on the wisdom of the liminal boundaries in a creative way. Of course, as Christian theology, it is inevitably emerging from a tradition that has found its most ready roots within a given framework of cultural diversity. As a writer born in the United Kingdom and educated in both natural science and the humanities and more recently living in the United States, in one sense I have a multiple cultural parentage, but in another sense a very myopic one given the sheer diversity of different cultural and religious traditions. The purpose of this book is certainly not to generate a kind of universalism within theological discourse, or to pronounce any kind of finality on what it means to be human, but to begin to set up some questions that provoke discussion and challenge preconceived ideas in the way that Ingold has attempted to do from an anthropological perspective, though, in his case, without much resolution. Theology is, of course, used to asking more questions than it answers, but I will also be attempting here to be both constructive and open-ended, to offer an argument and framework for thinking through the issues, but at the same time to make room for alternatives.

When Species Meet

If reflection on the human condition has set up premises about what it means to be human in a way that is distorting a more considered sense of what is distinctive about human beings in a way that leads, arguably, to narrowly conceived forms of exceptionalism in the light of characteristics of other animals, then perhaps reflection on the human encounter with those animal kinds will be productive. There are a number of ways to do this, but one of the prime aims of this book is to explore that encounter with other animals without losing a sense of human distinctiveness, to argue, further, that this distinction is best expressed in the light of that encounter and that reflection on such animal studies needs to be integrated into a theological anthropology. The latter roots human identity, in a primary sense, in a relationship with God as Creator of all that exists, of material and creaturely being as such. Theological anthropology as I am developing it here, accordingly, takes its bearings from an appreciation of God immersed with us, God incarnate as a human being like us. In addition, I point to those inner human experiences of God as Other; in theological language, the work of grace. A fully human life in theological terms is also expressed in community in horizontal relationships with others, including nonhuman others.

I argue in the section that follows this one that the way to achieve an outline of such theological anthropology as a more constructive task is through theo-drama, through bringing the world of creation into the human world of history. This is not done to demean the significance of that creation, but to elevate it and view human history as radically integrated into the evolutionary and ecological history of other creaturely kinds. I will also be dealing with explicit topics that are sometimes put under the bracket of theological ethics, such as justice and fairness, cooperation and charity. Of course, I am acutely aware that this discussion is limited and preliminary, but it provides an argument for a different form of theological ethics, one that is both self-consciously aware of its theological roots and deeply concerned about practices and how we are to live in order to begin to define human meaning in terms of concrete lives. I leave aside, however, in this volume, more specific examples of what this might look like in terms of case studies in the human treatment of other animals.[60]

As a way of setting up this constructive task, I turn my attention to a scholar who has achieved more than most in setting out a claim for the importance of other species in cultural anthropology. The boundary between culture and "nature," understood as somehow outside or apart from that culture, is thus problematized and made more fluid. This finds its theological parallels in attempts to develop a theological anthropology somehow apart from the created world in which we live. Although, as discussed above, David Kelsey has made bold steps toward including creation as a significant aspect of his threefold account of the human, if creation is reduced to the "quotidian," its specific sense of gift is weakened, since it becomes generalized merely as the context out of which human history and human culture arise. Instead, Donna Haraway offers a reminder to ex-

60. I intend to address issues such as animal rights/rites in a further monograph on the ethics of sustainability and its practices that will be developed in the coming years.

plore entanglements between human beings and other species, or "nature-cultures." Haraway starts with a grounded approach to human beings, so that "I am a creature of the mud, not the sky."[61] The symbionts that occupy each and every living human cell remain a fascination for her, so for her there is a vivid and real sense in which human bodies are pulsating with tiny companions. How does she arrive at this position? In the first place, she argues that four wounds serve to challenge human exceptionalism, understood as the belief that humanity alone is *not* a spatial and temporal web of interspecies dependencies. Drawing on Jacques Derrida, she takes the first three wounds from Freud, namely, (a) the decentering of the earth following the Copernican revolution, (b) the Darwinian revolution that placed humanity in the midst of other creatures, (c) the additional primacy to the unconscious in human psychology given by Freud, and adds a fourth: (d) the cyborg, which mixes up human and material reality.[62] It seems to me, however, that (d) is highly ambivalent for her project to resist human exceptionalism. Hence, while the cyborg overcomes the divide between organic and technical, it also seems to work against overcoming another divide that is crucial to her thought, namely, that between animal and human. While drawing on a distinct version of posthumanism, transhumanism clearly shows the ambivalence of this trajectory in terms of human practices.[63] Haraway herself denies the label "posthuman" on the basis that many human concerns, particularly feminist ones, are still crucial to her, and that cultural fashions, such as "posthumanism," will pass.[64] She is rightly critical, in my view, of Jacques Derrida's essay on his encounter with a cat, *The Animal That Therefore I Am,* because he fails to give enough attention to what the cat might *actually* be doing, thinking, and feeling; he fails, in other words, to map out what it might mean to live intersectionally.[65]

61. Donna Haraway, *When Species Meet* (Minneapolis: University of Minnesota Press, 2008), p. 3.

62. Haraway, *When Species Meet,* pp. 11-12.

63. I have discussed the significance of this aspect in relation to other animals in Celia Deane-Drummond, "Taking Leave of the Animal? The Theological and Ethical Implications of Transhuman Projects," in *Transhumanism and Transcendence: Christian Hope in an Age of Technological Enhancement,* ed. Ron Cole-Turner (Washington, D.C.: Georgetown University Press, 2012), pp. 115-30.

64. Haraway, *When Species Meet,* p. 17.

65. Haraway, *When Species Meet,* pp. 18-23. Haraway is using the term "intersectional" to refer in the primary sense to feminist critical theoretical interpretations of asymmetrical categorizations of women and humans, used in the first instance by women of color. Feminist

Haraway retells the story of primatologist Barbara Smuts, who decided to study baboons in Kenya in the Great Rift Valley near Lake Naivasha. Rather than sit immobilized on a rock, as standard scientific protocol suggested, she recognized that to really understand these creatures she needed to adjust what she did in the light of the baboon's social semiotics addressed to her and to the others in the troop. She found that gradually, instead of being treated like an "object," she was recognized as a "subject" with whom they could communicate.[66] However, this permission to allow baboons to be themselves by entering their world is not enough for Haraway. She presses for "situated histories, situated naturecultures, in which all the actors become who they are *in the dance of relating,* not from scratch, not ex nihilo, but full of the patterns of their sometimes-joined, sometimes-separate heritages both before and lateral to *this* encounter."[67] So also, ritualistic encounters between bodies express relationships in such a way that it is hard to deceive, so "An embodied communication is more like a dance than a word. The flow of entangled meaningful bodies in time — whether jerky and nervous or flaming and flowing, whether both partners move in harmony or painfully out of synch or something else altogether — is communication about relationship, the relationship itself, and the means of reshaping relationship and so its enactors."[68]

Haraway carves out a space for a new way of thinking not just for the humanities, but for the sciences as well. Ethnoprimatology, for example, is a newly emerging field, one that explores the anthropology of the human-primate interface.[69] This is not, as we might think from a Western perspective, an exotic or theoretical treatment; rather, humans have interacted with other primates for the entire period of *Homo* residence in most of Africa, East Asia, South Asia, Southeast Asia, Central America, and South America.[70] Ecological changes wrought by human presence

intersectionality, when applied to other animals, resists setting up some sort of analogous relationships with humans; rather, it teases out culturally *interlocking* systems of power and dominance and the weblike character of relationships (p. 309 n. 22). I engage with Derrida's essay in more detail in chapter 3.

66. Haraway, *When Species Meet,* pp. 23-25.

67. Haraway, *When Species Meet,* p. 25.

68. Haraway, *When Species Meet,* p. 26.

69. Agustín Fuentes, "Ethnoprimatology and the Anthropology of the Human-Primate Interface," *Annual Review of Anthropology* 41 (2012): 101-17.

70. Fuentes, "Ethnoprimatology and the Anthropology of the Human-Primate Interface."

are happening faster than they can be studied. Ethnoprimatology marks, significantly for my argument, both humans and other primates as coparticipants in shaping social and ecological space, rather than viewing the interface in terms of conflict and competition for resources. It also rejects the idea that ecosystems exist that are entirely free from human interference, or that studies of ostensibly wild systems give better insights than studies where primates live alongside human communities. The inclusion of the nonhuman other, as central in the examination of being human, offers a distinct way of approaching anthropological studies. There have been close affiliations between humans and other primates in physiological, phylogenetic, and behavioral senses since the dawn of the genus *Homo* in a way that makes an appreciation of such interrelationships particularly important for anthropology. However, this is not just in order to understand our own species, but also to understand other primates in general, in the light of the "monumental niche construction" by humans, sometimes referred to as the Anthropocene. Relationships range from benign to more violent, such as chimpanzee use of human crops in Bossou, Republic of New Guinea. A close study of behavioral and ecological factors allowed a suite of practical recommendations to be made to ameliorate the potential for violent interspecies interactions.[71] Further, alongside shifting economic, ethnic, and technological changes, human perceptions of other primates and the mythos surrounding them have a significant impact on their concrete ecology and behavior.[72] Viral pathogens, such as simian foamy virus and parasitic pathogens, have a complex and shared ecology between human and other primate species. But the key role in human alteration of a shared ecological niche has a significant impact on the evolution of other sympatric species.

Anthropologist Agustín Fuentes argues that given the dominance of human beings globally, there is selection for those primates that are best able to coexist with humans, such as macaque monkeys in South and Southeast Asia and baboons in sub-Saharan Africa. Fuentes has "observed the myriad ways in which humans look at, think about, consume, and cohabitate with other animals across the planet," so "the interface between

71. Fuentes, "Ethnoprimatology and the Anthropology of the Human-Primate Interface." See Kimberley J. Hockings and Tatyana Humle, "Best Practice Guidelines for the Prevention and Mitigation of Conflict between Humans and Great Apes" (Gland, Switzerland: IUCN/SCC Primate Spec. Group, 2009).

72. Agustín Fuentes, "Naturecultural Encounters in Bali: Monkeys, Temples, Tourists and Ethnoprimatology," *Cultural Anthropology* 25, no. 4 (2010): 600-624.

humans and other forms of life is neither uniform, nor simple."[73] There is considerable variety in how the human-alloprimate interface is worked out in different cultures, and some species are better able to adapt to living with humans than others. Apes and leaf monkeys seem less able to adapt to a shared living space with humans, so the outlook for the great apes is really bleak. In Asia, the dominant Hindu, Buddhist, and Shinto religious traditions and popular mythos create a baseline for sustainable relationships between macaques and humans. While a detailed treatment of such relationships would be of interest, the point of raising this issue is to show that human religious systems have coevolved alongside the companion creatures sharing the ecological space with humans. Christianity is something of an aberration in this respect, in that while its most ancient history to some extent took account of and appreciated the presence of other animals in its symbolism and liturgical practice, its more recent history in the Western world has stressed human exceptionalism.[74]

There is, nonetheless, a burgeoning contemporary literature on human/other animal intimacies that goes beyond that related to our nearest cousins, the primates. From attachments to pigs in New Guinea, foxhounds in England, and water buffalo in Nepal, to human-dolphin encounters in numerous locations, the list is both expansive and fascinating.[75] How far are such interactions "anthropomorphic" in the sense of reading human characteristics into the lives of mythical animals, or treating actual animals *as if* they are equivalent members of the human community, or actually sharing some of the characteristics of human persons as far as their inner states are concerned? Kay Milton argues that while the latter is the most promising, the use of this term is misleading, as it raises the question of which emotion or state can be attributed to other animals, something that cannot be reasonably tested out.[76] To assume other creatures do not have

73. Agustín Fuentes, "Social Minds and Social Selves: Redefining the Human-Alloprimate Interface," in *The Politics of Species: Reshaping Our Relationships with Other Animals,* ed. Raymond Corby and Annette Lanjouw (Cambridge: Cambridge University Press, 2014). I am grateful to Agustín Fuentes for giving me access to this chapter at the proof stage, before final publication.

74. For further discussion on this, see Celia Deane-Drummond and David Clough, eds., *Creaturely Theology: On God, Humans, and Other Animals* (London: SCM, 2009), and Deane-Drummond, Artinian-Kaiser, and Clough, eds., *Animals as Religious Subjects.*

75. John Knight, ed., *Animals in Person: Cultural Perspectives on Human-Animal Interactions* (New York: Berg, 2005).

76. Kay Milton, "Anthropomorphism or Egomorphism: The Perception of Nonhuman Persons by Human Ones," in *Animals in Person,* pp. 255-71.

such states may be just as problematic as assuming that they do. To avoid this problem Milton argues for a greater stress on human perception of other animals, so "egomorphism" relates to the insight that I understand a specific encounter insofar as they are "like me," rather than simply "human-like." We come to know ourselves, therefore, through intersubjectivity, but that intersubjectivity can be extended to human relationships with other animals. While helpful in some respects, this approach avoids the problem of working out what is really going on in the minds of the respective animals, so that the perception of other animals as like me could just as easily be delusionary. There has been a tendency in anthropological studies to oppose a constructivist approach that attributes characteristics to things versus direct perception that finds meanings in that environment. Instead, Milton argues that perception provides the raw material through which to think meaningfully about the world, and this lays the foundation for construction. But perception is not simply an armchair activity; rather, it takes place within the course of practical engagement with the world. The question then becomes, given the enlarged awareness of practical engagements with other animals, how might theological perception shift in response to that awareness?

Theo-Drama

While the concept of theo-drama is integral to the approach I am developing in this book, my own theological anthropology ends up being very different from that of Hans Urs von Balthasar, who inspired my interest in theo-dramatics. This is because of his constriction of theo-drama to human agents, and his relative lack of attention to scientific, bodily, and evolutionary aspects of human beings. Hence, while I find aspects of his discussion of the relationship between human and divine freedom particularly useful, his own explicit treatment of theological anthropology presents an approach that, ironically perhaps, is very different from the theological anthropology I am developing in this book.[77] Balthasar's treatment of theological anthropology restricts itself to human, ecclesial history and is focused on a particular interpretation of human perfection that somewhat bizarrely is still prepared to associate original sin and sexuality,

77. Hans Urs von Balthasar, *A Theological Anthropology* (Eugene, Ore.: Wipf and Stock, 2010 [1967]).

likening the latter to a degraded form of functional pleasure characteristic of other animals.[78] Further, while I agree with Balthasar that theologically Christology is presupposed in anthropology and sets up a theological horizon for considering human activity, I only touch on Christology in this work since I have already dealt with aspects such as the significance of the humanity of Christ for conceiving the meaning of image bearing in my previous monograph.[79] I have also had reason to challenge Balthasar's stereotypical view of humanity in terms of male and female difference.[80] Balthasar interprets Adam as different from other animals in that he is created first, unlike other animals, which are created in pairs; so that the delay in creation means that Eve is the "answer" and completion for what is lacking in the male.[81] His stress on the significance of the limitation of the incarnation in the maleness of Christ provides fuel for a sharp feminist critique.[82] Ironically, perhaps, he does admit to "even animals" having a life that shows a dramatic quality in their eroticism, play, defense of the family, song, and mortal combat, but is condescending in his suggestion that such a "natural dialectic" influences "simple people."[83] This is for him the first stage, the natural dialectic expressed in human sexual relationships. His is a progressive account of human history, so a second master-slave dialectic becomes shaped in domestic, clannish, tribal, and national existence that he draws from Hegel. There is a further, third dialectic between Jews and Gentiles expressed in Christian theology as the Old and New Testaments.[84] Hence, while he views, in a limited way, something of a dramatic narrative reaching into the life of natural systems, his interpretation is hierarchical, androcentric, and implicitly racist toward Jews in relation to Christians. Balthasar's attention to the significance of the resurrection for a theological anthropology is, however, a theological move on his part that I do not develop in any detail, preferring to leave this to

78. Balthasar, *A Theological Anthropology,* p. 89.

79. Deane-Drummond, *Christ and Evolution.*

80. Deane-Drummond, *Christ and Evolution,* pp. 247-52.

81. Balthasar, *A Theological Anthropology,* p. 308.

82. Balthasar, *A Theological Anthropology,* p. 308. So "He becomes human in one mode of being human [i.e., male] and not in another" makes little sense in the light of Christ's all-encompassing role as Savior of the world (brackets show my insertion). His distrust of sexuality as both "a humiliating punishment and an ennobling expiation" (p. 311) is culturally laden and perhaps reflects his limited experience as a celibate priest rather than anything more sinister.

83. Balthasar, *A Theological Anthropology,* p. 307.

84. Balthasar, *A Theological Anthropology,* p. 307.

a future work on pneumatology, where I intend to tackle more fully the relationship between "nature" and grace. Having redrawn, as it were, the scope of theo-dramatics as a framework for the present discussion, I then build up a richer account of theological anthropology by using sources drawn predominantly from the works of Thomas Aquinas. He could be equally accused of too strong an emphasis on anthropology, but because his works were influenced by Albertus Magnus, his teacher, and Aristotle, this orientates his theology in the direction that I intend to travel, namely, toward one that is more affirmative of the significance and lives of other creaturely kinds.

The particular evolutionary narratives that I pay most attention to in this book differ from those that occupied my interest in *Christ and Evolution.* In that book, I was most concerned to situate theo-drama against the very long sweep of evolutionary history, paying particular attention to different current evolutionary narratives that I considered most influential, including the debates between Simon Conway Morris's perception of what might be called a strong sense of evolutionary constraint in convergence and Stephen Jay Gould's stress on contingency.[85] Conway Morris argued for inevitable humans, so that if evolutionary history were to be replayed, then something like humans would appear again. Gould, on the other hand, stressed contingency, so that the appearance of the human being was little short of miraculous. But I argued that the difference between them was not as stark as this portrayal might suggest, in that Conway Morris also recognized contingent elements in the process, and Gould, at least in his mature work, acknowledged a degree of constraint. I situated theo-drama between these poles, arguing that there was an analogy with both inasmuch as theo-drama has a direction, one that in theological terms could be named divine providence and the coming of the reign of God, that is, eschatology; at the same time, there is considerable flexibility in working out these overall purposes, so that *improvisation* is a key characteristic of the unfolding of theo-dramatics. In the overall theo-drama, the central act is the life, death, and resurrection of Jesus Christ. Inasmuch as the goal of the Christian life is to become more like Christ in his humanity, the theo-drama for a believer is orientated toward becoming *imago Christi,*

85. Simon Conway Morris has set out his arguments in a clear and coherent way in *Life's Solution.* See also Stephen Jay Gould, *The Structure of Evolutionary Theory* (Cambridge: Harvard University Press, Belknap Press, 2002). For further discussion on this, see Deane-Drummond, *Christ and Evolution,* pp. 1-30.

and in this respect is countercultural.[86] For the purposes of this present monograph, and to make the discussion of the literature a little more manageable, I have engaged most closely with evolutionary theories that are of most relevance to anthropology, and as interpreted by anthropologists, rather than focusing more generally on evolutionary theory as such.

Returning to secular anthropology, Tim Ingold's own developed intention to break down the cultural and biological divisions comes through his notion of human cultural variation as *skill* grown through practice and training in a particular environment and the way we inhabit that environment.[87] What is crucial, however, is Ingold's insistence that human identity develops as a function of a placement within a relational manifold, hence "positionality."[88] But this is not in any way fixed since, inasmuch as theology bears some relationship to art, life is also about movement, and "the creativity of life processes is in their capacity to bring forth, rather than in the novelty of results compared with what has gone before."[89] I interpret the idea of theo-drama as, in one sense, a theological commentary on Ingold's concept of life as *movement,* a human becoming through deliberate placing of the human person in the movement of the play as a way of bringing forth not simply that which is unique to human beings, but structuring human life as part of a wider bringing forth. While such language might seem resonant with cosmic human origins, I will only touch occasionally on the grand narrative that this presupposes, and quite deliberately so. This is because insights about the human condition and the genealogical unfolding of the human species come alive most clearly when specific moments in that unfolding become the focus of attention. The radical and, for many scientists, bizarre Christian belief that the particular life of one Jew in human history bears on the lives of all other life, and even material existence as such, is at the heart of the Christian theo-drama.[90] If such a

86. I discuss this in more detail in Deane-Drummond, *Christ and Evolution,* pp. 256-87, where I examine the trend in which humans are attempting to take charge of their own evolution through transhuman narratives, that is, the deliberate transformation of the human that names human perfection in terms of freedom from suffering. This trend to transhumanism raises significant ethical issues that merit further discussion, but it is outside the scope of this monograph.

87. Tim Ingold, *The Perception of the Environment: Essays on Livelihood, Dwelling, and Skill* (London: Routledge, 2011).

88. Ingold, *Perception of the Environment,* p. xvi.

89. Tim Ingold, introduction to *ReDrawing Anthropology: Materials, Movements, Lines,* ed. Tim Ingold (Farnham: Ashgate, 2011), pp. 1-20, here 2.

90. A stress on historical aspects of Christology and its significance for how to think

perspective can be tolerated by being named as such, then readers who are not Christian can follow the arguments in this book. For I will argue that the puzzle of who human beings are comes not just from wrestling with ontological aspects of what it means to be human, but also through considering some specific *practices* — how, practically speaking, we might enact and perform that drama through a closer look at the grounds for specific ethical relationships with other animals.

The first part of this book is therefore a concerted effort to look at different facets of what Ingold names as the human condition; so reason, freedom, morality, and language all come into view. Such capacities have traditionally been used as a means to enhance human superiority over other animals, both in the classical understanding of human "nature" and in theological anthropology. Kelsey chooses to avoid using the term *imago Dei* almost entirely, even while concentrating on Christian practices of human societies. However, I will seek to show that if one explores the human/animal boundary set in an evolutionary context, the specific characteristics of humans become matters of degree, rather than marking out an absolute difference. While Ingold considered such reflections *ethnocentric* in their tendencies, given that such characteristics have been used historically by those from a particular set of cultural assumptions, my intention here is much less to map out a kind of universal human nature than to show that our sense of self-importance arising in the Western cultural tradition and its Christian expression needs to be appropriately qualified. It is in companionship with other animals and through recognition of their uniqueness, even through honest acknowledgment of the cultural boundedness of such a selection of complex characters, that we can begin to view what it means to be human.

Then, I explore in more detail what is arguably an intersection between biological and cultural anthropology in evolving social worlds. There is a growing consensus among evolutionary scientists and psychologists along with anthropologists that it was the ability of humans to co-

---

about the meaning of the human in terms of religious practice comes through clearly in José Pagola, *Jesus: A Historical Approximation* (Miami: Convivium Press, 2012). Here the way to think about how Christians should live is interwoven directly with an interpretation of the historical Jesus narrative in Scripture. It is theo-dramatic inasmuch as it stresses the concrete situation of the life of Christ, and in this sense compensates for the more abstract and often reified discussion characterized by the work of Balthasar. However, my attempt in this book is to ground the discussion of theo-drama another way, through close attention to the biosocial becomings of human beings in relation to other animals.

operate that marked out their success. But what might be the evolutionary patterns that formed the background to this cultural development? If evolution by natural selection is one facet in a more complex theory of inheritance, where does cultural and religious learning fit in? I argue that niche construction bears an *analogous* relationship with theo-drama in the way I understand it, in that both are perceptions of the human that bring meaning to human activity and that both suggest an active role for human beings in relation to other living creatures. Hence, human beings are not to be situated as if on a blank canvas, but together with other creatures they construct their world in a way that impinges on the very biological systems that have promoted their formation. In terms of Christian theological anthropology, such a construction stems from a relationship with God and is responsive to divine initiative, the way of grace. The temptation to stray away from the social world and construct worlds that are somehow detached from the fabric of creation in which human beings are grounded is a secular as much as a theological temptation. But the promise of an alternative practice is at hand through an interrogation of what justice requires in human-animal relationships and a reinterpretation, therefore, of human kinship with other animals. An inclusive, rather than an exclusive, interpretation of theological anthropology follows.[91]

91. A preliminary sketch of some of the ideas emerging from the perspective discussed in this chapter is in Celia Deane-Drummond, "God's Image and Likeness in Humans and Other Animals: Performative Soul-Making and Graced Nature," *Zygon* 47, no. 4 (2012): 934-48.

CHAPTER TWO

Human Reason and Animal Cognition

In considering the scope of rationality, it might seem surprising that in view of what we know about the marked intelligence of other animals, some theologians and philosophers still deny such a capacity to creatures other than humans. Furthermore, the theologian who is cited to support this view is, more often than not, Thomas Aquinas. Yet, to justify this position, the additional capacity for language is added to the suite of uniquely human characteristics, so that those reasoning powers associated with linguistic skills become the basis for separation and difference between human beings and other animals.[1] Herbert McCabe, therefore, goes so far as to claim: "It is because language is created by the human animal, and not biologically inherited that he or she has life, has self-movement, in a new sense, has freedom. With the appearance of the linguistic animal evolution becomes largely irrelevant."[2] McCabe is surprisingly resistant to an exploration of evolutionary modes of exploration as related to human cultures, largely, it seems, because he has not sufficiently recognized what scientists are calling nature/cultures and because he is insistent that "Evolution means Darwin or it means nothing."[3] Unfortunately, this has the unhappy consequence of a naïve association of evolutionary Darwinism with a form of genetic determinism now largely rejected by the scientific community, even if sometimes appearing in popular accounts of evolu-

1. While language is not explicitly discussed in these terms in Aquinas's works, this does not prevent authors such as Herbert McCabe and Anthony Kenny from coming to such conclusions. See Herbert McCabe's chapter "Animals and Us," in his *The Good Life: Ethics and the Pursuit of Happiness* (London: Continuum, 2005), pp. 95-114.

2. McCabe, "Animals and Us," pp. 107-8.

3. McCabe, "Animals and Us," p. 108.

tionary biology.[4] Added to this, the well-known negative ethical stance of Thomas Aquinas toward "brutes," then paraded as one of the most culpable aspects of the tradition by contemporary theologians wishing to expunge from Christian theology those elements that have worked against the treatment of animals, means that Aquinas has not been considered particularly promising as a positive dialogue partner in matters relating to other animals.[5]

There are, of course, some recent exceptions to this generalization. Judith Barad gives a comprehensive survey of Aquinas's position on the nature and treatment of other animals, arguing that his ontological position toward them clashes with his ethical stance.[6] Alasdair MacIntyre has undergone something of a U-turn, acknowledging his prior lack of treatment of human animality and dependency and recognizing common capacities between human beings and other animal kinds.[7] John Berkman has offered a helpful map of what a Thomistic theology of animality might look like by uncovering those places in the primary literature where Aquinas discusses lines of continuity and difference between human beings and other animals.[8] The question more specifically to be addressed in this chapter is the claim for unique powers of human reasoning in Aquinas, since this sets the stage for other capacities that carry the claim of superiority, which I will take up later, including freedom, morality, and language. Hence, exploring precisely what he claims other animals are capable of is important for working out what he means when he makes the claim for exclusivity

4. Anthony Kenny comes to similar conclusions. See Anthony Kenny, *What I Believe* (London: Continuum, 2007).

5. For a particularly strident example of a rejection of Thomistic metaphysics, see Francisco Benzoni, *Ecological Ethics and the Human Soul: Aquinas, Whitehead, and the Metaphysics of Value* (Notre Dame, Ind.: University of Notre Dame Press, 2007). I am not developing the ethical aspects of Thomistic metaphysics here, but it is sufficient to say that Benzoni argues that Thomas's ontology is entirely consistent with his instrumentalization of animals, and rejects both in favor of the process philosophy of A. N. Whitehead. I remain unconvinced by his arguments for debunking Aquinas as a potential source for ecological ethics, but his position is not uncommon. I intend to deal more fully with this criticism in a subsequent volume on ecological ethics.

6. Judith Barad, *Aquinas on the Nature and Treatment of Animals* (San Francisco: International Scholars Publications, 1995).

7. Alasdair MacIntyre, *Dependent Rational Animals: Why Human Beings Need the Virtues* (Chicago: Open Court, 1999).

8. John Berkman, "Towards a Thomistic Theology of Animality," in *Creaturely Theology: On God, Humans, and Other Animals,* ed. Celia Deane-Drummond and David Clough (London: SCM, 2009), pp. 21-40.

in humans. In order to assess this claim, I will argue that we need to appraise other aspects of his thought that qualify it, including his approach to reason in the natural world as such, or to put it more starkly, *nature as reason.* It is also possible to update some of his conclusions on the basis of what is known about the cognitive powers of other animals compared with humans. However, I will take this further in arguing for a recognition of what, more often than not, is missed by contemporary philosophers, namely, Aquinas's belief in reasoning as *graced* or subject to the work of the Holy Spirit. Surprisingly, perhaps, other animals in Aquinas also seem to have desires shaped by grace, but are understood as the more general work of God's *providence* rather than infused grace, as in humans. Such an approach to human reasoning would not be readily recognized by contemporary scientists. The dilemma opened up here could be avoided by confining theology and science to different levels of explanation, and this is a common reaction in facing what seem to be insurmountable problems in what science claims and theological tradition attests.[9] However, if, as Aquinas himself believed, the sphere of nature and grace are more closely entangled, then this may force particular questions about the interrelationship between religious experience and cognitive reasoning in a new way, thus opening up new questions not just for theology, but for science as well.

Aquinas on Rational Animals

Aquinas does seem to recognize from his interpretation of the first chapter of Genesis a relative degree of closeness between human beings and other animals compared with birds and fish. But Aquinas uses the Genesis text to argue that as humans are the only creatures that God seems to create in a direct way, this implies that "The highest degree of life, however, is in man." He interprets "beast" in the Genesis text as referring to wild animals, with oxen and cattle standing for domesticated animals and "creeping things" for snakes and other reptiles, while quadrupeds cover other types such as deer and goats. He also seems to allow for some change within this process by acknowledging the possibility of new species appearing, as long as these were drawn from latent "active powers."[10] Furthermore, for Aquinas the

9. John Haught, *God after Darwin: A Theology of Evolution* (Boulder, Colo.: Westview Press, 2007).

10. Thomas Aquinas, *Summa Theologiae, Cosmogony, Vol. 10 (1a. 65-74),* trans. Wil-

difference between human beings and other animals is sharper than that between different animal categories such as fish, birds, and land animals.[11] All living things have what Aquinas calls a soul, but he rejects the idea that the soul is simply a vital principle, or that it is corporeal as such; rather, it is "that which actuates a body."[12] For Aquinas, the distinctive aspect of the human soul relates to the mind or intellect, and he presumes that the body has no "intrinsic part" in the activity of understanding in humans, and therefore is able to subsist, and as such is to be thought of as incorporeal, even if the body is the means through which the soul of a human being comes to be embodied.[13] Aquinas aligns himself with Aristotle in naming the intellect as incorporeal and what he terms the "sensitive soul" of other animals as corporeal, that is, acting according to nonrational desires or appetites rather than according to the reasoning ability of human beings.[14] While this belief in a mind separate from the body might seem untenable in the light of contemporary knowledge of mental processes, the belief that the mind is not simply equivalent to brain function is not unreasonable.[15] Indeed, more recent neurobiological work shows that the difficulty of ascribing an activity to mind as reduced to material terms, that is, brain function, is still very much alive, and arguably a modern version of the distinction between soul and body.[16]

---

liam A. Wallace (London: Blackfriars, 1967), 1a, qu. 72. How much this is an incipient evolutionary theory is a moot point, but at least this qualifies the negative stance toward the "Chain of Being" cosmology that is another aspect of his thought that has been criticized by animal rights activists.

11. Aquinas, *ST, Cosmogony,* 1a, qu. 74.1.

12. Thomas Aquinas, *Summa Theologiae, Man, Vol. 11 (1a. 75-83),* trans. Timothy Suttor (London: Blackfriars, 1970), 1a, qu. 75.1.

13. Aquinas, *ST, Man,* 1a, qu. 75.2 See also, for example, Thomas Aquinas, *Summa Theologiae, Man Made in God's Image, Vol. 13 (1a. 90-102),* trans. Edmund Hill (London: Blackfriars, 1964), 1a, qu. 90.2, where Aquinas speaks of the creation of the rational soul as a direct act of God's creative activity. He also rejects the idea that the rational soul could be the work of angelic forces, since only God can create a soul directly. Aquinas, *ST, Man Made in God's Image,* 1a, qu. 90.3.

14. Aquinas, *ST, Man,* 1a, qu. 75.4.

15. Contemporary discussions of philosophy of mind are notoriously controversial and need not distract us here, except to suggest that working out a scientific basis for consciousness or other mental processes is still ongoing and is not likely to be resolved in the near future. See David Chalmers, *Philosophy of Mind: Classical and Contemporary Readings* (New York: Oxford University Press, 2002).

16. See, for example, discussion by Malcolm Jeeves, "The Emergence of Human Distinctiveness: The Story from Neuropsychology and Evolutionary Psychology," in *Re-*

So far, this portrait might imply a clear dividing line between humans and other animals in Aquinas, with reasoning as this watermark. Yet, there are qualifications to this interpretation. He recognizes, for example, that many animals act both according to responses to external sensations and out of an inner judgment about what might be useful or harmful. A lamb on seeing a wolf will flee because it knows it is a "natural enemy," and "a bird collects straw not because it pleases its senses, but because it needs it for building its nest."[17] He recognizes *aestimativa,* or an estimative sense, in other animals, meaning that they are able to grasp intentions that are not simply responses to sensation and have the power of memory to store these up for future use.[18] It is here that the difference between humans and other animals in their reasoning powers becomes clear, since intentions are perceived by the estimative sense in other animals, but in humans there is an active comparison, or cogitation, which Aquinas describes as "the particular reason."[19] For Aquinas, it is the capacity of human beings to deliberate about a particular end that marks out uniquely human capacities, while other animals can aim at an end but not deliberate on it, so that the movement toward this end is unpremeditated.[20]

Of course, Aquinas did not have the knowledge we possess of the relative sophistication of the cognitive acts of intelligent social animals, who do seem to have the capacity to deliberate on alternative courses of ac-

---

thinking Human Nature: A Multidisciplinary Approach, ed. Malcolm Jeeves (Grand Rapids: Eerdmans, 2011), pp. 176-205. His conclusion that mind and brain manifest duality without dualism is helpful. However, his decision to pick out relational aspects of image bearing rather than reasoning does not take sufficient account of the intersection between different facets of human being and acting; in other words, we have the capability of being able to relate to God *because* of the particular kind of cognitive reasoning that is endowed to us as human beings. His treatment of evolutionary psychology literature is also rather less critical than mine would be, though his attention to other animals as being nonthreatening to a consideration of human distinctiveness is very much in line with my own position.

17. Aquinas, *ST, Man,* 1a, qu. 78.4.

18. While Timothy Suttor in the Blackfriars translation uses the term "instinct" for *aestimativa,* my own preference is "estimative sense," since "instinct" is too loaded with meaning in contemporary usage. For further discussion of estimative sense, see Robert Pasnau, *Thomas Aquinas on Human Nature: A Philosophical Study of "Summa Theologiae"* (Cambridge: Cambridge University Press, 2001), pp. 253ff.

19. Aquinas, following the science of his time, and drawing on Avicenna, attributed this form of reasoning about particular things to "the middle of the head." Aquinas, *ST, Man,* 1a, qu. 78.4.

20. Thomas Aquinas, *Summa Theologiae, Psychology of Human Acts, Vol. 17 (1a2ae. 6-17),* trans. Thomas Gilby (London: Blackfriars, 1970), 1a2ae, qu. 6.2.

tion and have at least some lower levels of intentionality. There are heated debates on how far and to what extent other animals can perceive the thought processes of companion animals, that is, have a theory of mind. Observation of other animals does not prove convincingly what they might be thinking, though the clearest evidence seems to come from a study of quail bird behavior rather than from our closest living primate relatives.[21] In human beings, the capacity for memory is also more elaborated, since it is not just about a capacity for recalling events, but also a kind of inner reminiscence, "a quasi-syllogistic search among memories of things past in their individuality."[22] Yet, he allowed not just for the estimative sense and memory in other animals, but *also* for common sense and imagination. Differences and commonalities find clear expression in his claim that "Cognition and memory reach so high in man through their similarity to and connection with abstract reason, through a kind of overflow, not through anything belonging to the sense-soul as such. So they are not new powers but the same powers, more perfect than they are in other animals."[23] This makes it clear that the reasoning abilities of human beings are on a continuum with other animals, even though the capacity for abstraction makes human reasoning distinctive.[24]

What is particularly intriguing is that some of the insights that Aqui-

21. See Clive D. L. Wynne, *Animal Cognition: The Mental Lives of Animals* (Basingstoke: Palgrave Macmillan, 2001), pp. 19-23. I will discuss theory of mind again below and take up other aspects of cognition such as the representation of knowledge in other animals in the chapter on language.

22. Aquinas, *ST, Man,* 1a, qu. 78.4. Aquinas's subordination of memory to "instinct" or human cognition, along with his notion of sense consciousness, does not match with contemporary psychology. However, the point here is not to show that his science is in some respects naïve by contemporary standards, which in itself is hardly surprising given when he was writing, but that he attributes capacities to other animals that touch on those of humans, even if the two are distinct.

23. Aquinas, *ST, Man,* 1a, qu. 78.4. Note that Aquinas also speaks of "higher" and "lower" reason, following Augustine in other places (e.g., qu. 79.9), but he does not develop this way of distinguishing different powers of reasoning very extensively and insists that "higher" and "lower" reason are one and the same power, even if they result in different actions, so "higher reason" is associated with wisdom and "lower reason" with science. In this case, the power of abstract reasoning is connected to but distinct from the particular reasoning expressed as the estimative sense in other animals.

24. The ability of rational beings to perceive not just a good end, but to abstract and understand what that end means compared with the more specific reflection on particular ends in other creatures is also discussed in Aquinas, *ST, Psychology of Human Acts,* 1a2ae, qu. 11.2.

nas brought to bear on human psychology are actually being supported by recent cognitive science research. The terminology he uses may be archaic, but the basic concept that human rational decision making is deeply connected to our more ancient brain is only just coming to light. For example, Antoine Bechara argues that modern cognitive psychology often ignores the emotional aspects of decision making and assumes that decisions are made through a cost/benefit analysis.[25] Bechara found in experimental psychological tests that patients who could not process emotional information correctly due to ventromedial lesions of the prefrontal cortex still had unimpaired cognitive function. However, they were unable to make the choice between different options and had severely compromised decision-making abilities. His conclusion — that what is experienced existentially as reasonable decision making depends also in part on the more emotional parts of the brain — is consistent with Aquinas's view that while human reasoning ability is distinct from other nonrational animals in its capacity for abstraction, it still draws on the passions or estimative sense rather than being radically separated from it. Other scholars come to much the same conclusion, so that an article in *Frontiers in Psychology* by Andrew Wilson and Sabrina Golonka claims that "Embodiment is the surprisingly radical hypothesis that the brain is not the sole cognitive resource we have available to us to solve problems. Our bodies, and their perceptually guided motions through the world, do much of the work required to achieve our goals, replacing the need for complex internal mental representations. This simple fact utterly changes our idea of what 'cognition' involves, and thus embodiment is not simply another factor acting on an otherwise disembodied cognitive processes."[26]

25. Antoine Bechara, "The Role of Emotion in Decision-Making: Evidence from Neurological Patients with Orbitofrontal Damage," *Brain and Cognition* 55 (2004): 30-40. Bechara and associates claim that a new theory, the somatic marker hypothesis, distinguishes this view from alternatives. Hence, they claim that "The somatic marker hypothesis provides a systems-level neuroanatomical and cognitive framework for decision-making and the influence on it by emotion. The key idea of this hypothesis is that decision-making is a process that is influenced by marker signals that arise in bioregulatory process, including those that express themselves in emotions and feelings. This influence can occur at multiple levels of operation, some of which occur consciously and some of which occur non-consciously." Antoine Bechara, Hanna Damasio, and Antonio Demasio, "Emotion, Decision-Making and the Orbitofrontal Cortex," *Cerebral Cortex* 10, no. 3 (2000): 295-307. I am grateful to Hillary Lenfesty for drawing my attention to these sources.

26. Andrew Wilson and Sabrina Golonka, "Embodied Cognition Is Not What You Think It Is," *Frontiers in Psychology* 4 (2013): 1-13.

Aquinas situates humanity between angels and other animals, naming angels as those created beings who grasp truth and understanding without having to go through the process of reasoning as such. Human rationality aims at the truth in a way that is impossible for other animals but is known more perfectly by angels, so "angelic power of knowledge is not in a different general category from the rational power of knowledge, but compares with it as the finished to the unfinished."[27] On the one hand, there seems to be continuity in reasoning between humanity and other animals; on the other hand, there is continuity in knowledge between humanity and angels, as achieved through human abstract reasoning. In this respect, it is also worth mentioning "higher" and "lower" reasoning, terminology that comes from Augustine and that Aquinas compares with "scientific" and "opinative and ratiocinative" in Aristotle.[28] While the former attends to "eternal things," the latter attends to "temporal things." But for Aquinas, citing Romans 1:20, these two forms of reasoning are not clearly separated, for "in the order of discovery, our investigations lead us through the things of time to those of eternity . . . *non-empirical divine realities become distinct for us through understanding created things.*"[29] Confusingly, perhaps, in view of Aristotle's comparable but distinct categorization, Augustine names the lower form of reasoning "science" and the higher form "wisdom," and Aquinas adopts this terminology, arguing that the higher form governs the lower form.[30] While in contemporary Western culture it is harder to sustain the view that theological knowledge should set the parameters for scientific knowing, this is precisely what Aquinas suggests here, namely, that wisdom takes priority over scientific understanding.[31]

The estimative sense in other animals relates to what Aquinas calls "the appetitive power of the soul. By this power an animal seeks after what

27. Aquinas, *ST, Man,* 1a, qu. 79.8.

28. Aquinas, *ST, Man,* 1a, qu. 79.9. He does conclude, however, that scientific reasoning in Aristotle is not identical with higher reason in Augustine, which is more restrictive in its reference to eternal truths, because necessary truths are also in Aristotelian science, while "lower reason" is more expansive than the more restrictive opinative and ratiocinative reasoning in Aristotle.

29. Aquinas, *ST, Man,* 1a, qu. 79.9. Here he claims to draw on Saint Paul. Italics in original, so *"Invisibilia Dei per ea quae facta sunt, intellect, conspiciuntur."*

30. Aquinas, *ST, Man,* 1a, qu. 79.9.

31. There is insufficient space to discuss this aspect in detail here. I have dealt with this topic in Celia Deane-Drummond, *Creation through Wisdom: Theology and the New Biology* (Edinburgh: T. & T. Clark, 2000).

it knows, not merely going where natural inclination leads."[32] Yet because intellectual knowledge is universal, while sense knowledge is of concrete particulars, the intellectual appetite of human beings is different from the sensitive appetite of other animals.[33] More explicitly, the intellectual appetite is able to judge something particular in an abstract way as having a universal quality as *good,* as well as desiring nonmaterial goods such as knowledge and virtue as such. Reasoning and understanding are related as means and ends, so that reasoning is the way we arrive at knowledge of one thing or another, "so that strictly speaking we reason concerning conclusions, which become known through principles."[34] Aquinas draws a parallel between the relationship of intellect and reasoning and that between willing and the exercise of choice, which he calls free will. The intellectual apprehensive or cognitive powers are governed by intellect and reason, while willing and free will govern the appetitive powers.[35] An act of a human being is done from reason and will, that is, it is a deliberate, and therefore self-reflexive, act.[36] A human who acts without such deliberation displays acts of human beings but not properly speaking human acts, by which he seems to mean *distinctively* human acts.[37] For him, the "rational appetite, termed will," is self-motivated and aims at a defined end, whereas for those lacking intelligence the tendency to act is through a "natural bent" stimulated by something outside themselves, even if he allows for some "purposive perception" in other animals.[38]

It is the apprehension of something as good that allows those with reasoning powers to direct their attention to a good end in the exercise of

32. Aquinas, *ST, Man,* 1a, qu. 80.1.

33. Aquinas, *ST, Man,* 1a, qu. 80.2.

34. Aquinas, *ST, Man,* 1a, qu. 81.4.

35. Aquinas, *ST, Man,* 1a, qu. 83.4.

36. Thomas Aquinas, *Summa Theologiae, Purpose and Happiness, Vol. 16 (1a2ae. 1-5),* trans. Thomas Gilby (London: Blackfriars, 1969), 1a2ae, qu. 1.1. Here Aquinas compares the deliberative acts of humans with nonrational creatures, so "those actions which lie under his control are properly called human."

37. The implication that only those acts that stem from deliberation are properly human acts sets up an unfortunate thesis that only what separates humans from other animals is worthy of the label "human." Aquinas does qualify this statement by speaking of sensitive acts of humans, as I will discuss below, but not in a way that is usually recognized by either his commenders or his critics.

38. Aquinas, *ST, Purpose and Happiness,* 1a2ae, qu. 1.2. For Aquinas, the will is definitively a rational appetite directed toward a good end. Aquinas, *ST, Psychology of Human Acts,* 1a2ae, qu. 8.1.

the will. In this respect, Aquinas departs from other medieval scholars such as Duns Scotus who envisaged a separated will that was completely cut off from natural operations, including the intellect.[39] When compared with such views, Aquinas's position comes off surprisingly well in relation to contemporary cognitive science. For Aquinas, the will has two elements, both the means through will as a power and the end or purpose to which it is directed in an act, namely, volition.[40] The ability to separate these faculties in modern psychology has led Harvard psychologist Daniel Wegner to claim that the will is merely an "illusion"; strictly speaking, all he has shown is that an existential experience of will can be separate from action, a position that Aquinas would have supported inasmuch as he distinguished the two elements.[41] Furthermore, the "illusionary" nature refers to the "freedom" aspect of the will, which Aquinas also takes up in his discussion. Aquinas therefore acknowledged, following Romans 7:19, that while human acts are not necessarily those intended by reason, at the same time human beings do have the power to reason about their decisions in a way that distinguishes them from other animals.[42] However, both Scotus and Aquinas agreed, following Anselm, that the will had twin affections for justice and for advantage to oneself. Aquinas follows Aristotle in affirming that the will is not a separate faculty. Does the will require a virtue in the same way the sensory inclinations require virtues, such as temperance, in order to have a right attitude to things that are attractive according to the passions? Aquinas suggests it does not, in that the will does not require a virtue to make it directed toward the good. However, for Aquinas, where the good of the other is concerned, this does require virtue. The virtue of

39. See Rudi te Velde, "*Natura In Seipsa Recurva Est:* Duns Scotus and Aquinas on the Relationship between Nature and Will," in *John Duns Scotus,* ed. E. P. Bos (Amsterdam: Rodopi, 1988), pp. 155-70. I would like to thank Conor Cunningham for pointing me to this reference.

40. Aquinas, *ST, Psychology of Human Acts,* 1a2ae, qu. 8.2.

41. I will discuss Daniel Wegner again below. His supposition that the will can be mapped entirely by materialist explanations is based on evidence for malfunction following brain damage. While he has proved a separation of what might be loosely termed a feeling of will power and action or volition, he has not explained its ultimate origin, but just provided evidence for the material basis of its operations. See discussion in Daniel M. Wegner, "Précis of 'The Illusion of Conscious Will,'" *Behavioral and Brain Sciences* 27, no. 5 (2004): 2-45. Aquinas, on the other hand, acknowledged that there could be a separation of willed desire and willed action in time, such as willing health in general and then later seeking a means to bring this about. See Aquinas, *ST, Psychology of Human Acts,* 1a2ae, qu. 8.3.

42. Aquinas, *ST, Man,* 1a, qu. 83.1-3; see his discussion on free will, especially qu. 83.1.

justice allows the will to be directed to the social good of others, while the virtue of *caritas* allows the will to be directed toward the divine good in God; both in this sense transcend what is given in the natural operations of the will. The ability of the will to be in some sense transformed by grace is not found in Aristotelian ethics.[43]

Aquinas does allow that at times human beings may be driven by others or outside forces, but carrying out orders blindly means human beings are acting more like nonrational creatures. Properly human acts are, therefore, acts that come from deliberate and self-conscious willing on the part of the individual person.[44] Aquinas envisaged a reasonable human will as being *in command over* emotional forces common to other animals, and if such powers dominated, then that action was less than human.[45] While Aquinas did not go so far as to say that without emotion a decision made is *also* less than human, clearly Bechara's research in cognitive science suggests how crucial emotional elements are in order to make good decisions, whether or not they are acknowledged. Aquinas's discussion here points in two directions.

On the one hand, his elevation of human reason at the expense of emotional bodily actions has been the subject of contemporary criticism.[46] It is certainly unfortunate to portray those characteristics we share with other animals as somehow belittling human dignity. However, the temptation to reify intellectual ability is not confined to Thomistic thought, but is also characteristic of contemporary scholars such as Balthasar.[47] For Aqui-

43. I will discuss the way the moral life consists of acquired and infused virtues in chapter 4. What is remarkable here is that Aquinas is also arguing for a transformed will.

44. Aquinas, *ST, Purpose and Happiness,* 1a2ae, qu. 1.3. Aquinas also believed that the same physical act may be moral or not, depending on inner purposes.

45. Aquinas, *ST, Psychology of Human Acts,* 1a2ae, qu. 9.3.

46. See, for example, Janet Soskice, *The Kindness of God: Metaphor, Gender, and Religious Language* (Oxford: Oxford University Press, 2007).

47. I have had reason to criticize Hans Urs von Balthasar in this respect in "The Breadth of Glory: A Trinitarian Eschatology for the Earth through Critical Engagement with Hans Urs von Balthasar," *International Journal of Systematic Theology* 12, no. 1 (2010): 46-64. Aquinas also believed that other animals could not control their appetites, whereas human beings had active powers of consent. Aquinas, *ST, Psychology of Human Acts,* 1a2ae, qu. 15.2. Food sharing is a widely recognized phenomenon in primate societies. However, in experimental conditions Frans de Waal reports some evidence of restraint in response to perceived good for another. Frans de Waal, *The Age of Empathy: Nature's Lessons for a Kinder Society* (New York: Broadway, 2010). Of course, in this case, one could argue that the instinct toward protection of another overrides other self-preserving instincts, but it at least demonstrates that immediately satisfying appetitive instincts in other animals is not

nas, humans have the ability to be more detached from their appetitive desires and thus *consent* to a particular course of action, as well as having the ability to exercise deliberative choice or preference.[48] This feeling of consent, or, in philosophical terms, freedom of the will, is significant in his mapping of the psychology of human acts. It is also supported by recent research on primates that shows the distinctive ability of humans to self-consciously reflect on different alternatives.[49]

But there is, I suggest, another strand to his thought alluded to above that is much more affirmative of the emotions. He acknowledges, for instance, the positive aspects of sensitive appetites that are common to all animals, including humans. Importantly, there are occasions when he refers to principles of human acts being in the sensitive appetite, and not just through reason and the will. So, in his discussion of roots of sinful behavior, he names three principles, the intellect, the rational appetite, *and,* importantly, the sensitive appetite.[50] The sensitive appetites are distinguished in Aquinas into the concupiscible, which seeks after the good and avoids what is harmful, and the irascible, which defends against harm.[51] Aquinas believed that both appetites were subject to the estimative power or sense in other animals, but in humans they were, or could be, subject to a type of reason he called cognitive power.[52] At the same time, he recognized that reason alone was not sufficient to explain how humans act in response to various appetites, which were also subject to imaginative powers. Aquinas envisaged these various appetites in a hierarchy, so that the highest level of sensitive activity — the irascible appetite — comes into contact or touches the lowest rungs of reasonable activity. In this way, he

---

as automatic as Aquinas, and many others following him, has assumed. On the other hand, some scientists are now arguing that even human freedom of will is itself an illusion. See critical discussion of Wegner below under section on nature as reason. Wegner, "Précis of 'The Illusion of Conscious Will.'"

48. Aquinas, *ST, Psychology of Human Acts,* 1a2ae, qu. 15.3. Also discussed in qu. 17.2, where he claims that as soon as other animals perceive something as fitting or unfitting, they spontaneously move toward or away from it.

49. I will return to this issue in more detail in the following chapter on freedom. See, for example, Michael Tomasello and Josep Call, *Primate Cognition* (Oxford: Oxford University Press, 1997). The sheer diversity among primates should also not be forgotten.

50. Thomas Aquinas, *Summa Theologiae, Sin, Vol. 25 (1a2ae. 71-80),* trans. John Fearon (London: Blackfriars, 1969), 1a2ae, 78.1. I am grateful to Nick Austin for pointing me to this reference.

51. Aquinas, *ST, Man,* 1a, qu. 81.2.

52. Aquinas, *ST, Man,* 1a, qu. 81.3.

was ready to admit that other animals share in the capacity for friendship or hostility, as marks of the active irascible appetite.[53]

This might seem somewhat remarkable given the subsequent denigration of animal emotions in cultural history. However, in spite of this admission, Aquinas maintained that the purpose of other animals was to serve humanity. Even more remarkably, perhaps, given that he seems well aware of their capacity to suffer, he claims that other animals are punished "by divine law," even though they are innocent, for the sole purpose of punishing the human beings who own them, who are thereby "punished by their punishment or frightened by the sharpness of their pains or instructed by the meaning of the mystery."[54] Such an admission seems to emerge from a cultural blindness in ethical attitudes toward other animals and does not follow from his perceived ontological insights about them, which presumably he first learned to appreciate from his teacher Albert the Great.

Yet, in spite of what we might call the "graded" understanding of reasoning in other animals through the estimative sense and appetitive powers of the soul, Aquinas rejects the notion that other animals are capable of showing forth the image of God, even though he raises this as a possibility.[55] But, following Augustine, he considers the opposite scenario that God's gift of an intelligent mind in human beings means that whatever lacks intelligence cannot bear God's image.[56] The result of this dialogue is something of a compromise between these two possibilities. While Aquinas recognizes some likeness to God with respect to other creatures in that they exist and are alive, it is their capacity for discernment and intelligence that marks out human beings as bearers of the image, even if other creatures share in God's likeness.[57] This difference reflects what Aquinas considers to be the greater capacity for the highest good in human beings

53. Thomas Aquinas, *On Truth*, vol. 3, trans. Robert Mulligan (Chicago: Regnery, 1954), qu. 25.2.

54. Aquinas, *On Truth*, vol. 3, qu. 24.2.

55. Aquinas, *ST, Made in God's Image*, 1a, qu. 93.2. The statement, "It seems that God's image is to be found in irrational creatures," opens this question. I have discussed this aspect in more detail in Celia Deane-Drummond, "God's Image and Likeness in Humans and Other Animals: Performative Soul-Making and Graced Nature," *Zygon* 47, no. 4 (2012): 934-48.

56. By "intelligence" Aquinas means that which distinguishes human reasoning from other animals, rather than distinctions among human beings; Edmund Hill, translator's note, a, p. 53, in *ST, Made in God's Image*, 1a, qu. 93.2.

57. Aquinas, *ST, Made in God's Image*, 1a, qu. 93.2.

compared with other animals. It is the likeness "to the supreme wisdom in so far as they are intelligent" that makes humans intelligent animals capable of bearing God's image as such.[58]

He also considers the possibility that angels bear the image of God with respect to their intelligence, and inasmuch as there is "a certain imitation of God in man," human beings in a *bodily* sense might bear the image more perfectly compared with angels. But this last form of image bearing he rejects because it would mean that "even the animals would be after God's image," preferring the idea that image bearing is found more in angels than in humanity.[59] Hence, while he acknowledges that other animals bear the image of God "in the manner of a trace," for Aquinas only in the rational creature with an intellect or mind is the resemblance sufficient to be recognized as bearing the image of God; this is because it is only those areas of human life such as the spiritual, bodily, or imaginative ways of knowing that are ever capable of bearing a "trace" of the image.[60] In this way, he concludes that image bearing in the rational aspect of human nature bears the image in terms of both the uncreated Trinity and the divine nature. In the latter sense, "rational creatures seem to achieve some sort of portraiture in kind, in that they imitate God not only in his being and his living, but also in his understanding." In the former sense, the rational creature "exhibits a word procession as regards the intelligence and a love procession as regards the will."[61] Other creatures display "a certain trace of intelligence that produced them," and so offer "a clue that these realities may exist" with respect to word and love, in the way that a house shows something of the mind of the architect.

One might think from the above discussion that those who are un-

58. Aquinas, *ST, Made in God's Image,* 1a, qu. 93.2.

59. Aquinas, *ST, Made in God's Image,* 1a, qu. 93.3. I will come back to how Aquinas's idea of image bearing in men and women (qu. 93.4) might be adapted to incorporate other animals in subsequent chapters. God's image in men is considered in three stages: the nature of the mind is the first stage; the second stage is an attitude of knowing and loving God; and the third stage is knowing and loving God perfectly. The distinction between men and women was not made on the basis of any supposed superior powers of reasoning in men, but on the basis of differences in the second and third stages, drawn from a literal reading of Genesis that suggests women were created from men, from which he concludes that only men are capable of entering into image bearing in a perfected way. This is somewhat in tension with his view of image bearing as exclusively related to intelligent reasoning presented in qu. 93.2-3.

60. Aquinas, *ST, Made in God's Image,* 1a, qu. 93.6.

61. Aquinas, *ST, Made in God's Image,* 1a, qu. 93.6.

able to reason would no longer bear the image of God, but Aquinas rejects this idea. For him, human image bearing applies even in those who have, for whatever reason, lost their use of reasoning powers, where "this image of God is so faint — so shadowy, we might say — that it is practically non-existent, as in those who lack the use of reason; or whether it is dim and disfigured, as in sinners, or whether it is bright and beautiful, as in the just, as Augustine says."[62] Nonetheless, the idea of likeness of God in other creatures is still important for Aquinas, since it is the means through which he is able to claim that "God is the ultimate end for all things without exception." The difference is that human beings and rational creatures "lay hold of it in knowing and loving God, which non-rational creatures are not capable of doing, for they come to their final end through sharing some likeness of God, insomuch as they actually exist, or live and even know after their fashion."[63]

For Aquinas, happiness in human beings consists in being united with the uncreated good as an ultimate end through the intellectual process of understanding in the human mind, for "an act of mind forms the essence of happiness."[64] But he wants to include sensitive activity in this process as both antecedent to and consequence of this happiness. It is antecedent in that "sensation is presupposed to understanding," and it is a result in that at the resurrection there is a "flowing out from the beatitude of soul into the body and the senses such as to enhance their activities."[65] He, therefore, claims that in this world the "lower" happiness rises to the higher, while in "perfect bliss" the opposite is the case. This is a somewhat awkward result of Aquinas's belief in the human soul persisting after death through a kind of subsistent mental memory that then seems to take on bodily characteristics. How nonrational creatures can share ultimately in God's glory through their likeness, which he is ready to admit, and yet not be subsistent, is left unexplored. It would imply that God's glory is inclusive of all creation and all creatures, but only in humans is that glory expressed in an individuated manner with subsistent rational souls.[66]

62. Aquinas, *ST, Made in God's Image,* 1a, qu. 93.8.

63. Aquinas, *ST, Purpose and Happiness,* 1a2ae, qu. 1.8. This touches on the issue of natural law, which I will discuss in more detail below.

64. Aquinas, *ST, Purpose and Happiness,* 1a2ae, qu. 3.4.

65. Aquinas, *ST, Purpose and Happiness,* 1a2ae, qu. 3.3.

66. Contemporary theologians still wrestle with the issue of both wanting a more inclusive view of salvation and yet acknowledging a problem of envisaging a heaven where all individual creatures are raised. Yet the idea of persistence as memory in the mind of

A further way of dividing up intelligent activity reinforces this commonality and distinction according to theoretical or practical intelligence. The former seeks after the truth, and it is this activity that is associated with happiness and allows human beings through contemplation to converse with God and with angels. Contemplation, therefore, is sought for its own sake, and the mind reflects on a good within itself, that is, the truth of God; even though the final end is a good outside of itself, namely, God, it is reached in this life through "activity of the contemplative mind."[67] This religious, contemplative activity is the prerogative of human beings rather than other animals. Aquinas follows current thinking in that most, if not all, evolutionary biologists and anthropologists tie the specifically self-conscious religious activity to *Homo* species, even if claims are made that the ability to be religious is a naturally evolved human capacity.[68]

The latter, or practical intelligence, human beings share to some extent with other animals.[69] In this way, Aquinas can claim that "full practical wisdom or prudence is discovered in a person who has sound judgment about how things should be done, while a partial reflection of this is exhibited by some animals whose particular instinctive manifestations adapt them to tasks similar to those which tax human ingenuity."[70] He is also well aware of the way other creatures are able to show forth a type of wisdom, so that "Plain evidences are the wonderful instances of sagacity manifested by various animals, such as bees, spiders and dogs," but then suggests that this is a "natural determinism of [their] appetite" rather than

---

God is one way of expressing this tension, though in process thought this extends to human beings as well as other creatures. A useful view of alternative perspectives in light of ecological issues is in Ernst Conradie, ed., *Creation and Salvation,* vol. 2, *A Companion on Recent Theological Movements* (Berlin: LIT Verlag, 2012). Furthermore, how to envisage the resurrection is still a topic of conversation among those engaged in science and theology, and some authors have suggested that information persists after death in a manner that is not all that far from Aquinas's suggestion. See Robert John Russell, *Time in Eternity: Pannenberg, Physics, and Eschatology in Creative Mutual Interaction* (Notre Dame, Ind.: University of Notre Dame Press, 2012).

67. Aquinas, *ST, Purpose and Happiness,* 1a2ae, qu. 3.5.

68. This is an area of particularly focused current debate in science and religion, in which the explanatory power of evolutionary mechanisms is pushed to the limit. The tension relates to the extent to which evolutionary explanations are sufficient to explain religious belief, or are explanations of biological capacity for that belief. See further discussion in chapters 1 and 4.

69. Aquinas, *ST, Purpose and Happiness,* 1a2ae, qu. 3.5.

70. Aquinas, *ST, Purpose and Happiness,* 1a2ae, qu. 3.6.

anything approaching free choice.[71] But then we have to ask where such sagacity comes from. Aquinas says it comes from "a natural inclination to carry out the intricate processes planned by supreme art."[72] For Aquinas, it seems to be God-given rationality that is evident here, not the endowment of other animals with independent reason or choice as such. While this sounds strange to contemporary ears, his admission of forms of reasoning in other animals, even if mediated through the divine will, at least provides one way of affirming nonhuman creatures. The relationship between the existence of creatures in the Word and that of existing as such, however, is connected in that "they are of the same character analogously."[73] For Aquinas, other animals "have a certain resemblance of reason in as much as they share in a certain natural prudence, and in this respect a lower nature in some way attains to the property of a higher. This semblance consists in the well-regulated judgment that they have about certain things. But they have this judgment from a natural estimate, not from any deliberation, since they are ignorant of the basis of their judgment."[74] Biologists are engaged in heated debates about the relationship between primate and human cognition. Using primates as models for human evolution is fairly standard practice, but increasing evidence suggests that this may be over-simplified. The standard hypothesis is that evolutionary pressure for an increase in the mental capacities of primates may be related to increased social complexity, the so-called social brain hypothesis.[75] But some remarkable research on baboons by Shirley Strum suggests that this theory does not hold up in the light of field studies on baboons.[76] These studies show that the two challenges facing baboons are the ecological and the social, and that baboons have to navigate both simultaneously so that they reach their cognitive limits sooner than expected by the social brain hypothesis. Humans, on the other hand, in building complex social groups, have managed to separate off the social from the ecological. Distributed

71. Aquinas, *ST, Psychology of Human Acts,* 1a2ae, qu. 13.3. This bears on the question of freedom and agency, which I discuss in the following chapter.

72. Aquinas, *ST, Psychology of Human Acts,* 1a2ae, qu. 13.3.

73. Thomas Aquinas, *On Truth,* vol. 1, trans. Robert Mulligan (Chicago: Regnery, 1952), qu. 4.6.

74. Aquinas, *On Truth,* vol. 3, qu. 24.2.

75. Developed by authors such as Robin Dunbar, "The Social Brain Hypothesis," *Evolutionary Anthropology* 6 (1998): 178-90. I return to this issue in chapter 3.

76. Shirley Strum, "Darwin's Monkey: Why Baboons Can't Become Human," *Yearbook of Physical Anthropology* 149 (2012): 3-23.

cognition implies that the group as a whole has a cognitive capacity that is more than simply the sum of individual minds.[77]

Aquinas also admits to something of a halfway house between practical intelligence and theoretical intelligence when human beings engage in theoretical sciences rather than contemplation, where the object of attention is the material world. The ability of the human mind to perceive forms of things in the material world "reflect[s] some likeness of higher substances," and therefore anticipates the final happiness that is possible in contemplation. It is, however, anticipation only and therefore is interpreted in the light of true and complete happiness.[78] This is a type of natural theology as experienced explicitly through the sciences. While Aquinas's notion of "form" in material things is outdated, the process of arriving at a partial understanding of what is God through science chimes with contemporary reflections.[79] Although the natural theology of William Paley and others collapsed in the wake of Darwinian science in that it was no longer possible to find in natural forms evidence of a divine Mind,[80] the capacity for wonder in scientists when engaging with the natural world does have some parallels with the wonder experienced in religious activity, and this thread also seems to be behind what Aquinas is suggesting here in speaking of the anticipation of true happiness found in contemplation.[81]

77. How far and to what extent human beings show unique mental capacities for shared intention is presently under discussion. Michael Tomasello argues strongly that human beings are unique among primates in their ability to share emotional states and have shared intentions. Frans de Waal challenges this on the basis that negative evidence is weak, and that some behaviors among chimpanzees do not show any obvious rewards. See discussion and responses in Michael Tomasello et al., "Understanding and Sharing Intentions: The Origins of Social Cognition," *Behavioral and Brain Sciences* 28 (2005): 675-735.

78. Aquinas, *ST, Purpose and Happiness,* 1a2ae, qu. 3.6.

79. One could argue, perhaps, that those who advocate Intelligent Design are still holding on to such notions by suggesting that there is a directive rationality in evolution that is needed to explain the emergence of complex structures in living beings in addition to explanations through Darwinian forms of evolution by natural selection. For an intelligent analysis, see David Fergusson, *Faith and Its Critics: A Conversation* (Oxford: Oxford University Press, 2009), pp. 61-90.

80. As I discuss in the section below, I am not suggesting here that there was a parallel between design in the natural theology of William Paley and that of Thomas Aquinas; for Paley, design seemed to be imposed by God, while for Aquinas, it emerged from an inner God-given telos. In many respects, this latter view is more compatible with contemporary evolutionary theory.

81. For further discussion of wonder in the experience of scientists and theology, see

Nature as Reason

So far, I have suggested that Aquinas's understanding of reason in other animals blurs with his understanding of reason in humans inasmuch as a measure of reasonable activity is shared with other animal kinds that are, perhaps confusingly, named "irrational" because the strict notion of "rational souls" is reserved for human beings. Yet, he also argues that inasmuch as reasonable activities can be discerned in other creatures, they act by their share in divine, reasonable intentions. Furthermore, the animal body of humans is not left behind in his scheme of glorification, but perfected, even if mediated through a temporary subsistent rational soul. To understand this attribution of reason in other animals further, it is necessary to turn to Aquinas's understanding of reason in nature, or perhaps nature *as* reason.[82] By this is meant that the natural world is not separated off from reasonable activity in humans, but "human reason reflects the same intelligible structures of existence and action as are manifested in prerational nature, to which it brings understanding and the possibilities of a deliberate, organized realization."[83] The phrase "nature is reason" reflects this capacity of the created world to echo human acts, but as I elaborated above, the emphasis on a distinctive capacity for human abstraction and control is never in doubt. However, "these rational activities, in turn, are given coherence and direction by the natural processes out of which they stem."[84]

What is remarkable, perhaps, is that Aquinas's understanding of animal minds relative to human minds has not moved on in the scientific literature as much as one might anticipate. The cognitive capacity of other animals is such that there are still heated debates about whether they have a theory of mind, that is, whether they are able to base their actions on insight about what the other player is thinking. In some fascinating research, Sarah Clayton has proposed that scrub jays are capable of storing (caching) food and are sensitive to whether another conspecific is watching.[85] There

---

Celia Deane-Drummond, *Wonder and Wisdom: Conversations in Science, Spirituality, and Theology* (London: DLT, 2006).

82. I am drawing here on Jean Porter's superb scholarly work *Nature as Reason: A Thomistic Theory of the Natural Law* (Grand Rapids: Eerdmans, 2005).

83. Porter, *Nature as Reason,* p. 70.

84. Porter, *Nature as Reason,* p. 71.

85. Joanna M. Dally, Nathan J. Emery, and Nicola S. Clayton, "Cache Protection Strategies by Western Scrub-Jays *(Aphelocoma californica):* Hiding Food in the Shade," *Pro-*

are two hotly debated scientific explanations for this. The first is that such behavior implies a theory of mind, for the behavior varies significantly and is dependent on the specific circumstances, including the presence of others. A second, simpler explanation is that prior learning has occurred, and that the behavior is a simple application of rules learned. For example, the rule to cache away from onlookers could be learned. The advantage of the latter is that it requires less cognitive complexity, but to explain the remarkable flexibility in response, such as the apparent response to the presence of specific birds, virtually every behavior would have to depend on a prior learned rule.[86] Furthermore, some birds not only cache away from conspecific onlookers, they also recache prior cached stores close to onlookers after they are alone. To recache when they are alone, they would have to remember the distance between the original cache sites and the onlookers. How do they have the capacity for such advanced responses? Is it based on a theory of mind or not?[87] So was Darwin right or was he mistaken in believing in a graded continuity between humans and other animals?[88] Some remarkable research by Dutch scientists Elske van der Vaart, Rineke Verbrugge, and Charlotte Hemelrijk seeks to model cache behavior by devising consequences of theoretical decisions of a "virtual bird." Their research offers a variation on the hotly debated alternatives of a theory of mind or learned behavior.[89] The authors assume that the memory system of the virtual bird follows the basic pattern found in humans.[90] They also assume that memory is important, so that in their model

ceedings of the Royal Society B 271 (2004): 5387-90; Joanna M. Dally, Nathan J. Emery, and Nicola S. Clayton, "Food-Caching Western Scrub-Jays Keep Track of Who Was Watching When," *Science* 312 (2006): 1662-66; Gert Stulp et al., "Western Scrub-Jays Conceal Auditory Information When Competitors Can Hear but Cannot See," *Biology Letters* 5 (2009): 583-85; Uri Grodzinski and Nicola S. Clayton, "Problems Faced by Food-Caching Corvids and the Evolution of Cognitive Solutions," *Philosophical Transactions of the Royal Society B* 365 (2010): 977-87.

86. Derek C. Penn and Daniel J. Povinelli, "On the Lack of Evidence That Non-human Animals Possess Anything Remotely Resembling a 'Theory of Mind,'" *Philosophical Transactions of the Royal Society B* 362 (2007): 731-44.

87. I take up the issue of animal minds again in chapter 5, on language.

88. Derek C. Penn, K. J. Holyoak, and Daniel J. Povinelli, "Darwin's Mistake: Explaining the Discontinuity between Human and Nonhuman Minds," *Behavioral and Brain Sciences* 31 (2008): 109-78.

89. Elske van der Vaart, Rineke Verbrugge, and Charlotte K. Hemelrijk, "Corvid Recaching without 'Theory of Mind': A Model," *PloS ONE* 7, no. 3 (2012).

90. On human memory, see John R. Anderson et al., "An Integrated Theory of the Mind," *Psychological Review* 111 (2004): 1036-60.

the more often caching takes place, or recovery takes place, the stronger the memory will be. Furthermore, stress increases the likelihood of caching or recaching. Finding caches missing or the presence of a dominant conspecific increases stress and so further enhances caching. Their virtual model was premised on a single rule — increased caching during stress — and given their assumptions about what might cause stress, their results showed a remarkable correspondence with earlier field trials of birds that had responded to the presence of onlookers or dominants. But a model system is not the same as field experimentation, so it seems to me that the jury is still out on how far and to what extent scrub jays and other corvids might display a theory of mind. Aquinas would probably side with those scientists who argue, on the one hand, for a measure of continuity, but also, on the other hand, for a measure of discontinuity, one that does set human beings in some sense apart from other animals. So while the evidence from virtual bird models is fascinating, it is not necessarily conclusive.

The distinctively human experience of being able to reason in favor of a certain action and then carry it out, that is, the relationship between conscious will and action, touches on heated debates in current philosophy and psychology. The argument goes something like this: just because I am aware of a thought in my head that precedes a particular action does not necessarily prove a causal relationship between them, as there may be a common factor that gives rise to both simultaneously. In this case, the experiential awareness of the will is labeled illusionary because it cannot be proved with any certainty that it is inextricably tied specifically to the following action that is willed.[91] Wegner cites evidence from disorders that disconnect a willed intention from bodily action, such as alien hand syndrome linked with damage to the frontal lobe area of the brain, where one hand seems to act autonomously and independently of willed intention. Another example is hypnosis, where the perception is that actions are somehow involuntary and independent of the will. His main argument is that the processes of the mind that lead to willfulness may be distinct from those processes that lead to actions. In the classical tradition, the mind is divided into emotion, cognition, and conation, where conation is the willful part. But of particular interest here is this: What is the relationship between conation and cognition, and is there sufficient justification for these two categories according to modern psychology? Moreover, having a conscious will seems to be a prerequisite for freedom to be exercised; I will develop

91. Wegner, "Précis of 'The Illusion of Conscious Will.'"

this thought in the following chapter. Those arguing for metaphysical positions on the will have sometimes assumed that it is a fundamental aspect of human nature that escapes analysis by science. This seems to me to be mistaken, since there is no reason in theory why the will or the experience of the will cannot be analyzed and subject to experimental scrutiny, like any other area of psychology. As for religion, or belief in God in general, the experience of the will should not be a taboo topic. As Wegner points out, it is important to recognize the distinction between a person's self-conscious feeling of willing and the actual relationship with action that follows. A feeling of resolve or strength of will may or may not be related to action. Inasmuch as the feeling of conscious will is not absolutely related to the same mental processes that lead to action, Wegner is entirely correct.

However, Aquinas realized centuries before that there could be a distinction between what seems to us conscious will and the way we act. Furthermore, the experience of being a person, of being an agent, which I will return to in the following chapter, is authentic only if my mental perception matches up with actions. Where these are disjointed in a non-deliberate way, one has a disorder, rather than pointing up the will itself as "illusory." It is only illusory in the sense that it is not tightly connected to action in the way that intuitions about our wills may imply. But it is not illusory in the sense that the experience of the will habitually leads human agents to act in a certain way. The experience of the will situates itself between emotion and reason; in that it is not just a strong feeling of intention, the conscious will maps onto cognitive structures of the mind that are associated with higher reasoning powers, that is, the cerebral cortex. Hence, one would expect that other animals are not able to have the same sense of consciousness of the will that is common in human beings.

The inclinations of human beings that are shared with other animals are subject to further rational reflection, which Aquinas describes in terms of active consent. It is therefore incorrect to read natural law as if it could be simply read off an affirmation of biological processes as such.[92] The particular way of understanding nature is also relevant here, in that for scholastics it meant anything that is prior to human convention, so that the term "nature" or "natural" can include not just other creatures, but also human rationality as well as God's will as revealed in Scripture.[93] Once

92. A point also made by Porter, *Nature as Reason,* p. 75.

93. Jean Porter, *Natural and Divine Law: Reclaiming the Tradition for Christian Ethics* (Grand Rapids: Eerdmans, 1999), p. 77.

incorporated into the idea of natural law, the term "natural" tended to shed the meaning of sheer fact and have connotations of order, intelligibility, and goodness.[94] The alignment of goodness with the natural rests on the affirmation of the goodness of the natural order as such, so "those natural processes that we share with the animals are intrinsically valuable and form the basis for an important aspect of distinctively human forms of the natural law."[95] The equation of nature with reason came about because the orderly processes of the natural world were viewed as expressions of God's reason. The canonical text *Summa "Reverentia Sacrorum Canonum,"* written around 1184, describes other animals as having "the image of reason" equated with "imagination," and follows Ulpian in affirming that there is a sense in which other creatures also share in the natural law. It therefore speaks of the "natural justice" that directs other creatures as being in continuity with that which naturally directs human beings, even if, strictly speaking, natural law is confined to human societies.[96] Jean Porter attributes similar arguments to Philip the Chancellor, Roland of Cremola, and John of La Rochelle.[97]

Does Aquinas allow for any form of natural law in creatures other than humans? This becomes clearest in the questions in the *Summa* that lead up to his explicit exposition of the natural law. In the first place, he prefers to speak of the whole universe being subject to the eternal law, but nonrational creatures are moved by divine providence, rather than understanding God-given commands. However, "non-rational creatures

94. Porter, *Natural and Divine Law,* pp. 77-78. It is therefore a misreading of natural law to assume that the scholastics simply read of human morality from what was observed in the natural world, quite apart from the discussion noted above that elevated the human ability for abstract reasoning and consent regarding appetitive desires.

95. Porter, *Natural and Divine Law,* p. 80. Porter comments that while for scholastics other animals were not used as a guide for human behavior in any rigid sense, or subject to moral appraisal, they were prepared to admit that the lives of animals displayed an intrinsic goodness, and to ascribe intrinsic value to the integrity of animal behavior. Although Porter names the latter as being "unlike us" (p. 81), these are precisely the claims made by animal ethologists such as Marc Bekoff and Frans de Waal.

96. As evidenced in *Summa "Reverentia Sacrorum Canonum,"* Weigand no. 324-27, written around 1184, cited in Porter, *Natural and Divine Law,* pp. 86-87.

97. Porter, *Natural and Divine Law,* p. 115 n. 57. The importance of "natural" in natural law, even if understood in a scholastic sense as preconventional, is one reason why Porter rejects more truncated interpretations of natural law by scholars, such as Germain Grisez and John Finnis, who set nonrational or prerational nature in contrast to reason. They are therefore "forced to deny the moral relevance of all those aspects of our humanity that we share with other animals." Porter, p. 93.

. . . participate in divine reason by way of obedience: the power of divine reason extends to more things than come under human reason."[98] He likens this participation to the way our limbs are commanded by human will, without sharing in reason in any self-conscious way. Hence, "all creatures have a 'natural bent to what is consonant with the Eternal Law.' "[99] But where rational creatures share in this reason through intelligence, nonrational creatures share in it without awareness. The distinction is crystallized so that for rational creatures "their sharing is called law properly speaking, since law, as we have seen, belongs to the mind. Non-rational creatures do not hold law as perceiving its meaning, and therefore we do not refer to them as keeping the law except by figure of speech."[100] Aquinas seems, therefore, to perceive higher qualities in other animals as displays of divine providence and divine rationality, rather than inherent expressions of a rational mind. He uses a similar framework for understanding particular emotions that have purposive qualities, such as hope. While he acknowledges the presence of hope in other animals, for Aquinas the resemblance to human beings only goes as far as appearing to understand the future, for any human perception that other animals are able to do this is "bestowed by the divine intellect which does foresee the future."[101]

Prudence, or practical wisdom, as developed in Aquinas, is another virtue that shows the reasoning powers of humans in a particular way. At the same time, it is clear that the separation between humans and other animals is not abrupt, but flows from the specific cognitive capacities in human beings. For him, the common behavior of all members of a species suggests that prudence is only partially evident in nonhuman animals: "full practical wisdom or prudence is discovered in a person who has sound judgment about how things should be done, while a partial reflection of this is exhibited by some animals whose particular instinctive manifestations adapt them to tasks similar to those which tax human ingenuity."[102]

98. Thomas Aquinas, *Summa Theologiae, Law and Political Theory, Vol. 28 (1a2ae. 90-97),* trans. Thomas Gilby (London: Blackfriars, 1966), 1a2ae, qu. 93.5.

99. Aquinas, *ST, Law and Political Theory,* 1a2ae, qu. 93.6.

100. Aquinas, *ST, Law and Political Theory,* 1a2ae, qu. 91.2.

101. Thomas Aquinas, *Summa Theologiae, Fear and Anger, Vol. 21 (1a2ae. 40-48),* trans. John Patrick Reid (London: Blackfriars, 1964), 1a2ae, qu. 40.3. I will return to a discussion of virtues in other animals in chapter 4. The kind of hope experienced has resemblances with but only really anticipates the theologically infused virtue of hope.

102. Aquinas, *ST, Purpose and Happiness,* 1a2ae, qu. 3.6.

According to Aquinas, the least developed forms of prudence included memory and teachableness, and its fullest expression was found in human animals. There are plenty of references to this in Aquinas. A particularly useful citation comes from his engagement with Aristotle in his commentary on the *Metaphysics,* where he claims that

> from the fact that some animals have memory and some do not, it follows that some are prudent and some not. . . . Now those animals which have memory can have some prudence, although prudence has one meaning in the case of brute animals and another in the case of man. Men are prudent inasmuch as they deliberate rationally about what they ought to do. . . . Hence in other animals prudence is a natural estimate about the pursuit of what is fitting and the avoidance of what is harmful, as a lamb follows its mother and runs away from a wolf.[103]

Aquinas also believed that animals shared not only in memory, but also at a higher level, namely, experience, but only to a limited extent.[104] The difference between animals and humans seems to be related to capacity for art and universal reason in the latter, and customary activity and particular reason in the former.[105] He also thought the productive activity of art differed from that of prudence: "And these also differ; for prudence directs us in actions which do not pass over into some external matter but are perfections of the one acting, but art directs us in those productive actions, such as building and cutting, which pass over into external matter."[106] In light of current knowledge of animal behavior, their ability to reason in a planned way comes close to Aquinas's definition of art.[107] The relationship between the estimative sense and prudence is particularly clear: "He says that being wise 'is in few animals,' however, and not that it is in humans only, because certain other animals also have a share in prudence and some

103. Thomas Aquinas, *Commentary on Aristotle's "Metaphysics,"* trans. Richard J. Blackwell, Richard J. Spath, and W. Edmund Thirlkel (Notre Dame, Ind.: Dumb Ox Books, 1995), book 1, lesson 1, note 11.

104. Aquinas, *Commentary on Aristotle's "Metaphysics,"* book 1, lesson 1, note 15.

105. Aquinas, *Commentary on Aristotle's "Metaphysics,"* book 1, lesson 1, note 16.

106. Aquinas, *Commentary on Aristotle's "Metaphysics,"* book 1, lesson 1, note 34.

107. See, for example, Nicola S. Clayton and Nathan J. Emery, "Canny Corvids and Political Primates: A Case for Convergent Evolution in Intelligence," in *The Deep Structure of Biology: Is Convergence Sufficiently Ubiquitous to Give a Directional Signal?* ed. Simon Conway Morris (Conshohocken, Pa.: Templeton Foundation Press, 2008), pp. 128-42.

wisdom, inasmuch as through natural estimation they judge rightly about what should be done."[108]

In Aquinas's interpretation, there is what might be termed a theocentric reading of the quality of acts of other animals, which sets those creatures on a continuum with human beings and yet allows for a clear distinction between them. At the same time, the reasoning ability in humans as expressed in natural law is like a kind of overflow of that rationality present in the created world, beginning with life itself, and then finding expression in the lives of other animals and human beings. The difference is that humans are able to reflect self-consciously using their reasoning abilities. Aquinas did not have the knowledge we have today about cognitive powers of other animals.[109] If he had, he might have allowed for even closer correspondence between humans and at least some other animals. However, there are dangers in *not* marking out at least a distinction between humans and other social animals, even if the boundary becomes fuzzy in places. This is because even if we perceive the same or similar behavior in other animals, we cannot assume that their thought processes are the same as those of human beings. It might even be more respectful to conclude that there are some differences and, with Aquinas, acknowledge that the telos of the creature is that which is appropriate to that creature according to divine intent, rather than that according to human imagination.

While we might prefer to see the activity of an animal as more consciously autonomous than Aquinas implies, an acknowledgment of divine providence and purpose as such cannot be proved or disproved by scientific investigation, either in humans or in other animals.[110] Inasmuch

108. Thomas Aquinas, *Commentary on Aristotle's "De Anima,"* trans. Robert Pasnau (New Haven: Yale University Press, 1999), book 3, chapter 4, 427B6-8, §629, p. 323.

109. The cognitive powers of other animals can be surmised from tests on their intelligence, but since they are set up in accordance with how human beings think, it is difficult to avoid bias in such assessments. See Marian Stamp Dawkins, "Animal Minds and Animal Emotions," *Integrative Comparative Biology* 40, no. 6 (2000): 883-88. Marian Dawkins argues that there has been too much attention paid to animal cognition and not enough to animal emotions, which she believes are much older in evolutionary terms. Aquinas would have agreed with such a position, even if he does not have an evolutionary theory to explain it.

110. There are ways we might wish to map out what that purpose means in a theological sense. I have argued, drawing on a Thomistic understanding of natural law, that divine purpose is at least compatible with those forms of evolutionary theory that acknowledge constraint. See Celia Deane-Drummond, "Plumbing the Depths: A Recovery of Natural Law and Natural Wisdom in the Context of Debates about Evolutionary Purpose," *Zygon* 42, no. 4 (2007): 981-98. A full discussion of this aspect is outside the scope of this chapter.

as nature is perceived to reflect the wisdom and benevolence of God as Creator, the naturalness of a tendency provides prima facie evidence for moral legitimacy, and so, even if sifted through rational reflection, affirms the goodness of nature as such.[111] Importantly, Porter argues that the understanding of design that emerged in natural theology in the seventeenth century was very different from the way the scholastics understood creation to be a reflection of God's intelligence. In the former view, reasonable "design" is *external* to the creature, while for the scholastics the design was an integral part of the inner telos and form of the organism intended to promote its flourishing, rather than a function disconnected from it. In the scholastic view, "the goodness of a creature is inextricably bound up with its intelligible form, that is to say, with the ordered functioning proper to the kind of creature it is."[112] This is also important for understanding human nature, since even though rationality is elevated in the scholastic scheme, *isolating* any such function is inappropriate; rather, it has to be set within the overall well-being of the human being, humankind at large, and, it seems to me, creation as a whole.

But how might we envisage the move from "nature as reason" in a general sense as showing that the natural world is intelligible, to the more explicit expression of forms of practical reason, and then to the most sophisticated abstracted human reasoning abilities? Alasdair MacIntyre discusses this in his book *Dependent Rational Animals,* in which he acknowledges the particular intelligence of social animals, focusing particularly on dolphins. This allows him to recognize more clearly the common ground between humans and other animals. But the significance of this common ground is as much in human dependency, which he considers a shared characteristic with other animals, as it is in reasonable autonomy. It is the move from dependency to autonomy that is of interest in this discussion, for it lays out how we might map more general reasonableness in nature emerging into something rather more sophisticated in human reasoning, and therefore forming the basis for the ability to make complex moral decisions.[113] MacIntyre recognizes that entering into a mature adult world of reasoning is not something that is simply given at the outset of human life, but develops through

111. Porter, *Nature as Reason,* p. 136. The scholastics did realize that prerational nature does not lead in a simple or easy way to recommendations about social practices, so any recommendations are very general indeed.

112. Porter, *Nature as Reason,* p. 138.

113. I take up the twin issues of agency and morality in the two chapters that follow.

a child developing in the context of a network of familial social relationships.[114] This parallels the kind of care given to young that we find in social animals, but there is a crucial difference in that human beings can anticipate old age or look back in time and reflect on it in a way that social animals cannot.[115]

Like Aquinas, MacIntyre acknowledges that it is the development of the evaluative capacity in humans that is important, as well as the ability to imagine or envisage different future scenarios and the ability to stand back from particular human desires.[116] Drawing on the work of D. W. Winnicott, MacIntyre argues that to have a mature sense of self, which is necessary to be an independent, practical reasoner who is free from unhelpful forms of attachment, an individual must go through a period of creative mental activity manifested in play.[117] The eventual goal of that reasoning is toward what makes for our overall human flourishing, rather than simply satisfying immediate desires, that Bernard Williams names the "subjective motivational set."[118] Crucially, MacIntyre argues that mature thinkers will eventually seek to transform their inner desires to match what is considered good for their flourishing. He asks then, "What are the qualities that a child must develop, first to direct and transform her or his desires, and subsequently to direct them consistently towards the goods of different stages of his or her life? They are the intellectual and moral virtues."[119] But the acquisition of such virtues is only possible through

114. MacIntyre, *Dependent Rational Animals,* p. 82.

115. Aquinas also recognized the commonality with animals in mating and rearing young, but also the distinction in capacity for memory in that human beings are able to anticipate the future or reflect on past memories, as discussed above.

116. For Aquinas, discussions of different future scenarios inform his discussion of the will, while the ability to evaluate informs his discussion of reason, and the ability to stand back and distance ourselves from desires informs his sections on appetites. He did not, however, as far as I am aware, deal with the development of these capacities from childhood, even if he recognized that these capabilities were not present in children.

117. MacIntyre, *Dependent Rational Animals,* p. 85. MacIntyre does not, however, discuss the significance of play in providing ground rules for the subsequent emergence of fairness. See chapter 7, where I take this up in more detail.

118. Bernard Williams, *Moral Luck* (Cambridge: Cambridge University Press, 1981), p. 102, also cited in MacIntyre, *Dependent Rational Animals,* p. 86. MacIntyre is critical of Williams because he does not allow for the possibility that agents might have to learn to navigate a transition toward a mature recognition that the human capacity to discover reasons for doing things may not match their inner motivation, and thus acknowledge the limitation of their motivational set.

119. MacIntyre, *Dependent Rational Animals,* p. 87.

learning in a network of social relationships in which we gradually mature as human beings.[120]

Reason as Graced

The capacity for practical wisdom or prudence in human beings is something learned through education in the context of the familial or wider community. Aquinas also recognizes that the basic innate capacity for reasoning may vary with different individuals. He tended to treat other animals as having identical capacities depending on the particular species, rather than showing considerable variation between individuals in a species in the way recognized by contemporary ethologists.[121] But Aquinas also speaks of the capacity for that reason in humans as *graced* by the special infusion of the Spirit. Often somewhat of an embarrassment to contemporary philosophers, the idea of infusion is brushed to one side or not even mentioned in discussions about practical or theoretical reasoning. Yet the particular human capacity to experience grace colors Aquinas's views of the intellectual and moral virtues as well as the theological virtues of faith, hope, and charity. This has to do with the way Aquinas envisages human beings as located between angels and other animals. This does not mean, however, a loss of independence; rather, he views the possibility of a higher degree of independence the nearer a creature is to God, and thus the closer to reflecting the image of God.[122] Supposing grace to be infused into the intellectual virtues, therefore, is a natural outworking of this scheme. Overall, the work of grace is, therefore, primarily directed toward the reasoning process in Aquinas's scheme, so that four of the seven gifts of the Spirit are connected to reason, namely, wisdom, knowledge, understanding, and counsel. But he does allow for three gifts of the Spirit to be connected to appetite, namely, fortitude, piety, and fear.[123] The in-

120. In using the term "natural law," I am following the Thomistic definition elaborated by Porter as discussed earlier.

121. Individual variation in intelligence is characteristic not just of humans, but of other animals as well, as documented in Eduardo Mercado III, "Mapping Individual Variations in Learning Capacity," *International Journal of Comparative Psychology* 24 (2011): 4-35.

122. Hence, he speaks of a uniquely human mastery over inclinations. Aquinas, *On Truth,* vol. 3, qu. 22.4.

123. Thomas Aquinas, *Summa Theologiae, The Gifts of the Spirit, Vol. 24 (1a2ae. 68-70),* trans. Edward O'Connor (London: Blackfriars, 1974), 1a2ae, qu. 68.1.

tellectual virtues work through natural capacities but are supplemented by the work of God's grace, so that "wisdom is said to be an intellectual virtue in so far as it acts from the judgment of reason; it is called a gift in so far as its work arises from divine prompting."[124]

He, therefore, is prepared to speak of understanding not just as a cognitive capacity, but also as a gift.[125] For Aquinas, the gift of understanding relates to the human knowledge of faith and to appropriate acts. The gift of understanding seems to be that which is able to connect "eternal and necessary truths" with particular rules for human conduct. Since the eternal law exceeds natural reason, to know this law, Aquinas argues, our human reasoning powers need to be supplemented in some way by a gift coming from the Holy Spirit, and he calls this gift the gift of understanding.[126] In addition, he speaks of the gift of science.[127] If the gift of understanding perfects matters relevant to faith, the gift of science is about sure judgment so as to discern what is to be believed and what is not to be believed.[128] This comes not so much from a discursive process, as in the practice of human sciences, as from a revealed insight as to what the truth is about. He also distinguishes between the gift of science given to all who are "in grace" in discerning what to believe, and the gift of science as a means of bearing witness to that faith. Both the gift of understanding and the gift of science are therefore serving in some way the virtue of faith. For Aquinas, Christian theology is a science that receives its truth first by revelation, and only second by careful study.[129]

The gift of science is about human or created things, but the gift of wisdom points to "realities in themselves through being united with them," and therefore "corresponds more to charity which conjoins man's mind to God."[130] It is the gifts of wisdom and charity that inform all other patterns of right knowing and reasoning. T. C. O'Brien aptly summarizes Aquinas's position in his comment that "every human situation, whether of trying

124. Aquinas, *ST, Gifts of the Spirit,* 1a2ae, qu. 68.1.

125. Thomas Aquinas, *Summa Theologiae, Consequences of Faith, Vol. 32 (2a2ae. 8-16),* trans. Thomas Gilby (London: Blackfriars, 1975), 2a2ae, qu. 8.1–8.4.

126. Aquinas, *ST, Consequences of Faith,* 2a2ae, qu. 8.3.

127. Also called the gift of knowledge, but I am following Thomas Gilby in preferring this translation in this context; Aquinas, *ST, Consequences of Faith,* 2a2ae, qu. 9.

128. Aquinas, *ST, Consequences of Faith,* 2a2ae, qu. 9.1.

129. Thomas Aquinas, *Summa Theologiae, Christian Theology, Vol. 1 (1a. 1),* trans. Thomas Gilby (London: Blackfriars, 1964), 1a, qu. 1.6.

130. Aquinas, *ST, Consequences of Faith,* 2a2ae, qu. 9.2.

to evaluate the meaning of things or of trying to shape a specific course of action, involves judgment; the kind of judgment critical to salvation is one that is infused with the love of charity, that is, a *verbum spirans amorem.* Wisdom informed by charity is, however, simply the most eminent form that the experience of grace takes. These two stand for all the Gifts of knowing and of action that cover the conditions of the Christian life."[131]

The language of "gift" and "infusion" might imply rather a dualistic supernatural notion of God's grace working to intervene in an otherwise brutish human nature. Certainly, the hierarchical arrangement of other animals, humans, angels, and God in the scheme Aquinas adopts implies that God administers grace from above, rather than from below. Yet inasmuch as grace works to perfect what is in nature, it is possible to interpret infusion in the context of an emergence of awareness of the ever-present presence of God, rather than a dualistic version of grace as an alien force working in opposition to natural forces. Human beings in this interpretation would have a particular ability to experience grace in a particular way according to their general cognitive abilities; at the same time, the action of God's grace would not be limited by such abilities, otherwise the work of God would be most evident in those with high reasoning powers, which is clearly not necessarily the case. The experience of Jean Vanier's L'Arche communities suggests, if anything, the opposite, that God's grace is most often experienced with greatest intensity in a community that includes those whose mental functioning is impaired.

Grace, for Aquinas, also comes into the reasoning process when the passions work to distract the human ability to reason. While the admonition of others is a start, grace comes in to restrain the "lower" powers of passion and perfect reason in its contemplation of God. This understanding of the work of grace, which seems to detach reason from bodily nature, is unfortunate, and "It can sometimes look as if Aquinas's ideal for human nature is a life entirely free of the passions, a life of reason alone, with the passions held firmly under foot. The inevitability of our passions often seems to take on the aspect of a curse, a flaw in our nature that more times than not will prove fatal."[132] Aquinas seems closer to Platonic thought in this respect, though, in common with Aristotle, he allows for a positive

131. Thomas Aquinas, *Summa Theologiae, Father, Son, and Holy Ghost, Vol. 7 (1a. 33-43),* trans. T. C. O'Brien (London: Blackfriars, 1965), appendix 3: "The Sending and the Presence of the Persons," p. 265. I prefer the translation "Holy Spirit" rather than "Holy Ghost."

132. Pasnau, *Thomas Aquinas,* p. 262.

role of the passions if they come subsequent, rather than antecedent, to the directives of reason since they show an appropriate measure of commitment. Grace, therefore, in this aspect of Aquinas's thought, can only work in and through the passions that are guided by reason. This seems to be related to his elevation of reason as that which brings human beings closest to God. Robert Pasnau argues that Aquinas could give some weight to the primary role of the emotions if they were developed and cultivated through discipline and intelligence.[133] But such a scheme implies the influence of reason on emotions and not a positive appraisal of emotion on reason. Sara Shettleworth suggests that "students of human cognition are increasingly coming to appreciate that our own accounts of what we do as coming from conscious thought and rational decision may in fact be after-the-fact explanations of reactions to simple cues of the sort that other species might also respond to."[134]

Yet does Aquinas not precisely do this through his elevation of wisdom as connected with charity? While Aquinas's dismissal of the emotions in those parts of the *Summa* that deal with the passions may give the impression that he has not taken sufficient account of the emotions onboard, the central place of charity and wisdom as an intellectual virtue *embedded* in charity is important, for it gives a more positive view of the emotional life as more than simply antecedent to the work of practical wisdom or prudence. One of the problems may be that Pasnau's scholarly and erudite distillation of human nature in Aquinas's thought has largely restricted itself to close analysis of the first part of the *Summa*. For Aquinas, the function of wisdom is to contemplate the "simply ultimate," so consideration of the ultimate cause in any particular field is the work of wisdom, while the work of prudence or practical wisdom is directed to human acts.[135] The work of wisdom may be directed to wrong ends so that it can be focused on material goods, such as earthly wisdom, or on goods of the body, such as animal wisdom, both of which are limited; however, he reserves the harshest judgment of all for wisdom focused on "creaturely loftiness," which he calls "devilish," "because it copies the pride of the devil."[136] This implies

133. Pasnau, *Thomas Aquinas,* p. 263.

134. Sara Shettleworth, *Cognition, Evolution, and Behaviour,* 2nd ed. (Oxford: Oxford University Press, 2010), p. 243.

135. Thomas Aquinas, *Summa Theologiae, Prudence, Vol. 36 (2a2ae. 47-56),* trans. Thomas Gilby (London: Blackfriars, 1973), 2a2ae, qu. 47.1.

136. Thomas Aquinas, *Summa Theologiae, Consequences of Charity, Vol. 35 (2a2ae. 34-46),* trans. Thomas R. Heath (London: Blackfriars, 1972), 2a2ae, qu. 45.1.

that he is not as negatively concerned about bodily sins as his discussion of the passions might imply, but rather reserves the sharpest critique for that distortion of wisdom in the human will to power and arrogance that seeks to put humanity in the place that God deserves.

True wisdom, on the other hand, is directed to knowledge of the sovereign good and the ultimate end, which is God. The gift of wisdom "differs from the acquired intellectual virtue of wisdom. The latter comes through human effort, the former *comes down from above.*"[137] The gift of wisdom presupposes faith, understood as *assent* to divine truth, while wisdom as gift *judges* according to divine truth. In this case, wisdom manifests itself in the context of worship and the practice of piety where faith is professed. So "piety makes wisdom manifest too," and to such an extent that the two are equated, and "piety is wisdom and for the same reason also is fear. If a man fears and worships God he shows he has a right judgment about divine things."[138] While this might seem a somewhat optimistic view of the impact of worship and piety on human judgment, what he seems to be suggesting is that the true fear and worship of God are intimately connected with proper apprehension of the truth through the gift of wisdom. Piety and fear are appetitive powers rather than intellectual powers. This illustrates the way grace works to unite intellectual and appetitive powers, and is not simply restricted to the former. If the gift of wisdom works in judging the claims of faith, then the virtue of wisdom works in judging first principles of thought.[139] Yet the possibility for the gift of wisdom seems to emerge only where charity is present, which Aquinas understands as enabling human beings to have fellowship with God.[140]

Wisdom does not simply stay in worshipful contemplation of God, but directs human acts according to divine reasons in such a way that it is free from bitterness or toil.[141] Aquinas also suggests that there is a hierarchy of human capacity for wisdom based on different degrees of unity with God.[142] The lowest level is that needed for salvation and is given to all who are without mortal sin. Others "receive a higher degree of the gift of wisdom" and are able to direct not just themselves, but others, about

137. Aquinas, *ST, Consequences of Charity,* 2a2ae, qu. 45.1.

138. Aquinas, *ST, Consequences of Charity,* 2a2ae, qu. 45.1.

139. As also noted by translator Thomas R. Heath in Aquinas, *ST, Consequences of Charity,* note 19, comment on 2a2ae, qu. 45.1.

140. Aquinas, *ST, Consequences of Charity,* 2a2ae, qu. 45.2.

141. Aquinas, *ST, Consequences of Charity,* 2a2ae, qu. 45.3.

142. Aquinas, *ST, Consequences of Charity,* 2a2ae, qu. 45.5.

divine things. These gifts are given to those whom the Holy Spirit chooses; on this Aquinas cites 1 Corinthians 12:8-11. In this way, the first stage of wisdom is to shun evil, but the final stage also brings about peace so that everything finds itself in the proper place as judgments are directed according to divine intentions.[143] This hierarchy of stages in wisdom parallels in some respects his hierarchical interpretation of the different levels of image bearing possible for human beings discussed earlier in this chapter. At the same time, the work of the infused gift of wisdom does not replace the more mundane work of practical wisdom; rather, the gifts of grace infusing the moral virtues seem to foster a more complete reorientation of the human person toward God.[144] Prudence, as practical wisdom, is a virtue of practical reason compared with wisdom, which is a virtue of intellectual reason. Prudence as infused virtue, therefore, corresponds with the gift of counsel that acts to perfect prudence so that by being open to the movement of the Spirit it becomes guided by divine reason, but it is a perfection of practical human reason, rather than detachment from that reason.[145]

Some Interim Conclusions

The theological vision that Aquinas presents is one of human natural reason perfected by the power of the Holy Spirit working through those who are united to God in the fellowship of charity. While such a graced experience enables a stronger ascetic approach to material desires, it is an embodied rather than disembodied understanding of human nature transformed by God's grace. If the natural world is understood as ordered through the rationality of divine providence, the special task of humanity is one in which reason can become perfected in relation to a self-conscious awareness of divine truth. The action of grace in a human life is not limited to human reasoning powers, even if those powers enable human beings in a clearer way to make visible and self-conscious the divine intentions. The distinctive nature of human reasoning is its powers of abstraction, but the immateriality present in this case is qualified by consideration of cognitive

143. Aquinas, *ST, Consequences of Charity,* 2a2ae, qu. 45.6.

144. For further discussion, see Pamela Hall, *Narrative and the Natural Law* (Notre Dame, Ind.: University of Notre Dame Press, 1994), pp. 79-83.

145. Hall, *Narrative,* p. 85.

powers that are material and closer to the appetitive sense in other animals. Therefore, there are *degrees of reasoning* present across different species in a way that parallels the cognitive capacity of different creatures. What is surprising from this study is not that other animals also have some powers of reason, which clearly is the case from knowledge of animal cognition, but that the scholar most berated for his view of other animals also held similar views. Although naming the bald power of abstraction or symbol making as a uniquely human capacity perhaps requires some readjustment, the level and degree of that abstraction are recognized by contemporary scientists as being more advanced in humans. Wisdom as directed toward divine ends can therefore only be self-consciously experienced in humans, even if other animals might have forms of natural wisdom that could be envisaged, in some sense, as precursors of human wisdom. The evolutionary basis for that wisdom in social societies has yet to be worked out in any detail and raises fascinating questions for further research on other primates or other social animals.[146] The extent of that wisdom is likely to be closely correlated with the relative degree of animal agency that I will pick up in the chapter that follows. In other words, while grace as a work of the Holy Spirit does and can work on appetitive senses as well as the intellectual senses, inasmuch as it entails a graced freedom it shows forth the particular grace given to human beings rather than other animals. It makes more sense, therefore, to speak of the specificity of human acts as bearing the marks of humanity made in the image of God, rather than focusing just on deontological properties that are shared with other animals detached from the contexts of these acts. It also seems to me that Aquinas's view was orientated toward this approach as well, since his account of human reason and cognitive abilities in the first part is followed in the *Summa* by an even more extensive reflection on what it means to act well and in accordance with grace in the second and third parts.

146. While social creatures might be said to display a form of wisdom in social organization, such as ants, which are recognized in the Hebrew wisdom literature (e.g., Prov. 6:6), such wisdom lacks the inner freedom necessary for the full development of wisdom.

CHAPTER THREE

Human Freedom and Animal Agency

Regardless of the way the image of God is conceived, whether it be through ontological characteristics such as rationality or through more active categories including relational or even functional and performative characteristics, freedom is an ingredient in the meaning. Reasoning tied rigidly to specific thought processes is dysfunctional reason; obsessive or narcissistic relations are incompatible with human flourishing; and acting under coercion is problematic in terms of the good of the agent. Hence, all these understandings of what it means to bear the image presuppose a measure of human freedom, which is one reason why the Orthodox theologian John Zizioulas characterizes freedom as *the* characteristic that most distinguishes humans from other animals. At the same time, freedom of the will presupposes the possibility of deliberative reason. The shift away from purely ontological characteristics of human image bearing toward a more functional view of image bearing expressed as human acts has also been noted by others, but what is not often observed is that such a shift does not necessarily solve the ontological problem, since the distinctive functional capacity for humans to act in a certain way is itself dependent on a particular understanding of human freedom that is also understood in ontological terms.

Zizioulas also rejects the idea that rationality is the key characteristic of humankind, as discussed in the previous chapter. Rather than marry freedom with rationality in a manner akin to the thought of Aquinas, he associates human freedom with creativity, and, importantly, this serves to distinguish humans from other animals. For him, creativity is at the core of human identity, and this creativity is in tension with rationality, so "there is something in man's creativity that we could hardly attribute to rationality, since in fact it is its opposite. Man, and only Man in creating his own world can go very often against the inherent rationality of nature, of the world given to him: he can even destroy the given world. . . . Whatever involves succumbing to the given, this man has in common with the animals. Whatever is free from it, constitutes a sign of the presence of the human."[1] Here he seems to mean a positive understanding of human freedom as creativity that can choose to be *free from* internal necessity, rather than freedom understood in a negative sense as liberation from external compulsion. But why should human freedom understood as creativity be thought of in opposition to naturally endowed rationality? And why should it be somehow against the natural processes found in other animals? For Zizioulas, such positive human freedom is to be exercised correctly only in acknowledgment of God's intentions, rather than simply in a libertine, unbounded sense of individual free choice.[2] But again, we can ask, why are God's intentions somehow opposed to that which is found in the inherent rationality of nature, or if they are, what is the relationship between them? Another category that he argues is exclusive to the notion of human freedom is the tragic, but this is also bound up in the concept of a particular expression of human freedom in which "tragedy is the impasse created by a freedom driving towards its fulfillment and being unable to reach it."[3]

While his approach is well argued within an Orthodox theological framework, it jars with trends in some versions of evolutionary psychology that characterize the human freedom to act, including human morality, as grounded in an evolved capacity and religion, including belief in God, as either evolved or a "spandrel," a side effect of some other evolutionary function.[4] It is not my intention in this chapter to go into the

1. John Zizioulas, "Preserving God's Creation," lecture 3, *King's Theological Review* 12, no. 1 (1990): 1-6, here 2. He suggests further that if we consider what is found in God and not in creation, then this "forces us to seek the *imago Dei* in freedom" (p. 2). Yet, the aspiration for absolute freedom can never be attained because humans are finite creatures. For Zizioulas, this aspiration is fulfilled by humanity taking up its role as priests of creation.

2. He draws on Gregory of Nyssa's claim that *imago Dei* means "man's freedom to be master of himself." Zizioulas, "Preserving God's Creation," p. 2.

3. Zizioulas, "Preserving God's Creation," p. 2.

4. I discuss briefly the challenge of an evolutionary basis for religious belief in chapter 1. It is also discussed by a number of prominent authors in the science and religion debate, more specifically J. Wentzel van Huyssteen, *Alone in the World? Human Uniqueness in Science and Theology* (Grand Rapids: Eerdmans, 2006), and Wesley J. Wildman, *Science and Religious Anthropology: A Spiritually Evocative Naturalist Interpretation of Human Life* (Farn-

intricacies of scientific debate about the evolutionary origin of belief that humans are free agents or even into religious belief; for the purposes of my argument, it is sufficient to show that ever since Darwin there have been concerted attempts to break down the boundary between humans and other animals by explaining what used to be considered the exclusive province of humans in evolutionary terms. Religion and freedom are perhaps the last borders to be crossed. The questions that come to the surface, therefore, are these: On what basis might the fluidity of the boundary between humans and other animals be supported, and on what basis might it be resisted?

In other words, while on the one hand the acknowledgment of evolutionary commonality might seem a welcome step in seeking to show how strong anthropocentric theological positions are unsustainable according to contemporary scientific views, on the other hand, where such evolutionary views become emboldened as a means of explaining away religious or other metaphysical positions while often disguising an unacknowledged metaphysic, they can be subjects of intense philosophical and theological scrutiny.[5] So, simply making a claim that evolutionary biology has done theology a favor by challenging anthropocentrism inherent in it distinctly lacks nuance; a more accurate claim would be that, in acknowledging common traits with other animals, contemporary evolutionary science reminds humanity of its common biological origins, but that science is *also* premised on objective methods that themselves

---

ham: Ashgate, 2009). Scientists are not suggesting that animals are religious, although some ethologists permit the idea that this cannot be ruled out of court (Frans de Waal, personal comment following public discussion of his lecture "The Age of Empathy" at the American Academy of Religion, Atlanta, November 2010), but evolutionary psychologists are more likely to argue in a positivist way that the origin of human religion can be accounted for by entirely natural mechanisms, even if they are ready to admit that science does not then test the truth or otherwise of the claims of religion. Clearly, finding the biological basis *for the capacity for* religion does not amount to an *explanation for* religion. This is discussed in Jeffrey Schloss and Michael Murray, eds., *The Believing Primate: Scientific, Philosophical, and Theological Reflections on the Origin of Religion* (Oxford: Oxford University Press, 2009), especially essays by Michael Murray, for example, "Scientific Explanations of Religion and the Justification of Religious Belief," pp. 168-78; Alvin Plantinga's essay in that volume, "Games Scientists Play," is also useful in this context, pp. 139-67. See also below, chapter 4 on morality.

5. Conor Cunningham has discussed this issue in his erudite and detailed treatment of the topic in *Darwin's Pious Idea: Why the Ultra-Darwinists and Creationists Both Get It Wrong* (Grand Rapids: Eerdmans, 2010).

tend to distance humans from any sense of deep rootedness in the natural world.[6] Furthermore, and alongside this, more strident evolutionary psychologists speak of particular evolutionary functions in positive teleological terms of "design" that betray a particular metaphysical stance that is in tension with what might be termed a "purer" reflection of the prime engine of neo-Darwinian evolution being the nonteleological and relatively weak negative forces of natural selection.[7] This is important, since it undermines the very possibility of genuine freedom of action that is the core topic for this chapter. How far accusations of genetic determinism are accurate will depend on the particular evolutionary position being elaborated, but at least *between* evolutionary scientists there is a strong suspicion that in some accounts of evolutionary psychology, and its earlier sociobiological parent, rather too much weight is given to the impact of genes on human behavior.[8]

Before going any further, some philosophical clarity is needed to set out more explicitly what is at stake in this discussion, since, like the term "human nature," the term "freedom" covers so many different meanings. It is important to be clear which ones may or may not be relevant in relation to the boundary between humans and other animals and to point to both the commonality between the two and the distinguishing marks of humanity. Freedom can be construed in many different ways: *freedom of the will* relates to the deliberative action of human willing, but this is distinct from *freedom of choice,* which postulates different possible future scenarios prior to action.[9] In the classical tradition, will is distinct from the intellective capacity of reasoning, even though they are closely related.[10]

6. Tim Ingold has compared the approach to science by Charles Darwin and other evolutionary thinkers to a wedge; see Tim Ingold, "The Wedge and the Knot: Hammering and Stitching the Face of Nature," in *Nature, Space, and the Sacred: Transdisciplinary Perspectives,* ed. Sigurd Bergmann et al. (Farnham: Ashgate, 2009), pp. 147-62.

7. For further discussion of these internal debates, see Celia Deane-Drummond, *Christ and Evolution: Wonder and Wisdom* (Minneapolis: Fortress, 2009), pp. 60-94.

8. As evolutionary psychology has matured as a science, rather more extreme statements have become much more qualified, but the popularizers of that science still give the impression of more certainty about the explicative power of the scientific results than is really warranted.

9. See Robert Kane, *The Oxford Handbook of Free Will,* 2nd ed. (Oxford: Oxford University Press, 2011).

10. Voluntarism is the name given to the philosophical position that gives priority to the faculty of will over intellect. Philosophical categories of will are not readily mapped onto neurological categories of brain function, so even though the language of "will" is borrowed

Freedom of action, on the other hand, relates to free agency, a freedom to do this or that thing free of external barriers or internal constraints. Of course, the difficult question is how far *any* willing, choice, or indeed behavior is ever *genuinely* free of constraints. Evolutionary biologists and neurobiologists are more often than not strict determinists; that is, they assume that what appears to be human free will or free choice is only freedom in a limited, proximate sense, but rather, there are neurological, psychological, and "ultimately" evolutionary processes at work that limit which particular decision is made and which particular action is carried out by a given individual.[11]

Philosophical compatibilists are also deterministic in that while they acknowledge that human beings have a genuine inner sense of free will, that free will is part of a larger process and chain of events that are themselves deterministic. For compatibilists, as long as the immediate and particular choice comes from the desire of the individual, that choice is still reasonably called free, even if it is constrained by causes outside the agent. So for compatibilists, freedom is still possible even within a deterministic framework. It seems quite possible to me that evolutionary biologists could be compatibilist in this sense. Libertarians argue against determinism of this sort in favor of a genuine possibility or power to be able to do or act otherwise. An agent is only free if the conscious agent *could* have chosen differently. Marcel Sarot argues that Christian belief is only consistent with the libertarian variety of freedom, also named a liberty of indifference, rather than with compatibilism.[12] But a case could equally be made for compatibilism as being just as feasible within a Christian framework.[13]

---

by neuroscientists, what is being discussed is not normally will in the philosophical sense but existential consciousness of being an agent.

11. I discussed Wegner's influential but controversial argument for the illusion of the will in the last chapter.

12. Marcel Sarot, "Christian Faith, Free Will and Neuroscience" (paper delivered to the European Society for Philosophy of Religion, Soesterberg, the Netherlands, September 1, 2012). To be published in *Ars Disputandi,* in press.

13. Aku Visala, "Theism, Compatibilism and Neurodeterminism: A Response to Marcel Sarot" (paper delivered to the European Society for Philosophy of Religion, Soesterberg, the Netherlands, September 1, 2012). To be published in *Ars Disputandi,* in press. For an alternative, see Kevin Timpe, "Why Christians Might Be Libertarians: A Response to Lynne Rudder Baker," *Philosophia Christi* 6, no. 2 (2004): 279-88. I am grateful to Aku Visala for sending me a copy of his paper prior to publication and for pointing me to the paper by Marcel Sarot.

I suggest that both compatibilist and libertarian approaches to freedom have their limitations and that Aquinas makes significant moves to avoid the problems associated with both. For example, a compatibilist would have to assume that God puts in the human heart an irresistible desire to do something, but if that is the case, then the goodness of God could be challenged. This is one of the reasons why strong versions of determinism seem unpalatable, even if it might be possible to undertake philosophical gymnastics to prove that theoretically, at least, a person could be a Christian and a determinist. Yet libertarian views are no less problematic. For if human choices are completely free and not subject to any constraint, then they might seem arbitrary, for there would be no reasons why one might choose one course of action over against another. I suggest that Aquinas goes beyond these contemporary theoretical philosophical conundrums and offers genuine insights into how human free action can be understood.

Alongside what might be termed evolutionary deterministic pressures against theological accounts of human freedom, Jacques Derrida's essay that sets out to deconstruct philosophical anthropocentrism, entitled *The Animal That Therefore I Am,* is relevant.[14] In this essay, he describes his encounter, while naked, with his female cat, expressing his embarrassment *at his embarrassment,* for according to the Genesis text, only humans are characterized as self-consciously naked. His critique of Descartes's rational human being, clearly separated from animality, points back to the Judeo-Christian tradition. He weaves a literary web around embarrassment and the shame of that embarrassment and teases out its meaning for human identity. He plays with the idea of the animal as *subject,* which, because the animal is tentatively capable of *response,* challenges the common portrayal of animals in religious and philosophical traditions as only capable of "dumb" *reactions.* Of course, this does not elude the fact that other animals have subtly insisted on rather more presence in religious texts than is officially recognized, but this amounts to a rereading of theology, a reexamination of tradition for those hints and traces that the loudest voices in theology have at times so insistently attempted to erase.[15]

14. Jacques Derrida, *The Animal That Therefore I Am,* ed. Marie-Louise Mallet, trans. David Wills (New York: Fordham University Press, 2008). Note that this essay is becoming fashionable among those who work in cultural aspects of animal studies.

15. See Celia Deane-Drummond, Rebecca Artinian-Kaiser, and David Clough, eds., *Animals as Religious Subjects: Transdisciplinary Perspectives* (London: T. & T. Clark/Bloomsbury, 2013).

In Derrida's essay, human beings are portrayed in Genesis not only as those who are uniquely capable of shame, but also as those who have, by naming, power over other animals. This begins a process that, for Derrida, ends in the projection of other animals in a post-Cartesian world as not bearing *any* moral or ontological significance relative to the human condition. One of the crucial challenges for theological traditions must be to look closely at the porous boundary between humans and other animals that Derrida, quite correctly in my view, identifies. This includes the possibility of other animals having a degree of subjectivity, as well as humans being more like other animals in their basic emotional reactions that then inform the way they act. Derrida does not deny that there are differences between humans and other animals, which he terms the "abyss," but "the frontier no longer forms a single indivisible line but more than one internally divided line; once, as a result, it can no longer be traced, objectified, or counted as single and indivisible." It is, therefore, a "multiple and heterogeneous border," full of the "heterogeneous multiplicity of the living."[16]

However, although I find Derrida's account highly provocative in reminding us of the fluid nature of the human/other animal boundary, I suggest that Derrida's analysis has a number of critical flaws. The first is that human naming of other animals in Genesis does not necessarily need to be viewed as an abusive trajectory, as authors such as Zizioulas remind us. Rather, naming can more accurately be understood as a *free commission,* a particular vocation of human beings.[17] Second, the precise way that Der-

16. Derrida, *The Animal,* pp. 30-31. He is also critical of the crude nature of what he terms the "continuism of geneticism," p. 30.

17. For a critical discussion of the Genesis text, see David Clough, "All God's Creatures: Reading Genesis on Human and Non Human Animals," in *Reading Genesis after Darwin,* ed. Stephen C. Barton and David Wilkinson (Oxford: Oxford University Press, 2009), pp. 145-62. Also, David Clough, *On Animals: Systematic Theology* (London: T. & T. Clark/ Continuum, 2012), pp. 51-61. Clough relates the naming of animals to a general tendency for their classification in different theological tropes, a tendency that he finds unacceptable inasmuch as it puts human beings in a position of superiority. His concern in the latter book is to find, using a variety of theological sources, different ways to incorporate other animals in all their diversity into a specifically Christian systematic framework. Such a framework broadly incorporates creation, incarnation, and redemption as prolegomena for their ethical treatment in a subsequent volume. Perhaps surprisingly he does not, however, deal with animal subjectivity or agency, and even though he does recognize the possibility of morality and reason in other animals, he does not treat this topic in any detail. He picks up the theme of classification again in David Clough, "Putting Animals in Their Place: On the Theological Classification of Animals," in *Animals as Religious Subjects,* pp. 209-24.

rida portrays the internal mental world of his cat is not one recognizable by animal ethologists. While his account is almost seductive in its cleverness, it is just that, an expression of the extreme cleverness of a *very human* animal indeed. Third, there are intense difficulties associated with leaving human identity floundering in the wake of Derrida's deconstructive task that are inherent in his approach in terms of the *actual* valuation it places on the nonhuman world. His view of the human is highly speculative in the way that he envisages the significance of a particular existential encounter that is premised on a particular view of human beings. In other words, while Derrida might seem to challenge anthropocentrism in a fascinating and provocative way by reminding human beings of an encounter with an "other" self that is not human, and if at root his position presupposes the identity of human beings as one shorn from the very traditions that once put specific value on the creaturely and material world, then it seems to disguise a very thin modernist version of humanity that in its turn has relatively little motivation to give value to other life-forms. The shadow of Kant's rationalist position seems to feature much more prominently than he would care to acknowledge, since his is a highly abstracted account of the human. Mary Midgley, also writing from a nontheistic perspective, fares rather better in this respect, in that she, like Derrida, recognizes the difficulty associated with a separated rationality on the one hand and deterministic animalistic accounts on the other. Midgley therefore turns to a chastised account of evolution to help her interpret the meaning of human freedom in a way that Derrida does not.[18] But she is understandably wary of any approach that makes freedom illusory, or as she puts it, "thing-bound" rather than "person-centred."[19] While those concerned with animal ethics have often found inspiration in the deconstructive momentum of Derrida's position,[20] the actual basis for a more constructive approach has to come from elsewhere and is likely to be incompatible with the assumptions embedded in postmodern thought. I take up this issue again in the section on Hans Jonas below.

18. Mary Midgley, *The Ethical Primate: Humans, Freedom, and Morality* (London: Routledge, 2004), pp. 159-64.

19. Midgley, *The Ethical Primate,* p. 165. The somewhat stark alternatives Midgley sets up are still present, but there are others now occupying what could be called the median space that she seeks to carve out.

20. Including, for example, David Clough, *On Animals,* p. 74. Clough points to the variety of other animal kinds that Derrida mentions, though in practice Derrida's *Animals That Therefore I Am* text pays relatively little attention to this aspect.

The Question of Animal Agency

To clarify further the meaning of human freedom as free agency, we must ask in what specific sense other animals might be considered agents. This is a different way of treating the subject of freedom than most other approaches used in the science and religion literature, which on the whole have concentrated on either trying to find a general notion of freedom as integral to a material physical universe and integral to theodicy (so-called "free process" or "free will" defense) or arguing for the place of human — and scientific — freedom in the light of accounts of genetic determinism. Both accounts bypass consideration of other animals.[21] "Agency" is a broad term that designates the possibility for self-direction.[22] Helen Steward, drawing particularly on studies of early human development, argues that many nonhuman animals need to be considered as having a basic form of agency.[23] Her argument attempts to rule out the harsh line against animals being agents of any sort, rather than suggesting that other animals are capable of sophisticated propositional attitudes. She argues against those, such as Donald Davidson, who reject the idea that other animals could ever be *intentional agents.*[24]

Agency can be defined as having the ability to move what we think of as the body, as a center of a form of subjectivity, where intentional states (such as trying, wanting, perceiving) are attributed, and where movements of which body are nonnecessitated events, originating in the agent, and only secondarily in relation to environmental triggers.[25] In this sense, free agency is a *prerequisite* for the possibility of freedom, under-

21. See, for example, Ted Peters, *Playing God: Genetic Determinism and Human Freedom* (New York: Routledge, 1997); John Polkinghorne, *Science and Providence* (London: SPCK, 1989); Thomas Tracy, "Evolution, Divine Action and the Problem of Evil," in *Evolutionary and Molecular Biology: Scientific Perspectives on Divine Action,* ed. Robert John Russell, William R. Stoeger, and Francisco J. Ayala (Vatican City: Vatican Observatory,; Berkeley, Calif.: Center for Theology and the Natural Sciences, 1998), pp. 511-30.

22. The use of a term such as "free will" is unfortunate in theological terms if it implies a separate faculty from bodily existence. I have mentioned above the problematic tendency for notions of free will to be disembodied in Cartesian forms. See also further discussion in the section on Aquinas below.

23. Helen Steward, "Animal Agency," *Inquiry* 52, no. 3 (2009): 217-31.

24. He bases his argument on the assumption that other animals do not have language. Donald Davidson, *Subjective, Intersubjective, Objective* (Oxford: Oxford University Press, 2001).

25. This helpful definition is taken from Steward, "Animal Agency," p. 226.

stood as free choice, though animal ethologists are not known for using the language of freedom in describing animal behavior. There may be examples of simple animal movement, such as that of the paramecium, that appear to have agency but, on close examination, are governed by physical forces. The sheer diversity of animal species should not be forgotten in this discussion.

Steward believes that attributing agency to other animals is resisted in the academic literature, in the first place, because of cultural and religious forms of anthropocentrism. She also argues that, second, natural scientists eschew agency, as it might seem to imply some form of body/mind dualism. Furthermore, resistance to the idea of agency in other animals is related to parsimony, that is, only simpler explanations are acceptable. An empiricist approach rejects the agency of other animals because it distrusts any form of what is perceived as misplaced anthropocentrism — that is, reading into animal kinds habits of human society. Finally, for many philosophers under the influence of a rationalist Kantian ethic, agency is exclusive and amounts to a complex form of moral judgment. Steward, nevertheless, argues in favor of the basic intuition that animals are capable of agency. Yet, by ignoring ethology, Steward's account is disappointing, for she opens up the philosophical space for animal agency but then does little to show what evidence might be accumulating to support it. Ethologists have written significant work that questions a sharp boundary between animals and humans, though more often than not they write on how humans share the same emotional response as other social animals rather than on how other animals share some of the same cognitive functions.[26]

Steward also stops short of attributing to other animals anything like a theory of mind. Regardless of how intentionality might be mapped, it is clear that once beliefs about others or the world are present, then this is a capacity beyond that of internally directed responses. In this case, *first-order* intentions are said to be present, while if an agent considers the

26. See, for example, Frans de Waal, *Good Natured: The Origins of Right and Wrong in Humans and Other Animals* (Cambridge: Harvard University Press, 1996); Frans de Waal, *Chimpanzee Politics* (Baltimore: Johns Hopkins University Press, 1997); Frans de Waal, *The Age of Empathy: Nature's Lessons for a Kinder Society* (London: Souvenir Press, 2009); Marc Bekoff, *Animal Passions and Beastly Virtues: Reflections on Redecorating Nature* (Philadelphia: Temple University Press, 2006); Marc Bekoff, *The Emotional Lives of Animals* (Novato, Calif.: New World Library, 2007); Marc Bekoff and Jessica Pierce, *Wild Justice: The Moral Lives of Animals* (Chicago: University of Chicago Press, 2009).

mental state of others, then *second-order* intentions are reached. This can be expanded further, so that one could consider the mental state of the person who is thought about by the person who is close by as the *third order* of intention, and so on. For example, the latter is something like this: I want my children to believe that I expect them to be waiting for me at the after-school club at a certain time of day. While we may be naturally inclined to attribute second-order intentionality to other animals, careful ethological research shows in a more definitive way whether particular social cognition is involved or not.

Yet, assuming that intentions are *not* there in other animals may be problematic in that it fails to give them what might be termed "the benefit of the doubt." Popularizers of animal ethology are inclined to push for giving other animals the benefit of the doubt.[27] There seems no reason *not* to suppose that social animals are purposive in working out which actions to take in given situations. Examples of innovation in the cultures of social animals are not all that common, but there is a good case for social learning of given traditions among many different species of social animals, such as bird species, roof rats, and bottlenose dolphins and chimpanzees. Such learning seems to be spread by imitation of a neighbor, though the possibility of genetic predispositions to learn in a certain way cannot be ruled out.[28] The question becomes: How far can animals actively make choices other than those governed by affective states, including emotions, instincts, and learned desires?

Harvard philosopher Christine Korsgaard argues that humans have a deeper level of intentionality that allows them to make judgments in relation to particular norms or moral principles, so that they can choose actively either to follow such purposes or not. In this scenario, intentions do not simply exist in humans; rather they are actively assessed and adopted.[29] Furthermore, the extent to which humans show the capacity for *joint* attention does not seem to be characteristic of other primates; their cogni-

27. One such example is Jonathan Balcombe, *Second Nature: The Inner Lives of Animals* (New York: Palgrave Macmillan, 2010).

28. Bennett G. Galef, "Culture in Animals?" in *The Question of Animal Culture,* ed. Kevin N. Laland and Bennett G. Galef (Cambridge: Harvard University Press, 2009), pp. 222-46. The author admits that any concrete link between the evolution of animal traditions and the emergence of human cultures has yet to be proven.

29. Christine Korsgaard, "Morality and the Distinctiveness of Human Action," in *Primates and Philosophers: How Morality Evolved,* ed. Frans de Waal (Princeton: Princeton University Press, 2009), pp. 110-12.

tive capacity is quite simply not sufficiently sophisticated. Triadic joint attention that is the most sophisticated involves two individuals looking at an object with full awareness that the other is doing so. Dyadic joint attention is a mutual paying attention to the other, such as between mother and infant. If there is simply mutual looking at an object, this is a shared gaze. Chimpanzees seem to be capable of dyadic joint attention but not Old World monkeys or baboons.[30] A much greater range of social animals, including dogs and horses, are capable of shared gaze.[31] The evolution of joint attention may also relate to the capacity for language.[32] I suggest that it is important to acknowledge such distinctions in mental capacity across a range of social species, including humans, while recognizing shared elements. It would be incorrect, too, to envisage chimpanzees as somehow on the same evolutionary lineage as modern humans or as representing preliminary versions of mental capability that are then subsequently developed in *Homo sapiens sapiens*. The branching in evolutionary pathways is such that it is not possible to surmise an ancestral capability by surmising a particular, more limited capacity in chimpanzees. In other words, they are at best only weak markers of human evolution, so even if differences of degree are found, this does not give definitive evidence for the particular evolutionary trajectory in the *Homo* species. The significance for forms of joint attention and other capabilities for reason and agency is in relation to their own particular ecological niche, that is, creatures with a worth that is defined by their particular manner of flourishing. Only humans are capable of worrying about their own animality and its significance in relation to human self-identity; only humans discuss the fine points of what it means to express freedom; only humans are knowingly religious beings; and so on. But, in addition, human freedom does not make sense purely as an individual activity, but rather in the context of a community of other humans and other creatures who share to a greater or lesser extent capabilities for agency.

30. See a number of relevant essays in Tetsuro Matsuzawa, Masaki Tomonaga, and Masayuki Tanaka, eds., *Cognitive Development in Chimpanzees* (Tokyo: Springer-Verlag, 2006).

31. Shoji Itakura, "Gaze Following and Joint Visual Attention in Nonhuman Animals," *Japanese Psychological Research* 46, no. 3 (2004): 216-26.

32. Tao Gong and Lan Shuai, "Modeling the Co-evolution of Joint Attention and Language," *Proceedings of the Royal Society B* 279, no. 1747 (2012): 4643-51. See further discussion in chapter 5, on language.

Freedom, Agency, and Virtue in Thomas Aquinas

While a discussion of freedom, agency, and virtue in Aquinas could easily take up a complete volume, my intention is to draw him into this discussion inasmuch as it serves to clarify the particular concern of understanding a theological approach to human freedom in relationship with other creaturely kinds. He also prepares the ground for using Hans Urs von Balthasar in this constructive approach. But before I examine Aquinas's theological interpretation of freedom, it is useful to make a few preliminary remarks about how he navigates this difficult territory by distinguishing between voluntary, *voluntarium,* and a narrower category of those that are free, *liberum.* Voluntary acts are described as a *quality* of human acts according to internal principles and directed to a particular end. He claims that awareness of the goal and knowledge of that goal lead to voluntary behavior; where that purpose is lacking, the acts may follow, but they are not directed to an end. So "by saying that the source of voluntary activity by definition lies within the agent, we do not rule out this internal principle's being itself caused or moved by an external principle. It is not essential to a voluntary act that its internal principle should be the first principle."[33]

Other nonrational animals, on the other hand, in Aquinas's scheme, only ever respond to external stimuli, which impact their particular appetites and emotions and in turn lead to movement. For Aquinas, God could move a rational person to act by "setting in motion the will" or by presenting an object of desire to the person's senses that would then lead to a movement through bodily processes. Of course, Aquinas held to the view that the will, like reason, is also in some sense distinct from material processes in the body, but the main point here is that what Aquinas terms voluntary movement arises from the will of the agent, rather than from coercion. This immediately leads to the question of whether other animals can have any voluntary activity. Here the discussion becomes really fascinating. Aquinas does not, as one might have anticipated, reject the idea of voluntariness in other animals; instead, he argues that knowledge can be full or partial. Full knowledge recognizes not just a desirable goal, but also recognizes it deliberatively *as* desirable and considers the means to get to that end. Other animals have only partial knowledge in that they

33. Thomas Aquinas, *Summa Theologiae, Psychology of Human Acts, Vol. 17 (1a2ae. 6-17),* trans. Thomas Gilby (London: Blackfriars, 1970), 1a2ae, qu. 6.1.

are not able to appreciate the goal's purpose or significance. So "partial knowledge accompanies voluntary activity in a lesser sense of the term; it is present when there is perception of but no deliberation about the end, and the movement towards is unpremeditated."[34] Thus, while Aquinas denied that other nonrational animals could possess a full-blown faculty of "will," he did allow for *some* voluntary activity, but it is a partial voluntariness, and therefore would only make sense where those animals are moved to a particular end through some knowledge of that end. At the same time, given that he could not attribute a will to other animals, he also refused to attribute to them either moral praise or blame. In other words, they could not be held morally culpable for their acts. I will have reason to press Aquinas on this point in the light of what we know about many other highly social animals in a later chapter; for the moment, what is significant is that free will is largely confined to human beings, but voluntary agency is more inclusive.

We consider here in more detail how will relates to culpability, since this illustrates different facets of what it might mean for a human being to have free will. For Aquinas, the fully voluntary act proceeds from the will, but the free act, by contrast, proceeds from freedom of judgment, *liberum arbitrium*. He allowed for some voluntary activity in nonrational animals to the extent to which they were able to show volition and move toward a particular goal or end.[35] This means that all free acts are voluntary, but not all voluntary acts are free in the sense of deliberative freedom. This distinction maps reasonably well onto the distinction between freedom that is possible in human beings and a wider general agency that is possible for humans and other creatures. The distinctive aspects of human freedom compared with more general voluntary activity hold, even though the line is rather more blurred than Aquinas believed in that there is ongoing debate about the capabilities of other animals to be self-reflective and deliberate about their intentions. Aquinas recognized that it is the willing intention of the agent to act or not to act that leads to moral culpability. If a person does act, this might be either through a deliberately considered will to act or due to a different motivation, so leading to the well-known distinction between direct and indirect voluntary acts of the will, where only direct

34. Aquinas, *ST, Psychology of Human Acts,* 1a2ae, qu. 6.2.

35. In this way, while he denied the possibility of a will in nonrational animals, they were capable of a degree of volition, and thus voluntary activity. A deliberative form of voluntariness is not present in other animals according to his account. See Aquinas, *ST, Psychology of Human Acts,* 1a2ae, qu. 6.2.

voluntary acts are the prime intention.[36] He also distinguished between involuntary actions, which are against the will, and nonvoluntary actions, where the will is not involved. He further acknowledged the difference between actions that flowed directly from the will of a rational agent and those activities that are indirectly controlled through the will. He argued that violence could be done to the execution of the will in relation to its control over particular acts, but not in relation to the will in the absolute sense, which he believed was always directed to the good.[37] So, for Aquinas, the will is always orientated toward the good in human beings, for even evil *appears* as good to those who are responsive to "some decayed disposition."[38] Moreover, the extrinsic force of violence is against the intrinsic will of rational agents and the natural bent of nonrational agents insofar as, in the former, it acts on the secondary, controlling functions of the will. It is this negative action of violence on acts under the will's control that makes an act involuntary.[39]

Aquinas did allow for the possibility that acts done under the influence of the fear of evil, or lust toward what is perceived as good, could still be voluntary, while those done under compulsion are not.[40] However, there is an element of involuntariness in fear in that it involves an action against what is perceived as good. Aquinas pressed the case that an action, when under the influence of lust, was neither voluntary nor involuntary, for reason seemed to be suspended and so actions were outside the category of reasoned acts.[41] At the same time, this still meant that actions under the influence of lust were morally culpable because knowledge was not always missing and the will was capable of resisting passion that then led to irrational states of mind.[42]

36. Aquinas, *ST, Psychology of Human Acts,* 1a2ae, qu. 6.3. Examples of indirect voluntary acts include situations where the outcome is negative, but not the prime intention, such as the shortened life of a patient following pain-relieving doses of morphine.

37. This is one reason why Aquinas affirms that there is no absolute necessity in choices that are made under the guise of a particular good rather than that related to the universal good in which the will and the free choices incumbent on that will are of a more compatibilist type. See Aquinas, *ST, Psychology of Human Acts,* 1a2ae, qu. 13.6.

38. Aquinas, *ST, Psychology of Human Acts,* 1a2ae, qu. 6.4.

39. Aquinas, *ST, Psychology of Human Acts,* 1a2ae, qu. 6.5.

40. Aquinas, *ST, Psychology of Human Acts,* 1a2ae, qu. 6.6.

41. Aquinas, *ST, Psychology of Human Acts,* 1a2ae, qu. 6.7.

42. See also Aquinas, *ST, Psychology of Human Acts,* 1a2ae, qu. 10.3. Aquinas also speaks here of degrees of being transformed by passion, so that a "vehement rage of concupiscence makes a man beside himself or out of his mind." It is in this condition that "men be-

Freedom of the will in voluntary acts also relates to knowledge or ignorance. The particular case where this is important is when an action would be different if there had been greater knowledge. But where ignorance is itself willed, either deliberately or through not paying attention, then the person is morally culpable. Where ignorance leads to an evil act that is not intended, as when someone is accidentally shot at a firing range, then the person is not deemed responsible. Further, while the will relates to both good and evil, the good to be sought is properly called volition, *voluntas,* while the avoidance of evil is *noluntas.* It is only, therefore, in consideration of the details of how humans may act or resist action that a sense of the meaning of the freedom of the will becomes clear. Such a complicated heuristic could not be applied to other creaturely kinds because, quite simply, their powers of cognition are insufficiently developed.

Which takes priority in human action, free will or rational deliber-

---

come like the beasts, driven of necessity by passion; they are without the motion of reason, and, consequently, of will." At the same time, he insisted that it is in the will's power not to "will to lust" or to "consent to concupiscence." Furthermore, the resistance of emotion by reason is a matter of choice, rather than desire. Of course, Aquinas was not aware of contemporary studies of animal and human behavior that show our species as not only hypersocial, but also far more sexually promiscuous than other animals, including other primates. For a comparison of primate sexuality with that of humans, see Alan F. Dixson, *Primate Sexuality: Comparative Studies of the Prosimians, Monkeys, Apes, and Human Beings,* 2nd ed. (Oxford: Oxford University Press, 2013). For a critique of commonly held assumptions about sex in human communities, see Agustín Fuentes, *Race, Monogamy, and Other Lies They Told You: Busting Myths about Human Nature* (Berkeley: University of California Press, 2012), pp. 156-205. Yet, Aquinas is right to suggest that only humans are capable of suppressing that drive by using reasoning powers to bring sexual passion under control. Human ability to bring such passions under control in spite of this hypersexual tendency is remarkable. Religious motivation for that suppression based on Augustine's association of sexual activity with sin is well rehearsed. Aquinas adjusted that association by affirming human sexual activity in the context of loving relationships. For Eugene Rogers, this implies affirmation of homosexual relationships. See Eugene Rogers, *Sexuality and the Christian Body: Their Way into the Triune God* (Oxford: Wiley/Blackwell, 1999), pp. 87-139. Rogers also argues that the scriptural basis for Aquinas's ideas have been ignored because of too much attention to the first philosophically orientated parts of the *Summa.* Eugene Rogers, *Thomas Aquinas and Karl Barth: Sacred Doctrine and the Natural Knowledge of God* (Notre Dame, Ind.: University of Notre Dame Press, 1999), pp. 17-70. While broadly sympathetic with the view that attention to the philosophical aspects of Aquinas's thought has downplayed his theology, my own reading of the *Summa* is that it is replete with theological insights even prior to the third part, which is more explicitly theological. What would be more accurate is that a purely philosophical reading is an incomplete and partial reading, though Rogers goes further than this and argues that Aristotle should be understood as *absorbed into* his theological interpretation.

ation? Aquinas resists either alternative and argues instead that the will moves the mind and, at the same time, the mind sets the will in motion.[43] But the sensitive appetite in common with other animals was significant for Aquinas, in that it had the capability of taking over in particular concrete situations. However, for him, a truly human response is one where these passions are ruled not by "despotic dominion" but by "a kingly and civic dominion, as a freeman is ruled, who holds within himself the power of resistance."[44] It is this kind of control that Aquinas envisages in relation to the particular appetitive desires common to all animals, such as the desire for sex, food, and so on. The ultimate source of human willing, however, is theological; that is, it comes from knowing God as creator of the rational soul. Aquinas believed that the inclination of the will to the universal good also comes from God, and in this sense it is deterministic. God can also act on the will through grace, so that, as in graced reason discussed in the last chapter, "God moves us to will a determinate good, as when he quickens us by his grace."[45] He realizes, then, the limitations of the philosophical discussions of the will and includes the experience of grace in the will as a way of ameliorating its somewhat inflexible logic.

To summarize, so far Aquinas has argued that the ultimate direction in which the will moves is toward the good, at least as far as the human agent is concerned. So what is the relationship between this natural bent of the will toward the good and the experience of grace? In the first place, he argues that God is always needed in the primary sense because God is creator of all that is, so that being or existence is ultimately dependent on God, with God as prime mover. He speculates that in the condition of humanity before the Fall, a condition he calls "intact nature," it would be possible for that human nature to will the good inasmuch as it could will good acts according to acquired virtues.[46] But the transcendent good, which for him is the good of infused virtues, can only be both *willed* and *done* through

43. Aquinas, *ST, Psychology of Human Acts,* 1a2ae, qu. 9.1.

44. Aquinas, *ST, Psychology of Human Acts,* 1a2ae, qu. 9.3.

45. Aquinas, *ST, Psychology of Human Acts,* 1a2ae, qu. 9.6. God acts on the will in three senses: first, in relation to setting the will in motion, as discussed in 1a2ae, qu. 9.4; second, as a general characteristic of God as first cause of all that is created, as in Aquinas, *Summa Theologiae, Divine Government, Vol. 14 (1a. 103-109),* trans. T. C. O'Brien (London: Blackfriars, 1975), 1a, qu. 104.3, 105.5; and finally, through the special promotion of grace, as in Aquinas, *Summa Theologiae, The Gospel of Grace, Vol. 30 (1a2ae. 106-114),* trans. Cornelius Ernst (London: Blackfriars, 1972).

46. Aquinas, *ST, Gospel of Grace,* 1a2ae, qu. 109.2.

the work of grace.[47] Given, however, that human beings are never in the ideal condition they were in before the Fall, but are always and inevitably subject to sin, the possibility of acquired virtue through naturally endowed action is somewhat restricted. He compares this to the ability of a sick man to act; it is only after healing that this naturally endowed capacity to will the good can fulfill its proper function. So Aquinas, by joining freedom with reason, retains flexibility within a compatibilist approach and avoids the problems of either, supplementing it with a stress on the experience of grace. Thus, on the one hand, "man is the master of his acts, including those of willing and of not willing, because of the deliberative activity of his reason, which can be turned to one side or the other." On the other hand, the ultimate capacity to deliberate at all, or will at all, comes from God, so "the mind even of a healthy man is not so much the master of his acts as not to need to be moved by God."[48]

Willing the good is also complemented by the fact that Aquinas believed that the desire to love God above all things is connatural to all things — "even to any creature, rational and non-rational, and even non-living, in accordance with the kind of love which may benefit any creature."[49] So the basic orientation to love God goes all the way down, to material creation as such. However, "in the state of spoiled nature," the desire of the rational will is corrupted by sin and so "pursues a private good unless it is healed by God's grace."[50] It is this corruption of the desire of the will that then leads to a restriction of both willing and acting. With the gift of charity something new is introduced into the realm of grace-filled action, for while nature can love God above all things insofar as God is the source of the natural good, charity goes beyond this and loves God in a higher way by recognizing God as the source of all blessedness and in accordance with "a certain kind of spiritual communion with God."[51] From this it follows

47. I will be taking up the discussion of the relationship between acquired and infused virtues in the next chapter, on morality.

48. Aquinas, *ST, Gospel of Grace,* 1a2ae, qu. 109.3. By using "healthy" Aquinas is making a comparison with the sickness of sin, rather than mental health. However, given contemporary insights of modern psychology, the same could be said of those who are free from mental illness or psychological disorders that predispose a person to will and to perform sinful acts. Even in these cases, though, the acts are perceived by that person as good in a self-interested sense.

49. Aquinas, *ST, Gospel of Grace,* 1a2ae, qu. 109.3.

50. Aquinas, *ST, Gospel of Grace,* 1a2ae, qu. 109.3.

51. Aquinas, *ST, Gospel of Grace,* 1a2ae, qu. 109.3. Charity is always an infused virtue, rather than an acquired virtue.

that other animals could love God in a way connatural to them, but only animals capable of deliberative reason could show charity and deliberative acts of will, as explained above.

This leads on to a particularly interesting discussion of the Fall of Adam and Eve. For Aquinas, the freedom of the will meant that it was theoretically possible for the first parents of humanity to resist the temptation of the devil.[52] Furthermore, this situation came about through the corruption of desire, so that he interrogates the Augustinian pattern of sin that begins in that desire: first, in relation to concupiscence in sensuality, signified by the serpent; second, in relation to lower reason, signified by the woman; and third, in relation to higher reason, signified by the man.[53] His reply to this is to clarify the nature of temptation of the man as that which acts on the intellectual desire to be like God, and the sensual desire through sensible beings that are most akin to the man, namely, the woman and the serpent. Aquinas insisted that the devil was the principal agent but used the woman as an instrument because he believed that she was weaker than the man in that she was more readily deceived.[54] Clearly, the attribution of the woman as being less reasonable, more liable to deception, and the means through which the Fall of humanity, at least in its sensible aspects, came to pass is offensive in the context of contemporary appreciation of sexist prejudice. At the same time, the highest form of sin,

52. Aquinas, *Summa Theologiae, Parts of Temperance/Well Tempered Passion, Vol. 44 (2a2ae. 155-170),* trans. Thomas Gilby (London: Blackfriars, 1964), 2a2ae, qu. 165.1. Note, in using words such as the "devil" and "first parents," I am not thereby indicating a theological affirmation of the existence of such beings, but rather pointing to how such reflection illuminates for Aquinas the human condition.

53. Aquinas, *ST, Well Tempered Passion,* 2a2ae, qu. 165.2.

54. Such a view of women as weaker in terms of capacity for deception sounds pretty offensive to those with feminist sensibilities. Certainly, Aquinas was wrong to insinuate here and elsewhere that women were lesser beings with respect to reasoning capabilities or with respect to their reception of God's grace, even if he conceded that they were still in the image of God. However, evolutionary psychology that presses for essential differences between the way male and female brains function, such as that discussed in Simon Baron Cohen, *The Essential Difference: Male and Female Brains and the Truth about Autism* (New York: Basic Books, 2004), needs to be qualified by recognition of the spectrum of brain function in both males and females. Research that he cites that suggests women are more empathetic and males more constructive and systematic in their thinking, with tendencies reaching back to infancy, does not deal with the differential capacity for deception, and implies the possibility of hormonally related differences. The complexity of this issue relative to the influence of gendered communities in which people are placed should not be underestimated in the way it seems to be here.

namely, the desire to be like God, is attributed to the man as one who is tempted through the intellectual nature, even if the temptations of the sensual nature are mediated through the woman. Men are therefore more culpable than women in this respect, a consequence that has been largely ignored by current scholarship. He cites Augustine to support the idea that the principal means of temptation according to sensual desire comes through the woman. But the joining together of different facets of human nature in order to build up to the final act of human will and intellect to commit sin also shows a holistic appreciation of the nature of human willing and acting, rather than a dismissal of sensuality. Corruption of human will, therefore, builds on the bodily and emotional life, rather than being a simple act of detached deliberative reason. Furthermore, this implies that the agency of other creatures could also be corrupted insofar as they have the capacity to participate in a partial way toward a good end.

Further Steps on the Way: Hans Jonas's *Phenomenon of Life*

I am now going to discuss what might be termed Aquinas's graded understanding of agency and the distinctiveness of the human rational will and freedom to act by exploring more contemporary sources. While Hans Jonas has often been acclaimed as a philosopher who has offered a sophisticated critique of the work of Martin Heidegger, his particular approach to the philosophy of biology is relevant here because of the particular role he attributes to freedom and his attempt to include at least the idea of freedom beyond narrowly human terms.[55] It is also important because it grounds his particular view of the nature of human responsibility, which will be developed subsequently. His quarrel with Heidegger is about the way Heidegger's existentialism seems to desacralize the concept of nature through acceptance of the claims of the physical sciences. More explicitly, he believes that the root of Heidegger's existentialism amounts to a loss of eternity, a view shared with nihilism expressed in Nietzsche's disappearance of the world of ideas and ideals. This "spiritual denudation" of nature has profound moral consequences, for "There is no point in caring for what has no sanction behind it in any creative

55. *The Phenomenon of Life* has been described as "the pivotal book of Jonas's intellectual career." Lawrence Vogel, foreword to *The Phenomenon of Life: Towards a Philosophical Biology,* by Hans Jonas (Evanston, Ill.: Northwestern University Press, 2001 [1966]), p. xi.

intention."[56] Derrida, on the other hand, went further than Heidegger in the deconstructive task, but much the same critique can apply to his position as well, namely, that the natural world is desacralized, opening the way to an even more profound nihilism.

It is Jonas's more constructive task that is particularly pertinent in the present context. If we allow for the possibility of the border between humans and other animals being more open, as Derrida suggests, and for the possibility of genuine agency in other creatures, can we push this further open and ask metaphysical questions about the nature of life itself and of other animals in particular? This is, of course, a more constructive task that would be resisted by postmodern theorists like Derrida; but remaining in the ashes left by postmodern deconstruction does not, in my mind at least, take us very far, other than leaving us in an existential question that itself needs to be subjected to a stronger critical appraisal. I suggest that an outline for such a critique has already been fleshed out in Jonas's engagement with Heidegger, for his challenge to existentialism prefigures a challenge to postmodern theory.

The basis of Jonas's understanding of freedom is premised on the idea that all organic life-forms prefigure the mind, and the mind remains rooted in the organic.[57] He does not attempt to level out the distinctions between humans and other creaturely forms, but he believes that a contemporary way of interpreting Aristotelian ideas of "stratification" is indispensible.[58] There are opportunities for dualistic views to creep in here in that Jonas, in making the higher retain all that is in the lower, could open the door to denigration of the lower forms if the higher forms are thought to be complete expressions of the lower. Furthermore, the language of higher/lower like that in Aquinas and Augustine before him implies superiority. Yet, for Jonas, the scale of being can best be interpreted, first, according to graded capacities for perception expressed as the "freest objectification of the sum of being" and, second, through progressive freedom of action (p. 2). Here he is being bold in using the explicit language of freedom in areas other than a constricted anthropocentric understanding of the mind and will. He argues this view on the basis that mind is prefigured in the organic, taking this right down to the level of "metabolism" that he under-

56. Jonas, *The Phenomenon of Life*, p. 232.

57. Jonas, *The Phenomenon of Life*, p. 1.

58. This stratification is the dependence of the "higher on the lower" and the "retention of all the lower in the higher." Jonas, *The Phenomenon of Life*, p. 2. References to this book are placed in the text in the following paragraphs.

stands as the most basic level of all organic existence (p. 3). The core of his argument, therefore, is to show that "it is in the dark stirrings of primeval organic substance that a principle of freedom shines forth for the first time within the vast necessity of the physical universe — a principle foreign to suns, planets and atoms" (p. 3). For Jonas, grounding such "freedom" in the organic *as such* is not unrelated to its meaning in the human sphere inasmuch as it provides the ontological grounding for phenomena at the higher levels, and constitutes a breakthrough, even while not having conscious "mental" connotations.

Yet, he admits that the origin of such a capacity is unknown and remains a mystery. It is, in other words, the transition from inorganic to organic, the emergence of life, that is the most significant step and is capable of bearing the term "freedom." Once life appears as an independent identity from its purely material origins, the tension of being or not being emerges. The very possibility that this life might not exist shows "its very being is essentially a hovering over this abyss, a skirting of its brink," so becoming a "constant possibility rather than a given state" (p. 4). The polarity that exists between being and nonbeing is also characteristic of other basic polarities of self and world, form and matter, freedom and necessity. Jonas believes that, as these polarities are expressions of relationship, they also imply forms of transcendence, a "going beyond itself" (p. 5). Life shows a separate identity from lifeless matter, yet is still dependent on it, hence displaying freedom and necessity. Yet, accompanying the appearance of life is an ever-present fear of death, which resounds like "a never-ending comment on the audacity of the original venture" of becoming organic (p. 5).

Jonas's position bears some resemblance to Alfred N. Whitehead's process philosophy, in which mental processes reach down to material being, but there is a crucial difference in that Jonas insists that the nonlife-to-life transition is significant in a way that Whitehead ignores (see pp. 95-96). In this respect, Jonas's view is also distinguishable from the panvitalism characteristic of "early humans" where the whole world seems charged with life and the riddle to be confronted is death. Jonas's philosophy also speaks into the modern situation that puts more weight on sheer matter and a mechanical universe, where "death is the natural thing, life the problem" (pp. 7-9). For Jonas, the organic powers that culminate in human creativity, noted by Zizioulas above, form "a scale of freedom and peril" beginning with metabolism but gradually shifting to movement, desire, sensing, perceiving, imagination, art, and mind. Of particular significance is his idea that this progression is not inevitable, but rather is like an experiment accompanied by increasing risks where the freedom of humanity may end in either disaster or success (pp. xxiii-xxiv). In this respect, his position is rather more preferable to the optimistic trajectory inherent in the pan-psychic thought of authors such as Pierre Teilhard de Chardin. Jonas intends to counteract what he perceives to be the prevailing "ontology of death" that informs the materialism that has embedded modern scientific views ever since the Renaissance. He also believes that the "materialistic monism of science" broke new ground once it included within its explicative power the living kingdom (pp. 42-44). Here we find the problematic boundary of nonlife to life pushed back to the first primeval instantiation of life, yet denuded of teleology. Jonas summarizes well the weak negative force of natural selection in his proposal that, "Strained through their sieve, the fortuitous is held to turn constructive — and with no 'cunning of reason' there results the paradox of advance through mischance, of ascent by accident" (p. 51).[59]

In such a context where evolution by natural selection has come to dominate contemporary views of life, his proposal for a strong metaphysical version of freedom as *the* characteristic of life pointing toward a common transcendence is daring and provocative. He certainly runs the risk of being accused of recovering a version of vitalism that envisages particular energetic powers existing in life-forms.[60] But this risk can, perhaps, be avoided if he rests his claim on a metaphysical position that eschews using vitalism as an appropriate scientific methodology. More serious, however, in the context of the present discussion, is the risk that when the language of freedom is made a common denominator of life, it begins to lose its more explicit and specific demand in the human sphere. While I will take up elements of Jonas's analysis in seeking to portray life in dramatic rather than static categories, once freedom becomes so all-embracing it becomes harder to specify the precise dynamic of what freedom means for the human condition. In other words, what is the point of such extension, other than putting emphasis on the shared mortality of humans with

59. Modern evolutionary biologists are more inclined to allow for a greater degree of constraint than Jonas allows in terms of the possible patterns that evolution might take, rather than the raw contingency that he implies here. See Simon Conway Morris, ed., *The Deep Structure of Biology: Is Convergence Sufficiently Ubiquitous to Give a Directional Signal?* (Conshohocken, Pa.: Templeton Foundation Press, 2008).

60. For a historical overview, see Matthew Wood, *Vitalism: The History of Herbalism, Homeopathy, and Flower Essences,* 2nd ed. (Berkeley, Calif.: North Atlantic Books, 2000).

other creatures, the common struggle to sustain life in the face of death? Furthermore, if freedom becomes such a fundamental category of being, of life, then ethical reflection is in danger of becoming at times constricted rather than enabled by such a category. Aquinas's more elaborate scheme of freedom of choice, voluntary acts, and the freedom of the will that is still capable of being transformed by God's grace reveals itself as even more necessary in the light of this discussion.

Human Freedom and Other Animals in Hans Urs von Balthasar

How might different facets of freedom be developed further in a theological sense? To fill this out, I will draw on the work of the influential Roman Catholic theologian Hans Urs von Balthasar, who was himself influenced by the writing of Thomas Aquinas. Balthasar's approach to the theological meaning of freedom is constructive insofar as he manages to avoid the shibboleth created by the opposite and equally problematic tendencies toward divine freedom as a vehicle for the denial of finite human freedom, or the secular alternatives in the humanist absolutization of human freedom understood as the freedom of the individual to choose. Both alternatives clash with the evolutionary rationalization of human freedom of will as merely a surface consciousness disguising deep-seated evolutionary drives. Balthasar's motivation is strictly theological, for underlying the freedom of God is divine love that permits humanity its freedom. In the first part of his trilogy *The Glory of the Lord,* he discusses the metaphysical basis for freedom. Significantly, human freedom awakens as *freedom of consent* in the experience of another; for Balthasar this is the first awakening of the "I" in relation to the "Thou" of the mother.[61] Balthasar is naïve inasmuch as a baby's first smile may not imply the kind of self-recognition that he assumes it does.[62] Freedom of consent is a "fundamental freedom that

61. Hans Urs von Balthasar, *The Glory of the Lord: A Theological Aesthetics,* vol. 5, *Realm of Metaphysics in the Modern Age,* ed. Brian McNeil and John Riches, trans. Oliver Davies et al. (Edinburgh: T. & T. Clark; San Francisco: Ignatius, 1991), p. 616.

62. Melvin Konner summarizes cross-cultural research that shows that adults more or less consistently across cultures interpret smiles in social greetings in infancy. Even anencephalic infants show reflex smiling, as do blind infants. While there is some evidence of differential smiling to a stranger or to the mother when social smiling first emerges around two months, the smile of recognition is not properly formed until four months after birth. What is apparent, however, is that the ability of an infant to smile markedly impacts on the

enables us to affirm the value of things and reject their defects, to become involved with them or to turn away from them."[63] He also seems to recognize some kinship here with other animals, in that he allows for what he terms "sub-human nature" being a "singularly illuminating touchstone for the value of a metaphysics," rejecting the mechanical materialism of Descartes, while resisting the Hegelian continuity that views different forms of nature as ways or stages of the Absolute Spirit.[64] He rejects the former because it cannot interpret the "glorious freedom of the essential forms," while resisting the latter because in Being we find "a superior and playful freedom beyond all the constraints of Nature."[65] But, for him, this freedom of Being is not self-explanatory, for "the freedom of non-subsisting Being can be secured in its 'glory' in the face of all that exists only if it is grounded in a subsisting freedom of Absolute Being, which is God," so its gloriousness is not hardened into a mathematical necessity but remains an "event of an absolute freedom and thus of grace within its open ended sway in which each 'pole' has to seek and find its 'salvation' in the other pole."[66] Within such communal relations of love, "we have all been permitted entry . . . Our mother too . . . And the animals with which I play."[67]

Here Balthasar somewhat astonishingly seems to be allowing for the inclusion of companion animals within the core sphere of human freedom understood in terms of loving relationships; but he fails to consider social species that are not human companions. Of course, it might be argued that Balthasar was writing at a time when ethology was not so well developed as it is today. However, even at that time there was an awareness of the close evolutionary relationship, at least relatively speaking, between humans and other social primates. He also seems to envisage other animals as being included in the human sense of freedom by the way that companion animals become involved in the lives of human beings, rather than any sense

---

mother's subjective sense of a bond and the cementing of a love relationship. This is thought to have an evolutionary advantage in that the death of very young infants in most of evolutionary history is common, so making such a loss less traumatic to the mother concerned. See Melvin Konner, *The Evolution of Childhood: Relationship, Emotion, Mind* (Cambridge: Harvard University Press, Belknap Press, 2011), pp. 219-26.

63. Hans Urs von Balthasar, *Theo-Drama: Theological Dramatic Theory,* vol. 2, *The Dramatis Personae: Man in God,* trans. George Harrison (San Francisco: Ignatius, 1990), p. 211.

64. Balthasar, *Glory of the Lord,* 5:621.

65. Balthasar, *Glory of the Lord,* 5:621.

66. Balthasar, *Glory of the Lord,* 5:625.

67. Balthasar, *Glory of the Lord,* 5:635.

of other animals being subjects in their own right. Furthermore, what he calls "entry" is a reference to the light of being and love that is open to all creatures by the fact of their creaturely existence. Being, presented as "sublime and serene," is a metaphysical category hovering from the beginning to the end of human existence that, for him, puts even the terrors of this world into perspective. Even human beings are "accidental" relative to that light of Being. Such metaphysics sounds somewhat unconvincing to ears tuned in to contemporary scientific ways of thinking about the world, but at least it has the beneficial effect of qualifying the stronger notes of anthropocentrism in his work.

Yet before we reach the conclusion that his strong metaphysics of Being has forced him to adopt an all-inclusive model of finite freedom, this account needs to be qualified in two ways. First, his most developed account of freedom of consent in the second volume of *Theo-Drama* is the human capacity to be "present to myself" and recognize my uniqueness, but in a way that acknowledges the uniqueness of countless others because the "light of being expands me beyond limitation" and, crucially, "just as the animal lacks this expansion beyond itself and, accordingly, also lacks self-knowledge."[68] It is this reification of freedom that for Balthasar seems to make it distinctively human, since even where it is reduced to rationality or the will it amounts to a "subhuman, instinctual level"; freedom of consent is always a universal opening to all being that is only possible in human beings, generating an indifference such that there is a letting be of the good for its own sake, rather than for the sake of the gain involved.[69] This level of abstraction can, perhaps, be mapped onto what psychologists call third-order intentionality in terms of its level of abstraction, and thus would not reasonably be attainable by other animals. Yet, the fact that Balthasar seems in *Glory of the Lord* to hint at inclusiveness at what might be termed the "foothills" of such capacity is important.

To understand Balthasar's concept of finite freedom, a second important "pole" of freedom as *autonomous motion* needs to be taken into account. This aspect of freedom is concerned with *self-realization,* and it is this that seems to be characteristic of humanity in a completely exclusive sense, echoing to some extent John Zizioulas's account of freedom as

68. Balthasar, *Theo-Drama,* 2:209. Balthasar, in a somewhat surprising way, then goes on to support his argument by using Col. 1:16, which speaks of "all things" being created through Christ, but most exegetes will press for an interpretation that is inclusive of other creaturely kinds.

69. Balthasar, *Theo-Drama,* 2:209-11.

creativity. Balthasar's view of autonomy is very different from humanist philosophy, in that it does not draw on libertarian models; rather, it is connected with obedience understood in relation to Christ. Using New Testament texts such as 2 Corinthians 3:17, "where the Spirit of the Lord is, there is freedom," he presents the case that freedom in the power of the Holy Spirit is the opposite of addiction; rather, citing 2 Corinthians 5:15, he maintains it is "to live no longer for themselves, but for him who died and rose for them."[70] This, for Balthasar, issues in service, both for God and for others. Alongside this idea of freedom as autonomy, properly understood through the lens of service, he retains a traditional understanding of human image bearing, such that it "raises man far beyond all other beings of the world," and moreover, these other beings are "inferior beings," echoing his earlier assessment in his discussion of humanity as a microcosm.[71] Such anthropocentrism is in tension with other aspects of his thought that stress the creaturely basis for human life and its shared finitude alongside other creatures. Drawing on ancient interpretations, he understands image bearing as a "making present" and so implies a special relationship to God and a special representative of God that sets humanity apart from all other beings. Yet, for him, the image-bearing nature of humanity is always incomplete because it needs to be fulfilled through another in male and female relations, through the experience of grace, through humanity's response to God's call, and through relationship with Christ. All aspects touch on freedom in different ways, and the christological dimension serves to shape the nature of the mission of humanity, which, for him, is a freedom that is the opposite of addiction, a freedom marked by service of God and others.[72]

One reason why Balthasar's account of human freedom is problematic is that he retains a stereotypical view of women as associated with particular stereotypical roles in the home and bound to the natural world. Here he speaks of man as being perfected by woman, who is his "answer," and also, significantly, that man "symbolises freedom, but now, how wound round he is by clinging ivy, which often threatens to choke him — by wife

70. Hans Urs von Balthasar, *The Glory of the Lord: A Theological Aesthetics*, vol. 7, *Theology: The New Covenant*, trans. Brian McNeil (Edinburgh: T. & T. Clark; San Francisco: Ignatius, 1989), p. 403.

71. Hans Urs von Balthasar, *The Glory of the Lord: A Theological Aesthetics*, vol. 6, *Theology: The Old Covenant*, trans. Brian McNeil and Erasmo Leiva-Merikakis (Edinburgh: T. & T. Clark; San Francisco: Ignatius, 1991), p. 90.

72. Balthasar, *Glory of the Lord*, 7:403.

and children, home and profession and a knot of cares."[73] His sexual stereotyping is particularly problematic and rests on a form of essentialism that is arguably the very opposite of what he is seeking to promote, namely, a way of thinking that resists reductionist tendencies in modernity. For him, all other species converge on the human in a way that, quite frankly, jars with contemporary understandings of the paleontological and archaeological record. He takes the latter position not so much from a proper understanding of evolutionary biology as from ancient works of the early church, by supposing that humanity is a microcosm of all that is in the universe as a whole, so that "All the realms and genera of living things converge in him; no animal species is alien to him. He contains them all, as superseded and discarded forms in which he can mirror himself and, as in fables, recognize the features of his own character."[74]

Hence, while he claims that other animals are not "alien" to human beings, his mistaken trajectory of human evolution as one that leaves behind "discarded" forms reinforces a strong sense of human superiority. For him, human beings are "the synthesis of the world," yet at the same time "above it."[75] He dissociates humans from other animals by their ability to reason, so that "animals are swept away by the waves of sexual drives which ebb and flow like the sea, whereas man can experience *eros* in a more inward, sublimated way and, through love, make for it a lasting abode in his enlightened heart."[76] Here we have an attitude toward other animals as driven entirely by sexual and other sensate instincts and presupposing a profound lack of agency. While I am not suggesting that other animals actively choose their sexual partners, to portray animals as driven by sensual instincts is stereotypically anthropocentric in that it assumes that other animals do not have the capacity to willingly associate with others, form friendships, etc. Balthasar's attitudes toward animals have, as far as I can discern, received no critical attention, partly because he hardly ever mentions other animals, in spite of his frequent reference to creation and creaturely being, but also no doubt because of the anthropocentric bias of his commentators.

73. See, for example, Hans Urs von Balthasar, *Man in History* (London: Sheed and Ward, 1968), pp. 308-9. His stereotypical views of women have been the subject of sharp critique, especially by feminist scholars, as I have discussed in Deane-Drummond, *Christ and Evolution,* pp. 249-51.

74. Balthasar, *Man in History,* p. 43.

75. Balthasar, *Man in History,* p. 44.

76. Balthasar, *Man in History,* p. 44.

In the second part of *Theo-Drama,* Balthasar portrays the work of God's infinite freedom in Trinitarian terms in relation to human freedom as analogous to a theatrical performance. God is the playwright, the Holy Spirit is the stage director, and the central act of the *theo-drama* comes to be expressed through the incarnation, crucifixion, and resurrection of Christ.[77] In his later works, he spells out the specific task of human freedom in terms of mission. Human persons have a role to perform, but only when this role is united to their mission given by God do person and role become fused in the manner found in the person of Jesus Christ.[78] Freedom is expressed, therefore, through practical action.

This approach bears some resemblance to David Kelsey's relatively compressed account of freedom in his monumental theological anthropology as bearing the marks of eccentricity, in which he is at pains to distinguish the meaning of call and response in human relationships of freedom from that of the creature's response to God.[79] For Kelsey, Jesus' faithfulness to his mission came eccentrically — from its focus "outside" himself in the power of the eschatological Spirit. While this turn against what Kelsey calls "unqualified autonomy" is an important line of defense against cultural individualism, he seems to envisage the work of the Spirit in Jesus' free response as somehow "outside" and therefore "eccentric" to his life; so "Jesus' own human response to the one he calls 'Father' is eccentric. It has its center outside Jesus himself, in the power of the eschatological Spirit."[80] This implies in an almost Hegelian sense that the locus of freedom is detached from Christ's bodily existence, and therefore, by example, our own existence. This is unfortunate since it is in tension with other aspects of his thought that stress the need to ground particular cases of the meaning of freedom in concrete examples — freedom, he argues, makes most sense when interrogated according to particular

77. See Hans Urs von Balthasar, *Theo-Drama: Theological Dramatic Theory,* vol. 1, *Prolegomena,* trans. George Harrison (San Francisco: Ignatius, 1988).

78. Mission is a basic concept in Balthasar's Christology. Here he makes clear that Christ's mission extends beyond the human community to the universe as a whole. Yet, Christ's mission is also one that relates obedience and freedom, but this is achieved through the work of the Spirit. Hans Urs von Balthasar, *Theo-Drama: Theological Dramatic Theory,* vol. 3, *The Dramatis Personae: The Person in Christ,* trans. George Harrison (San Francisco: Ignatius, 1992), pp. 149-250, 515-24.

79. David Kelsey, *Eccentric Existence: A Theological Anthropology,* vol. 2 (Louisville: Westminster John Knox, 2009), pp. 829, 834.

80. Kelsey, *Eccentric Existence,* p. 829.

circumstances. There is also no reference to the possibility of freedom or agency in other animals.

The future hope and coming kingdom also look to the transformation of human finite freedom into ultimate freedom by participation in infinite freedom. For Balthasar, the theological task is to work out how finite freedom can act in relation to infinite freedom without being swallowed up by the latter, and how infinite freedom can make room for finite freedom without surrendering its own nature as infinite.[81] While Balthasar avoids more extreme anthropocentrism by resisting the belief that only human souls are saved in heaven, his final vision of the future is remarkably intellectual in tone, and free creativity is constricted and construed in intellectual and spiritual terms.[82]

If Balthasar had paid rather more attention to other animals, apart from somewhat cursory remarks about companion animals and his limited discussion of sexuality, perhaps this tendency toward epic thinking would not have emerged.[83] Ben Quash proposes that Balthasar has fallen into the trap of epic thinking himself, in spite of his denials. For example, with respect to freedom, obedience has the last word in Balthasar, Quash maintains, comparing him unfavorably with Barth in this respect, and insisting that he interprets obedience in an ecclesial way that leads to a lack of human creativity.[84] I agree that obedience in Balthasar comes over at times as cold and institutional; he even occasionally claimed, in my view in a quite horrifying way, that "Every 'dialogue-situation' was excluded —

81. Aidan Nichols, *No Bloodless Myth: A Guide through Balthasar's Dramatics* (Edinburgh: T. & T. Clark, 2000), p. 63.

82. See, for example, Hans Urs von Balthasar, *Theo-Drama: Theological Dramatic Theory,* vol. 5, *The Last Act,* trans. George Harrison (San Francisco: Ignatius, 1998), p. 474.

83. For a commentary on epic thinking in Balthasar, see Ben Quash, *Theology and the Drama of History* (Cambridge: Cambridge University Press, 2005). Ben Quash describes Balthasar's own definition of epic thinking as "an element of *necessity* at the heart of events and happenings that take place . . . this is one way of choosing to read the interaction between God and his creatures. . . . At its worst . . . epic is the genre of a false objectification" (p. 42).

84. Quash, *Theology and the Drama,* pp. 158-59. Quash's association of Balthasar with epic, Hegelian thought has some justification in my view, but also for other reasons as well, namely, his tendency for a stereotypical view of the sexes and the intellectualization of freedom characterized as a male trait, with associated denigration of women (and animals). While Kevin Mongrain notes that Balthasar is influenced strongly by Irenaeus, it seems that, as far as his eschatology is concerned, this note becomes much weaker. See also Kevin Mongrain, *The Systematic Thought of Hans Urs von Balthasar: An Irenaean Retrieval* (New York: Herder and Herder, 2002).

by a corresponding agreement of [Adrienne von Speyr's] soul — so that it became experientially clear that the obedience of the Church can and at times must have all the reality and relentlessness of the Cross itself, both in the authority which commands and the faithful who obey."[85] However, this somewhat rigid conservatism understood as conformity is not the only note in his theology, and elsewhere he speaks in a much more positive way about future hope including human creativity.[86] Proper attention to other animals can, therefore, act in the service of constructing a theology of freedom that remains robustly grounded in creatureliness. Moreover, I suggest that, given Balthasar's understanding of freedom as primarily expressing agency rather than simply theoretical judgment, nonhuman animals can also be included in his notion of freedom as *participation,* as well as in his notion of freedom as *consent.* The mission of humanity reflects the particular *density* of that participation in relation to freedom as autonomy. Perhaps we might even surmise that animal freedom in nonhuman kinds, inasmuch as they do not suffer from internal anxiety about their actions in relation to their identity as humans do, is also thereby closer to that freedom found in Christ, where personal identity and role are united.[87] Yet, there is also a distinction, for while it cannot be said that nonhuman animals possess an autonomy that is directed by a divinely ordained *mission* in the way that is possible for humans in Balthasar's thought, there is no real reason why they cannot be included in the participation in the divine life that is enabled by the grace of the Holy Spirit.

85. Hans Urs von Balthasar, *First Glance at Adrienne von Speyr,* trans. Antje Lawry and Sergia Englund (San Francisco: Ignatius, 1968), p. 70.

86. The freedom of the perfected life is freedom expressed in creativity that echoes, to some extent, Zizioulas. For Balthasar, "The earthly experience it [the creature] has on the basis of its freedom teaches it that what is most precious is not so much its decision in favor of the good (even if this may have been immensely difficult and meritorious) as its creative activity." Balthasar, *Theo-Drama,* 5:402. The note of creativity in his own work is on occasion overshadowed by a tendency for overdogmatic assertions about God, so that the rich possibilities for theo-dramatics become eclipsed in a presumption for what Karen Kilby calls a "God's eye" view of the world. In this respect, he fares rather worse than Thomas Aquinas, who incorporated to a greater extent apophatic elements into his discussion about God. See Karen Kilby, *Balthasar: A (Very) Critical Introduction* (Grand Rapids: Eerdmans, 2012), pp. 162-67.

87. See also Kelsey, where he argues for reflective capacities of humans that allow them to reject (he uses the term "cross-grain") a basic personal identity as reconciled bodies in Christ, but at the same time are able to respond to the creative invitation of God. Kelsey, *Eccentric Existence,* p. 834.

In theological terms, it is in the context of infinite freedom that these finite freedoms flourish; indeed, human freedom as flourishing should not be detached from that of other finite creaturely kinds. Bear in mind also the different degrees to which different animal kinds might be capable of such participation, according to their own differential capacity for flourishing in different ways. It is in the light of such infinite freedom that the relative difference between human and other animal freedoms becomes one of degree, rather than of absolute difference. Both have the capacity to be agents in a sense that is meaningful for that species. Yet by linking together animal and human freedom, we are reminded again of the inadequacies of individualization; freedom is freedom in community, a community that includes all creaturely beings. Hence, lines of continuity and distinctiveness serve to emphasize that the particular role of human freedom and its capacity for good or ill is joined with service for God and neighbor, where neighbor is understood in an inclusive, rather than exclusive, sense. Decisions about how to exercise our freedom in relation to these others become moral and ethical ones — but given the discussion so far, I would press for that good to be based on inclusive, rather than exclusive, parameters.

Some Interim Conclusions

The topic of human freedom is one over which there have been centuries of heated philosophical and theological debate. A short chapter cannot do justice to it, and I am acutely aware of limitations of space. However, I can make preliminary remarks about those features of freedom that are important for understanding the human condition. First, freedom is not single but multifaceted, so freedom means freedom of choice, freedom of the will, freedom of consent, freedom to act, and so on. The tension between compatibilist forms of freedom that express a deterministic approach and a libertarian insistence on the genuine possibility of alternatives shows that forms of compatibilism are arguably easier to reconcile with evolutionary and neuroscientific approaches to free will. However, even if we can concede that a libertarian position is not the only option for a Christian theological perspective, a purely compatibilist approach is counterintuitive. Aquinas managed to avoid both such difficulties by combining a sophisticated account of free will with reason alongside an overall, more fundamental orientation of the will to the good. His affirmation of the goodness of appetitive sensitive desires of all animal kinds was qualified by his understanding of sin as entering in through concupiscent desire that was untamed by deliberative reason. But his appreciation of the partial knowledge that could lead to genuinely voluntary acts in other animals opens up the possibility of a richer understanding of agency, even though this was not developed very far in his work. Furthermore, his appreciation of the distinctiveness of human freedom maps onto contemporary appreciation of, and debates about, the relative sophistication of human cognitive powers of attention, levels of intention, and theory of mind. Hans Jonas's attempts to bring a measure of freedom into matter and other forms of life is fascinating because, like Aquinas, he points to a transcendent source that speaks of a wider communal understanding of freedom. While I have argued that those elements in his thought that point to a process philosophy of being are less than fully convincing, his clear recognition of the significance of other animals is innovative. The same cannot be said for Hans Urs von Balthasar, whose treatment of other animals is impoverished and limited at best. However, he brings in the theological metaphysical framework of theo-drama and the absolute freedom of God that shows the different facets of human finite freedom as freedom of consent and freedom of autonomy. The latter is not so much a libertarian version of freedom as it is freedom of obedience. The language of obedience seems starkly opposed to what one might think freedom entails. Certainly, if this is interpreted as self-inflicted punishment or wooden, unthinking obedience to ecclesial authority, it is deeply problematic. However, if it is viewed through a Thomistic lens, then it becomes rather more theologically convincing. In this case, freedom of obedience would be related to the will, to the ultimate good in God, and to the promise of the beatific vision. Such obedience would not represent a masochistic suppression of desire but a liberating desire transformed by the presence of God's grace. Freedom would then be freedom to grow in the virtues and the freedom to resist vices, but it would be not so much a Pelagian struggle to earn salvation as an open reception of God's grace, a living out according to the infused virtues and according to a transformed will and transformed reason. Such reasoning and willing, furthermore, are not detached from animality but serve to transform it according to the pattern set forth by the Son. But here I am starting to touch on the next topic of discussion, namely, the virtues and the moral life.

CHAPTER FOUR

Human Morality and Animal Virtue

This chapter begins to address what is arguably a crucial topic in any discussion of human nature, namely, not just what it means to be an agent, but what it means to be a *moral* agent. While the relationship between morality and other animals has traditionally sought to find expression in specific *ethical* practices in relation to other animals, in other words, a discernment of their moral *status,* in this chapter I will argue that our understanding of human morality is illuminated in distinctive ways by closer attention to the variety of lives of other social animals, including the possibility that at least some of them express forms of morality that are distinctive to their own social worlds. Raising this as a possibility rather than ruling it out gives permission to explore more deeply facets of the origin of human moral capacities and sentiments, understood both in evolutionary and theological terms. Hence, instead of defining moral agency in Kantian exclusive terms that restrict such a possibility to human agents alone, who have, as I argued in chapter 3, capacities for distinctive forms of reasoning, the definition of morality is now enlarged so those creatures that show deliberation and choice according to social norms, even if not abstracted choice, are potentially included. I believe it is not helpful necessarily to use a completely different term for such morality in order to recognize distinctive capacities of humans in this respect. However, I distance myself from those evolutionary psychology accounts that bolster their arguments by finding a direct evolutionary connection between moral agency in humans and latent capacities in other animals. In some cases, such a trajectory can even be highly misleading for interpreting human moral nature. Instead, based on an expansive understanding of human evolution developing in supercomplex and what might be termed hypercooperative communities that are themselves strongly shaped by dynamic ecological relationships, I argue that we need to envisage the moral lives of other animals as also emerging in complex social communities, even if not on the same scale as found in human societies. At least some of these communities of other animals need to be understood as interacting and interlacing in complex ways with human communities. I am presupposing, of course, that cooperation in a community is distinct from moral agency; cooperation can certainly be for good or ill, but discussion of human morality makes most sense in relation to a consideration of the good for that community and when viewed through this lens. This takes the argument considerably further than the reasoning I have developed in earlier work, namely, that other social animals need, in some cases at least, to be thought of as moral agents, with at least incipient moral capacities relevant for their own worlds, such as empathy, justice, fairness, and so on.[1]

Of course, while the temptation to draw a straight line between social insects and human sociality needs to be resisted in the way that Sarah Coakley has indicated in her Gifford Lectures and elsewhere,[2] there are still highly social and intelligent animals that are "in between" present-day humans and social insects. Such highly social animals are, in some cases at least, capable of forms of moral agency that are most appropriate to their own social worlds. Sociality and even cooperation are certainly *not* coterminous with morality, but the former is a prerequisite for the latter. The question is, then, are some aspects of moral behavior required for human moral life in a way that is also characteristic of the regulation of the social worlds of other highly cooperative animals? Why is this significant? Some evolutionary psychologists believe that this is significant as it is part of their argument for the evolution of moral capacities in human beings. But this may be very difficult to prove with any accuracy. In this chapter, I will suggest that while exploring the evolution of human morality does

1. The most expansive version of this argument is in Celia Deane-Drummond, "Are Animals Moral? Taking Soundings through Vice, Virtue, Imago Dei and Conscience," in *Creaturely Theology: On God, Humans, and Other Animals*, ed. Celia Deane-Drummond and David Clough (London: SCM, 2009), pp. 190-210.

2. Sarah Coakley, *Sacrifice Regained: Reconsidering the Rationality of Religious Belief*, inaugural lecture, October 13, 2009 (Cambridge: Cambridge University Press, 2012), and her more recent Gifford Lectures, "Sacrifice Regained: Evolution, Cooperation, and God" (delivered at the University of Aberdeen, Scotland, April 17–May 3, 2012). Available online at http://www.abdn.ac.uk/gifford/about/ (accessed March 18, 2013). I return to a discussion of cooperation in more detail in chapter 6.

certainly close the perceived gap to some extent between humans and other social creatures, it also shows up distinctive characteristics of human beings in their currently evolved state, namely, *Homo sapiens sapiens.* The capacity of human beings for abstract thought has engendered forms of the moral life that encompass complex social and institutional organization in a way that is completely distinctive, and arguably unique for our species. Such developments have taken millennia to emerge, and prior to that human beings lived in much smaller hunter-gatherer societies that had close interrelationships with other animal species. Hence, the emergence of human morality could not have been arrived at in isolation from animal communities, but in close relationship with them.

Are there theological starting points that help us navigate this extremely difficult territory? I will suggest that retrieving aspects of Aquinas's understanding of the passions, virtues, and gifts is illuminating because it points to specific characteristics of human morality that are lost to the discussion once it is constricted to evolutionary accounts of moral origins. Furthermore, a theological account of the moral life shows up weaknesses in the arguments for what might be termed strong evolutionary naturalism filtered through the lens of scientific positivism. For reasons of space, what could be considered prerequisites for the moral life will be taken up in much more detail in subsequent chapters, including the evolution of communication in chapter 5, that of cooperation in chapter 6, with a more detailed treatment of specific moral capacities such as fairness in the discussion of the evolution of justice in chapter 7, and the evolution of empathy, conscience, and interspecies friendship in chapter 8. I have become acutely aware in writing this chapter that the themes here could easily be expanded into a full-length monograph, but my intention is to give pointers for further development and raise questions that are most relevant to the overall argument of this book rather than attempt a full or comprehensive discussion of either human morality or the virtuous life.

Introduction

In this section, I intend to discuss briefly arguments for the evolution of morality in humans. There is a vast wealth of literature on this topic, but arguments for evolutionary origins draw on the universality of aspects of morality across cultures and often tie together moral and religious beliefs so that religion is sometimes viewed as serving to stabilize moral systems.[3] Finding positivistic examples of what might be termed rampant human evolutionism is not difficult. This becomes particularly striking in the discussion of the evolution of morality and religion by authors such as Richard Joyce and Donald Broom.[4] It is easy to see the problematic aspects of Joyce's discussion; his positioning of moral concepts in evolutionary terms leads to his argument for doubting their validity.[5] But this argument is weak, not least because natural selection in theory could undermine belief in anything, even evolutionary science. Confidence in strictly genetic evolutionary claims for morality is also not nearly as solid as Joyce implies. He seems to harbor a narrowly conceived understanding of evolution that depends on genetic or "innate" capacities rather than on a richer account that includes epigenetic, cultural, and symbolic inheritance systems.[6] Second, even if a case for a neo-Darwinian account can be made, it is likely to have been selected for in a way that corresponds with truth claims about reality rather than in an arbitrary way. The case for undermining humanist concepts of morality is taken even further by Steve Stewart-Williams, who, while rejecting evolutionary ethics, argues against concepts of human dignity on the basis that they reflect a pre-Darwinian anthropogenic view of the universe that now has to be rejected.[7] In addition to his more specific argument against human dignity, he rejects the possibility that there can be *any* objective moral truths.[8] But

3. A host of authors could be cited here, including Richard Joyce, *The Evolution of Morality* (Cambridge: MIT Press, 2006); Jan Verplaetse et al., eds., *The Moral Brain: Essays on the Evolutionary and Neuroscientific Aspects of Morality* (Dordrecht: Springer, 2009); John Lemos, *Common Sense Darwinism: Evolution, Morality, and the Human Condition* (Chicago: Open Court, 2008); Nicholas Wade, *The Faith Instinct: How Religion Evolved and Why It Endures* (New York: Penguin Press, 2009); Susana Nuccetelli and Gary Seay, *Ethical Naturalism: Current Debates* (Cambridge: Cambridge University Press, 2012).

4. Joyce, *The Evolution of Morality;* Donald Broom, *The Evolution of Morality and Religion* (Cambridge: Cambridge University Press, 2003).

5. Joyce, *The Evolution of Morality.* Here he speaks in terms of a "belief pill" that he represents in terms of natural selection, so that if our ancestry has encouraged concepts like obligation, property, virtue, and fairness, then we should be skeptical of their positive value without further evidence. For further discussion, see pp. 180-81.

6. For an alternative approach to evolution, see Eva Jablonka and Marion Lamb, *Evolution in Four Dimensions: Genetic, Epigenetic, Behavioral, and Symbolic Variation in the History of Life* (Cambridge: MIT Press, 2005).

7. Steve Stewart-Williams, *Darwin, God, and the Meaning of Life: How Evolutionary Theory Undermines Everything You Thought You Knew* (Cambridge: Cambridge University Press, 2010).

8. Given that the nihilism he finds is a logical outcome of evolutionary biology, he

this is a philosophical metanarrative that need not cohere with evolutionary accounts of human becoming. It is also not clear what the basis for coming to a particular decision might be. Further, as I will show below, recognition of the biological fluidity of species boundaries does not need to align with rejection of human distinctiveness. He also resists equating the natural with goodness, arguing that all that evolutionary theory can do is give an account of what happens in evolutionary terms; our moral decisions are then more informed as a result. But he is disingenuous in arguing that evolutionary theory dispenses with *any* form of right and wrong, so independent grounds need to account for particular beliefs, for evolutionary theory itself presupposes a particular epistemology and basis for truth claims.[9]

I am not intending to devote too much attention to the evolution of religion here, except to note that critical views of such a model are surfacing even within the scientific community. Paul Bloom, for example, argues that there is little evidence for specific religious beliefs being tied to specific moral practices, but rather, the latter are more likely associated with other human practices.[10] His criticisms bring to the surface the sheer difficulty of drawing conclusions from associations and correlations between highly complex human practices that cannot be simplified to a biological phenotype, but consist of a complex combination of capabilities and cultural traits.[11] Jeff Schloss argues convincingly that "morality" consists of a constellation of interacting group and individual traits that include, at minimum, an interacting combination of moral sentiments, concepts, behaviors, and social institutions. A prerequisite for each is a combination of capacities, but alongside this are rather more problematic specific claims for universals *in content* having an evolutionary origin. Evidence for an evolutionary origin of moral behavior also emerges from a study of animal social behav-

---

rejects the idea that evolutionary biology should provide the starting point for moral reflection; instead, he argues that we have to decide what we value first and then allow evolutionary biology to give guidance. Stewart-Williams, *Darwin*, p. 256. But if this is the case, what is presupposed in coming to decide what is of value?

9. Stewart-Williams, *Darwin, God, and the Meaning of Life.*

10. Paul Bloom, "Religion, Morality, Evolution," *Annual Review of Psychology* 63 (2012): 179-99.

11. See Jeffrey Schloss, "Darwinian Explanations of Morality: Accounting for the Normal but Not the Normative," *Zygon* (2013). See also Philip Clayton and Jeffrey Schloss, eds., *Evolution and Ethics: Human Morality in Biological and Religious Perspectives* (Grand Rapids: Eerdmans, 2004).

ior, including play behavior, while that for moral sentiments and moral concepts is weighted more toward psychological studies on human beings. But the scope of what moral emotions entail spreads out on a number of different axes that map onto particular behaviors. In evolutionary terms, these parse out in the following manner: harm/care, fairness/reciprocity, in-group loyalty and authority/respect, purity/sanctity.[12]

Matt Rossano's evolutionary account of religion attempts to "spiritualize" each axis in order to reinforce group norms by a supernatural incentive. Those moral virtues that are universally admired are *wisdom,* defined as creativity, curiosity, open-mindedness, and love of learning; *courage,* defined as bravery, persistence, integrity, and vitality; *humanity,* defined as love, kindness, and social intelligence; *justice,* defined as citizenship, fairness, and leadership; *temperance,* defined as forgiveness, humility, prudence, and self-regulation; and finally *transcendence,* defined as beauty/excellence, gratitude, hope, humor, and spirituality.[13] He also argues that religions map onto three different types of religious practice: (a) intrinsic, referring to committed believers; (b) extrinsic, in which participation is for practical or utilitarian purposes; and (c) questing, which entails a seeking orientation and a greater sense of wonder and mystery. But aspects of his account can be challenged on a number of fronts. First, while the axes of the moral emotions bring some clarity to the discussion of the range of moral sentiments, this oversimplifies how each moral axis depends on the other. Respect, for example, is integral to the practice of fairness; care in evolutionary terms needs to be related to in-group loyalty; purity and sanctity are connected to perceived harm; and so on. The universality of moral sentiments across different cultures is also not necessarily evidence of their evolutionary origins, and the definitions are so broad that it is hard to discern their meaning in evolutionary terms. In this respect, Schloss's comments are particularly perceptive, for moral sentiments need to be distinguished from but related to moral behaviors, concepts, and social institutions for a clearly articulated evolutionary account of their origins. Envisaging the God concept as a supernatural "add-on" simply does not do justice to how God is actually perceived in relation to the moral life.

However, rather than draw on studies of other animal worlds to map out the possible behavioral origins of morality or possible analogous hu-

12. Matt J. Rossano, *Supernatural Selection: How Religion Evolved* (New York: Oxford University Press, 2010), p. 175.

13. Rossano, *Supernatural Selection,* p. 189.

man moral sentiments, I will be asking how far and to what extent animal social worlds enable us to perceive more clearly distinctive aspects of human moral life in its *relationships* with other animal worlds. Claims by some evolutionary psychologists to "explain" complex human moral traits trigger understandable objections by sociologists such as Christian Smith, who presses for a closer recognition of the distinctive aspects of human societies. For him, "Human culture is always moral order," and "Human persons are nearly inescapably moral agents."[14] Following a definition of "moral" used by Charles Taylor, he presses for moral to be a *normative* claim that engages with our own individual desires in a self-reflexive manner; humans have "second-order desires" that permit metareflection on those desires.[15] He objects to evolutionary accounts of morality from an ensuing lack of moral standards by which to judge actions.[16] Certainly, attempts to explain the normative in evolutionary terms have yet to yield convincing results, but that does not mean that evolutionary considerations or considerations of other animal worlds can be dispensed with.

Animal Social Worlds

While I am very sympathetic to Smith's characterization of human social and moral life as distinctively self-reflective and his objections to reductionist accounts of much evolutionary psychology, I suggest that even though he acknowledges that humans are also animals, he may have passed over a little too hastily potential insights about human social and moral life from a study of other animal worlds. Alasdair MacIntyre in his *Dependent Rational Animals* admits that his earlier work did not pay sufficient attention to the lives of other animals in seeking to understand human moral life.[17] For him, a close study of animal worlds shows human dependencies that correspond with those in other animals, including a more detailed treatment of social animals such as dolphins. But the main lesson he draws from this analysis of other animal worlds is the need for prior recognition

14. Christian Smith, *Moral, Believing Animals* (Oxford: Oxford University Press, 2003), p. 7. See also Christian Smith, *What Is a Person? Re-thinking Humanity, Social Life, and the Moral Good from the Person Up* (Chicago: University of Chicago Press, 2010).

15. Smith, *Moral, Believing Animals,* p. 9.

16. Smith, *Moral, Believing Animals,* p. 37.

17. Alasdair MacIntyre, *Dependent Rational Animals: Why Human Beings Need the Virtues* (Chicago: Open Court, 1999).

of dependence and vulnerability before developing independent practical reasoning. But does such recognition also, to some extent, elevate human beings from that sense of dependency? And further, is this *all* that other animals can bring to an understanding of human morality — simply a deeper recognition of dependence? Close reading of the works of ethologists such as Marc Bekoff suggests otherwise. Bekoff, in common with most biologists, tends to assume perhaps a rather too facile evolutionary account of the behavior of other animals. But his observation of moral capacities in some social animals, which has arisen mostly from his observation of play behavior in canids, opens up the possibility of not just what might be termed the biologically "normal" moral realm, but also the "normative" moral realm.[18] Bekoff, writing with philosopher Jessica Pierce and following from decades of close observations on canids, claims: "We propose certain threshold requirements for given species to have morality: a level of complexity in social organization, including established norms of behavior to which attach strong emotional and cognitive cues about right and wrong; a certain level of neural complexity that serves as a foundation for moral emotions and for decision making based on perceptions about the past and the future; relatively advanced cognitive capacities (a good memory for example); and a high level of behavioral flexibility."[19] Significantly, they name not just cooperation as evolved, which I will treat further in chapter 6, but also, from a close study of social play, forms of *justice* understood as fairness, which I will take up in chapter 7. Justice here is defined as a "set of social rules and expectations that neutralize differences between individuals in an effort to maintain group harmony."[20] Some biologists want to take this further and argue for moral lessons to be learned from the study of primates, for example, human societies, but this form of evolutionary naturalism is, it seems to me, completely unjustified.[21] Fur-

18. Robert Bellah develops a fascinating comparison between play behavior in animals and the emergence of religious rituals. This account illuminates the discussion of religious belief and no doubt impacts the emergence of moral behavior. I will take this up again in a subsequent chapter on justice, which connects directly with the question of fairness in play. See Robert N. Bellah, *Religion in Human Evolution: From the Paleolithic to the Axial Age* (Cambridge: Harvard University Press, Belknap Press, 2011), pp. 74-97, 109-16.

19. Marc Bekoff and Jessica Pierce, *Wild Justice: The Moral Lives of Animals* (Chicago: University of Chicago Press, 2009), p. 13.

20. Bekoff and Pierce, *Wild Justice,* p. 121.

21. See, for example, Frans de Waal, *The Age of Empathy: Nature's Lessons for a Kinder Society* (New York: Three Rivers Press, 2010). One of the problems associated with his

ther, even the weaker claim that the moral lives of other animals provide concrete evidence for an evolutionary basis for moral behavior in humans is also highly speculative, given the very different evolutionary trajectories of those animals under study and given hominid evolution. But I suggest that the lives of other animals *are* illuminating in ways that go further than simply reminding human beings of finitude and dependency, even if those lessons are highly significant. As Bekoff and Pierce suggest, morality is always species specific, in humans as much as in other social animals.

It is inappropriate, therefore, to judge the acts of other animals as "immoral" based on human moral systems in the manner characteristic of medieval bestiaries. Rather, their acts are moral or otherwise according to the norms established in their social worlds. Research in animal behavior shows that some social animals experience a wide range of moral sentiments, including positive emotions such as love, joy, and pleasure, alongside emotional experiences such as empathy, grief, and forgiveness.[22] Bekoff and Pierce even suggest that "Animals form friendships, are caught lying or stealing and lose face in the community, they flirt, their sexual advances are sometimes embraced and sometimes rejected, they fight and make up, they love and they experience loss. There are saints and sinners, bad apples and good citizens."[23] Is this unjustified anthropomorphism? Is the observation of "normativity" a reading *into* animal behavior that is simply a less reflective "conformity" to certain rules? Not, I argue, if it is viewed as a heuristic tool to understand how other animals think and act more clearly.[24] And not if the criterion of flexibility that Bekoff suggests is factored in, for this implies the possibility that the animal *could* have acted otherwise. Furthermore, neurological evidence points in the same direction. Mirror neurons involved in human social emotional reactions to others are also active in the same circumstances in those animals that have them. Spindle cells, also called *Economo* neurons, seem to process social emotions in humans and are involved in social attachment and empathetic reactions. They have been discovered in social species, including not just the great apes but also whales, where their appearance predated that in humans.

"Tower of Morality" model is that even if it is more sophisticated than the veneer theory, it tends to assume that there is a direct evolutionary trajectory from apes to humans.

22. Marc Bekoff, *The Emotional Lives of Animals* (Novato, Calif.: New World Library, 2007).

23. Bekoff and Pierce, *Wild Justice,* p. 45.

24. See Deane-Drummond, "Are Animals Moral?"

If "vice" and "virtue" are defined in relation to the moral framework for that species, then other animals can be said to display such characteristics, even if their exercise is far less sophisticated in terms of reflexive self-awareness compared with humans. Of course, if "normative" in this context means a "detached" self-conscious second-order desire in relation to a group norm, it seems unlikely that the canids and highly social animals that Bekoff and other ethologists pay attention to display such a characteristic. So too, if the definition of "morality" is tied into Kantian deliberation, that automatically excludes careful consideration of other animals' lives. But, as I hope to show below, even if we wish to use that definition as developed in a particular cultural context in the Western world, thereby excluding many other cultures and societies, human morality is much more distorted if it is abstracted in a way that ignores the concrete biological and ecological worlds in which human development takes place.

To elaborate this further, I intend to comment briefly on work that is still under development in cultural and social anthropology. Here I will be asking, what are the ways in which evolutionary accounts of human becoming can actually *illuminate* our understanding of human distinctiveness, including moral distinctiveness, in a way that avoids some of the problematic formulas associated with the denigration of other species? One way to do this is through perceiving human evolution on a long trajectory in relationship with other hominids. Present-day humans are not simply a species, *Homo sapiens,* but a subspecies within a species, *Homo sapiens sapiens.* We are *doubly* imbibed with wisdom. But how are we to perceive human becoming? Certainly, the categorization of "species" is a way of labeling a suite of characteristics that served that group well in its evolutionary survival. But if we go back to the millennia in which *Homo* came to be prominent, we find not just one but many coexisting lineages. Further, anthropologists are beginning to appreciate that it is not enough just to pick out one characteristic as if *that* were the defining moment in human evolution. Instead, building on recognition of what can be termed the emergence of super-sociality, it is the evolution of the community *system as a whole* in its ecological, social, and neurological dimensions that is relevant, which in turn impacts on the subsequent historical, psychological, cultural, and eventually moral and religious becomings.[25]

25. Agustín Fuentes, "The Community Niche as Focal Context in Assessing Pleistocene Human Evolution," *Current Anthropology,* in preparation. I would like to thank Agustín for sharing work in progress.

The mapping of specific characteristics at each stage shows profound overlap in capacities between different hominids and hominins.[26] Of course, the fascinating question is *why Homo sapiens sapiens* was so much more successful than other hominin groups that coexisted with it. One possible answer is that there was no single trait involved, but a multiplicity of factors that influenced the development of a community niche and moral norms in a particular way. Early hominins also shared strong social reciprocity. In this model, symbol creation appeared relatively late, but cultural innovation permitted positive feedback. To put this more simply, humans learned by *doing,* which involves a multiplicity of characteristics otherwise known as the apprentice model, suggested by Kim Sterelny.[27] But the puzzle remains as to what allowed one group, *Homo sapiens sapiens,* to persist when the other recognizably different groups of modern hominins did not. Although the cultural characterization of *Homo neanderthalensis* has often been cast in a negative light, there is some discussion as to how much overlap with *H. sapiens* took place.[28] The discovery of genetic transfer between the groups implies at least in some cases interbreeding.[29] Ian Tattersall believes that the excitement over such a discovery is premature, and that any gene transfer reflects occasional "hanky-panky" rather than a blurring of community boundaries.[30] Hence, the fluidity of boundaries is certainly there across time, even if eventually distinctions between different coexisting hominin groups, including

26. I am not going to rehearse the lineage between different hominids here, except to say that very primitive hominins existed as early as seven million years ago, with premodern hominins *Homo ergaster* being relatively short-lived, with other hominins such as *Homo erectus, Homo floresiensis, Homo heidelbergensis, Homo neanderthalensis* all, with the exception of *H. floresiensis,* predating, perhaps with the exception of *H. erectus,* or persisting at least for a limited time with *Homo sapiens.* See Bernard Wood, "Reconstructing Human Evolution: Achievements, Challenges, and Opportunities," *Proceedings of the National Academy of Sciences USA* 107 (2010): 8902-9.

27. Kim Sterelny, *The Evolved Apprentice: How Evolution Made Humans Unique* (Cambridge: MIT Press, 2012).

28. Stephen Mithen has suggested that Neanderthals communicated by music. Stephen Mithen, *The Singing Neanderthals: The Origins of Music, Language, Mind, and Body* (Cambridge: Harvard University Press, 2008).

29. See discussion in Joao Zilhao, "The Emergence of Language, Art and Symbolic Thinking," in *Homo symbolicus: The Dawn of Language, Imagination, and Spirituality,* ed. Christopher N. Henshilwood and Francesco D'Errico (Amsterdam: John Benjamins, 2011), pp. 111-31.

30. Ian Tattersall, *Masters of the Planet: The Search for Our Human Origins* (New York: Palgrave Macmillan, 2012).

the first *H. sapiens* and *H. neanderthalensis,* are such to keep communities glued together for the most part. Having said this, deciding on the classification of any given hominin archaeological remains is still hotly contested and not always easy to discriminate. The fact that there was *some* transfer suggests that the two "species" were cross-fertile, but the fact that this did not happen to any large extent implies geographical and cultural separation.

Intersubjective and Intermoral Evolution

Finally, and to my way of thinking crucially, what about the evolutionary relationships between *Homo* and other social animals? The argument I have made for a strong community niche in *Homo* evolution above does not mean that it was closed or not actively interacting with its environment. Indeed, the definition of community niche *includes* an ecological dimension. Can we go further and ask about the possibility of social interaction not just between hominids, but also between phylogenetically unrelated species? Naming the significance of other animals in human lives is associated with the work of Barbara Noske, an anthropologist who was one of the pioneers of the idea that animals should not be thought of simply as passive and acted upon by human beings, defined in terms of separation from other animals; rather, animals *themselves* need to be viewed through an anthropological frame, namely, an "intersubjective nonreductionist" approach that helps envision what other animals are like.[31] This bears some relationship with anthropomorphizing as a heuristic tool, which I mentioned above. Agustín Fuentes has also pioneered intersubjective methodologies with alloprimates,[32] developing this further to argue for a community niche construction model in hominid evolution that takes account of the concrete ecological worlds of the human as embedded in their social worlds.[33] Matei Candea has conducted similar work with meer-

31. Barbara Noske, "The Animal Question in Anthropology: A Commentary," *Society and Animals* 1, no. 2 (1993): 185-90.

32. Agustín Fuentes, "The Humanity of Animals and the Animality of Humans: A View from Biological Anthropology Inspired by J. M. Coetzee's *Elizabeth Costello,*" *American Anthropologist* 108, no. 1 (2006): 124-32; Agustín Fuentes, "Naturecultural Encounters in Bali: Monkeys, Temples, Tourists and Ethnoprimatology," *Cultural Anthropology* 25, no. 4 (2010): 600-624.

33. Fuentes, "The Community Niche as Focal Context in Assessing Pleistocene Hu-

kats, but there the intention was for human "observers" to have little or no influence on the meerkats' behavior in the interests of "interpatience."[34] More imaginative, perhaps, are those that deliberately seek the possibility of intersubjectivity from an anthropological perspective in a way that parallels to some extent the experience noted by Marc Bekoff in his study of canids from an ethological perspective.[35] Rather than discuss other animals in general and in acute awareness of their variety of form and social behavior, I will focus in what follows on a particular multispecies ethnographic case study that I have found highly illuminating, as it is so unexpected because it focuses specifically on the interrelationships between humans and a social species. For this I am going to explore the relationship between *Homo* and *Hyaena.*

The latter have historically commonly been associated with negative attitudes in human communities, not least because they consume all bodies, including the bodies of the dead. Consider comments on hyenas by that great naturalist Albertus Magnus in the monumental *Summa Zoologica:*

> The hyena is an animal about the size of a wolf which often inhabits the sepulchers of the dead. It also gladly frequents horse stables. It learns from frequent listening and calls people and dogs by name. It kills the ones it has fooled by calling them and devours them. Sometimes it also deceives people with a wretching sound of vomit. It is said that hunting dogs that come in contact with its shadow lose their bark. It is also said that it can change its color at will. Some also say that every animal which crosses its path sticks to its tracks. Jewelers also relate that this beast bears a precious gem in its eyes, or to be more accurate, in its forehead. The hairs on the neck of this animal are like those of a horse's mane. Some say its vertebrae are so rigid that it cannot bend its neck without twisting its entire body. Jorach also says that it is sometimes male and sometimes female and that it collects poison on its tail. But this Jorach often lies.[36]

---

man Evolution." I will come back to this idea again in a later chapter (6) on the evolution of cooperation, where it is of direct relevance.

34. Matei Candea, "'I Fell in Love with Carlos the Meerkat': Engagement and Detachment in Human-Animal Relations," *American Ethnologist* 37, no. 2 (2010): 241-58.

35. S. Eban Kirksey and Stephan Helmreich, "The Emergence of Multispecies Ethnography," *Cultural Anthropology* 25, no. 4 (2010): 545-76.

36. Albertus Magnus, *On Animals: A Medieval Summa Zoologica,* vol. 2, trans. Kenneth F. Kitchell and Irven Michael Resnick (Baltimore: Johns Hopkins University Press,

While some of this reflects secondhand knowledge and prejudicial attitudes about hyenas that eventually filtered into bestiaries, Albertus Magnus was unusual as a philosopher and theologian in actively seeking firsthand experience of the animals under discussion. It is also significant that he was the teacher of Thomas Aquinas.[37] The observation of Jorach is actually accurate inasmuch as it is difficult to distinguish the sex of a hyena.

In a highly original work, Australian anthropologist Marcus Baynes-Rock investigates the relationship between hyenas and humans through a narrative ethology in the Muslim town of Harar, Ethiopia.[38] Spotted hyenas *(Crocuta crocuta)* living in the town are not just tolerated by the human population but they depend on foods supplied from anthropogenic sources to survive. The lives of both humans and hyenas are intricately linked, extending even to religious practices. In a fascinating account, he recounts that even as far back as 4.4 million years ago hyenas were associated with early hominins, the Ardipithecines, so much so that if hyenas had not been present many more remains would have been discovered. Half a million years later, the hominin *Australopithecus anamensis* is associated with hyena remains, and 3.6 million years ago further evidence for such association continues. Baynes-Rock portrays beautifully the dramatic evidence for the relationship of hyenas and *Homo* over 3 million years ago:

> Later still, 3.6 million years ago, at a place now known as Laetoli in Tanzania, a volcano now extinct was belching ash into the air above an ancient landscape that was not dissimilar from that of the present. The ash fell with rain and filled wide depressions in the ground surface, creating beds of light grey mud, across one of which three hominins ventured onto the plains from the woods to the south. There were three individuals, a male, a female and a juvenile — the earliest

1999), book 22, chapter 1, §106. See also Albertus Magnus, *On Animals: A Medieval Summa Zoologica,* vol. 1, trans. Kenneth F. Kitchell and Irven Michael Resnick (Baltimore: Johns Hopkins University Press, 1999).

37. Space does not permit discussion of this here, but several commentators have noted that the hasty castigation of Thomas Aquinas as having an inevitably negative influence on human relationships with other animals is premature. See, for example, chapters by John Berkman, "Towards a Thomistic Theology of Animality," and Celia Deane-Drummond, "Are Animals Moral?" in *Creaturely Theology,* pp. 21-40, 190-210.

38. Marcus Baynes-Rock, "Hyenas Like Us: Social Relations with an Urban Carnivore in Harar, Ethiopia" (Ph.D. diss., Department of Anthropology, Macquarie University, Australia, 2012). I am grateful to Agustín Fuentes for pointing me to Marcus Baynes-Rock's work and to Marcus Baynes-Rock for permission to draw on his, as yet, unpublished thesis.

> known nuclear family — and their footprints became incontrovertible evidence of the bipedality of their species. The sodden ash crystallized and cemented quickly in the heat of the sun. Then, soon afterwards, another layer of sodden ash filled the depressions, miraculously preserving the moment in time for paleontologists to discover millions of years later. . . . And among the other animals whose footprints were preserved at Laetoli were the ubiquitous hyenas.[39]

He points out that the damaged bones of our earliest ancestors had previously been interpreted as evidence for a "killer ape," which persisted in the literature for over three decades.[40] Instead, close examination of the markings on the hominid bones revealed such hominids were not killer apes at all but rather victims of ferocious carnivores, and the most likely culprits were leopards and hyenas. The point is that human beings have been associated with hyenas for as long as their history permits, and it is only relatively recently that hyena distribution has become so constricted. *Homo ergaster, Megantereon whitei,* and *Pachycrocuta brevirostris* (giant hyenas almost as tall as the hominids themselves!) coevolved, eventually by 0.5 million years ago being replaced by the smaller spotted hyenas. Furthermore, the only African species persisting in Europe after the glacial cycles were hyenas and humans, hyenas finally disappearing from Europe and Asia a little before ten thousand years ago.[41] Why is this so crucial? I suggest it is crucial because human becoming, including human morality, has not happened in isolation from other species, but in coevolutionary contexts. There is evidence that strong social bonds were forged as a result of human beings needing to protect themselves from predatory carnivores,[42] and much the same could be said for the development of moral norms in human societies. Further, human identity has drawn on millennia of coexistence with other species and millennia of becoming in relation to other related hominid kinds. A given species is a convenient marker for

39. Baynes-Rock, "Hyenas Like Us," p. 22.

40. This idea is also taken up in more detail in Robert W. Sussman and C. Robert Cloninger, eds., *Origins of Altruism and Cooperation* (New York: Springer-Verlag, 2011). The book was the result of a conference that took place in 2009 that argued persistently that human beings should be thought of as prey rather than predators, and that human sociality emerged in such a context.

41. Baynes-Rock, "Hyenas Like Us," p. 33.

42. For a fascinating account of this aspect, see Sussman and Cloninger, *Origins of Altruism and Cooperation.*

biologists to use to classify the distinct characteristics of *H. sapiens sapiens.* In evolutionary terms, "human nature" and even morality are about human becoming and have emerged in association with other animal kinds. Eventually, the capacity for revelation, for a direct relationship with God, opens up a new social world, one where God features in human morality in self-aware humans. But this shift to a religious sense of morality *must* have been explored in a community context, rather than through the classic dyadic portrayal of an original isolated Adam and Eve. Baynes-Rock's account of the lives of the hyenas shows that in Harar the social relationships of the hyenas have coevolved and are coevolving with those of humans, so that humans' community life, including their moral and religious practices, maps onto their association with hyenas. Greater stress should therefore be placed on envisaging human nature not as a sharp marker separating us from other animal kinds, but as a particular way of being a social animal, one that is remarkably different from but also has learned in association with other animal kinds. Such association has gone back as far as paleontology into the nether reaches of prehistory and beyond.

The story, however, does not end here, because what is particularly significant is Baynes-Rock's detailed elaboration of intersociality in his narrative ethology. He admits at the start that we need to understand how hyena social worlds form; for example, cues include use of mouth, nose, and genitals, though hyenas' sexuality is often hard to discern, leading to suspicions and associations with witches, evil spirits, and so on. However, in Harar hyenas are held in positive regard and are fed regularly by human beings in special feeding sites; their lives are woven into the religious life of the community and they are thought to protect against negative spirits associated with mental illnesses. Baynes-Rock watched and followed the hyena groups in different locations in the city, and on one occasion his relationship with a particular hyena took an unexpected course. He argues that his research ethics committee that adjudicates the particular way humans are permitted to investigate the lives of other animals still assumes that consent could not be given by another species, but this, along with other assumptions, such as that they do not have the capacity to make their own decisions or communicate their desires, was a mistake, presumably based on a lack of field experience.

Baynes-Rock watched the hyenas at the same feeding place each night and wore the same clothes. Hyenas were generally very nervous of humans and tried to keep a safe distance. But one hyena was bolder than most, and he came to be known as "Willi," which means "early" in Harari. This hyena allowed his curiosity to take over and allowed Marcus[43] to come near him on a number of occasions. Willi played with another young hyena called Baby, but then came over to Marcus and invited him to play by giving him a play bite. He comments, "I might have refused the invitation . . . when one is amidst the unfolding of research, refusal of play feels like exerting control over the relationship (and so over the data I was collecting) . . . it also felt very natural to respond to the invitation; it triggered something in me as a mammal."[44] Later, Marcus was able to pat Willi and rub his fur. Willi continued to bite, and Marcus wondered what this might mean: Did he think that the food offered was strips of skin or was he looking for something else? Use of the mouth is part of social contact for hyenas, and the play bite is hard, as they have a tough skin. He became convinced Willi was trying to engage in play with him, and gradually a close relationship developed with Willi actively seeking his human companion out, and vice versa. Willi began with initial forays into the old town on his own. But after a while Marcus started joining him on some journeys, and on these occasions Willi accepted Marcus's presence. Willi then took a more active role and positively led Marcus to his den. Willi seemed to be treating Marcus as if he was another conspecific, in that such invitations to visit dens are also given to other hyenas in near proximity to their own. Marcus describes the unfolding relationship in the following way. The first response is an instinctive reaction that is almost formulaic. The second level is where the other animal tries to gain a sense of the intentions of the human. At the third level there is recognition, and the animal responds differently to that particular human compared with others of the same species. The fourth level involves communication and an attempt to interpret each other's behavior. The fifth level is when a mutually beneficial relationship is reached. The sixth level is a relationship for its own sake, and the seventh is where there is subjective coidentity and mergence. Marcus argues that *this* level was opened up when he was able to see the hyena through Willi's eyes, and vice versa.

But during the three-month break in research Willi had bitten Abbas, who had regularly sat with Marcus and was associated with him. He seemed to base his judgment about other people on their relationship with

43. I am using the first name of the researcher here in order to put emphasis on the subjectivity of the exchange, and because the hyena is referenced by the first name given to him.

44. Baynes-Rock, "Hyenas Like Us," p. 84.

Marcus. Burissey, an offspring of a high-ranking hyena of the same clan, had watched Willi play with Marcus and also tried to interact, but her interaction was more akin to hunting, rather than play behavior. Both hyenas became far bolder at the feeding site than the others, leading to problems with feeding the other hyenas. One hyena called Dibbey also became very aggressive toward Willi and bit him on the rump. Marcus laments, "I cannot take full responsibility for the harms that were done because I was never in control. Willi and I were both novices following paths that were unfolding before us. . . . I find that I am ethically obliged to apportion some of the responsibility to Willi."[45] This reflection on what happened shows the uniquely human capacity for human beings to reflect on and consider the outcomes of an ongoing relationship. He later spoke of Willi's initial hesitation to admit him back into his social world, but eventually there was acceptance. Baynes-Rock had no doubts in attributing to Willi the emotion of forgiveness.[46]

Of course, one question that we might ask is this: In the light of such an experience, would it be appropriate to develop such a close tie with a "wild" animal again, given the negative impacts it seems to have had subsequently on the function of the group? Were the insights gained worth it? These are difficult ethical questions that need to be pondered by anthropologists working in this terrain, and such questions reveal the particular human responsibility of being the dominant partner in such a relationship. Regardless of the significance of such results on ethical dimensions of research practice, is it possible to argue for not just intersociality but also intermorality? Certainly, if Baynes-Rock is right and hyenas, when observed more closely, demonstrate significant capability for subjectivity and second-order desires, then it makes sense to think of their group behavior in terms of *normativity* and not just blind *conformity.* But this means that their moral world adapts to and is adjusted to the way humans choose to behave in relation to them, and vice versa. Baynes-Rock provides evidence that it was the traditional religious belief that hyenas had the capacity to kill and consume unclean spirits that persisted even after the population had converted to Islam, and that seems to set in place close protective relationships with hyenas in the Hararge region of Ethiopia.[47] Clearly, much

45. Baynes-Rock, "Hyenas Like Us," p. 96.

46. Baynes-Rock, "Hyenas Like Us," p. 77.

47. Baynes-Rock also comments that hyenas in the region have adapted their behavior to human societies by refraining from attacking livestock and people in return for security and food offered by the local population at particular feeding sites. See Marcus Baynes-Rock,

more research needs to be done in showing how human moral frameworks have adapted to and engaged with the changing patterns of social life in those animals with which humans have interacted. This is not, of course, to suggest that all early hunter-gatherer societies had benign or necessarily positive relationships with other animals in the way that seems to have developed in Harar society, but rather that their social worlds responded to the social worlds of other animals in highly complex ways. What is important is that there are particular places known as *multispecies commons* that show particularly clearly the social, biological, and historical entanglements in human and other animal societies interwoven with ecological processes. Such entanglements are evident in densely populated areas. Hyenas living in such conditions have to adapt to a lack of clearly defined boundary conditions between clans.

The particular boundary marker practices operational in a nonurban context, such as marking up scented paste on grasses or creating clusters of white droppings, are not available to them in an urban context, as the growth of grass is suppressed and droppings are cleared up. In the urban context, therefore, the boundary between clans was not easy to discern, so in practice clans had shared areas in some urban regions where territorial disputes were worked out. The two hyena clans of Harar in Ethiopia resolved their differences at a particular site outside the gate at Argobberi. Baynes-Rock comments, "The gate at Argobberi is more than an edifice. It is a mutually constructed, historicised, politicized meaningful place in the minds of both hyenas and humans who participate in the dramas which are enacted there."[48]

In addition, the local people assume hyenas are like themselves in social organization, believing that they hold meetings and communicate through hyena language to other conspecifics and to those humans who can understand their language, and they also believe that hyenas have an understanding of and a capacity for revenge. Hyenas who attack livestock are "disciplined" and may be killed by other hyenas, and if humans insult hyenas, then humans can expect retribution. For the locals, at least, a hyena thinks like a human being.

But what might it mean for our human moral world to be so closely

---

"Local Tolerance of Hyena Attacks in East Hararge Region, Ethiopia," *Anthrozoös* (2013). I am grateful to Marcus Baynes-Rock for sending me a copy of this article.

48. Marcus Baynes-Rock, "Life and Death in the Multispecies Commons," *Social Science Information* (2013). I am grateful to Marcus Baynes-Rock for sending me a copy of this article while still in press.

informed by the lives and practices of other animals in a multispecies commons? I suggest that important clues in this direction come to the surface in Thomas Aquinas's account of other animal lives.

Aquinas on the Passions and the Virtuous Moral Life

Aquinas's rendition of the moral life sought to make clear not just the way human beings were influenced by their passions,[49] but also how the excellences in virtue should be sought and practiced. He also understood the moral life to be framed within a rational ontological structure of morality that took its bearings from the natural world, namely, the framing of natural law. I could easily devote the whole of this section to natural law theory and its checkered history in shaping moral life in human societies. I will, however, defer a more thorough discussion of natural law to the chapter on justice, as it makes most sense in relation to what justice requires and as this was the context in which the most thorough discussion of natural law took place in Aquinas's monumental *Summa Theologiae*. Natural law could also be thought of as a moral concept rather than a moral sentiment or moral behavior. It is a concept that frames the moral context rather than being an explicitly moral sentiment even if, arguably, natural law is perceived as having deep roots in the natural world. It is also highly relevant when considering that other aspect of the moral life, namely, the institutional one. Instead, in this chapter I confine my attention to the passions, virtues, and gifts, and even this constriction will necessarily be compressed. Here I want to ask questions about the passions, virtues, and gifts in Aquinas that show up specifically the lines of continuity and discontinuity between human and other animal worlds. How might, in other words, the possibility of intermorality actually cash out in theological terms?

While the influence of Aristotle on Aquinas's understanding of the virtues is often assumed, fairly recently a number of authors have challenged the assumption that his understanding of the virtues follows Aristotle, or at least that the perfected moral life significantly departs from Aristotle. This is important since Aristotle puts emphasis on a biological

49. A passion is defined in its narrowest sense in Aquinas as an act of the sensitive appetite when the appetite is responding to deliverances from the senses. For emotions, there needs to be some cognition as well. If passions are thought of in a less restrictive way, then there are intellectual or volitional passions, or at least analogues to those passions.

understanding of the human in a way that his contemporaries did not. The challenge relates to the relationship between acquired virtues, infused virtues, and gifts. Aquinas's list of acquired virtues follows the four that characterize those of Aristotle, namely, practical wisdom, courage, justice, and temperance. The theological virtues of faith, hope, and charity are always infused. The gifts of the Holy Spirit, on the other hand, are piety, courage, fear of the Lord, wisdom, understanding, counsel, and knowledge. While earlier commentators believed that acquired virtues were retained alongside those infused by the action of God's grace while not negating human volition, recent scholarship challenges this idea in favor of a believer *only* having infused virtues; therefore, a person in a state of grace in William Mattison's analysis "cannot possess the acquired cardinal virtues," and for Eleanore Stump Aquinas's ethics becomes "non-Aristotelian."[50] A close reading of these articles makes it clear that acquired virtues are *not* somehow in parallel with infused virtues, but rather are transformed by God's grace. What were for some years something of an embarrassment for philosophers, namely, infused virtues, become instead the linchpin orientating the proper moral life. Inasmuch as Aristotle does not take account of the action of God in the moral life, this becomes non-Aristotelian, but it would, it seems to me, be quite incorrect to claim this strongly as if Aristotle had *no* influence over the way Aquinas perceived human moral life.

The interesting question is, then, not just whether Aquinas's ethics is ultimately non-Aristotelian, but whether the transformations he suggests are convincing or not. Renée Mirkes, in an article published in 1998, resonates with my own interpretation in that she refuses to split apart the acquired and infused virtues, and even though the latter are the measure of what virtue is like, "each infused moral virtue is related to its acquired counterpart as the determining or perfecting principle, that is, that which actualizes the potency of its corresponding acquired moral virtue."[51] She also distinguishes between human virtue that is transformed in infused virtue and that absolutely perfect moral virtue that is totally transformed by grace. But she resists in a way that is correct any argument for the perfection of nature that somehow downplays its importance.

50. William Mattison III, "Can Christians Possess the Acquired Virtues?" *Theological Studies* 72 (2011): 558-85; Eleanore Stump, "The Non-Aristotelian Character of Aquinas Ethics: Aquinas on the Passions," *Faith and Philosophy* 28, no. 1 (2011): 29-43.

51. Renée Mirkes, "Aquinas on the Unity of Perfect Moral Virtue," *American Catholic Philosophical Quarterly* 71, no. 4 (1998): 589-605, here 591.

Indeed, I will argue that Aquinas had a greater sensitivity to the social worlds of other animals than Stump and Mattison suggest. Such sensitivity was likely to have been influenced by his teacher Albertus Magnus. He not only, like Aquinas, read Aristotle closely, but he also was one of the first philosophers who dedicated considerable time to actual observations of other animals. This compares with later constructivist theorists that avoided due consideration of other animals entirely.[52] It is therefore highly instructive to explore the original *Summa Zoologica* of Albertus Magnus briefly in order to tease out more specifically the way Aquinas was likely to have thought about other animals or at least his starting point in that venture. The *Summa Zoologica* is a two-volume work in which Albertus lays out details of his observations. His account is meticulous for the time and includes a commentary on morphology, physiology, and anatomy. A considerable number of pages in the second book are devoted to the causes of the generation of animals: for example, sexuality in its manifold expressions and the powers of reproduction, including Aristotle's odd view that the soul was in the semen and not in the intellect.

Far less space comparatively speaking is spent on the human animal, so that human animals are discussed in a way that is interwoven with aspects held in common with other animals. Considerable space is devoted to generation and sexual activity in all animals, including human beings.[53] He discusses the Aristotelian idea that the soul is in the semen, meaning that through it animals have the power of generation. But this sets up a contrast in that the rational soul is caused by the intellect, rather than by the generative powers of the semen, characteristic of the sensible soul.[54] According to Albertus, human beings are exceptions to other animals in having a "rational soul." Albertus seems to want to separate the rational soul, which "has nothing in common with the operation of a bodily organ in any way whatever," from the intellect, which is "divine, that is perpetual and uncorruptible." But like Aristotle, he departs from Plato in naming the

52. Albertus Magnus, *On Animals,* vol. 1 and vol. 2.

53. He devotes considerable space to describing in graphic detail the pleasures of sexual intercourse, but his account is not unexpectedly stereotyped in aspects of his characterization of male and female relationships in humans, so that while he acknowledges the importance of mutual pleasure in intercourse, he compares human females with mares in their desire for sexual activity. See Albertus Magnus, *On Animals,* vol. 2, book 15, chapter 7; vol. 2, book 18, chapter 4, especially §72.

54. Albertus Magnus, *On Animals,* vol. 2, book 16, chapter 12, §65.

vegetative and sensible soul as having a form of potency in the material as such rather than external potency.[55]

Although only a small fraction of the book is devoted to an explicit study of human beings, he has no problem in speaking of animal virtues, for "every perfection and imperfection in animals exists in accordance to their perfect or imperfect participation in the animal virtues." But there is a qualification: for him, perfection is measured relative to human beings, so that "we should first determine what the true nature of the most perfect animal is."[56] What is interesting, though, is that in the sensible soul, the vegetative soul also exists as a partial power according to the being of the sensible soul. But the being *(esse)* is the act and effect of the essence and its form, which is "unique for each individual animal." So he speaks of "living" as the mode of being for plants, "sense" as the mode of being for sentient beings, and "understanding" as the mode of being for intelligent beings. The perfection of the vegetative soul and the sensible soul comes, for Albertus, through participation in reason in some way. He is prepared, however, to label virtues according to the gradations of the soul, so that "temperance and chastity are present according to the functions of the vegetative soul; humility and gentleness, however, and likewise fortitude and many other virtues, are present according to the desires and angers of the sensitive soul. This could only be the case if the vegetative and sensible souls were in the human according to the being *(esse)* of the intellectual soul, for otherwise the soul would not be receptive to a good rational order."[57] The idea of a *nested* hierarchy makes sense, so the relationship of a triangle to a quadrangle is the relationship of the vegetative soul to the sensible soul. The perfection of humans, then, was perceived in relationship with the powers shared with other animals that are taken up and transformed by reason.

In chapter 2 of book 21, he takes up the theme of prudence in other animals in a way that resonates with Aquinas's account. He argues, therefore, that "some animals have a sort of prudence with respect to gathering things for themselves, but they are nevertheless not subject to instruction." Here he comments on the activities of bees and ants. He argues, though, that some animals are capable not just of hearing and giving an instinctive

55. Albertus Magnus, *On Animals,* vol. 2, book 16, chapter 12, §67.

56. Albertus Magnus, *On Animals,* vol. 2, book 21, chapter 1, §1. This chapter is headed, significantly, "On the Highest Perfection of Animal Which Is the Human."

57. Albertus Magnus, *On Animals,* vol. 2, book 21, chapter 1, §2.

response, but also of hearing sounds and interpreting them. So "many animals do many things in response to human voices."[58] He adds that some animals are capable of learning from experience and "have a kind of imitation of art, even though they do not attain art."[59]

But his categorization of some humans as animals is interesting here; he claims that pygmies are not human because they lack abstract reasoning. He writes, "Some, moreover, flourish so much in the instruction of hearing that they even seem to signify their intentions to one another, as does the pygmy, which speaks, although it is an irrational animal nonetheless." Here "reason is a power of the soul drawing out the universal from the specific or syllogistic figure [*habitude*] and bearing from it principles of art and sciences through similar figures."[60] For him, pygmies are in a different category because their nature does not seem to lend itself to the ability to reason abstractly. But he does attribute the capacity of imagination to monkeys: "the genus of monkeys, more than all the other brute animals, appraises [*estimere*] that which is beneficial and that which is capable of causing injury, doing so from sense, imagination and memory."[61] He allows for the possibility of "imperfect practical syllogisms," but it is a "phantasm" arising from that which is seen, rather than from universal considerations.[62] He is prepared to consider the possibility that monkeys are also "human likenesses." And here he uses biological categories to consider why this is the case, such as structure of head, use of fingers, bend at elbow, etc., in a way that is remarkable, especially considering the way theologians subsequently stressed that which sharply distinguished human beings from other animal kinds.

Rather than stress any non-Aristotelian account, it therefore would be more preferable to argue for a transformed account since, while the metaethical analysis is different, Aristotle and Aristotelian mediation through Albert the Great still strongly influence the shape of what constitutes the virtues in Aquinas.[63] However, to avoid any misunderstanding,

58. Albertus Magnus, *On Animals,* vol. 2, book 21, chapter 2, §10.

59. Albertus Magnus, *On Animals,* vol. 2, book 21, chapter 2, §11.

60. Albertus Magnus, *On Animals,* vol. 2, book 21, chapter 2, §11, brackets in original.

61. Albertus Magnus, *On Animals,* vol. 2, book 21, chapter 3, §17, brackets in original.

62. Albertus Magnus, *On Animals,* vol. 2, book 21, chapter 3, §§17, 18.

63. Working out more precisely the relationship between "nature" and "transformed nature" was a recurring challenge in the discussion amongst scientists, philosophers, and theologians at the Center of Theological Inquiry study year in which this chapter took shape, so the pattern set forth by Aquinas can be illuminating in all sorts of respects.

it is helpful to consider more precisely the relationship between reason, what might be called the "lower appetites," and virtue in Aquinas, since this aspect is crucial to his portrayal of the moral life. I contend that this is just as important as reflection on the infused virtues and gifts that recent philosophical scholarship has rediscovered, which could be thought of as closer to the angelic end of the spectrum where humanity occupies that place in between other animals and angels. For Aquinas, virtue understood in terms of the fulfillment of capacity is only truly present when there is a concomitant possibility of acting or not acting, and a disposition to act well according to a good end.[64] But the possibility of acting well or not is according to reason, so that those powers of life below the conscious level cannot possess virtues. Hence, "if any opposition arises as a result of these powers, it will be mediated through our sensory desire which can be affected by the command of reason (and therefore be described as 'human,' and a possessor of human virtue)."[65] The question of whether virtue could ever be found in nonhuman animals is also raised in the first question, article 4. Aquinas's reply to that is interesting, for he draws on Aristotle in order to consider more fully what it means for virtuous powers to be in the sensitive, nonrational parts of human nature. He elaborates further: "An act is called human not just because it is done in any old way by or through a human being — for some things are shared with non-human animals and even plants — but because it belongs distinctively to a human being. What is distinctive about human beings, compared to these other things, is that human beings are in control of their own actions. . . . Human virtue, then, can be located in whatever is the principle of an action of which a human being is in control."[66]

The sensory desires are not brought into line by a kind of forcing by reason; rather, virtue consists in the "completeness in the sensory desire that will enable it to obey reason easily."[67] If, on the other hand, reason follows the inclinations of the aggressive and sensual parts, this amounts to sin. It follows from this that the aggressive or sensual aspects of human acts cannot be virtuous independent of reason, but insofar as the aggressive and sensual dispositions "follow the direction of reason without any

64. Thomas Aquinas, *Disputed Questions on the Virtues,* ed. E. M. Atkins and Thomas Williams, trans. E. M. Atkins (Cambridge: Cambridge University Press, 2005), "On the Virtues in General," Art. 1, reply, p. 7. Art. 2, reply, p. 14. Hereafter cited as *DQV.*

65. Aquinas, *DQV,* "On the Virtues in General," Art. 3, replies to objections, p. 18.

66. Aquinas, *DQV,* "On the Virtues in General," Art. 4, reply, p. 22.

67. Aquinas, *DQV,* "On the Virtues in General," Art. 4, reply, p. 23.

struggle," then that act is virtuous.[68] But while Aquinas insisted that the whole of human nature needed not just reason, but "also the lower parts of the soul and indeed the body," he also held that "The intelligence, though, is entirely free from matter, that is why its activity is not involved with physical things." As for the aggressive and sensual parts, these also shared in the nonmaterial, and so were intermediate since they obeyed reason, so "Virtue is found in them, then, just to the extent to which they are raised above the material and obey reason."[69]

Clearly, in the light of current developments in neuroscience, the belief that reason is distanced from the material does not make so much sense. However, the activity of the mind cannot be reduced to material neurological brain function, and in this sense Aquinas was perfectly correct. He was, nonetheless, careful to speak of intelligent creatures. Hence, his exclusion of other animals from the virtuous life was related to his belief that they lacked the ability of reason to inform their sensual and aggressive appetites, so "those powers do not share in reason at all. That is why non-human animals cannot have the moral virtues."[70] It is the corruption of the reason by misdirected emotions and wrongful desire that leads into sin.[71] But in other places he seems to allow the possibility of reason in nonhumans, so that "Human beings and other rational creatures are able to achieve a higher end than other creatures."[72] Further, "every creature possesses some likeness to God by virtue of being something good. A rational creature is like God in one further respect, in that it is intelligent, and in a further respect when it is perfected."[73] Other animals can be said to be in the likeness of God in their created goodness.[74]

What about the difference between acquired and infused virtues, and how might transformed human "nature" in infused virtues be understood? Certainly there is a sense in which "God works in us without us,"[75] and

68. Aquinas, *DQV,* "On the Virtues in General," Art. 4, replies to objections, p. 24.

69. Aquinas, *DQV,* "On the Virtues in General," Art. 4, replies to objections, p. 25.

70. Aquinas, *DQV,* "On the Virtues in General," Art. 4, replies to objections, 12, p. 26.

71. Aquinas, *DQV,* "On the Virtues in General," Art. 4, replies to objections, 13, p. 26.

72. Aquinas, *DQV,* "On Charity," Art. 1, replies to objections, 15, p. 114.

73. Aquinas, *DQV,* "On Charity," Art. 1, replies to objections, 8, p. 113.

74. I discuss this in more detail in Celia Deane-Drummond, "God's Image and Likeness in Humans and Other Animals: Performative Soul-Making and Graced Nature," *Zygon* 47, no. 4 (2012): 934-48.

75. Thomas Aquinas, *Summa Theologiae, Virtue, Vol. 23 (1a2ae. 55-67),* trans. W. D. Hughes (London: Blackfriars, 1968), qu. 55.4. Aquinas is citing Augustine here, rather than necessarily making the claim that this definition is completely sufficient.

acquired virtue "is not of the same species as infused virtue,"[76] but even if the origin and goal are transformed, that does not imply a *separation from* grounded human nature. The language of "different species" is confusing to modern readers if this implies some kind of radical dualism, but would be more akin to how most biologists envisage species today, that is, as a loose concept that shows a distinction arising from an emerging capacity. As Mattison points out, it is the "form" that is distinguished in Aquinas, so the idea of transformation is accurate.[77] He explicitly rejects Pelagianism in holding that natural principles are in some sense sufficient for eternal life, but he also resists the idea that eternal life is not mediated *through* what is natural.[78] The infused virtues are related to the final end of eternal life, "the last state of blessedness that the human being can attain" that in some sense "exceed[s] the abilities of the principles natural to us and that order us to our supernatural end."[79] Human beings are human inasmuch as they are situated between animals, which are directed to sensual pleasure, and angels, which are directed to contemplation and possess intelligence.[80] The goals of infused and acquired virtues are different in each case: for example, acquired temperateness looks to the goods in relation to this life, while infused temperateness is orientated toward God's law and the final end.[81] Each of the four acquired virtues has analogies with the infused virtues, but also with the gifts of the Holy Spirit. The important point here is that the gifts of the Spirit are a result of an ongoing relationship between a human person and the third person of the Trinity, who dwells in that person. The way this comes to be expressed is most obvious in Aquinas's discussion of charity. Hence, the disposition of charity is not an intermediary between God and the subject, but characterizes an inner-personal relation, so the unity is one of affection "as that between a lover and a loved one. . . . For the action of loving passes directly to God, as the loved one, rather than indirectly through the disposition of charity."[82] Temperance becomes fear

76. Aquinas, *ST, Virtue,* 1a2ae, qu. 63.4, also in qu. 55.4; see Aquinas, *DQV,* "On the Virtues in General," Arts. 9-10. Here we can add, what does different "species" mean? Even Mattison argues for a transformed nature, rather than separation from it.

77. Mattison, "Can Christians Possess the Acquired Virtues?" p. 567.

78. Aquinas, *DQV,* "On Charity," Art. 1, objection 12 and reply, pp. 107, 113.

79. Aquinas, *DQV,* "On the Virtues in General," Art. 10, reply, p. 65.

80. Aquinas, *DQV,* "On the Cardinal Virtues," Art. 1, reply, p. 244.

81. Aquinas, *DQV,* "On the Virtues in General," Art. 10, replies to objections, 8, 10, p. 68.

82. Aquinas, *DQV,* "On Charity," Art. 1, replies to objections, 3, p. 112.

of the Lord, and justice becomes piety. But I suggest that in this scheme the human moral world of the acquired virtues overlaps with the spiritual world of infused virtues understood as energized by the Holy Spirit.

Andrew Pinsent has argued recently that Aquinas's understanding of the gifts given by the Holy Spirit and necessary for a religious understanding of perfection in the moral life is decidedly *second personal* in the sense that it involves an active relationship between God and the human subject.[83] He also contends that the gifts have been underrated in interpretation of Aquinas's ethics and are in fact crucial to understanding the goal of the moral life. Although Aquinas seems to recognize the difficulty in separating gifts and virtues, especially infused virtues, he attempts to distinguish them in that, although both have their origin in God rather than in human reasoning, the spiritual nature of gifts is that which *predisposes* a right action before God, as well as the action itself.[84] Pinsent interprets the gifts as being the penultimate foundation of or principle of the moral life, following the ultimate theological principal virtues of faith, hope, and charity, rather than a transformation of or building on existing virtues.[85] Rather like infused virtues, anyone, including children and those with mental disabilities, can possess gifts even alongside acquired vices.

But the activity of gift is not coercive but free, and in this sense specifically Pinsent argues that the psychological analogy of *joint attention* most readily describes the working of gifts in the human heart, so that it retains a sense of human agency while involving God in a personal way.

83. While I would not go quite as far as Pinsent does and suggest that the attention to the gifts eclipses all understanding of Aquinas's account of the moral life in Aristotelian terms, his approach gives welcome attention to the life of grace as transforming the moral life of the believer. See Andrew Pinsent, *The Second Person Perspective in Aquinas Ethics: Virtues and Gifts* (London: Routledge, 2012).

84. Aquinas therefore claims that "a gift, in so far as it is distinguished from infused virtue, can be said to be that which God gives to dispose a person for his motion; it makes man follow God's promptings well." Of course, this is complicated by the fact that some virtues are also gifts, but in this case the different ways of functioning would be described as virtue or gift, so wisdom can be an intellectual virtue in some cases, and a gift in others, where it arises through divine prompting. See Thomas Aquinas, *Summa Theologiae, The Gifts of the Spirit, Vol. 24 (1a2ae. 68-70),* trans. Edward D. O'Connor (London: Blackfriars, 1974), 1a2ae, qu. 68.1.

85. Pinsent, *The Second Person Perspective,* pp. 30-34. He also develops the idea of beatitudes and fruits, giving a virtue-gift-beatitude-fruit (VGBF) structure to the moral life in Aquinas. Aquinas's discussion of beatitudes and fruits seems to be his way of integrating scriptural references in the Christian moral life, rather than anything more significant, and Pinsent has overstated his case in this respect.

This perspective is helpful in that it allows a particular way of viewing human moral perfection informed by the notion of gift received by the grace of the Holy Spirit through joint attention to a specific task. It allows the subject to be a free agent, but to be aware of and responsive to God's presence. The notion of friendship or kinship, however, could do much the same kind of work, and that extension would connect with Aquinas's belief that charity is friendship with God.[86] Whether second personal or friendship is used, both are ways of considering and expanding the notion of human morality that is *intersocial* in a way that is *analogous with* but certainly not *identical to* the possibility for intersociality between humans and between humans and other animals. In the case of gifts, human beings act out the moral life in accordance with the perfected moral sphere in friendship with God according to the life of the Spirit.[87] For other animals the shift in human moral behavior will not be as sharp, but there still will be an adjustment in human moral action in receptivity to what is perceived as of value for and to the other.

For all its insights, the second personal analogy does tend to weaken the importance of the collective in moral decision-making, as if gifts of the Holy Spirit were received in a highly personal and individual manner somewhat in isolation from the wider human community. While this protects individual autonomy that has become increasingly significant in present-day cultures, in evolutionary terms a sense of collective agency was more likely to have been important, both in religious life and in the overlap between human and other animal lifeworlds. Furthermore, the new scholarly emphasis on the life of grace and the gifts and the work of the Holy Spirit in the moral life in Aquinas's thought is meaningful for the

86. I have discussed the possibility of extending Aquinas's notion of friendship to nonhuman creatures in Celia Deane-Drummond, *Genetics and Christian Ethics* (Cambridge: Cambridge University Press, 2006), pp. 229-44. I will take this up again in the final chapter.

87. Such questions open up a whole series of issues dealing with the way the Holy Spirit might be said to be active in the human community and in other creatures. This discussion would require a monograph in its own right on pneumatology. Aquinas does not rule out the possibility that gifts can include powers of action that involve both reason and appetite. He also claims that, like infused virtues, gifts can be given to children and to those who have impaired reasoning. His logic could therefore extend the possibility that gifts could be given to other animals that are capable of a subjective sense of self, as well as human subjects, but as far as I am aware this is not taken up in his discussion. Of course, those who deny the possibility that other animals can have such self-consciousness would rule out such a possibility, and a certain minimum level of brain function would seem to be required as a prerequisite for such activity, quite apart from higher reasoning powers.

religious community, but it seems to me that it is just as significant for the moral life to consider his close attention to human relationships with other creatures, with their passions, emotions, and estimative sense. If attention is given to just the former work of grace, then human moral life tends to be split off from the bodily emotive and ecological contexts in which human lifeworlds are situated. If, on the other hand, too much emphasis is given to biological forms, then the possibility of a transformed human moral life in communion with the work of the Holy Spirit is lost.

Aquinas seemed to follow Aristotle rather than Plato in his understanding of the human soul as a nested hierarchy incorporating plant and animal souls, who also were capable of a kind of immaterial existence.[88] His understanding of different "grades" of virtues bears close relationship with his understanding of the transformation of the image of God into God's likeness, also following a threefold pattern. Animal passions in this scheme are not so much rejected as incorporated into graced nature. I will explore next to what extent he envisaged moral behavior in other animals, including a rich emotional life. He certainly attributed to them the emotion of hope that he also claims elsewhere is, in humans, an infused virtue. Albertus Magnus, his teacher, insisted on close observation of the natural world, and allowed other animals to have an imaginative capacity, even if they lacked the power of abstraction required for universal knowledge. This goes considerably further toward attributing subjectivity in other animals compared with René Descartes, for example, who was to heavily influence subsequent scientific developments.

Some Interim Conclusions

When I started working out how to develop this chapter, I thought I would devote considerably more attention to specific virtues of the moral life, such as prudence, charity, temperance, and so on, and ask questions about how these might have evolved in the human community in relation to perceived precedents in other animals. Instead, I found that a prior question needed to be addressed first, namely, in what sense can human moral becoming be understood? For that, I had to pay attention to the literature on the evolution of morality, with a slanted reference to the related

88. See Deane-Drummond, "God's Image and Likeness in Humans and Other Animals."

burgeoning literature on the evolution of religious belief. That was important because the way human social worlds have evolved impacts how morality has come to be understood. Morality is not properly understood, therefore, as simply the abstracted decision making of a rational subject in detachment from the social world in which the subject is embedded. Of course, the kind of morality possible in human beings is certainly not identical to that in other creatures, but allowing for the possibility of morality in other agents is illuminating in understanding both their lifeworld and that of human beings.

The difficulty is how we arrive at an account of human distinctiveness, while not wanting to sever recognition of human selves as evolved beings living in close ecological relationship with other creatures for most of their evolved history. I contend that human attitudes and relationships with other animals are a significant ingredient in parsing out the moral and even religious life of human beings. In Harar, Ethiopia, examples of close interaction between *Homo sapiens sapiens* and *Crocuta crocuta* show an intermeshing of social and moral worlds in a way that challenges prior conceptions. It opens up the concrete possibility of intersubjectivity in a way that follows directly from discussions in the first few chapters on animal reason and agency. I have also suggested the possibility that human morality can be thought of as intermoral as well as intersubjective inasmuch as morality developed alongside and in interaction with the moral worlds of other creatures. But more important, perhaps, it reminds interpreters of Aquinas to pay as much attention to his treatment of other animals in parsing out the moral life as to his focus on the life of grace and gifts. While the latter is a reaction to scholars who have focused simply on the Aristotelian *habitus* in acquired virtues, so too, the lack of attention to passions and the animal worlds is equally problematic. Gaining a Thomistic sense of human morality and animal virtue shows both the perfection to which human beings are called in grace and the human nature grounded in passions held in common with other animals.

CHAPTER FIVE

Human Language and Animal Communication

Perhaps of all the qualities purported to be most characteristic of humans, language is the one that is more often than not cited as a basis for arguing that humans should exercise supremacy over other creatures. Yet analysis of the way other creatures communicate with each other illuminates both common and distinctive evolutionary bases for human language and the way it developed and diversified in social communities. After touching on philosophical issues of why language has become of such central concern to present-day humans, I intend in this chapter to build on the discussion in chapter 2 of how animal minds work, including human minds. Without a closer look at these facets, it is difficult to make a reasonable comparison of communication systems between different species in the biological classification group Animalia, which takes in birds, fish, mammals, insects, and so on. I have touched on these issues in earlier chapters on reason and freedom, but this needs to be more explicit in this chapter, since knowing the fine-tuning of the way human minds work is necessary to understand their particular requirements for human communication and what might be considered highly distinctive facets of human language. Furthermore, symbolic and language development contributes not just to communication as such, but arguably to thinking itself. I will also give some specific examples of animal communication systems to illustrate the sheer variety in different species. As an intermediary between animal communication and the full-blown development of complex human language, I will discuss symbol making in early hominids and the possible reasons for its evolutionary development. There are plenty of gaps in the scientific literature that are revealed in some of the heated controversies on the way human language evolved, the acquisition of language in human infants, as well as perhaps even more controversial attempts by humans to teach their language to other animals. It will soon become evident that questions over language evolution and acquisition are not only topics for highly charged debates in the scientific literature, but they are also extremely complex. This chapter will offer a sketch of that literature and argue for the place of theology in language evolution. I will suggest that theology has the potential to be humanizing in that it demonstrates distinctive aspects of human being that become most obviously evident through an analysis of human language becomings.

Human Language

What is extremely noticeable for those interested in the historical development of the meaning of human nature is that a concentration on language as *the* prime characteristic of human beings is a relatively recent, twentieth-century phenomenon. Aquinas, for example, mentions human speech in his *Summa Theologiae* almost in passing and in reference to how angels could possibly communicate with one another, given that they do not have the kinds of bodies, and presumably vocal chords, that humans do.[1] He ends up suggesting that angels communicate not so much by words but by willing mental thoughts to become evident to one another. Furthermore, ordinary speech, on the one hand, is inward in that it involves persons speaking in their heads to themselves through their inner thoughts, for by definition the mind is "an inner word."[2] On the other hand, speech is also outward. The possibility of speech through exterior or sensible signs was not, interestingly, confined to the use of the voice, but for him could also include a nod of the head or a gesture of tongue or fingers, a practice that would be impossible for angels. In naming speech as both inward and outward, and in naming outward speech as more than simply the spoken word, Aquinas was on the right track in terms of reflection on both the origin and the significance of language in humans and other creatures. While he did not discuss the possibility of speech in other animals, it would be

1. Thomas Aquinas, *Summa Theologiae, Divine Government, Vol. 14 (1a. 103-109),* trans. T. C. O'Brien (London: Blackfriars, 1994), 1a, qu. 107.1.

2. The context in which he uses this phrase is the following: "Now when the soul applies itself to actual thought about something retained habitually, a person is talking to himself; we even refer to the mind as an inner word." Aquinas, *ST, Divine Government,* 1a, qu. 107.1.

entirely fitting within his scheme to envisage other animals having some of the gestural means of communication but lacking the interior speech characteristic of both humans and angels.[3] However, he was not particularly interested in human speech as that which makes us human; rather *reason* occupied his attention.

Of course, as Charles Taylor points out, reason and language are not all that far apart in that for Aristotle humans are the rational animal, which itself means an animal who possesses the word, *zøon logon echon.*[4] Taylor argues that if human beings are now labeled as the language animal, then this raises the issue of how puzzling language actually is, especially if it is framed in the context of communicating through music, art, dance, and other symbolic forms. In this chapter I want to contribute to the unraveling of this puzzle by shedding light on the evolutionary basis for language acquisition understood in the broadest sense.

Different theories exist about the ways language itself is used. Designative theories of language make meaning unmysterious and unpuzzling: what is spoken is related directly to the world or state of affairs.[5] Expressive theories of language, on the other hand, resist tying in an explanation by correlative relationships to something else, but only in relation to another expression. Designative theories are more in keeping with scientific modes of thinking, while expressive theories are more in keeping with subject-related properties characteristic of theology and the humanities more generally. It is clear that scientific and evolutionary accounts of language origins will lean toward a metaphysical approach that is designative, whereas theological accounts will be more expressive. Designative theories are about the use of language as an instrument of control in gaining access to knowledge; hence, scientific language is characteristically formulaic.[6] The expressivist reaction to this in various forms of what can loosely be

3. I have discussed the place of humans in relation to angels and other animals in Celia Deane-Drummond, "In God's Image and Likeness: From Reason to Revelation in Humans and Other Animals," in *Questioning the Human: Perspectives on Theological Anthropology for the 21st Century,* ed. Lieven Boeve, Yves De Maeseneer, and Ellen Van Stichel (New York: Fordham University Press, 2014).

4. Charles Taylor, *Human Agency and Language: Philosophical Papers* (Cambridge: Cambridge University Press, 1985), p. 217.

5. Taylor also points out that such a direct correlation between words and states of affairs ends up with behaviorist theories, such as that of Burrhus Frederic (B. F.) Skinner; Taylor, *Human Agency and Language,* p. 220.

6. Taylor, *Human Agency and Language,* p. 226.

termed Romanticism resisted the idea that words correspond with things, for the capacity of reflective awareness is needed to turn what something is into a category, so humans, unlike rats, can recognize a triangle as being part of the family of triangles and not just react to it as a sign.[7] In terms of function, capacity for expressive use of language is highly distinctive for human communities, while some designative forms of communication may be possible for other social animals.

In this chapter I am going to attempt what may seem like an impossible task: to draw on some insights emerging from designative theories and incorporate them into a metaphysical position that is more expressive. Taylor believes that the classical lack of distinction between words and reason was modeled on a discourse model of thought, which in Plato related to ultimate reality in Idea, so that by laying it out in words the meaning becomes clear.[8] Words are "external clothing" to express inner discourse thought of the mind. Augustine adapted Plato's ideas in order to explain how God acted as Creator through the Word; creation bears an analogous relationship to God, as words to human thought. In this view, *all* of creation becomes a sign, a signifier of the handiwork of God. This idea that everything is a sign of divine language is expressive rather than designative in its basic philosophy, and leads to the possibility of semiological ontologies. For Taylor, it is the nominalist rebellion against a semiological view of the universe that creates the space for making human language important.[9] But the trajectory of Taylor's position is that expressive semiological views of the world have no place within a designative theory, and vice versa. The empiricist view of language traces it out in terms of an assemblage of different instruments that can be controlled and contained. By contrast, language for the expressivist, according to Taylor, "is something of the nature of a web, and to complicate the image, is present as a whole in any one of its parts. To speak is to touch a bit of the web, and this is to make the whole resonate. Because the words we use now only have sense through their place in the whole web, we can never have a clear oversight of the implications of what we say at any moment."[10]

7. Even Aquinas recognized this crucial distinction that humans have the ability to abstract the things in the world in a certain way. Charles Taylor cites J. G. Herder as being particularly influential in the eighteenth-century reaction to designative theories of language. Taylor, *Human Agency and Language,* pp. 227-28.

8. Taylor, *Human Agency and Language,* p. 222.

9. Taylor, *Human Agency and Language,* p. 223.

10. Taylor, *Human Agency and Language,* p. 231.

Further, it is in the expressivist view that language opens up to include other creative expressions of human beings, such as poetry, music, art, dance, and so on. Theology and the designative descriptions of science occupy different language worlds that seem impossible to reconcile. But maybe Taylor's contrastive account is rather too simple, and a more complex understanding of the way language has evolved and is used in different contexts, oscillating between designative and expressive modes, can help elaborate a portrait of human nature that takes account of different ways of understanding the meaning of language. In addition, an interaction between them can open up new insights for what might be called chastened versions of expressivism that are rather more aware of insights emerging from the sciences. He gestures toward such a possibility himself by arguing that expressivism has become far more pervasive than most will care to admit, and is behind the reason why language seems enigmatic to contemporary scholars. But he does not take the next step and argue for a more comprehensive and self-conscious relationship between designative and expressive theories. Before we get to that point, an exploration of concrete aspects of other animal minds shows the specifically distinctive characteristics of human language.

Animal Minds

Confusingly, perhaps, philosopher Jesse Prinz labels a language theory expressive when there is a focus on its function as a means of expression of thought, rather than that which enables thought, thereby including a wide range of scholars under the umbrella of expressivism, from empiricists such as John Locke to rationalists such as Noam Chomsky.[11] More recently, psychologists have shifted to what could be termed cognitive theories of language in making the claim that the primary function of language is *cognition* rather than expression, hence returning to the older association of language and rationality.[12] Strong claims that language is always a prerequisite and indeed *necessary* for cognition to be possible at all seem exaggerated. However, if these theories are even partially correct,

11. Jesse Prinz, *Beyond Human Nature: How Culture and Experience Shape the Human Mind* (London and New York: Norton, 2012), p. 174.

12. Experimental methods to test the ability of language to facilitate mental tasks include what is termed "shadowing," in which spoken words heard through headphones prevent "thinking aloud" in the head and seem to inhibit a range of tasks. See discussion in Prinz, *Beyond Human Nature,* pp. 174-75.

then understanding cognition is important in working out precedents for facets of language evolution and language acquisition and how this might then impact on subsequent brain development. This is particularly the case in working out the distinctive aspects of human cognition that allow a flexible acquisition of language as opposed to envisaging language as so constrained by modular mechanisms that there is little variation. But if Prinz is correct that Stephen Pinker has been tempted by the lure of the universal at the expense of a consideration of the huge variety in language formation,[13] Prinz leans toward the opposite error, namely, to deny that there are any shared cognitive capacities that are important in human language development. Language may be a human invention, but it is not an invention detached from biological precedents. The debate, therefore, needs to be about not just the subsequent variety that ensued, but about what these precedents might be, whether it be in cognition or in broader systems of communication and symbolizing, including, for example, music. So it is probably a mistake to believe that other animals "think" if this term means they have mental representations of language. But denying they can "think" in this way is still compatible with animal intelligence, if we think of that intelligence in terms of solving problems; they might even have "minds," if this is understood as the cerebral capacity required for such problem-solving intelligence.[14] A crucial question is how far the mental function in humans is an evolved capacity; while some psychologists are still skeptical about the commonality between human and other animal minds, the case for at least evolutionary elements in mental function seems much more likely than the alternative that all human mental, including linguistic, functions arose *de novo*.[15]

One of the most prevalent accounts in textbooks recounts the observation by researchers in the late 1950s that Japanese macaque monkeys learned that if sweet potatoes were washed from sand in the sea they were more palatable as food.[16] Researchers found that the practice spread to other macaques. The crucial question is: Do those macaques that take up the habit genuinely *imitate* the other macaques or do they each simply

13. Prinz, *Beyond Human Nature,* p. 190.

14. Clive D. L. Wynne, *Animal Cognition: The Mental Lives of Animals* (New York: Palgrave Macmillan, 2002), pp. 3-4.

15. In this respect, I am convinced by Wynne's argument; see Wynne, *Animal Cognition,* p. 6.

16. See, for example, Marc Bekoff and Dale Jamieson, *Readings in Animal Cognition* (Cambridge: MIT Press, 1995), pp. 99-100.

learn to do the same thing? Genuine imitation requires a theory of mind, namely, that the macaque observer considers what the other macaque is thinking and realizes why it is washing the potatoes. A simple observation of the spread of behavior will not tell us the answer. However, the *pattern* of behavior in a genuine imitation would be expected to be slow at the start and then speed up as more and more macaques copy one another. On the other hand, if the behavior was relearned each time, the spread would be much more even. Observations suggest that the latter is the case, so it seems doubtful if genuine imitation is going on. Scientists have also described behavior that is not genuine imitation but not simple relearning either, in terms of *stimulus enhancement,* so that close proximity to the actor encourages similar behavior in another as attention is drawn to the same activity. Rather similar is the idea of social facilitation, which is a spontaneous tendency to copy the other, rather than a deliberate act of imitation.

An ingenious experiment with Japanese quail in the late 1990s set out to discover if genuine imitation could take place.[17] Chana Akins and Tom Zentall set up a low treadle that could either be pecked or trodden on in order to gain access to food. Birds that observed others step on the treadle were more likely to step on it themselves compared with birds that had not observed the demonstrators. But when half the demonstrators were given food, the observers copied by stepping on the treadle but only when they observed the reward of food, indicating genuine imitation was taking place. The authors refrained from coming to the conclusion that imitation was through perspective taking, but considered the underlying mental mechanisms unresolved. Subsequently, the same research group found that pigeons are able to imitate two actions in sequence rather than one simple action.[18] Genuine imitation also seems to be taking place in other species, like marmosets and budgerigars.[19] There are, of course, difficulties in that it is impossible to know what precisely is going through the minds of other animals.[20] Suitable controls need to be set up to make sure

17. Chana K. Akins and Thomas R. Zentall, "Imitation in Japanese Quail: The Role of Reinforcement of Demonstrator Responding," *Psychonomic Bulletin and Review* 5, no. 4 (1998): 694-97.

18. Nam H. Nguyen, Emily D. Klein, and Thomas R. Zentall, "Imitation of a Two Action Sequence by Pigeons," *Psychonomic Bulletin and Review* 12, no. 3 (2005): 514-18.

19. John M. Pearce, *Animal Learning and Cognition* (New York: Psychology Press, 2008), p. 310.

20. I discussed this example briefly in chapter 2, including a theoretical virtual bird model that weighs against the possibility of a theory of mind.

that simple emulation is not taking place. This is a response to the physical properties of the container, for example, through learning about its properties, rather than genuine imitation of a living demonstrator. This can be tested by mechanically making containers move without the demonstrator being present, known as the "ghost" control.

The controversy as to how far other primates genuinely respond to the thinking of conspecifics relates to the difficulty of distinguishing between whether the subordinate observer has acted on the basis of realizing what the dominant primate might be thinking and whether it is a simple act of associative learning.[21] For example, the observation that a subordinate chimpanzee will only take food that has never been visible to the dominant may mean simply that food is not sought when the dominant is visible and food is placed in a given area, rather than that the subordinate knows that the dominant has seen the food. Derek Penn and Daniel Povinelli are particularly skeptical about whether there is any evidence for a theory of mind in other species, believing that the only really conclusive evidence is possible if behavior can be predicted without observable cues.[22]

However, even if it is difficult to show that other primates possess a theory of mind, there is growing evidence for specific aspects of mental function present in other species. The discovery in 1977 that monkeys, chimpanzees, and pigeons could exercise what is known as transitive inference, in which learning seemed to go beyond the information given, came initially as a surprise, as it was originally thought to be confined to children with relatively advanced cognitive skills.[23] This relatively developed ability may be related to the evolutionary advantage of being able to rank others successfully in the wild. It is also a cautionary tale in terms of making categorical statements based on what other animals are assumed *not* to be able to perform.

21. Associative learning is, as the name implies, a way of learning that *associates* two events with each other. Only taking food when the dominant is not present would be an associative learning process rather than the more complex idea of perceiving that the dominant has seen the food and is likely to want it, and so for *this reason,* only taking food when the dominant is absent.

22. Derek C. Penn and Daniel J. Povinelli, "On the Lack of Evidence That Non-human Animals Possess Anything Remotely Resembling a 'Theory of Mind,'" in *Social Intelligence: From Brain to Culture,* ed. Nathan Emery, Nicola Clayton, and Chris Firth (Oxford: Oxford University Press, 2008), pp. 393-414.

23. In this case, for example, if A > B and B > C, the inference is that A > C. Wynne, *Animal Cognition,* pp. 153-55.

There are also controversies around whether other animals can have reasoned behavior such as tool use, insight, or other abstract forms of reasoning. In this case, it is difficult to show what psychologists term *genuine tool use* in which an animal shows a flexible and reasoned exploitation of a tool, rather than habitual behavior. Similarly, behavioral observations that are used as evidence that other animals have the ability to reason in an abstract way or arrive at what could be termed *genuine insight* are often just as explicable through simpler theories, such as trial-and-error learning or experience. However, examples of tool use in chimpanzees involve a series of intricate actions in selecting, constructing, and employing tools. Chimpanzee termite fishing, for example, is done on termite mounds that have no visible entrances and in which the insects are deeply buried. Such termite fishing is not simply a response to the perception of insects. The chimpanzee must know the season when it is appropriate to pick open a hole and in what place to pick the hole, that is, just above the nocturnal emergence tunnel when the sexual form of the termites appears. Therefore the chimpanzee has to be able to recognize a sealed exit and only use a suitably long and flexible plant stem.[24]

Complexity of behavior, such as the tool use described above, may even be a more useful marker of ape culture than definitions of local variation that cannot be explained by ecology or genetics. Richard Byrne proposes that a hallmark of ape culture can be defined as that which shows intricate complexity of behavior and near ubiquity among a contiguous population.[25] Byrne believes that such complex behaviors are very unlikely to be discovered by a single individual and so reflect cultural learning.

Yet, aspects of animal minds that take us perhaps even closer to the possibility of language include the ability to form categories.[26] Arguably five levels of categorization exist, beginning with simple discrimination, then categorization by rote, open-ended categorization according to perceptual similarity in a class, concept formation, and abstract relations. Some scientists claim evidence for pigeons forming concepts. They con-

24. Richard Byrne, "Culture in Great Apes: Using Intricate Complexity in Feeding Skills to Trace the Evolutionary Origin of Human Technical Prowess," in *Social Intelligence*, pp. 147-60, here 152-53.

25. Byrne, "Culture in Great Apes," p. 153.

26. See, for example, Jacques Vauclair, "Categorisation and Conceptual Behaviour in Nonhuman Primates," in *The Cognitive Animal: Empirical and Theoretical Perspectives on Animal Cognition,* ed. Marc Bekoff, Colin Allen, and Gordon M. Burghardt (Cambridge: MIT Press, 2002), pp. 239-45.

ducted experiments in which pecks at images were rewarded where trees were visible, but were not rewarded in their absence. When new photographs with trees were presented, the birds showed a similar response, implying that they had worked out a category called "tree." Pigeons could also be trained to distinguish between different tree species, but not between different subspecies of oak.[27] The representation of knowledge in this case is most likely to be in the form of a "concrete code." Similar results pertain to what is termed analogical reasoning, in which chimpanzees given the correct training can work out the relationships between objects and apply them to a new context, be it in shapes or pictures of other animals.[28] Information that is of a more abstract nature develops in humans after the age of five years and concerns representations of relationships between things. Some relationships may be associative ones of familiarity with "concrete codes" rather than genuine abstractions. All or most animals can form concrete codes, but present knowledge suggests that only some primates can form abstract representations.[29] Metamemory is the ability not only to recall events, but also to have an awareness of how much might be recalled and its accuracy. Monkeys can, in experimental conditions, show that they remember and have some awareness of how much they can remember, but the results are not fully conclusive.[30] A measure of that awareness is made much easier by specific language skills, which brings us to the second topic under discussion.

Animal Communication

For Michael Tomasello, the precedent for the development of human language is not so much cognition as communication, with communication among social groups providing the trigger for such a development.[31] But

27. Pearce, *Animal Learning and Cognition,* pp. 171-84.

28. For example, a dog is to a puppy as a cow is to a calf is worked out according to analogical reasoning. Chimpanzees can show this with some training. Pearce, *Animal Learning and Cognition,* p. 187.

29. Pearce, *Animal Learning and Cognition,* pp. 187-89.

30. Pearce, *Animal Learning and Cognition,* p. 208.

31. Michael Tomasello, *Constructing a Language: A Usage Based Theory of Language Acquisition* (Cambridge: Harvard University Press, 2005). For him, the essence of language is its symbolic dimension. Here he presents a convincing battery of evidence against Chomsky's theory of universal grammar.

this means that it becomes relevant to explore the types and significance of animal communication. The simplest form of interaction among co-specifics is a stimulus followed by a response, such as the stereotypical display type. Male and female stickleback fish, for example, display an elaborate courtship ritual in response to mating instincts.[32] Communication is only properly named when one animal influences another by transmitting specific signals, but the line between a specific signal and other types of information transmission is not always easy to judge. The specific communication may not necessarily be an active process; an example of passive signaling could be the bright red color of rainforest frogs, to show that they are unpalatable. Signals use a variety of senses, including the visual, olfactory, electrical, tactile, and auditory senses. The specific message of the signal will in some cases be influenced by the environment, such as alarm calls warning of the presence of a predator, and the meaning is inferred by the behavior of the one receiving the information. In evolutionary terms, both the signaling and the receiver's response will be selected if the overall fitness is increased as a result, that is, if it has survival value.

Shettleworth argues that much of the way animal minds work is likely to be *modular,* in that developing appropriate ways of processing and using different kinds of information from a completely undifferentiated system is likely to take much too long. This is particularly true in communication between short-lived species such as ants and bees.[33] However, it seems more likely that modularity is connected with *neurobiological evolution,* rather than function, such as associative learning or numerical discrimination. This means that functionally similar behavior may result from rather different neural, molecular, developmental, or cognitive mechanisms. This is important since observations of similar behavior, such as tool use in different species, do not necessarily reflect underlying similarity in cognitive mechanisms. The way that such molecular or cognitive mechanisms have evolved will be distinct for that species according to the particular selection pressures, thus confirming the idea that each species has evolved skills to solve particular problems in a particular way.

The signals used in other animals most commonly reflect concerns about sex, predators, aggression, and food, with a fairly small signal set

32. For further discussion, see Sara Shettleworth, *Cognition, Evolution, and Behaviour,* 2nd ed. (Oxford: Oxford University Press, 2010), pp. 508-10.

33. Shettleworth, *Cognition, Evolution, and Behaviour,* p. 550.

that may be graded in intensity.[34] The signals used are usually discrete, that is, other animals rarely combine signals to create new meanings; if the combination does occur, it does not seem to connect with the original meaning of components. There are also differences in behavior of the signaler according to who is present; this is known as the audience effect, and scientists have studied this phenomenon in, for example, chickens, ground squirrels, and some primates. Eavesdroppers who seem to observe the exchange between signaler and receiver therefore influence the signaler. In this case, the term "eavesdropper," like other terms, including "mind reading," "manipulation," and "deception," has a functional, scientific meaning, rather than being connected specifically with suppositions about the particular thought processes in other animals. Peter McGregor suggests that communication should never be viewed simply as a signaler-receiver dyad, but rather in terms of networks of relationships where there is always an eavesdropper.[35] This is particularly the case where there is a high intensity of signaling, where the signal is intended for more than one receiver. But what if the behavior of the receiver changes, and this impacts the behavior of the sender? The crucial scientific question now is "whether sophisticated conditional control [of the sender's behavior] by the behavior of the receivers can be distinguished from the control of the sender's understanding of whether the receivers are getting the intended message."[36] In other words, is this being processed through cognitive processes in the sender's understanding that the receivers are or are not getting the message, or is this just an automatic reaction in response to the receivers' particular behavior? I discussed a similar problem earlier in relation to working out whether dominant and subordinate monkeys demonstrated a theory of mind in their behavior related to food acquisition.

The biological terminology used to describe communication systems in other animals is worth rehearsing briefly here.[37] If a sender reliably gives a response to an object or event compared with a generalized condition of excitement, this is known as *production specificity.* If the receiver, on the other hand, reacts even if the receiver cannot see the object or event, this is known as *context independence.* The combination of production specificity

34. Shettleworth, *Cognition, Evolution, and Behaviour,* p. 514.

35. Peter McGregor, introduction to *Animal Communication Networks,* ed. Peter McGregor (Cambridge: Cambridge University Press, 2005), pp. 1-6.

36. Shettleworth, *Cognition, Evolution, and Behaviour,* p. 516, brackets added for clarification.

37. See discussion in Shettleworth, *Cognition, Evolution, and Behaviour,* pp. 515-16.

and context independence leads to what is called *functionally referential signals.* As a rule, human beings show the capacity to go further than this and show *situational freedom* or displacement, in which food or danger can be referred to even if it is not visible to the signaler at the time. Relatively few other animals show this capacity, but the communication of honeybees is an important exception.

A particular ritualized behavior of bees known as "the waggle dance" is one communication system that has been studied in some detail. Bees who have found a food source return to a hive and, after a straight run, waggle their abdomen from side to side with an angle to the vertical that reflects the angle of the location of the food source from the sun. The vigor of the dance and the amount of buzzing also reflect the quality of the food source.[38] Later experimenters challenged the early research by suggesting that bees were merely responding to the odor on the returning bee, rather than the specific abdominal angle. In a clever experiment, researchers found a way to distinguish between the location signal from the waggle dance and the odor of the food that the bees also displayed because the angle of the dance in a lighted hive is orientated toward the light, rather than vertically. Hence, by lighting the hive, researchers discovered that the incoming bee will change the angle of the waggle according to the light, and if indeed the waggle dance is directing the behavior of other bees in the hive, then they would fly off in this direction away from the food source, rather than the direction indicated by the common odor from the dancing bee and the food source. The hypothesis was proved correct, and the bees predominantly followed the angle of the waggle dance. Covering up the photoreceptors of the dancing bee with paint added further experimental control, as then there would be no light effects on the angle of waggle. Most of the other bees in this case arrived at the site indicated by the waggle dance, indicating that the food odor is a secondary rather than a primary cue. There is also discrimination in the way that information is used according to the experience of the bees witnessing the dance. In this way, "The spatial information in the dance may primarily be used by naïve bees just beginning to forage or those that have not been foraging recently, whereas the dancer's odour or even its dancing alone serves to re-activate experienced foragers, which then visit sites they already know."[39]

38. Early experiments on bees were done by Karl van Frisch; see Shettleworth, *Cognition, Evolution, and Behaviour,* pp. 516-20.

39. Shettleworth, *Cognition, Evolution, and Behaviour,* p. 520.

Chickens have the ability to raise alarm calls and seem to discriminate between raccoons and hawks, with the number of alarm calls going up with the size of the predator.[40] However, they may also give alarm calls indicating the presence of a harmless creature, so the discrimination in this case is not all that good. Food calling in chickens might not be genuine; it might just elicit a scanning response rather than the specific information to search for food. Chickens given a few grains of food did not display such a marked scanning response to the food call, indicating that this reaction is a genuine communication about food rather than simply eliciting a scanning response. In this case, the food call would not give the receivers new information as the food had been found already, and therefore they did not display a marked response.

Vervet monkeys are able to discriminate rather better than chickens about which species are predators, but this also develops with age, even though older vervets do not seem to be involved in teaching this capacity.[41] It is also hard to tell if their alarm call represents a signal about running to trees and taking cover, or if it is genuine information about a leopard. Vervet monkeys do not seem to be all that sensitive to what those on the receiving end of their messages need to know, and they will continue to call even if their cospecifics are already safe in trees or even calling themselves. Diana monkeys protect their cospecifics by sounding alarm calls in the presence of predators. Diana monkeys, when experimentally given repeated artificial alarm calls for their predators, eagles or leopards, show a gradual habituation, that is, they become gradually desensitized to what is considered a threat when the alarm is first given. However, if only one artificial alarm is given repeatedly, then habituation is specific to that perceived threat, and not to other threats. Hence, an alarm for eagles does not diminish response to alarm signals for leopards. This, fascinatingly, suggests different underlying cognitive mechanisms for each predator.[42] Shettleworth suggests that, on the one hand, where different classes of situations requiring different responses exist, such as hiding in the case of an eagle or climbing trees in the case of a leopard, then it is more likely that functional reference to those predators will evolve.[43] On the other hand, a change in intensity of call will evolve when there is only one type of response.

40. Shettleworth, *Cognition, Evolution, and Behaviour,* pp. 521-26.
41. Shettleworth, *Cognition, Evolution, and Behaviour,* pp. 524-26.
42. Shettleworth, *Cognition, Evolution, and Behaviour,* pp. 527-29.
43. Shettleworth, *Cognition, Evolution, and Behaviour,* p. 532.

Peggy Hill suggests that vibration may be the primary means of communication in some animal groups, and it is ubiquitous in vertebrates and arthropods.[44] The receiver will detect vibration signals in the common substrate to the signaler, such as the ground. Such a skill is also reflected in the sensitivity of other animals to detect earthquakes in advance. In some cases where acoustic communication has been assumed by experimentalists, the actual communication is in fact through vibration. In woody vegetation, for example, vibration is an order of magnitude that is faster as a means of communication than acoustic methods. Vibrations are also less likely than acoustic methods to encounter confusing problems such as echoes.[45]

Talking Animals

One experimental way of trying to discern lines of continuity and discontinuity between humans and other animals is through humans trying to teach other animals human language. While controversial, the early experiments reveal some interesting facets of the human/animal boundary that are worth exploring here. Clever Hans was a horse that lived in Germany at the end of the nineteenth century who was trained by Mr. von Olsen to recognize numbers. Hans appeared to have the mathematical ability of a fourteen-year-old human being and would stomp his hoof in response to specific questions, including those that involved addition, subtraction, multiplication, and division, and including the use of integers and fractions. Stomping his foot five times, for example, followed by a pause and six stomps, meant five-sixths. He could, apparently, work out calendar dates and timing on clocks in a way that at face value seemed astonishing. He also was able to use letters in an alphabet according to a chart that showed the position of the letter according to row and column, and answer accurately questions about pictures, such as, "What is the lady holding in her hand?" Even Professor Stumpf, who was the leading psychologist of the time working at the University of Berlin, was convinced that the horse showed genuine abilities.[46] One of Stumpf's research students, Oskar Pfungst, was not sure, and he decided to observe in detail both Hans and

44. Peggy S. M. Hill, *Vibrational Communication in Animals* (Cambridge: Harvard University Press, 2008), pp. 1-8.

45. Hill, *Vibrational Communication in Animals,* p. 203.

46. Wynne, *Animal Cognition,* pp. 9-12.

his trainer. He found that Hans could only answer a question accurately if the person asking it already knew the answer and was visible to Hans. When the trainer asked Hans questions inside a tent, his performance collapsed. He concluded that the person questioning Hans bent his head in an involuntary way, and Hans had the ability to pick up this cue and respond accordingly. The account showed Hans's remarkable sensitivity to inadvertent cues rather than his specific mathematical abilities. This example shows how easy it is to be convinced that a particular behavior reflects a particular skill found in humans, whereas Hans's skill was rather different but still extremely highly developed.

Apes can also be trained in something like human language in a way that does seem to reflect genuine learning, rather than a response to human cues in the manner of Hans the horse. The language taught is sign language. Washoe the chimpanzee learned 132 signs after five years; Koko the gorilla learned 250 signs after four years; and Nim the chimp learned 125 signs after three and a half years. These are remarkable achievements, even though when compared with young humans the difference becomes clear, since Koko learned in four years what an average child could learn in one month.[47] Ape language projects are themselves controversial as they are testing the abilities of apes directly in relation to humans, even though human language came into being about 100,000 to 500,000 years ago, while humans diverged from their closest living relative about 5,000,000 to 6,000,000 years ago.[48] Hence, one would not expect common abilities in linguistic capacity to be retained given the length of time from the divergence. Clive D. L. Wynne goes further and suggests that ape language projects have generated relatively little scientific evidence of specific linguistic or comprehension skills in other animals.[49] It seems to me that the experiments also reflect a particular desire to make other animals communicate with humans in a way that is like us, rather than try and see how their own communication systems might serve their specific particular ends and goals, their own telos.

A species that is often claimed to have a language is dolphins. Dolphins use "click" sounds to navigate through echolocation. But they also have signature calls that are pure in tone and specific to a given dolphin. They are also able to imitate other sounds that they hear and can be taught to recog-

47. Wynne, *Animal Cognition,* pp. 165-70.
48. Wynne, *Animal Cognition,* p. 161.
49. Wynne, *Animal Cognition,* p. 171.

nize human systems of communication. Louis Herman and his colleagues at the University of Hawaii used two bottlenose dolphins, Akeakamai and Phoenix. Phoenix was trained to recognize noises generated by a computer, while Akeakamai was trained to recognize gestures by humans.[50] A trainer used goggles to get over the problem of possibly giving away unconscious cues and rewarded Akeakamai if she responded correctly to the gestures, and she learned around fifty signs. While the number of commands was relatively small, the researchers wanted to know if Akeakamai could show displaced reference, that is, respond to a command where the object in question was out of sight. Most of these tests were successful. A few sentences were constructed so that the meaning depended on the order of the words. In these cases, Akeakamai was tested using 193 novel sentences and performed correctly in 85 percent of cases. "Pipe hoop fetch" meant take the hoop to the pipe, while "Hoop pipe fetch" meant take the pipe to the hoop.

The possibility that dolphins in the wild have some sort of communication that is analogous to human language has since been an area of active research.[51] Signature whistles develop in the first few months of life. Female dolphins have distinct signature whistles that identify their presence to other members of their group. The young males seem to copy their mother's signature whistles, whereas young females develop their own individual calls. Males leave their group relatively early on, so it may not be as necessary for them to develop distinct calls. Much of the time dolphins imitate each other's whistles rather than expressing their own signature whistle. Frequency of use increases when they become separated from the group. This behavior may encourage group cohesion when they cannot see each other. Imitating one another's whistle may also be a way of calling a group together or requesting help. A wild dolphin that was temporarily captured used its own signature whistle frequently for the first half hour, but then

50. Louis M. Herman, Douglas G. Richards, and James P. Wolz, "Comprehension of Sentences by Bottlenosed Dolphins," *Cognition* 16 (1984): 129-219. Akeakamai means lover of wisdom. In her case gestures signaled a particular word, and when in a sequence they acted like sign language.

51. Peter L. Tyack, "Development and Social Functions of Signature Whistles in Bottlenose Dolphins *Tursiops truncates*," *Bioacoustics* 8, no. 1-2 (1997): 21-46. More recent studies are skeptical about the extent to which signature whistles reflect genuinely distinct individual calls, or merely natural variation in a common call. See Brenda McCowan and Diana Reiss, "The Fallacy of 'Signature Whistles' in Bottlenose Dolphins: A Comparative Perspective of 'Signature Information' in Animal Vocalizations," *Animal Behaviour* 62 (2001): 1151-62.

started to emit the signature whistle of the oldest member of the group. Wynne concludes that it would be wrong to describe this form of communication as a language; rather, it is a "simple system of identification calls."[52] While this might seem disappointing given the degree of intelligence displayed in learning human gestural forms of communication, the behavior in the wild needs to moderate any conclusions drawn from the more artificial conditions set up in trying to teach dolphins human language.

Parrots can also be trained to learn human language using their developed powers of mimicry.[53] Irene Pepperberg taught an African grey parrot, Alex, to recognize objects by color, shape, material, and quantity.[54] Alex was able to answer very complex questions, such as, what is the shape of the green wood? Pepperberg did not test the specific ability of Alex to use grammar, but she uncovered other cognitive abilities. All such research shows the remarkable capacity of other animals and the sheer variety and diversity of their systems of communication that are finely tuned to the specific ecological needs of each species. The lessons from history also show how careful humans need to be of drawing too hasty conclusions about the relative closeness of analogy about how human and other animal minds work, especially when discussing whether other animals can adopt human language. Humans, in their developed capacity for situational freedom in their use of language, in which an object or event can be talked about in its absence, do seem to have an enhanced capacity for deception and lying. Shettleworth believes that there is little convincing evidence that other animals deliberately signal incorrect information to each other, or that they show other forms of intentional deception.[55] However, attempts to set a clear marking boundary between humans and other animal species through language are inappropriate, for the human/other animal boundary is rather fuzzier than it might appear at first sight, where aspects of what allows human beings to express themselves in language are present in the cognitive communicative capacities of other species. But vocalization in humans is not part of an ascending trajectory from simpler species, for some species are more advanced than humans in their forms of communication even if the species are relatively simple. What is not yet certain, and a matter of

52. Wynne, *Animal Cognition,* p. 176.

53. Wynne, *Animal Cognition,* p. 173.

54. Irene Pepperberg, *Alex and Me: How a Scientist and a Parrot Discovered a Hidden World of Animal Intelligence and Formed a Deep Bond in the Process* (New York: Harper Perennial, 2009).

55. Shettleworth, *Cognition, Evolution, and Behaviour,* p. 515.

heated debate, is how far other species have elements that are in some way parallel to human language acquisition. There are significant distinctive features of *Homo sapiens* in their linguistic vocalizing capacities that shape particular features of human culture and religious expression.

Human Language

Overall, such studies on the ability of other animals to express human language show a high degree of intelligence in other species. Asking questions about whether or not languages exist in other animals may be less interesting than asking if there are *features* of human language that are shared with other species. All but the very simplest of human sentences are recursive, that is, they show patterns in patterns. An example might be: "Mary remembered the time when Sara told Isabella that she did not like driving in her car as it was very rusty." The cognitive ability to compute such complex information is not found in other species. Noam Chomsky is unusual in arguing for a sudden transition to the ability to acquire language in modern humans, pressing the case for an innate universal grammar built into the structure of human minds in a faculty that seems to be separate from other cognitive faculties. Chomsky bases his argument on the fact that children cannot learn languages by consciously forming rules since they learn far too rapidly. His solution to the problem is that language is innate. However, evidence for the existence of such universal grammar is weak, and similar results can be explained by a more generalized statistical learning approach to following certain rules that is also characteristic of other animals. Statistical approaches are also unconscious in that patterns are tabulated and then generalized, but they do not appeal to a specialist language mechanism in the brain. Even when their teachers are incompetent, as long as competency exceeds a certain minimum, rules are absorbed and applied with greater accuracy.[56] There also seems to be a period in early life when language needs to be acquired if learning is to be achieved. But this is equally explained by the possibility that the capacity for statistical learning builds up progressively, so that in infancy only simple associations are possible, building up to more and more complex

56. Prinz has examined the evidence put forward by Chomsky for innate language skills and dismantled each argument on the basis of the simpler theory of statistical learning. Overall, this argument seems convincing. Prinz, *Beyond Human Nature,* pp. 137-69.

linguistic associations. If children are deprived of social contact during the sensitive period, then by the time they are eventually exposed to language their statistical learning capacity would be too developed and so would be overwhelmed.[57] In other words, a general statistical learning capacity for following rules and actual language acquisition grow correspondingly with each other. So-called genetic defects in language acquisition seem to have more general effects on the memory of linguistic information than on the linguistic rules themselves.

A more fundamental question, perhaps, is precisely how language evolved in humans. There are different scholarly debates as to how this came about.[58] One model suggests that full syntax developed out of a simpler spoken protolanguage. The protolanguage itself would have developed from semantic representations that did not show grammar but did express themselves in phonetic vocalization. A second, alternative model is that gestural sign language developed first, including full syntactic messages, and this was followed by its expression through the medium of speech. Here the emergence of vocal delivery (speech) is synonymous with a fully developed grammatical system. Hence, while the first model implies a very simple ungrammatical language first, which then became more complex, the second model indicates that the vocalization occurred after syntax had been worked out through the use of signs. Initially, the basic unit of expression may have been manipulative rather than referential, so that, like many animal communication systems, a word such as "eagle" could invite a particular response in the hearer, rather than a deliberate reference to a particular object, in this case, a bird of prey. The problem in the specific case of the evolution of human language is which came first: syntax or words? Alison Wray asks, "how mentally adept at problem solving could we have become *without* developing language?"[59]

Phonetic production does appear to require a particular configuration of the vocal tract that at first sight seemed specific to human primates. However, the difference between humans and apes may have been exaggerated. Our unusual laryngeal arrangement may have evolved for other reasons and then was exploited by the need for phonetic expression. Other

57. This is the ingenious work of Elissa Newport, cited in Prinz, *Beyond Human Nature,* pp. 163-64.

58. For a good review, see Alison Wray, "Introduction: Conceptualizing Transition in an Evolving Field," in *The Transition to Language,* ed. Alison Wray (Oxford: Oxford University Press, 2010), pp. 1-18.

59. Wray, "Introduction," p. 4.

animals are able to perceive patterns comparable with human vowels, so it seems more likely that humans harnessed these capacities, rather than evolved them *de novo*.[60] W. Tecumseh Fitch showed, using some experiments with dogs, that the larynx in dogs becomes retracted and lowered when a dog barks, so that the capacity for speech is likely to be more pronounced in other animals compared with the simple evidence from skeletal remains. The phonetic capacity to make sounds is therefore present, even if the neural capacity underlying the structures of speech is not yet present. He suggests that "the evolution of language presumably entailed complex conceptual structures, a drive to represent or communicate them, and systems of rules to encode them. The evolution of speech required vocalizations of adequate complexity to serve these linguistic needs, entailing a capacity for vocal imitation and learning, and a vocal tract with a wide phonetic range."[61] In this he is aligning himself with the second model, in which speech *followed* linguistic needs.

There are conflicting theories about precisely how human language evolved; some argue that it appeared relatively suddenly, others that it evolved relatively slowly and emerged either from animal calls or gestures. But other questions remain, such as, what was the purpose of language? Was it primarily to facilitate thought, or was it used in social communication earlier than this? Another question relates to the relationship between speech and musical development. One particularly fascinating and original study by anthropologist Dean Falk argues that the way language emerged in humans was through the development of "motherese," that is, the babbling of a mother to her child, rather than through a drive to represent complex conceptual structures.[62] Falk goes further back in time compared with the theory talked about above regarding the development of protolanguage, and her idea is sufficiently original to be called a third alternative of how human language evolved. She believes that the focus on the recent evolution of *Homo sapiens* around 200,000 years ago makes the origin of language too recent in evolutionary history; rather, she explores the idea that this evolved at the time of the earliest human ancestor's divergence from other primates some 5 to 7 million years ago.[63] This is particularly

60. Wray, "Introduction," p. 5.

61. W. Tecumseh Fitch, "Comparative Vocal Production and the Evolution of Speech: Re-interpreting the Descent of the Larynx," in *The Transition to Language,* pp. 21-45, here 24.

62. Dean Falk, *Finding Our Tongues: Mothers, Infants, and the Origins of Language* (New York: Perseus Book Group/Basic Books, 2009).

63. Falk, *Finding Our Tongues,* p. ix.

important for our present discussion, since it puts the origin of that distinctive form of human language much further back in history when human beings were even closer in evolutionary terms to other primates. She also argues that the clues to the emergence of language can be observed in the way mothers speak to very young children; a musical-sounding motherese exists in all human societies.[64]

The basis of her argument is as follows.[65] When our ancestors began to walk on two legs in an upright stance, the relative narrowing of the birth canal meant that babies were born who were not as well developed as other primates, and these newborns could not cling to their mothers in the manner of other apes and monkeys. She believes that before slings were invented mothers had to put babies down while they gathered food; while the babies fussed, the mothers sought to soothe them with musical words, marking the beginning of protolanguage. Babies are known from our present experience to respond particularly well to music. Unlike other theorists who suggest that music was an unwanted evolutionary "spandral" emerging from speech, or those who suggest music evolved prior to speech, Falk suggests that music and speech evolved in step with each other, reflected in the gradual increase in the right and left side of the brain respectively. She believes that the remarkably early expression of artistic ability in hominins reinforces the belief that musical development emerged early on in the evolutionary record. She draws parallels with the present development of musical, linguistic, and artistic skills in early human development.

Her comparison between chimpanzees and humans is also particularly instructive. She notes that despite the close similarity between chimpanzees and humans in many aspects of behavior, chimpanzee mothers treat their infants very differently than humans treat their young, in that chimpanzee mothers are vocally nearly silent toward them, even though they are very noisy in other respects.[66] Chimpanzees of either sex are also known to kill newborns, sometimes for food, and those infants most vulnerable are those who have wandered away from their mothers. Bonobos

64. Some anthropologists have challenged Falk in suggesting the lack of universality of motherese in some societies, such as West Samoans or working-class African Americans. Closer research shows that both these groups do display motherese, even if it is moderated by some cultural constraints. See Falk, *Finding Our Tongues,* pp. 92-94.

65. Her argument is summarized helpfully in the preface; Falk, *Finding Our Tongues,* pp. ix-xi.

66. Falk, *Finding Our Tongues,* pp. 2-3.

are less aggressive, which may be related to the sexual promiscuity of females, as males are less likely to kill their own offspring. Mothers of both species are highly protective of their infants, and their infants cling to their bodies, initially on the front, but later on their backs.[67] While chimpanzees and other primates are able to express a variety of emotions through vocal or vibrational signals of varied intensity, noisy protests are largely confined to weaning, or if the baby becomes separated from its mother.[68] Some grunts are used to initiate travel, or mothers may occasionally utter soft vocalization when examining their babies. Overall, communication between mother and baby in other primates is specific to a given command or in response to difficult circumstances.

The difference between humans and other primates is that human babies learn early on to utter spontaneous vocalizations that give way to babbling. Nonhuman primates rarely kill their own offspring, but parent-inflicted infanticide is relatively common in many human cultures.[69] This practice may have emerged to allow survival of older siblings where food was particularly scarce. The cries of a human infant can signal hunger, pain, or anger that is recognizable by the mother and is designed to elicit emotions and protective responses. Yet, in industrialized societies the main reason babies cry seems to be to reestablish contact with mothers. In both humans and chimpanzees, crying, such as it exists in the latter, peaks about six weeks of age and in the late afternoon and early evening, which is when the chimpanzee mother is preoccupied with building a sleeping nest.[70] Less industrialized societies allow their infants to sleep with their parents for many years, in some cultures until children are eight years old. Falk suggests that lullabies found universally across human cultures probably emerged before motherese developed. The rhythm, regularity, and simple structure of lullabies help to shape and control the emotions of infants, and babies grasp the emotional content of the songs.

67. Falk, *Finding Our Tongues,* pp. 3-9.

68. See above, Falk, *Finding Our Tongues,* pp. 16-18.

69. Sarah Blaffer Hrdy believes this practice of parentally inflicted infanticide in early humans emerged in prehistoric times, and marks a difference from other primates, where killing of offspring from fellow primates rather than their own offspring is rather more common. Sarah Blaffer Hrdy, *Mother Nature: A History of Mothers, Infants, and Natural Selection* (New York: Pantheon, 1999), p. 519. Hrdy's credentials as a feminist scholar have sometimes been questioned in that she draws on traditional scientific methods for her anthropological works, even if asking questions in a rather different way.

70. Falk, *Finding Our Tongues,* pp. 30-31.

In considering the evolution of human language, Falk goes back to prehistory. The relatively short early hominid species *Australopithecus afarensis,* living around 3 million years ago, while walking upright, had not yet developed a narrow birth canal, and their adult and infant brain sizes were in the same range as those of chimpanzees.[71] What is also remarkable is that *Homo florensiensis,* a human species that lived on the island of Flores until around 17,000 years ago and hence was contemporaneous with *Homo sapiens,* also had an Australopithecene-like pelvis. It was only when the birth canal became much smaller that infants no longer had the ability to grip with their hands. Discovery of the *Homo erectus* skeleton in East Africa dating from 1.6 million years ago and nicknamed "The Strapping Youth,"[72] which shows a smaller pelvis size and a relatively larger cranial capacity than Australopithecene, suggests that the babies of this species were likely to have undergone considerable development in the first year. The delay in neurological development would also lead to slower motor development so that clinging onto the mother would have been increasingly difficult to achieve. Although it is not entirely clear when baby slings were invented, they were one of the earliest tools used, and in *H. erectus* were probably made of animal hides.

For Falk, the really interesting transition is the ancestor of *H. erectus* that had started to develop a narrow birth canal but had not yet invented baby slings. Narrow birth canals would select out those babies born with larger brains and favor those that had slower brain development. Falk makes the fascinating suggestion:

> Travelling mothers would have stopped periodically to relax with their babies, as ape mothers do. When foraging, however, mothers would have needed both hands to pick berries, dig for roots, or gather other resources, and "aunts" or siblings would not always have been available to hold their infants. Only one option would have remained: to put the baby down . . . the infants must have been extremely distressed by this development. . . . I believe the loss of constant contact between mothers and infants was pivotal for humankind. Most important, it helped our ancestors find their voice.[73]

71. Falk, *Finding Our Tongues,* p. 49.

72. Other nicknames are "Turkana lad" or WT 15000. The skeleton was discovered by Alan Walker and Kamoya Mimeu, and it is the earliest relatively complete skeleton known for *Homo erectus.* The cranial capacity is twice that of Australopithecene and two-thirds that of modern humans.

73. Falk, *Finding Our Tongues,* p. 55. This idea was first published in Dean Falk, "Pre-

Motherese itself is accompanied by facial expressions and body language, taking into account broader facets of social communication beyond simply verbal exchange. Motherese does not just convey information; initially, it conveys emotional meaning that contributes to infants' emotional and social maturation.[74] Motherese also contributes to linguistic development by allowing infants to become familiar with sound combinations and grammar, including words and clauses, even as it builds on the recognition of the quality and rhythm and melody of the mother's language learned even while the fetus is still in the womb.[75] Stressing syllables in spoken language, as in motherese, helps infants see where one word ends and another begins. Remarkably, six-month-old infants can distinguish all the sounds in all the world's languages, about six hundred consonants and two hundred vowels.[76] However, by the time they are a year old, the forty or so sounds important for their native tongue are perceived particularly well, while discrimination in foreign speech decreases, showing that they have become culturally bound in their listening skills.

On the basis of comparative work between humans and other species, Shettleworth rejects the general process view of how human minds work in which animal intelligence is ranked according to a hierarchy of learning processes, beginning with intelligence, through to associative learning and abstract problem solving, and culminating in the emergence of language. Shettleworth's preference for an accumulating modular view would fit in, to some extent, with Falk's hypothesis, but Falk's account also shows more precisely how the specific building blocks of human linguistic ability might have arisen in evolutionary terms. While it is controversial in that it is speculative, it seems to me to be reasonable in the light of current knowledge and more intuitively and logically satisfactory compared with the alternatives that assume the emergence of gestures prior to vocalization. The different models are not necessarily mutually exclusive. Once a musical form of language had developed, there is no reason why it could not be co-opted for other, more sophisticated cognitive tasks, and the relative flexibility of human brains was likely to be an advantage. The relationships between the capacity to symbolize and ritual, music, and what might be termed full-blown language is, however, complicated, and I will return to this issue below.

---

linguistic Evolution in Early Hominins: Whence Motherese?" *Behavioural and Brain Sciences* 27 (2004): 491-541.

74. Falk, *Finding Our Tongues,* p. 73.

75. Falk, *Finding Our Tongues,* pp. 75-76.

76. Falk, *Finding Our Tongues,* p. 78.

Controversy remains, however, concerning how far the human brain retains a modular structure characteristic of other animal species and how far it is flexible in its patterns of development. Evolutionary psychologists have tended to stress the modular Swiss army knife model of the human brain, while philosophers have tended to stress its flexibility. The Swiss army knife model is not convincing if it tries to explain all aspects of human behavior, especially the more complicated ones. There are areas of the brain that seem to be related to linguistic ability and the acquisition of languages, but this needs to be distinguished from the computational power of human brains to adapt to different conditions and to use language to express complex abstract ideas. Although some genes are associated with speech, such as the FOXP2 gene, even this gene probably has a more general function than simply permitting language development, as it is also found in other animals, including mice and birds, as well as in other tissues in the intestines, lungs, and heart.[77] The suggestion that language emerged when group sizes became too large to permit tactile grooming is also a possible facet in the development of language from its earliest beginnings; if Falk is correct in arguing that motherese was prior to protolanguage, it may be that this prompted the transition from motherese to protolanguage and, with increasing social complexity, to more developed forms of language.

Peter Munz is deeply skeptical of the ability of cognitive science to explain how the human mind works. He believes that its recourse to viewing the brain as merely a stepwise building up of information fails to consider human language's inventive capacity, and he describes language skills in humans as "three-dimensional."[78] He means by this term the ability to go beyond the information given; it is distinguished from earlier two-dimensional languages that have evolved in direct response to what is observed and are domain-specific. For him, two-dimensional languages can

77. Wolfgang Enard et al., "Molecular Evolution of FOXP2, a Gene Involved in Speech and Language," *Nature* 418 (August 22, 2002): 869-72. See also Massimo Piattelli-Palmarini and Juan Uriagereka, "A Geneticist's Dream, a Linguist's Nightmare: The Case of FOXP2," in *The Biolinguistic Enterprise: New Perspectives on the Evolution and Nature of Human Language Faculty,* ed. Anna Maria Di Sciullo and Cedric Boeckx (Oxford: Oxford University Press, 2011), pp. 100-125. This paper shows clearly how hard it is to come to solid conclusions about a firm genetic basis for language evolution; while there are certainly genetically based prerequisites, even the FOXP2 gene affects a wide range of functions other than simply language.

78. Peter Munz, *Beyond Wittgenstein's Poker: New Light on Popper and Wittgenstein* (Farnham: Ashgate, 2004), pp. 142-43.

never engage in "Imaginings, fantasies, hypotheses, guesses, hopes, and so on."[79] While his critique is appropriate where scientists are making claims beyond the evidence, I am now rather less convinced that *all* cognitive scientists commit the kinds of errors he is suggesting, in that the relative complexity of human language in its power of abstraction and reflection is recognized and acknowledged by scientists themselves, even if they might resist labeling the difference between humans and other animals in quite the way that Munz proposes.

Philip Lieberman's most recent book on human uniqueness stresses what he views as an essential characteristic of the way human minds work compared with other animals, namely, the unpredictable quality of the human mind and its flexibility. Drawing on a range of neurological evidence, he presents a strong counterargument against a modular approach to evolutionary psychology, and in this respect coheres with the more philosophically sharp critique of Peter Munz.[80] He is correct in my view to resist Chomsky's more deterministic models of language emergence. He is also right to challenge the genetic basis for human behavior presupposed in much of the work of contemporary scientists such as Stephen Pinker, Richard Dawkins, Sam Harris, and Marc Hauser.[81] While Lieberman is correct to challenge "Just So" stories in evolutionary psychology, his seeming dismissal of any useful insights on human behavior emerging from a study of early hominids seems in my opinion to be too extreme, as is his insistence that human minds are so completely different from those of other animals that their study says little about the human condition. So, according to Lieberman, our cognitive capacities may be similar to those of people living 250,000 years ago, but because humans now live in drastically different ways — different from even five decades ago, and never mind our ancestors living in the eighteenth century — that means that the way humans have acted and continue to act is both highly unpredictable and innovative.[82] But just because our lives now are clearly different from those of our forebears, does that *necessarily* prove that there are no common and consistent tendencies to act in particular ways? A combination of flexibility with at least *some* shared or universal characteristics seems more likely; otherwise, humans would have virtually nothing to learn from

79. Munz, *Beyond Wittgenstein's Poker,* p. 143.

80. Philip Lieberman, *The Unpredictable Species: What Makes Human Beings Unique* (Princeton: Princeton University Press, 2013).

81. Lieberman, *The Unpredictable Species,* p. 2.

82. Lieberman, *The Unpredictable Species,* p. 2.

human history. Further, for him, humans "think" but other animals just have "conditioned reflexes."[83] He has, therefore, in spite of his cautious approach to the most dominant voices in evolutionary psychology, fallen foul to a somewhat exaggerated form of anthropocentrism. When he does draw on a study of nearest primate relatives or earlier hominid history in his discussion, he uses it to marshal the distinctiveness of humans over against other animal kinds, rather than to stress commonality.[84] He also reverses the overall direction of evolutionary psychology by starting from the present and working backward through history. So, for example, arguments for the contemporary cultural explosion in human creativity are filtered back through particular criteria that he sets up, first through traces for its evidence in early hominids and second through its comparative lack in our nearest primate relatives.[85] His recognition of the subtle influence of culture, including gender, on the development of language is, however, of interest, most of all because he views the cultural/biological boundary as hard to discern.[86]

Munz also addresses the question of how the unique features of human language might have evolved. He believes that the increase in brain size was a crucial step. He also believes, against Terence Deacon, that the ability of humans to symbolize is not the interesting issue; the crucial question is how that symbolization differs from the ability — such as it exists — in other animals.[87] Munz proposes, controversially, and to my mind somewhat weakly, that the enlarged brain in hominids was a *liability* rather than an asset. Early hominids found themselves with a somatic marker, too large a brain, that had need of articulation, and the three-dimensional language that followed compensated in evolutionary terms for the liability imposed by the enlarged brain size.[88]

83. Lieberman, *The Unpredictable Species,* p. 20.

84. He does seem to anticipate such a criticism by noting in his final chapter in a qualified way some aspects of human behavior that have a genetic component, such as shyness/extroversion, found in chimpanzees and humans. But this is intended as a qualifier for his overall thesis that stresses human uniqueness, rather than an admission that such characteristics are of primary importance. Lieberman, *The Unpredictable Species,* pp. 189-93.

85. Lieberman, *The Unpredictable Species,* p. 147.

86. Lieberman, *The Unpredictable Species,* pp. 199-206.

87. Terence W. Deacon, *The Symbolic Species: The Co-evolution of Language and the Brain* (New York and London: Norton, 1997); Munz, *Beyond Wittgenstein's Poker,* p. 144.

88. Munz, *Beyond Wittgenstein's Poker,* pp. 144-45. A somatic marker is a term taken from Antonio Damasio, and is a "feel" without any clear definition, so a two-dimensional language is inadequate to envisage such a concept. Antonio R. Damasio, "The Somatic Marker

While Munz is caustic toward those who argue for the evolutionary advantages of an increase in brain size in humans, his own case for the evolutionary liability of the brain as a prerequisite to the evolution of human language is not all that convincing. In the first place, if an increase in brain size was a liability, why do early hominids show a progressive increase in brain size leading up to *Homo sapiens,* unless the argument is made that *only* when the brain reached a certain size in hominids did it become a somatic marker and thence simultaneously paved the way for the emergence of three-dimensional language? But if this is the case, then why was it a selective advantage for babies born with smaller brains, following the shift to an upright stance and a narrow birth canal, to continue to develop that brain *again* after birth? One would have expected that there would be no advantage in such a strategy of late maturation, unless the enlarged brain was a genuine selective advantage.

In Falk's hypothesis the early emergence of those elements required for protolanguage to begin in the first instance through the mother-baby bond, and further complexities in language development emerged later. The need to convey hopes, fears, imaginary scenarios, and so on is rather more likely in my opinion to be triggered by a mother soothing her baby than by a disorientating recognition that our brains are too big for our needs. It is, nonetheless, impossible to be definite about how far early hominids had anything approaching three-dimensional language or how far motherese existed in our earliest ancestors. What is clear, however, is that while religious belief expressed in recognizable and recorded forms emerged later in evolutionary history, and sometime after the evolution of the somatic body and brain of *H. sapiens,* it is not necessarily futile to imagine a much earlier emergence of the capacity for symbolic modes of thought and self-reflexivity.

Humanity as Symbolic Species

Anthropologist Terence Deacon is well known for his argument for the distinctive human capacity for symbol making.[89] He argues in particular that

Hypothesis and the Possible Functions of the Prefrontal Cortex," *Philosophical Transactions of the Royal Society B* 351, no. 1346 (1996): 1413-20. Marker signals arise in bioregulatory processes, including but not exclusive to feeling and emotional states.

89. Deacon, *The Symbolic Species.* The underlying evolutionary idea that behavior change impacts on evolution is also common to other animals. What is distinctive about

human language is different from other forms of animal communication and that human minds have coevolved with language; in other words, distinctive features of human minds and human communication in language run parallel in evolutionary terms. Furthermore, it is not enough just to examine the brain and work out that it provided prerequisites for the development of language; rather, Deacon proposes that the use of symbolic ideas literally changed the human brain in a positive feedback process. So "the first use of symbolic reference by some distant ancestors changed how natural selection processes have affected hominid brain evolution ever since."[90] But his readiness to use the language of uniqueness when referring to the human species is unfortunate if it implies a sudden break or oppressive sense of superiority over other animal kinds. He raises, however, one of the crucial difficulties associated with the evolution of brain and language, namely, that there is no direct access to the brains of the earliest hominid ancestors. He also believes that comparisons between human language and animal communication systems may be misleading, even if humans share in the ability to communicate through nonvocal gestures. But resisting the temptation of authors like Chomsky, who favors an innate theory of language in order to account for the complexity inherent in any language, he raises the issue that there are no simple languages in living species, so language appeared to arise *de novo* in humans. Deacon therefore names the symbolic, the ability to associate a combination of words with things, as the crucial difference between humans and other species. He argues, therefore, in favor of the existence of a much simpler language appearing in hominid prehistory *after* what he sees as the Rubicon for capacities for symbolic thinking is crossed, and this appearance of language was then followed by further development of the human brain.[91]

Words are complex in that they are capable of being interpreted in different ways and as such are known, following Charles Sanders Peirce, as interpretants. An interpretant may be a mental image, another related word, or a definition. It is the ability to elicit other words in association with the word in question that leads to the symbolic basis of word meaning, so words that are abstract like "justice," "false," and so on are symbolizing based on particular concrete experiences. Deacon draws on Peirce's

---

hominids who could symbolize was that this impacted significantly on the kinds of evolutionary pressures they then subsequently faced. This connects with the evolutionary concept of niche construction that I will discuss in more detail in the following chapter.

90. Deacon, *The Symbolic Species,* p. 322.

91. Deacon, *The Symbolic Species,* p. 45.

categorization of the semiotic relationships of icons (where there is a similarity between sign and object), indexes (where there is a correlative temporal or physical correspondence), and symbols (which are more abstract according to agreed rules). Deacon says the iconic and indexical abilities are present in other animal forms of communication.[92] For Peirce, and Deacon following him, language is a subset of signification; this contrasts with Ferdinand de Saussure's approach, which categorizes sign use as a variety of language. Viewing language as a part of a broader semiotic system is more convincing.

Deacon and other biologists, such as William Noble and Iain Davidson, assume a hierarchy in the development of signification, so that symbol formation, in which words are related to agreed conventions distinctive to human communities, develops after human communication through indexical gestures and iconic gestures.[93] Andrew Robinson, in a study that explores the world of Peircean signs in relation to theology, argues that hierarchical models of language evolution are too simplistic if they imply that indexical or iconic forms of language are simply left behind.[94] Rather, using examples drawn from modern physics, he shows that iconic signification feeds into and elaborates further the way in which symbols are used. Robinson's argument for the development of what he terms a semiotic language matrix, envisaging a combination of all aspects of semiotic development, seems convincing. Yet, to call such complex linguistic capacity the "ultimate threshold" in human evolution[95] may itself be too strong since it implies, like the symbolic model that it draws on, the importance of *one* special capacity in *Homo sapiens* that was then responsible for the cultural revolutions noted in the Upper Paleolithic

92. Deacon, *The Symbolic Species,* pp. 69-83.

93. William Noble and Iain Davidson, *Human Evolution, Language, and Mind: A Psychological and Archaeological Enquiry* (Cambridge: Cambridge University Press, 1996), pp. 218-24. The authors argue for the relatively late evolution of human language. J. Wentzel van Huyssteen follows their lead, arguing for a late appearance in Upper Paleolithic not just of language, but also of symbolism. J. Wentzel van Huyssteen, *Alone in the World? Human Uniqueness in Science and Theology* (Grand Rapids: Eerdmans, 2006), pp. 228-33. My own reading of the literature indicates that an earlier rather than later evolution for language is to be preferred; see further in note 107 below.

94. Andrew Robinson, *God and the World of Signs: Trinity, Evolution, and the Metaphysical Semiotics of C. S. Peirce* (Leiden: Brill, 2012), pp. 146-50.

95. Robinson, *God and the World,* p. 150. It would be more accurate to say that this shift represented a significant threshold in language evolution, which along with other changes contributed to an important shift in human evolution.

era. As I will be developing in the following chapter, a community niche model favors evolutionary development understood in terms of a host of factors that are themselves responsive to and yet serve to shape the conditions under which human beings became themselves. Nonetheless, a portrait of the specific evolution of human language as present in iconic and indexical representation in early hominids and gradually increasing to fully articulate speech in *H. sapiens* makes sense and is consistent with the paleontological record.

Robinson places full legisign[96] competence in early humans, including *Homo habilis* and *Homo ergaster,* with increasing use of vocal symbols in *Homo erectus* and *Homo heidelbergensis,* and fully articulate speech emerging with *H. sapiens* and possibly *Homo neanderthalensis.*[97] However, if that is the case, then the shift toward symbolic legisign capacity appeared first in *H. habilis* and so could not be used to explain the distinctive success of *H. sapiens* compared with all the other hominid species of the genus *Homo.* The advantage of this scheme, however, is that the process of acquiring language is gradual, with the possibility for symbolic articulation appearing in earlier hominids prior to vocalized language in *H. erectus.* There is

96. Legisigns are signs generated according to some rule for the purpose of signification, such as a letter or word written on paper or other medium. They express, in Peircean language, *Firstness* in that they refer to the sign vehicle itself, but *Thirdness* in that it is more than a direct correspondence but reflects a rule. If there is no rule relationship, but simply the presence of something else in a single form, such as a leaf blowing in the wind, marking the presence of the breeze, then this is called a *Sinsign:* it shows a combination of Firstness with respect to the sign vehicle and Secondness with respect to the object. The simplest relationship of all is something like a color sample, so it is a qualisign, an embodiment of the quality it represents, and thus shows Firstness with respect to the sign vehicle and object. When the relationship between sign and object is put under scrutiny, then there is a movement from the Firstness of the sign vehicle to Secondness, and that leads to icon, index, and symbolic formulation already discussed, according to Firstness, Secondness, and Thirdness respectively. However, Peirce went further than this in that he named Thirdness, which reflects not simply a relationship between sign and object but a relationship to interpretant. Here the scheme becomes a rheme in relation to Firstness, a dicent in relation to Secondness, and an argument in relation to Thirdness. The most complicated use of language, therefore, is the ability to construct an argument. For further discussion, see Robinson, *God and the World,* pp. 39-43. While ingenious, Peircean categorization of signification is complex and hierarchical, but may not even be complex enough in its description of language. Robinson's insistence that icons and indexical modes of relationship feed into the symbolic is therefore a sensible modification, though finding the evidential basis for such a shift is far more challenging.

97. Robinson, *God and the World,* p. 151.

some evidence that Neanderthals had the hyoid bone required for speech.[98] Even if *H. neanderthalensis* could also express fully articulate speech, this does not contribute to the explanation of the relative success of coexisting *H. sapiens*. If full-blown language is of genuine evolutionary importance, it is more likely to have been in its distinctive form in *H. sapiens*. Ian Tattersal is skeptical about any claim for symbolic thought in pre–*H. sapiens* ancestors, believing that evidence, such as the existence of hand axes or shelters built by *H. ergaster* and *H. heidelbergensis* respectively, is not conclusive evidence for symbolic thinking.[99] He also recognizes the difference between *H. neanderthalensis* and *H. sapiens* in terms of the latter's ability to remake the world. The increased cultural complexity coincident with the ability to combine different semiotic phases through symbolic communication and iconic representation still does not explain why this shift occurred when it did, or the selection pressures that prevailed at the time. For Deacon, the Upper Paleolithic revolution was dependent on behavioral changes forced by external pressures from climate and ecology; for Robinson, it was dependent on a new complexity in semiotic competence; for Tattersal, it was the *de novo* appearance of symbolic thought and language, even if anatomically modern humans were around 200,000 years ago. How far that new competency might be related to the capacity for "doodling" in the way Robinson suggests is highly speculative,[100] but the benefits of such an approach are that it puts more emphasis on the playful, imaginative

98. David Frayer was one of the first to argue for Neanderthals being capable of speech based on the discovery of the hyoid bone from a 60,000-year-old Neanderthal specimen from the Kebra Cave in Israel. See David Frayer, "Cranial Base Flattening in Europe: Neanderthals and More Recent *Homo sapiens*," *American Journal of Physical Anthropology*, suppl. 14 (1992): 77. Other anthropologists vehemently resist this, arguing that the soft tissue of the larynx will never fossilize and so it cannot be demonstrated. Spencer Wells believes that the possibility of speech is a possibility that has not as yet been disproved. Spencer Wells, *Pandora's Seed: Why the Hunter-Gatherer Holds the Key to Our Survival* (London: Penguin Books, 2011), p. 100. FOXP2 genes have also been found in Neanderthal remains, indicating that the genetic prerequisites for speech were present. John Shea, "*Homo sapiens* Is as *Homo sapiens* Was: Behavioral Variability versus 'Behavioral Modernity' in Palaeolithic Archaeology," *Current Anthropology* 52 (2011): 1-35.

99. Ian Tattersal, "A Possible Context for the Emergence of Human Cognitive and Linguistic Abilities," *Euresis* 4 (2013): 31-39.

100. Robinson, *God and the World*, p. 155. Robinson argues that speech allowed our hands to be freer from their previous use as a means for making gestures, so permitting a combination of iconic and symbolic representation. Although offering fairly weak evidence, he points out that abstract geometric forms that coexist with the Paleolithic cave art lend support to his speculations (p. 156).

aspect of human behavior that tends to be missed out in discussions on the evolution of language. It also implies a shift in capability sometime after anatomically modern *H. sapiens* appeared that is hard to explain.

Alan Barnard also notes the difficulty of mapping the evolution of language. But his stress is not so much on communication as on the ability of language to facilitate thought, rather than communication, a distinction that leads to "I language" and "E language" respectively.[101] I language is about narrative and mythology, about entering a world that is more than simply a practical discussion about hunting, gathering, tool making, and so on.[102] But Barnard uses symbolic thought in a looser sense than that confined to Peircean representative categories of language-object relationships. Rather, it seems to refer to the generalized ability to think in a more abstract or even in an aesthetic and mystical way through use of an inner language of thought.[103] In this way, symbolic thought for Barnard is not simply confined to linguistics, but points to a different way of being in a social community.[104] The advantage of this scheme is that it opens the door for ritual and other performative practices in shaping symbolic ways of being in the world, so mythology and ritual are in mutually reinforcing relationships to one another. For him, "symbolic humanity represents a stage of thought beyond the material."[105] By that he means that what is referred to is not simply connected with the practical day-to-day means of survival, though if "beyond" implies some kind of restriction to antimaterial gnostic speculative claims for truth, this would also be a distortion. But, like the other writers discussed above, Barnard agrees that symbolism preceded syntax and language formation. What is particularly interesting, however, is that Barnard places music, ritual, and art in between symbolic thought

101. Alan Barnard, *Genesis of Symbolic Thought* (Cambridge: Cambridge University Press, 2012). Barnard names "I language" as used by Noam Chomsky to characterize internal language associated with thinking; so for him it is "language in the guise of cognitive science," while "E language" is external language used in communication (p. 84). Barnard also raises in this context the possibility of "P language," Platonic language, existing as a detached language independent from people. I am less sure that such a language makes sense, since Platonic forms of language still communicate something about the social worlds that humans occupy; that is, it would be very difficult to presume a purely abstract language form that has no relation at all with human experience.

102. This distinction coheres with the earlier discussion above of language as a means for cognition.

103. Barnard, *Genesis of Symbolic Thought,* pp. 1-5.

104. Barnard, *Genesis of Symbolic Thought,* p. 87.

105. Barnard, *Genesis of Symbolic Thought,* p. 96.

and language acquisition. This makes sense of language as a way of thinking about the significance of particular practices.

Another more intermediary hypothesis is that of Stephen Mithen, who argues that music was crucial in the development of language. In his highly original book *The Singing Neanderthals,* the "Hmmmmm"-ing of Neanderthals in Europe coexisted with the emergence of linguistic humans.[106] But Mithen makes the evolution of the FOXP2 gene critical for language acquisition; while he is cautious about attributing all linguistic ability to one gene, he is convinced of its genetic basis. In the light of the earlier discussion about language development and symbolic thought, it seems to me rather more accurate to argue for a biological prerequisite for vocalized language formation, for such results do not readily explain why vocal language began to be used, but rather how it was biologically possible that such language could evolve. Mithen specifies that the earliest known symbolic engravings from the Blombos Cave are 70,000 years old, but he thinks language evolution occurred much earlier than that. Large quantities of red ochre from Klasies River Mouth Cave on Cape Coast in South Africa are in deposits of 125,000 years ago, and some pieces show up as "pencils." He argues, furthermore, that red is an ambiguous color in nature, hence it was most likely the first color used in a symbolic way. For Mithen, the earliest vocalized language found in *Homo ergaster, Homo heidelbergensis,* and *Homo neanderthalensis* was holistic, manipulative, multimodal, musical, and mimetic; hence, he calls this the "Hmmmmm" theory.[107] Philip Lieberman offers a variant on Mithen's thesis. Unlike Mithen, he strongly resists a modular structure of the brain, as discussed earlier, but also through his own research he has attempted to prove that the structure of the Neanderthal vocal tract and tongue position is such that they could not have produced vowel sounds *i, u,* and *a,* all of which are needed for more effective vocal speech.[108] The advantage of the musical

106. Steven Mithen, *The Singing Neanderthals: The Origins of Music, Language, Mind, and Body* (London: Orion/Phoenix, 2005), pp. 246-65.

107. An alternative protolanguage to the Hmmmm theory is that words appeared first but without grammar. This is also speculative, but it seems to me to be less convincing, since the primary selection pressure for vocalization is the demands of social life, and a holistic language involving sound related to specific tasks rather than nongrammatical language is best suited to this function. Holistic language is where none of the syllables used map onto a particular action in a specific way, but the sound signifies a specific task to be done or action performed. Mithen, *The Singing Neanderthals,* pp. 147-49.

108. Lieberman, *The Unpredictable Species,* pp. 137-40.

theory of Mithen is that it ties in with Falk's theory of language evolution that builds on motherese but is less specific. In other words, motherese was just one of the musical types of language that were around in the earliest ancestors. Much of this is, of course, speculative, as it is a debate about whether the first real word was "Mama" or "Yuk," alerting the infant to repellent materials such as rotting meat or feces.[109]

Toward a Theology of Human Language

If one of the key biological differences between modern humans and other animals is the ability of human beings to think at some distance from specific visceral needs, then theology is, to use Peircean categories, at bare minimum Thirdness, about interpretation of Firstness and Secondness, and, perhaps beyond that, Fourthness, the interpretation of interpretation.[110] Such a view ties in with Barnard's interpretation of a preliminary symbolic thought giving way to ritual, language, and eventually mythological thought, which in turn requires more and more complex language formation.[111] In this sense, theology could be seen as a crowning moment in human linguistic development; at the same time, it is still an ambiguous gift, carrying with it the possibility of oppression as well as liberation.[112]

109. Mithen favors the "Yuk" hypothesis, though Falk argues for the "Mama" hypothesis. See Mithen, *The Singing Neanderthals,* pp. 203-4.

110. Peirce did not suggest a category of Fourthness. I am suggesting this playfully as a way of showing how theology works to reflect on third-order reflections and arguments.

111. Barnard uses the term "P" (Platonic) language to refer to language developed in the absence of other agents. Barnard, *Genesis of Symbolic Thought,* p. 84. This is somewhat unfortunate if it implies that religious language is like that, somehow detached from the material and everyday relationships. Rather, mythological language sought to make sense of these relationships and give them deeper meanings by linking them to particular myths.

112. Deacon names the mystical or religious imagination with its capacity to reflect on the significance of mortality as "the source of what is most noble and most pathological in human behaviors. . . . But the dark side of religious belief and powerful ideology is that they so often provide twisted justifications for arbitrarily sparing or destroying lives. Their symbolic power can trap us in a web of oppression, as we try through ritual action and obsessive devotion to a cause to maintain a psychic safety net that protects us from our fears of purposelessness." Deacon, *The Symbolic Species,* p. 437. While no doubt indicating an atheistic bias in his assessment, the type of practice he envisages here is an unthinking practice that resists reason, which is a good reason for arguing in favor of theology as reasoned reflection on practice. Where theology resists reason, it amounts to fideism, and such theologies could be oppressive.

But theology from within a religious perspective is more than simply a sophisticated form of symbolizing; if it were flatly that and that only, it would amount to a form of idolatry.[113] Religious symbols expressed in theological language are an attempt to articulate profound religious experiences, but they are always broken in that their attempts always fall short of the experiential revealed reality that they seek to embody. A variation in what might be called the flattening out of religious symbolic thinking to finite explanations is attempts to explain the differential language of revelation through altered states of consciousness, as if such states induce the imagination to act in specific ways and as if that can account for the content of the beliefs that emerge.[114]

Theology is necessarily abstract in its deliberations, but that does not mean that the content of religious practices that are the subject of its reflection is similarly detached or mythological in form. So there is a danger in associating religion just with advanced mythological forms of thinking in that it tends to detach from the very social and communicative practices of love and relationships that are the core reasons for its success. Compassion for others and the ability to articulate what that meant fuel religious experience and practices along with associated theological discourse as much as abstract notions about the meaning of God as Creator. Those persons who are cognitively impaired in their ability to communicate verbally are still able to communicate through showing nonverbal cues to express affection or distress. In the so-called advanced societies in the West, where the level of cultural complexity has tended to distance human beings from each other, the simpler forms of communication found among those with cognitive impairments arguably offer an opportunity for the reeducation of those who have become too abstracted from the concerns of everyday living. In the practice of the worldwide

113. Interpretations of religious symbols as simply instances of symbolic thought forms are therefore, according to this view, idolatrous, for religious revelation is equated with finite forms in which it is expressed through symbol. Robert Cummings Neville, *The Truth of Broken Symbols* (Albany: State University of New York Press, 1996), pp. ix-xi.

114. As found in, for example, William Downes, *Language and Religion* (Cambridge: Cambridge University Press, 2011), pp. 249-50. The assumption in this case is that altered states of consciousness account for the change in content of language in a particular way. Further, the assumption is that such experiences require detachment from the everyday, so "Images of and dialogue with imagined supernatural powers — mediated by the prophet/shaman — resolve inconsistencies in a validating context unconstrained by the actual world" (p. 250).

network of the L'Arche communities, for example, where those with learning difficulties and those without share their lives together, the emphasis is on the mutual healing experienced through togetherness and welcoming the stranger, rather than developing a culture simply emerging from philosophical abstraction.[115] I am not arguing that philosophy is unimportant — far from it — but rather that theology as a discourse carries within its heart a corrective in relation to the concrete that is arguably lacking in analytical forms of philosophy. A theology of language, therefore, to be true to the variety of forms of communication among human beings, including those who have impaired functions, needs to be able to take into account the religious benefits of that variety, and the way God can be experienced within those communities where language does not necessarily show the high level of abstract and grammatical complexity that it is capable of expressing.

In a similar fashion, it is possible to argue that the presence of God can be felt where boundaries between seemingly different others are pushed to one side and the common ground of creatureliness and communication between and with others comes to the fore instead. Just as I argued that we need to recognize the possibility of intermorality in the previous chapter by recognizing the shared evolutionary basis for an intertwined world of human and other animal normative practices, so too human language becomes richer when understood in relationship with other animal minds. I dealt with the variety of those minds and the variety of the different possible communication pathways above, yet even within one species there will be considerable variation in the way each animal thinks and communicates. The diversity is immense and something to celebrate. For that diversity leads to the possibility of rich forms of interaction and communication with other species. It is no accident that some of the earliest recorded examples of cave art are representations of other animals. That is not to suggest that humans throughout history have had an affiliative relationship with other species. Practices among human communities toward other animals are extremely diverse. What I am suggesting is that human language, including the language of theology, was shaped at least in part by a knowledge and awareness of commonality with and yet difference from other animals. The human-animal boundary has

115. The therapeutic power of living in such communities is attested by Matt Edmunds in his book *A Theological Diagnosis: A New Direction on Genetic Therapy, "Disability," and the Ethics of Healing* (London: Jessica Kingsley, 2011), pp. 179-95.

fascinated human beings throughout recorded history,[116] but this reflects a latent interest that would have developed much earlier than this in our early ancestors. Although it would be speculative to postulate when the first humans recognized other species in word form, what in the Genesis scriptural account is traditionally viewed as the naming of the animals, it is likely to be early in terms of the lexicon of words used. Young children consider other animals to be agents just like humans, so it is possible that the earliest hominids thought of them as having agency as well.

The tradition of human beings keeping companion animals is as ancient as *Homo sapiens* itself, thus showing the ability of two species to live together and find ways of communicating with each other without necessarily sharing a common language. Stephen Clark suggests that companion animals become incorporated into familial relationships,[117] and in this sense familial bonds may be more powerful than those generated through linguistic means alone. I am not suggesting by this that this common bond in creatureliness elides the differences between human beings and other animals. Although there is a strong temptation to think of other animals as having similar cognitive capacities to humans, it is rather more compassionate to be realistic about what is known from comparative cognitive research on other animal minds, as well as their capacity for communication, and reflect this in our theological approaches to other animals. Theological language *about* other animals should not, therefore, adopt animals as if they were simply young or immature members of our own species.[118] Indeed, if we do make this comparison, it could be damaging to the status of other animals, since when measured up against the specific capacities

116. See, for example, Angela Creager and William Chester Jordan, eds., *The Animal-Human Boundary* (Rochester, N.Y.: University of Rochester Press, 2002).

117. For a good summary of his view, see Stephen Clark, "Enlarging the Community: Companion Animals," in *Introducing Applied Ethics,* ed. Brenda Almond (Oxford: Blackwell, 1996), pp. 318-30. Clark, interestingly, argues that the ability to relate to other animals well would have been a selective advantage, and domestication may have happened by humans selecting in those animals characteristics that were appreciated in their own young (pp. 321-22). This is different, of course, from the suggestion that it is ethically responsible to treat them as if they were our young.

118. Andrew Linzey does this in his discussion of other animals as comparable with human children. This to my mind is a mistake since this is a weak metaphor; the only comparison being that both are under the care of human others, rather than any analogy of responsibility toward other animals. See Andrew Linzey, *Why Animal Suffering Matters: Philosophy, Theology, and Practical Ethics* (Oxford: Oxford University Press, 2009), pp. 36, 151-68.

of children, even alloprimates show far weaker capabilities. Instead, our comparison should reflect on the degree to which other animals have developed unique capacities to solve particular problems within their own worlds.[119]

What, then, are we to make theologically of the particular uniqueness of human culture in its relative plasticity and interpretation of others' actions, not just on the basis of past competition or cooperation, but on the basis of networks of belief and ability through language to develop metarepresentational concepts? Language serves to foster a culture in human beings that has both a behavioral and a cognitive differentiation and flexibility that far outstrip those of other animals. Humans can, therefore, actively shape their environment in a way that goes far beyond that found in other animals. Even where we find common elements of behavior between human beings and other animals, it is often difficult to reach any certainty about the commonality of underlying cognitive mechanisms.

Evolutionary issues aside, the contribution of theology in developing symbolic language about religious belief and a way of expressing that belief is a qualified dependence on language. That language permits different facets of theology to emerge over time and distance from the historical events themselves. The Synoptic Gospels, for example, are very different in flavor than the later Johannine account, the latter reflecting a greater degree of abstraction and reflection in the light of philosophical Hellenistic ideas than the former. The powerful symbolic force of the Word/Logos that became flesh and dwelt among us in John's account serves to generate a paradox: the transcendent God envisaged as greater than human beings now dwells in the material flesh of human form. The language put into the mouth of Jesus according to the Johannine Gospel account reflects the powerful symbolic images of his status as both human and divine: he describes himself as the Way, the Bread of Life, the Truth, the Light, and so on. The question now becomes: Does such language serve to *distance* the figure of Jesus from human culture, or does it *ennoble* it by showing forth the particular capacity of human beings in a way that expresses the deepest religious truth as that which befits the particular capacities for symbolic

119. This is a theme repeated again and again in the biological literature, not least in commentaries on the unique aspects of human language. See Louise Röska-Hardy, "Introduction — Issues and Themes in Comparative Studies: Language, Cognition and Culture," in *Learning from Animals: Examining the Nature of Human Uniqueness,* ed. Louise S. Röska-Hardy and Eva M. Neumann-Held (Hove, U.K., and New York: Psychology Press, 2009), pp. 1-12.

language characteristic of the human species? I am inclined to think the latter, that is, that the Gospel of John exemplifies a particularly *human* way of expressing religious belief, even if it is certainly not the *only* way of expressing that belief. Furthermore, John's Gospel reflects an implicit sophiological structure in that it echoes the language of Sophia that has an ancient religious pedigree, worked out through centuries of religious reflection and struggle.[120] In addition, even if the theological language used is highly symbolic, that does not necessarily imply either a dualistic approach to the material world or that a distancing from other creaturely kinds will follow in its wake. Further, such abilities have to be set in the context of human beings in community, rather than envisaging such abilities as characteristic of individuals in isolation. It is therefore to the crucial idea of cooperation in community that I turn in the chapter that follows.

120. See Celia Deane-Drummond, *Creation through Wisdom: Theology and the New Biology* (Edinburgh: T. & T. Clark, 2000), pp. 48-52.

CHAPTER SIX

Evolving Social Worlds: Theo-Drama and Niche Construction

I am now coming to what is arguably one of the pivotal arguments in this book, namely, how to think about the human in and through the significance of how humans are perceived to act, understood as a conversation between specific evolutionary perspectives and a specific way of framing theological discourse on the human. The introduction to this chapter necessarily lays out aspects of the evolutionary literature that will inform this discussion as a way of setting up an opening for a fruitful conversation. The selection of literature on evolution used will of necessity be restricted, but still is, I will maintain, consistent with a respectable and emerging consensus in evolutionary theory. The particular evolutionary focus I have chosen for this chapter will be the broader one of cooperation and the evolution of conscience as significant for religious experience, rather than the evolution of religion as such. I lay out where the evolution of religion arguments are situated in relation to this work in chapter 1, and I do not wish to be distracted by that here. I also build on a discussion of the evolution of morality and the evolution of language fleshed out in the two prior chapters. This chapter sets the stage for a more detailed discussion of altruism that follows in chapter 8.[1]

1. One of the issues of confusion is that "altruism" is used in biological terms to denote particular behavioral consequences, which seem on the surface to be negative in relation to reproductive consequences, whereas when this term is used to describe the moral life, it often includes a concern for positive motivating factors. See further discussion in chapters 4 and 8. Cooperation is a wider category that when used in a biological sense includes both altruism and collaboration. The main focus of this chapter is collaboration and cooperation, rather than altruism as such. I also tend to avoid using the terms "cost" and "benefit," as they are associated with utilitarian frameworks, even though such usage is common in the

What I am attempting in this chapter, instead, is to draw out facets of the evolutionary questions related to *why* humans have the kinds of complex social and cultural worlds that they do, and offer a theological interpretation.[2] In order not to tie this discussion into any one specific scientific approach, and to give a flavor of the dynamism across the range of scientific evolutionary approaches and its emerging horizons, I have tried to give a sample of the different scientific discussions and competing ideas, ranging from evolutionary biology to cultural anthropology, rather than to be exhaustive in any one specialist area. This is deliberate insofar as the theological discourse I am attempting to develop also attempts to look at the broad sweep of how humans interact and engage with each other as part of a wider understanding of what that interaction entails, namely, as participants in a theo-drama.

The more constructive theological task is also situated in the context of efforts by contemporary theologians to develop a theological anthropology that has ethical import, first in David Kelsey's theological anthropology, *Eccentric Existence,* and second in Sarah Coakley's Gifford Lectures. My own preference for understanding human meaning theologically is through a theo-dramatic interpretation of human existence, developing strands of thought in Hans Urs von Balthasar, but taking these strands in a new direction. I will argue that such a constructive approach to theology bears an analogous relationship with the anthropological and ecological idea of niche construction, which is becoming increasingly more prominent in evolutionary thought. Furthermore, and significantly, such niche construction should not be thought of as detached from other animal kinds, but in some sense *entangled with* them. This renders the theo-dramatic task *inclusive* rather than *exclusive,* a way of seeing God in relation to humans and other creaturely kinds in terms of dynamic performance, incorporating insights from evolutionary science, while being aware of different methodological presuppositions. The relationship between theological and particular biological modes of expression is, I suggest, an analogous one. Hence, just as discourse about God is in some sense analogous to what can be found and discovered in the human sphere, so theologi-

---

scientific literature, and it is sometimes difficult to avoid when speaking about evolutionary function such as fitness.

2. Even within these limitations, this area is incredibly complicated, so when encountering this literature for the first time, one is apt to feel adrift in a sea of interconnecting and in some cases competing theories, some of which are supported by a priori mathematical analysis, while others emerge from observation and field data.

cal discussion bears a similar relationship with secular anthropology: it is a reasoned interpretation of that discourse through the lens of faith. In this way, an understanding of the human through theological reflection can never be reduced to or contained within evolutionary biology in the manner that is sometimes portrayed in theistic evolution, even though there are family resemblances in both discourses that help us articulate in a richer way what it means to be human.

Introduction

So where to begin? In the vast literature on evolutionary biology currently available, even those who have prior training in biological science can feel overwhelmed by the sheer diversity of data, alongside competing theories jostling for the pole position. Of course, some evolutionary biologists might say that such a myriad of opinions merely reflects the diversity of meme variants that are currently available, and that those that survive through history are selected for in evolutionary terms. Yet, it is relatively rare for scientists to turn the focal lens back on themselves and describe their own mythmaking in terms of evolutionary symbol systems. This seems to be because evolutionary theorists have a strong sense of being critical realists, as articulated by philosopher Roy Bhaskar,[3] that what is under discussion in evolutionary biology reflects something about the concrete truth of the world that is more than simply human constructive abstractions of it.

With this qualifier in mind, I wish to emphasize what I consider one of the most important discussions in evolutionary biology in recent years, summarized helpfully in Eva Jablonka and Marian Lamb's *Evolution in Four Dimensions*.[4] The kernel of their argument is as follows. First, as in most books on evolution, their focus is on heredity. However, they broaden out an understanding of heredity understood in neo-Darwinian terms by going beyond genetic analyses. Contrary to common perceptions associated with the random mutation of genes, they suggest that *some* heritable variations are nonrandom in origin, including information acquired during the lifetime of the individuals concerned. Finally, they argue that heritable evo-

3. Roy Bhaskar, *A Realist Theory of Science* (London: Verso, 1997).

4. Eva Jablonka and Marion Lamb, *Evolution in Four Dimensions: Genetic, Epigenetic, Behavioral, Symbolic Variation in the History of Life* (Cambridge: MIT Press, 2005).

lutionary change does not simply follow genetic selection; it also follows from *instruction* between individuals. Their diagnosis of the problem to date stems from what might be termed a narrow neo-Darwinian restriction in the mechanism of evolutionary theory following a strictly reductionist interpretation in terms of the mutation of strands of deoxyribonucleic acid (DNA) followed by natural selection. Epigenetics has shown that not all information passed to the next generation is in the form of DNA, and they label this the second form of inheritance. The third form of inheritance is perhaps more difficult to fathom in that it is behavioral and is passed from one individual to the next. The final form of inheritance is that of symbolic systems, as discussed in the previous chapter, and is arguably unique to the human species.

The point is that evolution by natural selection works on heritable variation, and that this variation can arise from different means, only one of which is strictly genetic. Of course, there will always be those biologists who seek to explain the other three systems of variation in the terms of the first, that is, genetic inheritance, as in the early work of sociobiologists such as E. O. Wilson, who envisaged culture as being kept firmly on a "leash" of genetic restraint. Inasmuch as genes set up certain broad parameters or finite limitations within which such variation can exist, there is some truth to this statement. But I suggest that it is a clarification rather than a confusion to name four distinct dimensions of variation, since they will have their own dynamics that are not identical to that arising out of the first system of inheritance traditionally framed through the selection of genes, or even the subsequent impact of different environments and stages of development on the expression of those genes.

Such a new view of evolutionary theory relieves the pressure often felt by those in the humanities when engaging in dialogue with evolutionary biologists "because it is no longer necessary to attribute the adaptive evolution of every biological structure and activity, including human behavior, to the selection of chance genetic variations that are blind to function."[5] Significantly, too, the language used here is *dimensions* of evolutionary selection, which implies that different evolutionary processes are to some extent entangled. Hence, what is going on at the genetic level is distinct from but, at the same time, consistent with what is happening at the epigenetic, behavioral, and symbolic levels. Consistency is not the same as explanatory focus, so that what is significant at the symbolic level may be meaningless

5. Jablonka and Lamb, *Evolution in Four Dimensions,* p. 2.

at the genetic level, and vice versa. One of the frustrations of those trained in the humanities reading some renditions of evolutionary psychology is its seeming reluctance to let go of the first dimension in favor of the second, third, and even fourth dimensions of evolution. And those philosophical commentators on science have sometimes accused it of a univocal approach to reality that excludes other ways of knowing and being in the world.[6] What seems to be happening here, however, is an *internal critique* within evolutionary science as such that opens up not just different ways in which genes are passed down from one generation to the next, but different patterns and modes of inheritance as well.[7] Of course, many of these ideas are not completely new and were aired as far back as when Lamarck first posited his scientifically respectable interpretation of inheritance alongside Darwinian alternatives of pangenesis.[8] The point is that even the first dimension of inheritance is proving rather "looser" in terms of its dynamics. So-called "causal" relationships between genes and behavior are based on correlative studies that may lead to misleading deterministic views of an inheritance of behavior or disease along with associated ethical alarm bells.

Yet, more interesting still is the idea that variations in *phenotype* are themselves subject to selection processes and, like genotypes, phenotypes act as inheritance systems in their own right.[9] This is particularly important once the evolution of social worlds is considered, since phenotype includes behavioral differences. Socially mediated learning includes the passing down of practices within the family. Jablonka and Lamb introduce this idea through mythical creatures called "tarburniks," a play on the Jewish

6. Nicholas Lash, *The Beginning and End of Religion* (Cambridge: Cambridge University Press, 1996), p. 80.

7. I have discussed this aspect in Celia Deane-Drummond, ed., *Brave New World: Theology, Ethics, and the Human Genome* (London: T. & T. Clark, 2003). However, what is new and significant in this context is that what might be termed the new dynamic form of molecular biology and the highly complex regulation of these genes along with specific environmental influences on mutation, for example, has not percolated sufficiently into discussions of evolutionary biology, which tend to hold on to a description of the gene as a unit of inheritance that changes in frequency in response to random mutations. Furthermore, if the genome acts as a unit, rather than as a collection of discrete genes, this opens up the possibility of a *directed* form of genetic change, rather than one that is entirely random.

8. For a discussion of Lamarck, see Jablonka and Lamb, *Evolution in Four Dimensions*, pp. 12-27.

9. Genotype is the sum total of the genetic endowment of an organism, while phenotype is what can be observed, traditionally thought of in terms of outward expression of genotype, though that assumes a close linkage between genotype and phenotype.

word for "culture." In this scheme, children who are introduced to a food substance by their mothers will find that they have an automatic preference for that food as an adult. The basic insight here is that individuals can learn from the experiences of others. This is not intended to imply an active or intentional passing on of information, but rather it is passed on to others who are in the same social environment. This applies to habits, skills, and preferences and is not just within kin, but can be beyond this as well. Diversity of behavior, such as mating preferences or changes in alarm calls, will impact on evolutionary fitness, but behavior could be mediated through shifts in "cultural" processes acquired through social learning. In this case, a definition of culture is "a system of socially transmitted patterns of behavior, preferences, and products of animal activities that characterize a group of social animals."[10] Socially mediated learning, on the other hand, is defined as "a change in behavior that is the result of social interactions with other individuals, usually of the same species."[11] This is one behavioral inheritance system (BIS); there are three.

The first BIS could be classified as a simple transfer of behavior-influencing substances, such as preferring carrots over juniper berries. It is well known that mothers who consume certain foods will influence the food preferences of their offspring.[12] Strict *socially mediated* learning depends on observing the behavior of experienced others and using that information to adopt a similar behavior. Early on in life young chicks will "imprint" the first large moving object that they see, and follow that devotedly. They will also model a choice of mate on that of the image of their parents, in some cases leading to later attempts to mate a human carer. As adults many different species will adopt more complex behaviors that follow from observing the activities of others. In the United Kingdom, for example, where milk is commonly delivered to households in bottles with small aluminum foil tops, blue tits discovered that they could remove the lid and drink the creamy milk from the bottle. This habit started to spread in the population and was widespread by the 1940s. The way that tits opened up the bottles was diverse, showing that this was not an example of imitation; rather, each bird used the information acquired from observation and found its own way of breaking open the bottle tops. Other behavioral practices, such as singing in whales and birds, are passed on by

10. Jablonka and Lamb, *Evolution in Four Dimensions,* p. 160.
11. Jablonka and Lamb, *Evolution in Four Dimensions,* p. 161.
12. Jablonka and Lamb, *Evolution in Four Dimensions,* pp. 162-65.

genuine imitation, classified as the third BIS, in which individuals copy the behavior of the one observed. The point is that it is the *behavior* that is passed on, irrespective of the underlying genotype, so that small alterations in song, for example, can spread in subpopulations and increase variety accordingly. But the genotype also sets the broad framework in which particular learning can take place, so that some species such as birds always learn songs easily, while other species do not; canids, to give another example, have a highly developed sense of smell that is prior to their recognition of specific communication of olfactory signals. In the specifically human case, imitation is not "blind" but intentional and goal directed, and this depends on the relative sophistication of mental processes. Jablonka and Lamb comment that one of the most striking aspects of almost all cases of behavioral inheritance systems is "the active role that the animals play in acquiring and transmitting information."[13] Direct roles would include active teaching, but indirect roles are significant also, so that animals actively participate in shaping the environment in which they are selected.

I will return to this idea of "niche construction" below, as it is crucial for the argument. Broader issues than simply BISs are also at stake here, for the sheer mobility of animals and their plastic response to new situations are important in shaping the possibilities on which evolution by natural selection can act, whether at a genetic, epigenetic, or behavioral level. So, according to Patrick Bateson and Peter Gluckman,

> Organisms were doubtless usually passive in the initial stages of biological evolution driven by environmental change, but they could also have been active. This is the key conceptual point in understanding how plasticity and behavior can drive evolutionary change. By their mobility, in the case of animals, or facility to disperse, in the case of plants . . . organisms often expose themselves to new conditions that may reveal heritable variability and open up possibilities for evolutionary changes that would not otherwise have taken place.[14]

Also important in setting the scene for what follows is the concept of "entanglement" between different species, so that, particularly in the

13. Jablonka and Lamb, *Evolution in Four Dimensions,* p. 176.

14. For a specific discussion of freedom and agency, see chapter 3. Patrick Bateson and Peter Gluckman, *Plasticity, Robustness, Development, and Evolution* (Cambridge: Cambridge University Press, 2011), p. 103.

field of anthropology, there has been a much greater appreciation of the actual relationships between humans and other animals, and other animals' impact on human lives.[15] This means that ethnographic studies on humans living in close proximity with alloprimates, for example, could no longer afford to confine their interests just to human societies in isolation. Rather, as Agustín Fuentes suggests, there is a sense in which the ethnographic tools used for anthropological investigation need to give "agency, in symbolic, social and ecological senses, to the human alloprimate interface. This inclusion of the nonhuman other as central in the examination of being human has also emerged as the core narrative in the embryonic field of multispecies ethnography."[16] Here, the divide that Tim Ingold has pointed out[17] between what cultural anthropologists do in terms of looking at explicit characteristics of human cultures as the defining mark of human beings living in diverse societies and the work of evolutionary biologists, who tend to view differences between humans and other animals in a progressive sense of increasing complexity, becomes bridged in new and interesting ways.

This leads to the fourth dimension of evolution, the symbolic inheritance system, forged originally in the work of Ernst Cassirer and taken up by neurobiology professor Terence Deacon and discussed in chapter 5. Rationality, linguistic ability, art, and religion are all features of the ability to symbolize. Symbol-based culture passes on from one generation to the next. It is more than simply imitation, as it involves an understanding of the relationships between words, not simply their repetition. As every educator will know, it is not enough to regurgitate words "parrot fashion"; students must show the ability to learn new and novel combinations in different circumstances. Humans are able to abstract meanings to a general metaphysical and symbolic level that is quite impossible for other animals, even if they have systems of signs.[18] Human cultures are unique in the

15. As surveyed in Pat Shipman, *The Animal Connection: A New Perspective on What Makes Us Human* (New York: Norton, 2011). I will come back to this in chapter 8.

16. Agustín Fuentes, "Ethnoprimatology and the Anthropology of the Human-Primate Interface," *Annual Review of Anthropology* 41 (2012): 101-17.

17. Tim Ingold, "Humanity and Animality," in *Companion Encyclopedia of Anthropology*, ed. Tim Ingold (New York: Routledge, 2002), pp. 14-32. Ingold believes that those who seek for specific characteristics, such as reason, language, etc., are really examining the "human condition" informed by particular cultural prejudices, rather than what might be properly called biological characteristics of human nature. For further discussion, see chapter 1.

18. See chapter 5 on language, where I take this up in more detail.

pervasiveness of symbol systems in behavior such as food preferences or in songs that lack such symbolic association in other animals.[19] Symbol systems may be fictional and future orientated or creative in relation to historical incidents and past time. How human beings as a group have been able to cooperate and arrive at agreed symbolic systems, including those symbols used in science and theology, is perhaps a good example of the complex metalevels that are possible in the ability to symbolize: human beings are symbolizing their own symbolizing!

Debates in the Evolution of Cooperation

One of the more interesting debates that has surfaced in evolutionary theory deals with the evolution of cooperation. Cooperation is not necessarily morally good, since it is not always directed for good ends. In biological terms, the value judgments about whether cooperation should be termed morally good/bad will not be made; what is of most interest is the benefit to species survival, often parsed out as benefit in evolutionary terms.[20] Cooperation is, however, particularly interesting to explore in the context of human evolution and what allowed human communities in particular to flourish. Hominids were able to outcompete their rivals, but what was specific about the way hominid species evolved, and *Homo sapiens* in particular, that allowed them to do this effectively? In this case, comparison between humans and other primates may be a distraction in terms of accounting for the specific evolutionary pathway, since chimpanzees are reflexively xenophobic. Even though bonobos are temperamentally more like humans, it is not clear if their ancestor was more chimpanzee-like or not. Sarah Blaffer Hrdy argues that there is a tendency to project a violence-prone temperament onto our hominid ancestors from observa-

19. Jablonka and Lamb, *Evolution in Four Dimensions,* p. 205.

20. The ethical implications of cooperation are therefore not as simple as they might seem. See discussion in Jean Porter, "The Natural Law and the Normative Significance of Nature," *Studies in Christian Ethics* 26, no. 2 (2013): 166-73. Nigel Biggar makes much the same point in N. Biggar, "Evolutionary Biology, 'Enlightened' Anthropological Narratives, and Social Morality: A View from Christian Ethics," *Studies in Christian Ethics* 26, no. 2 (2013): 152-57. Nonetheless, Biggar names evolutionary game theory as still orientated around a utilitarian paradigm of selfishness and draws a cautionary note in relation to evolutionary theory in general, though a critique can, it seems to me, also come from within evolutionary biology rather than from other disciplines.

tions of chimpanzees.[21] Instead, human beings routinely show the capacity to identify with and share with others. Specific hunter-gatherer societies, such as the Ju/'hoansi culture studied by Polly Wiessner, for example, are socialized from early life to share with others.

Hrdy's main argument is that tendencies for genuine gift-giving are rare in other species except those that engage in cooperative breeding. Furthermore, how far the urge to share specifically among human primates is "hard-wired" in the way Hrdy prefers[22] is perhaps a debatable point, unless a correlation with neurological changes during gift exchange is considered evidence for such processes. She suggests, therefore, that the tendency to give gifts was an earlier, originating impulse, and that other, more violent tendencies emerged later, as a result of an inability to live in larger and more impersonal groups. A more general capacity in the ability to read another's mind is clearly a crucial prerequisite of such processes and marks off the relative sophistication of cooperation in human species compared with primates.[23] Crucially, Hrdy argues that humans were *emotionally modern* in their ability to understand others before linguistic and other cultural capacities emerged.

She draws such conclusions from a detailed study of comparative primatology and from ethnographic studies of childhood in foraging societies. While there is debate about the extent to which chimpanzees can possess genuine cooperative tendencies, Hrdy insists that such ambiguity is not found among foraging societies, and that humans are deeply invested in what others think about whether they are competing or cooperating.[24] Overall, her argument that humans evolved language *after*

21. Sarah Blaffer Hrdy, *Mothers and Others: The Evolutionary Origins of Mutual Understanding* (Cambridge: Harvard University Press, Belknap Press, 2009), p. 21. How far she is correct in suggesting that the sharing that goes on among chimpanzees is "tolerated theft" rather than genuine sharing behavior is a debatable point on which I will not dwell in this chapter, since it reflects prior conceptions about cognitive capacities in other primates.

22. Hrdy, *Mothers and Others,* p. 25.

23. Michael Tomasello, *Why We Cooperate* (Cambridge: MIT Press, 2009).

24. While some experiments show that it is possible chimpanzees can recognize what another wants or intends, it takes special training to pay attention to what others think or know when they are cooperating, even though they may do so when they seem to be competing. See discussion in Joan B. Silk, "Who Are More Helpful, Humans or Chimpanzees?" *Science* 311 (2007): 1248-49. This is clearly at odds with the views of authors such as Frans de Waal, so clearly this is still a matter of intense scientific debate. One of the problems with the latter is that experiments were conducted in laboratory conditions. See also further discussion of altruism in chapter 8.

they were able to connect with each other emotionally makes biological sense. But why did that emotional ability evolve? Two standard theories — the mind-reading mums hypothesis and the Machiavellian intelligence hypothesis — seem to have their corollaries in other animals.[25] Similarly, both apes and humans are able to imitate each other and seek out faces and eyes, registering the expression they see. But a more fundamental point is that there is a difference between the way infants and apes are reared. Unlike hunter-gatherer mothers, most primate mothers are compulsively possessive and dedicated to their babies no matter what their condition, even if their infant is severely incapacitated. A human mother seems to be more conditional in her devotion, and in hunter-gatherer societies will practice infanticide by drowning, abandoning, or burying the infant alive when it is perceived to be defective.[26] If there is social support in caring for the infant, the possibility of abandonment is reduced, and importantly, hunter-gatherer mothers allow others to come close to their infants and hold them. !Kung infants were held by their mothers disproportionately compared with infants in Western societies, but they were also held by others in the social group. In the great apes, mothers are the only ones who hold their new infants. In human hunter-gatherer communities that have been studied, other members of the community called alloparents hold infants; in Hadza communities, for example, they do it 85 percent of the time. The practice of sharing infant carrying occurs in around 87 percent of foraging societies that have been documented.[27] But in spite of the heavy influence of attachment theory, research has also shown alloparenting in about half of all primates, and such alloparenting increases reproductive success. Marmosets and tamarins, like humans, may deliberately harm their infants and are also in the same family, Callitrichidae.

25. The mind-reading mums hypothesis speculates that early in hominid evolution the mothers' bond with their infants provides the foundational source of emotional sociality. But this does not explain why this is a characteristic of all humans. The Machiavellian intelligence hypothesis, on the other hand, portrays humans as innately deceptive, using their intelligence to plan for their future through deception or manipulation. But other primates are also capable of competitive social relations.

26. "Defective" might include characteristics such as low birth weight, limbs that are missing, coming too close to the birth of another sibling, or the lack of social support. See Sarah Blaffer Hrdy, *Mother Nature: A History of Mothers, Infants, and Natural Selection* (New York: Pantheon, 1999). Once breast-feeding starts, the attachment to the mother overrides any other conscious considerations.

27. Barry Hewlett, "Human Relations Area Files," in *Diverse Contexts of Human Infancy* (Englewood Cliffs, N.J.: Prentice-Hall, 1989), cited in Hrdy, *Mothers and Others,* p. 77.

The most likely circumstance for such drastic behavior seems to be a lack of perceived support by alloparents. But humans are the only great apes with alloparental care.

The presence, therefore, of important others in the lives of humans seems to be critical. A selection pressure toward collaborative relationships could therefore have started from infant-other relationships in collaborative breeding. I remain agnostic here as to whether such collaborative tendencies are subject to analysis through what I have termed the genetic dimension of evolution, or whether they are inherited through behavioral or symbolic means, or a combination of all factors. Michael Tomasello has conducted research on very young children and found that even children younger than eighteen months have a natural tendency to help others, which implies, but does not prove, a "natural" responsiveness prior to any cultural learning.[28] Sarah Blaffer Hrdy concurs, "Within the first two years of life, infants fortunate enough to be reared in responsive caretaking relationships develop innate potentials for empathy, mindreading and collaboration, and often do so with astonishing speed. Such behavior is the outcome of complex interactions between genes and nurture, and this drama is played out on the stage of developing brains."[29] Hunter-gatherer societies can provide reasonable proxies for what happened early in evolution, but given the time gap, uncertainties are bound to remain. Differences in the time that humans take to mature, known as the extension in post-weaning dependency period, are also significant in that humans take significantly longer than other primates, again, elevating the need for a strong system of alloparental care.[30] Hrdy argues that the emotional capacity for intersubjectivity emerged much earlier than most other scholars suggest; she places this in the early Pleistocene rather than the late Pleistocene, or even later along with language, symbolic thinking, and art, finding its first ap-

28. His experiments have involved controls where there was little or no encouragement to help. He distinguishes different elements in cooperation, such as generosity (giving goods), helping others in tasks, and passing on information. Tomasello, *Why We Cooperate,* pp. 1-47.

29. Hrdy, *Mothers and Others,* p. 286.

30. If alloparents were not available, then mothers would have to invest more time for each infant, thus making additional child rearing more difficult. For a discussion of post-weaning dependency, see Melvin Konner, *The Evolution of Childhood: Relationships, Emotion, Mind* (Cambridge: Harvard University Press, Belknap Press, 2011), pp. 281-85, 441-49. Alloparents are those members of a community, especially other relatives, who take on some of the roles of the parents in child rearing.

pearance 30,000 years ago in the magnificent cave paintings of Chauvet in France or in the Altimira cave in Spain.

Can such complex evolutionary dynamics be given a theoretical basis? Martin Nowak attempts to do just that by using a mathematical model, drawing on game theory, in order to model cooperation in collective groups.[31] Nowak argues that the adaptations to inclusive fitness theory emerging from the mismatch with field experiments are mathematically inept, and he has courted biological controversy by rejecting inclusive fitness theory (IFT) in favor of multilevel selection theory (MLST), in which selection works at the level of groups, either between individuals in a group or between groups. E. O. Wilson joined forces with Nowak, and they published a controversial article in the journal *Nature.*[32] A benign view of this controversy is that each group of scientists is speaking a different language or perhaps promoting different perspectives, rather than one paradigm attempting to replace the other.[33] Because multilevel selection has been a minority view ever since Darwin's *Origin of Species,* this is at least partly correct. But the heated and dramatic engagement between biologists over this issue suggests that both models reflect more fundamental commitments that cannot easily be dislodged. Part of the problem is that even though the two different models are showing different features, both are entering the same territory, namely, how to explain eusociality. Those who argue for multilevel selection are viewed as "defectors" that need to be punished by those in the more narrowly defined IFT group. Furthermore, if IFT works, then many scientists are reluctant on the basis of parsimony to seemingly add another layer of explanation through MLST. To a nonspecialist, MLST intuitively makes more sense, since it seems unlikely that IFT is sufficient because it focuses too much on individual actions and reactions rather than considering group dynamics that have for centuries been the province of sociology in general and re-

31. Martin Nowak with Roger Highfield, *Super Cooperators: Altruism, Evolution, and Why We Need Each Other to Succeed* (New York: Free Press, 2011).

32. Martin Nowak, Corina Tarnita, and Edward O. Wilson, "The Evolution of Eusociality," *Nature* 466 (2010): 1057-62. http://www.ped.fas.harvard.edu/people/faculty/publications_nowak/NowakNature2010.pdf (accessed March 18, 2013).

33. David Sloan Wilson, for example, argues that it is more reasonable to hold to *both* inclusive fitness theory *and* multilevel selection theory, since these are experimental tools that can be used for different purposes. See David Sloan Wilson, "Clash of Paradigms" (2012). http://www.thisviewoflife.com/index.php/magazine/articles/clash-of-paradigms (accessed March 18, 2013).

ligious communities in particular. As a culture, the most recent tendency in the Western world has been to focus on individuals rather than groups, even though appalling practices have been and still are committed in the name of group "cleansing." Of course, here the opposite problem emerges, namely, the coercive nature of group dynamics. Reputation issues are also likely here: scientists who have built their careers on one or another model and who depend on funding on the basis of that model are unlikely to shift. E. O. Wilson at the end of his career can take risks, but his opponents will (may?) attach his radical shift in views to a diminishing intellect.

This example shows the drama explicit in social collaboration that appears, ironically, in the specific practice of the science of collaboration and *its* symbol systems. One of the explanations for the passion with which such debates are conducted has to do with a realist philosophy underlying science, namely, that it represents the truth about *material* reality, and it is this that is at stake. While good scientists are open to the possibility that their models may be wrong, there is also a sense in which they are creating their own symbolic worlds, even while drawing on what seems to be discoverable in the natural realm. But how did human beings develop such capacities for complex thought?

Alan Barnard associates symbolic thought with the shift from *Homo erectus* to *Homo sapiens,* arguing that hunter-gatherer societies today show a purer form of symbolic thought.[34] He also maps the capacity to make metaphors as a stage beyond symbolic form. He suggests that symbolic thought arose much earlier than many scholars have supposed, after the use of fire and before rituals, music, and art development, which means that symbolic thought was also prior to the full development of language. The difficulty in any reconstruction is whether symbolic thought arose prior to or after the development of language in anatomically modern humans.[35] Based on the possibility that early language developed and then disappeared and then reappeared again after symbolic thinking, and drawing on the finding that the anatomical basis for language development was

34. Alan Barnard, *Genesis of Symbolic Thought* (Cambridge: Cambridge University Press, 2012). I would agree with this inasmuch as it is probably easier to analyze symbol systems and their development in hunter-gatherer societies, and that other human societies can learn from this experience. To claim, with Barnard, that we have "lost some of our 'humanity'" (p. 3) makes sense in the light of his analysis of the ideologies of hunter-gatherer rather than post-Neolithic cultures (see below). See more detailed discussion of symbolic thought in chapter 5.

35. Barnard, *Genesis of Symbolic Thought,* p. 101.

much earlier, he suggests that a form of language could have appeared prior to symbolic thinking, so that behavioral and anatomical modernity coincided.[36] Terence Deacon argues for a coevolutionary model of language and symbols, but Barnard presses for symbolic thinking after language development.[37]

German Dziebel challenges the out-of-Africa model for human origins and argues for an out-of-Americas model, based on the strength of the kinship structures found here.[38] But it is the ability to tell stories that arguably is the hallmark of symbolic meaning systems and is what makes us human. Significantly, "narrative is so embedded in the advance of language, and vice versa, that these must have preceded the *Homo sapiens* Out of Africa migrations."[39] Significantly, the movement of human cultures into the Neolithic phase brought with it a revolutionary change in the meaning of what it is to be social. For hunter-gatherer ideology with its close-knit, small-scale kin communities, accumulation is equated with not sharing and immediate consumption is regarded as social. For Neolithic and post-Neolithic societies, on the other hand, with the introduction of agriculture and social hierarchy, and the growth of cities, accumulation is seen as a means to save and is a social activity, while immediate consumption is antisocial.[40]

The above implies that close anthropological studies are needed to tease out what it means to be social. Hence, game-theoretical models of eusociality based on cost-benefit analysis will only apply to those forms of human sociality that depend on economic patterns of thinking and acting and are only likely to work where such presuppositions hold true.[41]

Finally, this discussion of the evolution of cooperation would not be complete without brief reference to Kim Sterelny's work *The Evolved Apprentice.* Rather than tying in the evolution of cooperation to a crucial adaptation, such as cooperative breeding by Sarah Blaffer Hrdy or

36. The view that there was a gap between behavioral and anatomically modern humans has presented a puzzle for anthropologists. Barnard, *Genesis of Symbolic Thought,* p. 115.

37. Barnard, *Genesis of Symbolic Thought,* p. 121.

38. His argument is difficult to prove since cultural innovations may change the center in a migratory movement, while being retained in the periphery.

39. Barnard, *Genesis of Symbolic Thought,* p. 121.

40. Barnard, *Genesis of Symbolic Thought,* pp. 122-24.

41. The elegance of the mathematics and its self-presentation as "hard science" rather than the "softer" observational sciences should not, in other words, lead to blindness about how far it is applicable in different societal contexts in the field.

the evolution of conscience by Christopher Boehm, Sterelny argues that there is no key adaptation or "magic moment" in the history of human cooperation. Rather, it depends on "the evolution and stabilization of a set of positive feedback loops that connect technology and the division of labor with cooperation, with social learning and with informationally engineered developmental environments."[42] Significantly, he argues that cooperative foraging depended on technology and expertise that were then shared between and across generations. He presses for a combination of information pooling, ecological and economic cooperation in relation to targeting specific "high-value" large-game resources, and reproductive cooperation, acting as a third "leg" in the evolution of cooperation. Importantly, he argues that different forms of cooperation could have been stabilized by affiliative emotions, namely, trust.

Steps in Theological Anthropology

Sociality as a highly significant component of how to think about human beings is central to many theological interpretations of the human, ranging, for example, from Alistair McFadyen's interpretation of the human individual through social relationships, and more explicitly, human mirroring relationships with God as the Trinity, through to a more eucharistic focus in the work of Eastern Orthodox theologian John Zizioulas.[43] But how are theologians to respond to such a burgeoning and dizzying array of literature on the evolutionary biology of the sociality of the human? One response is simply to ignore it altogether. This seems to be the case in David Kelsey's otherwise majestic *Eccentric Existence.* The starting point for his thesis is one that puts emphasis on the relationship between humans and that which is "grounded outside themselves in the concrete ways in

42. Sterelny also rejects Wrangham's idea that the crucial social change in human evolution was the ability to cook food, a hypothesis that I do not have the scope to go into in more detail in this chapter. Nonetheless, Sterelny could be criticized for portraying his view as not stressing a key adaptation, since in his case it is dependent on the human ability to respond to feedback. He would probably reply that such abilities are much more general compared with models that assume a key innovation in human culture. Kim Sterelny, *The Evolved Apprentice: How Evolution Made Humans Unique* (Cambridge: MIT Press, 2012).

43. Alistair McFadyen, *The Call to Personhood* (Cambridge: Cambridge University Press, 1990); John Zizioulas, *The Eucharistic Communion and the World* (London: T. & T. Clark, 2011).

which the triune God relates to all that is not God, including humankind."[44] While his presentation of this view of God is an attempt to safeguard the God/human distinction, viewing a fundamental human social relationship as somehow "outside" the human feeds an image of supernatural agency. Kelsey does not intend this and so begins with a discussion of grounded, creaturely existence that he discusses in terms of "energy systems."[45] This is the "proximate" context into which humans are born, and from Kelsey's perspective biblical Wisdom's theology of creation provides a good starting point for such reflection. The "ultimate" context is not this world, however, but "the active creativity of God."[46] He is provocative here in naming such dependency as a kind of living on "borrowed breath" that was shared even in the person of Jesus Christ, whom he understood as displaying a "radical dependence on God's continuing to relate to him creatively."[47] Such active creativity is by no means confined to the human sphere, as the Creator is generously attentive to the well-being of all creation, so "its otherness is the necessary condition of being anything besides God for God to love freely and in delight."[48]

Kelsey makes a crucial move, namely, he envisages the creaturely relationships in which humankind is situated in the light of what he calls the "quotidian," "the everyday finite reality of all sorts — animal, vegetable and mineral — in the routine networks that are constituted by their ordinary interactions."[49] That network "defines the spaces and times of our everyday lives and provides us with fellow agents sharing these spaces and times . . . a society of everyday being."[50] Such an account cries out for an ecological

44. David Kelsey, *Eccentric Existence* (Louisville: Westminster John Knox, 2009), 2:1008.

45. Kelsey, *Eccentric Existence,* 1:160.

46. The inverse of the use of the terms "ultimate" and "proximate" compares with that of evolutionary biologists, where "ultimate" is often used to refer to evolutionary roots and "proximate" to more immediate behaviors. While the use of the language of "ultimacy" is falling out of fashion, the contrasting sense in which what is driving particular changes in human communities is striking. Tinbergen's metaphysical naturalism (see, for example, Niko Tinbergen, "On Aims and Methods of Ethology," *Zeitschrift für Tierpsychologie* 20 [1963]: 410-33) can be replaced by metaphysical theism where God is seen as the originator of evolutionary change, but Kelsey does not attempt such a strategy as he seems to want to keep the work of God as an independent "force" of creativity.

47. Kelsey, *Eccentric Existence,* 2:1012.

48. Kelsey, *Eccentric Existence,* 1:165.

49. Kelsey, *Eccentric Existence,* 1:190.

50. Kelsey, *Eccentric Existence,* 1:190.

or evolutionary interpretation, but on this Kelsey remains silent. This is important since when he develops the second part of his theological anthropology viewed through the lens of eschatological consummation, the active presence of other creatures seems to have disappeared from view, so that the final phase of reconciliation from all that is not of God embeds a rather more restricted form of human sociality. The occasional references to other creatures as expressive of different modes of God's glory show a willingness to refute the claim that human beings are the pinnacle of God's glory in a superior sense.[51] But if other creatures are such reflections, why is there such limited attention to concrete aspects of social relationships apart from what might be termed a basal quotidian? This is all the more ironical since his timidity about naming humans through the concept of *imago Dei* seems to have surfaced, at least in part, from his sensitivity to the way such a concept could be used to aggrandize the human over against other creaturely kinds, a view that he believes is now no longer viable.[52] However, even though his intention is to create a triple rather than a single narrative, drawing on a biological metaphor that gives a "triple helix" structure to his theological anthropology, it is not clear how the first strand in its specific relation to other creatures feeds into or is interwoven with the other two strands, apart from its role as a reminder of human creaturely and bodily existence.[53] Such a structure also allows Kelsey to stress the continuous action of God's creative activity, but it is a disappointment that such activity in relation to the second and third strands seems rather less expansive compared with the first strand. In other words, his view of the human has not, at least inasmuch as it reflects future hope, taken sufficient account of human interrelation with and engagement with other creatures. His view of human community is, therefore, focused on the religious community as it informs particular practices of faith.

I do suggest, however, that Kelsey has provided hints in his project of the ways in which other creaturely kinds may be significant in mapping human sociality. Rather more explicit in its engagement with evolutionary theory is Sarah Coakley's determined effort to rehabilitate the idea of sacrifice, but not so much by referring to intra-ecclesial claims as by exploring

51. Kelsey, *Eccentric Existence,* 1:316.

52. Kelsey, *Eccentric Existence,* 1:29-31. There are other reasons for his rejection of this concept, including his belief that *imago Dei* suffers from a single narrative logic that he believes is unhelpful.

53. The three strands are, as named above, creation, eschatological consummation, and reconciliation, in contrast to the traditional "narrative" of creation, fall, and redemption.

evolutionary theories of cooperation, with Martin Nowak's mathematical modeling of game theory playing a prominent role.[54] Coakley's attention to biological aspects of cooperation is certainly a positive shift, especially in view of the relative hesitancy of many academic theologians, particularly in the U.K., to engage seriously with scientific understanding. Her writing betrays a lyrical, almost musical quality that builds a narrative step-by-step but not without some philosophical hedging, making clear that for her, engagement with science is not simply a theological gloss to what is being argued for in the scientific literature, but is something much more profound. She is careful, too, to display the utilitarian elements in Nowak's thesis, crafting alternative ways in which theology might engage with evolutionary theories. Nowak argues for five mathematically based rules for cooperation, including a novel idea of network reciprocity.[55] However, these ideas are less important to Coakley than the explicitly religious idea of sacrifice, which she brings alongside biological accounts of altruism from her contact with Nowak and the Cambridge zoologist Timothy Clutton-Brock, who had studied the behavior of meerkats. But here she confronts an acute problem.

If, as she argues correctly with MacIntyre, it is inadequate to portray science and theology on the same "flat plane" of explanation, then what purpose are cooperative theories of evolutionary biology really serving in her theology? She seems to want to argue in favor of a bold form of natural

54. Such contact seemed to stem initially from her self-description of her liaison with mathematician Martin Nowak as a "forced marriage" engineered by generous funding from the John Templeton Foundation. From this followed the confession of the liberation of a once narrowly interested classics scholar, both in her inaugural lecture (Sarah Coakley, *Sacrifice Regained: Reconsidering the Rationality of Religious Belief,* inaugural lecture, October 13, 2009 [Cambridge: Cambridge University Press, 2012]) and her more recent Gifford Lectures, "Sacrifice Regained: Evolution, Cooperation, and God" (Gifford Lectures, University of Aberdeen, Scotland, April 17–May 3, 2012; online: http://www.abdn.ac.uk/gifford/about/ [accessed March 18, 2013]). See also the fruit of that collaboration in an interesting collection of essays: Martin Nowak and Sarah Coakley, *Evolution, Games, and God: The Principle of Cooperation* (Cambridge: Harvard University Press, 2013); a further collection of short essays dealing with ethical aspects is published in a special issue of *Studies in Christian Ethics,* May 2013, including S. Coakley, "Evolution, Cooperation and Ethics: Some Methodological and Philosophical Hurdles," *Studies in Christian Ethics* 26, no. 2 (2013): 135-39. This collection of essays was most concerned with the ethical implication of evolutionary theories of cooperation, but less on a practical level of applied ethics, and more on theoretical implications for metaphysics, and metaethics.

55. For an outline of this position see Martin Nowak, "Five Rules for the Evolution of Cooperation," in *Evolution, Games, and God,* pp. 99-114.

theology that she takes from Aquinas's fifth way as representing a movement from science to God.[56] However, she rejects the idea that scientific reasoning is commensurate with theology in any simple correspondence. On the other hand, the natural theology to which she subscribes is also pointing to the idea of sacrifice, which in itself has a problematic resonance in the theological and biological world, associated as it is with narratives of violence.[57] She boldly and critically appraises René Girard's seeming acceptance of violence and scapegoat narrative of Jesus' significance. While Girard's account of Christology is certainly unconvincing in this respect, his attention to sociological issues is perhaps more important than Coakley allows for here. Evolutionary biologists more often ascribe to both the selfishness hypothesis *and* that of cooperation, rather than simply one or the other, in that the overall trajectory of evolution is not perceived in terms of a good end in the way required for theological interpretation of divine providence. Coakley insists that cooperation rather than violence is at the heart of Christian reflection, but to do that through a natural theology she has to confine herself to one evolutionary account and reject the other. At the same time, she takes cooperation to be that defined in biological terms by a costly form of behavior that benefits the population as a whole. Altruism then builds on this definition by being "a form of (costly) cooperation in which an individual is motivated by good will or love for another (or others)."[58] Here Coakley is incorporating a particular biological view of altruism and aligning it with the Christian tradition of sacrifice, understood

56. Coakley's rendition of Aquinas as a basis for natural theology understood as a way of arguing for God in the traditional sense is somewhat weak, given that most interpreters of Aquinas, myself included, would resist such an explanation of his thought as accurately representative. For a fuller discussion of Aquinas's position, see Eugene Rogers, *Thomas Aquinas and Karl Barth: Sacred Doctrine and the Natural Knowledge of God* (Notre Dame, Ind.: University of Notre Dame Press, 1999).

57. Biologists normally use the language of "cost" rather than "sacrifice" in describing, for example, the evolutionary benefits of cooperation. Coakley is well aware of this herself, as she is aware that mathematical modeling may not be a suitably accurate description according to empirical approaches. She is also aware of the dangers of reading too much human history into the lives of other creatures, a false anthropomorphism, and reducing the human to mechanical reductionist accounts. See Coakley, "Evolution, Cooperation and Ethics," pp. 137-38. But the question remains: How far is it appropriate to associate discussion of biological "costs" with "sacrificial" metanarratives? Could it reinforce the possibility of inappropriate self-debasement for the sake of the other?

58. Coakley, "Evolution, Cooperation and Ethics," p. 137; also in Sarah Coakley and Martin Nowak, "Introduction: Why Cooperation Makes a Difference," in *Evolution, Games, and God,* pp. 1-34, here 5.

as sacrifice for others. But from a historical perspective there remains a profound ambiguity in her use of the language of sacrifice; in other words, is the language of sacrifice really resonant with extreme cooperation or extreme violence? Or perhaps both?

I am not sure that the shadow of Girard's analysis can be dispensed with quite as easily as she seems to claim, however refreshingly novel her particular approach. Certainly, in the history of the Judeo-Christian tradition sacrifice has been associated with violence toward other animals rather than positive cooperation with them. The shining Christian examples of what might be termed supercooperation can still be subject to evolutionary explanatory indexes of gene survival, even though Coakley argues that this is insufficient. But should we rely on such extreme examples to argue the case for God? Of course, if Christian reflection on the inspiring lives of moral exemplars, stemming from the theological idea that Christ redeems suffering, is presupposed, then the biological notion of sacrifice might take on a different meaning entirely. But this is not what Coakley intends; for her, biological sacrifice somehow *leads into* theological notions, at least up to a point. Hers is a natural theology of sorts in that the two narratives come together and point to one another, though Coakley is too sophisticated a thinker to suggest any sort of synthesis. Yet there is still a gap in credibility, but this gap is most pronounced only if evolutionary biology is rendered univocally consistent in the way Coakley implies, rather than being subject to the very varied and controversial interpretations that I have alluded to above. For example, there may be different biological tools that are rather more appropriate to explain extreme sacrifice compared with game theory models of cooperation.

We have here a mirror image of the problems associated with Kelsey's anthropology. Kelsey begins explicitly with God as Creator, paying lip service to creaturely kinds, but takes away their significance when considering creaturely redemption and the eschaton. Coakley, on the other hand, begins with a hidden view of God that she hopes will come into clearer view through close attention to what is happening in the creaturely world. Kelsey's address is directed to the ecclesial community. Coakley is bolder, moving into the public sphere. But will biologists ever be convinced by her attempt to lure them into a form of natural revelation? The views of sacrifice emerging from theology and her interpretation of evolutionary biology are about as paradoxical as they can be when brought alongside each other. If sacrifice in theological terms is thought of, instead, as a means to express symbolic thought, and that is the inspiration for what might be termed extreme acts, then a pattern of inheritance through symbolic means still becomes possible in naturalistic terms. What I am suggesting is that scientists, *qua* scientists, are hugely creative when it comes to rethinking how humans might come up with their explanatory frameworks, even deeply held religious ones. I doubt, therefore, that such a shift will pass muster among scientists, even if it could serve a useful purpose in bringing theology back into serious conversation in the public sphere.

What might be an alternative? I agree with Coakley that it is vitally important to try as best we can, and with all the limitations in epistemology that this might imply, to listen to scientific discussions. The question then becomes, how are such discussions dealt with theologically? I believe we can find some resonance with science by showing in structural form the way theology can chart its course, not on the same flat plane, but by way of convergence. Both evolutionary theory and theological analysis are diverse and hotly debated. Both represent advanced forms of symbol systems that this chapter is attempting to tease out. But theology is also more than this, for it can be a deliberate way of standing inside rather than outside a participant observer. And here I suggest that Hans Urs von Balthasar's notion of theo-drama is crucially important.[59] Here I want to develop his particular theological dramatics not so much in the light of the broad evolutionary debate characteristic of tensions between the stress on contingency in Stephen Jay Gould and the teleonomy implicit in Simon Conway Morris, for example. Rather, I intend to pick out those aspects of his thought that bear on human sociality understood in dramatic terms and then, in a section below, build on what I think is a crucial aspect of the evolutionary discussion, namely, niche construction and human/animal relationships. Balthasar, like Kelsey, gives some provocative hints at paying attention to the creaturely world, especially in *The Glory of the Lord,* which is expansive in scope. But like Kelsey, who also appears influenced by Barthian modes of thought, he seems to downplay the significance of other creatures in creating eschatological horizons that remain narrowly subscribed to exclusive human communities. It is possible to argue for

59. His five volumes of *Theo-drama,* which followed in the wake of his ten-volume *Glory of the Lord,* are an impressive collection of works that show him to be a highly original and at times idiosyncratic thinker. I have used his theology to good effect in Celia Deane-Drummond, *Christ and Evolution: Wonder and Wisdom* (Minneapolis: Fortress, 2009). I discuss evolution in the context of debates between Stephen Jay Gould and Simon Conway Morris.

an expansion of this scope so that it is more inclusive of other creaturely kinds.[60]

Before going further, it is worthwhile to take a closer look at Balthasar's understanding of the human in the context of his theo-dramatic perspective. Theo-drama is a type of narrative, a way of seeing human beings in relation to their religious world. At best, it aims to resist the idea of a *grand narrative,* if this means an exclusive universalizing category in some way apart from the human observer. One of the most striking aspects of the fieldwork discussed in the various anthropological texts cited above is the sheer variety of forms of human social experience. The temptation to look at this variety of forms through particular grand narratives is exceptionally strong, and perhaps cannot be avoided entirely when sociality is approached through evolutionary theory. Hence, those grand narratives that still allow for a considerable degree of flexibility in terms of what might be called "minidramas" are rather more enticing than those that seem to fix human social behavior in particular ways.[61] Anthropologists working in field situations inevitably become to some extent "participant observers" in that they share in the life of the communities in which they take part, and so learn from their human experiences some of the important norms for a particular social group. Balthasar suggested something similar when he argued that there was no standpoint from which human beings could position themselves as if they were somehow "outside" or "apart from" theo-drama. This is particularly true if we consider the way Scripture is used according to Balthasar's interpretation. Scripture is not some objective text that permits avoidance of a dramatic decision.[62] Rather, "Scripture mirrors the drama and can only be understood in reference to it, it

60. See, for example, Celia Deane-Drummond, "The Breadth of Glory: A Trinitarian Eschatology for the Earth through Critical Engagement with Hans Urs von Balthasar," *International Journal of Systematic Theology* 12, no. 1 (2010): 46-64.

61. It is possible, perhaps, to use the term "narrative" if it is suitably qualified, as in Matthew Ashley's discussion of the use of the Bible. J. Matthew Ashley, "Reading the Universe Theologically: The Contribution of a Biblical Narrative Imagination," *Theological Studies* 71, no. 4 (2010): 870-902.

62. David Sloan Wilson, for example, has used scriptural texts as a basis for drawing up what he terms a biblically based "genotype" that he believes primes alternative religious practices or "phenotypes" in local communities. He justifies this language on the assumption that religious communities follow the same patterns of inheritance as ecological systems, flowering in alternative phenotypes. David Sloan Wilson, "Religion and Spirituality in the Context of Everyday Life" (public lecture, Center of Theological Inquiry and Center for the Study of Religion, Princeton University, October 4, 2012).

is part of the drama. It does not stand at some observation post outside revelation. And insofar as it is part of a greater whole, it points beyond itself to its content, and its content is the *pneuma,* which is always more than the *gramma,* the letter."[63] But arising out of Scripture is the view central to the idea of theo-drama that God has made his own the "tragic situation of human existence, right down to its ultimate abysses; thus, without drawing its teeth or imposing an extrinsic solution on it, he overcomes it" (2:54). His discussion of spirituality is pertinent here as well, since a tension between spirituality and theology appears where spirituality is viewed as a lyrical and existential recollection of aspects of the past life of Jesus and theology reacts by more universalistic epic modes of speech. If, therefore, we speak of God as unknowable, absolute, transcending all that we know, then it still remains a discourse about God. The reaction to such an objectification is to focus on theo-praxy, the lived experience in protest of such objectifications. The answer, for Balthasar, is to rediscover the dramatic dimension of revelation. In this context, human beings address God and others in a single social relationship. Such theo-dramatic action unfolds "in the context of God's action, which challenges the believer, takes him over and appoints him to be a witness" (2:57).

The apostles are also witnesses to the dramatic way in which God works in the believer's life not as an uninvolved observer, but as deeply involved and handing on the drama of both Christ's life and theirs. Balthasar does not, therefore, reject all notions of epic existence, but only those that encourage a standing outside, rather than a standing within. A believer, therefore, by being in tune with God, represents not so much resignation in the face of an authority figure or acting out of fear of punishment as "the readiness to step into whatever role in the play God has in mind" in a way that still is capable of distinguishing the actor from the role played. This may take the form of active resistance, but also of patience and acceptance of suffering. For Balthasar, "Christian suffering is at least equally as fruitful for the salvation of the world as external activity. Thus, no Christian is obliged to leave the stage and the action: in suffering and dying he is still playing his part in the theo-drama" (2:60). His stress on sacrificial obedience is controversial, and inasmuch as it reclaims the idea of sacrifice, it coheres with aspects of Sarah Coakley's approach mentioned above. Crit-

63. Hans Urs von Balthasar, *Theo-Drama: Theological Dramatic Theory,* vol. 2, *The Dramatis Personae: Man in God,* trans. George Harrison (San Francisco: Ignatius, 1990), p. 58. Page references have been placed in the text.

ical here, however, is a readiness for suffering, rather than an obligation to suffer. So suffering may be accepted as part of a theo-dramatic role, but not sought after deliberately. Furthermore, the Christian in the theo-drama has to discern whether suffering is creative or not; there may be occasions when active resistance rather than passivity is called for.

The difference between a Christian acting in a theo-drama and social action resting on secular hope emerges from a distinct belief in the ongoing if inchoate presence of the Jesus event, which in some sense both guarantees the future kingdom and contains something of the fullness that is to follow (2:76). Importantly, for Balthasar, theo-drama understood as action does not represent simple "busyness," but rather, it can be as much about a surrender of attitudes, formed and shaped by the multiple perspectives that emerge in the scriptural accounts. Yet, the focal point is the life of Jesus as portrayed in the Gospels, so "Jesus Christ, in his dramatic role, which encompasses all dimensions of the world and of history, becomes the norm of every real and possible drama in the personal and public domains" (2:83). But Christ is not some kind of representative for human imitation; rather, Christ is envisaged as a being who is able to enter the abyss of all that is tragic, and here God's grace is asserted and reconciliation becomes manifest in terms of God's glory (2:84). Does this restrict human action in some way? Balthasar opposes such a view by pointing to the doctrine of creation: in a sense "everyone is already within the norm that is to appear definitively in Christ" (2:85). In this way, "conscience does not address itself to an absolute freedom that is its own starting point but to a freedom that is indebted and responsible" (2:85). Such norms are "relatively correct" prior to Christology.[64]

His view of humanity presupposes, therefore, a specific understanding of Christology and Christ's place in the theo-drama. While I am critical of features of his interpretation of Christology inasmuch as his vision of the cross leans too much toward an understanding of God in punitive categories, his construction of human life in terms of theo-drama is still, I suggest, helpful, for it allows interesting parallels to be drawn with evolutionary ideas about niche construction that I will elaborate further below. He also sets up his theo-drama, in the first instance, through a prior discussion on theological aesthetics, allowing a theological affirmation of the natu-

64. Balthasar has been criticized for presenting a view that leans more toward "epic" narrative understood in a negative sense. Crucial in this respect is the interplay between his understanding of freedom and obedience. For further discussion, see chapter 3.

ral world but without confusing the world of creation with that of God, understood through his development of the idea of the analogy of being. Nonetheless, if his views are to become more in tune with ecological and evolutionary understanding, a much greater emphasis needs to be placed on the evolved and ecological worlds in which human beings are situated. It is here, I suggest, that we find the making of what it means to be human. Not simply in a bald obedience to God detached from the creaturely world, but in dynamic relationship with it. The world of the human then becomes expanded historically through theo-dramatic inclusiveness, but it also becomes expanded spatially through greater attention to the niche in which humans are situated as biological beings where species are not separated sharply from one another, but where they meet. Yet we will end with a qualifier here, in that theological understanding always and necessarily admits to its limits. Hence, mystery that is revealed is still mystery that can never be grasped in its entirety. The eye of faith is required and even then is incomplete, so "'Absolute knowledge' is the death of all theo-drama, but God's 'love which surpasses all gnosis' is the death of 'absolute knowledge.'"[65]

Niche Construction Theory (NCT): A New Evolutionary Approach

One of the advantages of using the broad concept of niche construction is that while it has often been neglected in the scientific literature dealing with evolutionary processes, arguments touting its importance are accumulating. It seems highly unlikely, therefore, that its significance will be reduced, since it adds another layer of complexity that serves to qualify simpler models that assume a kind of linear equation of genotype, the sum total of the genetic endowment, plus environment equals phenotype, or outward and observable expression of that genotype. Jeremy Kendal and his coauthors suggest that "the defining characteristic of niche construction is not the modification of environments per se, but rather the organism-induced changes in selection pressures in environments."[66] Niche construction represents a philosophical shift in the way evolutionary

65. Balthasar, *Theo-Drama,* 2:89.

66. Jeremy Kendal, Jamshid J. Tehrani, and F. John Odling-Smee, "Human Niche Construction in Interdisciplinary Focus," *Philosophical Transactions of the Royal Society B* 366 (2011): 785-92.

processes work, so that while some have incorporated aspects of NCT in their frameworks, more radical is to approach evolutionary questions under the umbrella of NCT, rather than adding it on to previous models.[67] It is particularly interesting in my view as it provides a significant bridge between the biological sciences and the human, cultural sciences. Standard evolution theory is "externalist" inasmuch as the environment is viewed as an external factor acting in order to select those internal properties that are most adapted to that environment. Natural selection in this view is the "ultimate" category that explains phenotype, including behavioral differences, and devalues "proximate" causes. Hence, standard evolution theory can still include niche construction, but the "ultimate" explanation is still rooted in natural selection. In NCT, the idea of "causation" becomes problematized. So the "dichotomous proximate and ultimate distinction" is replaced by "reciprocal causation."[68] In this way, niche construction works with natural selection in the evolutionary process in a dynamic interchange. Niches are themselves part of the inheritance process, so that an *interactionist* theory replaces an *externalist* theory. Niche construction emphasizes not just genetic and cultural inheritance, but also ecological inheritance, in dynamic interaction with the first two.[69] But envisioning cultural aspects as separate from ecological inheritance seems too constraining. Ecological and cultural inheritance under a broader "ecological" category carries the advantage of perceiving a developmental context in which the physical niche is not separated from the social niche.[70]

In a recent review, Agustín Fuentes argued that "We are in the midst of significant enhancements in complexity and diversity in evolutionary theory, with the role for behavioral modification of social and ecological

67. The mathematical expression of NCT is straightforward. Standard evolutionary theory assumes an organism's state is a function of the organism and the environment ($dO/dt = f[O,E]$) and changes in the environment are simply a function of that environment ($dE/dt = g[E]$). NCT, on the other hand, allows for the organism to be able to change the environment, and so can be expressed mathematically as $dO/dt = f(O,E)$ and $dE/dt = g(O,E)$.

68. Kendal, Tehrani, and Odling-Smee, "Human Niche Construction," p. 786.

69. This threefold model of Laland et al. compares with the four dimensions of evolution suggested by Jablonka and Lamb. The difference in this case is a greater emphasis on the ecological aspects; the latter allow for niche construction but place this in the context of behavioral change and symbolic change as two of the four dimensions of evolution. Kevin N. Laland, F. John Odling-Smee, and Marc W. Feldman, "Cultural Niche Construction and Human Evolution," *Behavioral Brain Sciences* 23 (2000): 131-75.

70. F. John Odling-Smee, "Niche Inheritance," in *Evolution: The Extended Synthesis*, ed. Massimo Pigliucci and Gerd B. Muller (Cambridge: MIT Press, 2010), pp. 175-207.

spaces, and their inheritance, becoming a key factor."[71] This means that trait-based selection is far too simple; rather, plasticity is critical in allowing a greater degree of diversity in phenotype without necessarily involving changes in the genotype. This is particularly useful because it opens up the evolutionary significance of behavioral and symbolic systems, so that a good definition of niche construction is "the building and destroying of niches by organisms and the synergistic interactions between organisms and environments"; hence, the organisms themselves "modify the evolutionary pressure acting on them, on their descendants and on unrelated populations sharing the same landscape."[72] The interrelationship between ecological, biological, and social niches becomes stressed, rather than each being treated in isolation. Information acquiring can therefore be placed on three levels, population genetic, ontogenetic, and cultural. In this case, the passing on of cultural inheritance and socially learned knowledge depends on preexisting information that is inherited through genetic or ontogenetic processes. One of the distinguishing marks of human societies is the speed at which humans are able to respond to new challenges based on prior learning. Their abilities to respond at quicker rates compared with most other complex organisms give them a distinct advantage in evolutionary terms, and they can respond in flexible ways even when faced with the same challenges. This plasticity and flexibility is not included in standard models of the evolution of human behavior according to natural selection. Hence, even where selection pressures are invoked as a means to explain changes in behavior, characterizing that behavior as an adaptation to a single selective pressure is far too simplistic. In the evolution of hominids, a good case can be made that it was cooperation between groups, in particular, that created a niche that then accounted for the success of hominins and the first members of our own genus, *Homo erectus* and *Homo ergaster.*[73]

The success of *Homo sapiens* compared with Neanderthals arises in this model because of their ability to construct long-distance trade routes.

71. Agustín Fuentes, "Cooperation, Conflict and Niche Construction in the Genus *Homo,*" in *War, Peace, and Human Nature: The Convergence of Cultural and Evolutionary Views,* ed. Douglas P. Fry (Oxford: Oxford University Press, 2013), pp. 78-94, here 78.

72. Fuentes, "Cooperation, Conflict and Niche Construction," p. 80.

73. See Donna Hart and Robert W. Sussman, *Man the Hunted: Primates, Predators, and Human Evolution* (Boulder, Colo.: Westview Press, 2008), and Agustín Fuentes, Matthew Wyczalkowski, and Katherine C. MacKinnon, "Niche Construction through Cooperation: A Non-linear Dynamics Contribution to Modeling Facets of the Evolutionary History in the Genus *Homo,*" *Current Anthropology* 51 (2010): 435-44.

This argument from archaeological evidence is consistent with Nowak and Highfield's mathematical case for human beings' characterization as "supercooperators."[74] Yet, the language that Nowak and Highfield use suggests that they envisage cooperation less in terms of niche construction and more in terms of another strand of neo-Darwinian selection that works according to models such as indirect and direct selection, reputation, and so "cooperation constructed humanity," rather than the other way round. While this is qualified by the idea that cooperation "generates the possibility for greater diversity by new specialization, new niches and new divisions of labor," it "makes evolution constructive and open ended." The overall emphasis seems to be on cooperation as a trait selected for throughout evolutionary history, where "Cooperation was the principle architect of 4 billion years of evolution."[75] The driving force of natural selection is therefore still preeminent in this account, so it is *natural selection* that uses five means of cooperation to turn "the essentially competitive drive of evolution" to cooperative process.[76]

Overall, then, integrated cooperation was a vital component of the primate niche that modified the social and biotic environments that changed the selection pressures in those populations. As social relationships became more complex in hominids, cooperation created a feedback between social and biotic ecologies leading to niche construction. In the last 10,000 years or so, cooperation, coordination, and niche construction moved to an even larger scale, and allowed the possibility of large-scale intergroup violence, but also the promise of large-scale cooperation.[77]

The Evolution of Conscience

If human beings are evolved to be in biosocial cultural communities, where their behavior shapes the very tapestry of the environment in which they

74. Nowak and Highfield, *Super Cooperators.*

75. Nowak and Highfield, *Super Cooperators,* p. 280. They do recognize that with the arrival of culture humans were able to "detach" to some degree from "chemistry, genes and DNA" (p. 275), but the full significance of this and how the two kinds of cooperation (cultural and gene-based) are related to each other are not explored.

76. Nowak and Highfield, *Super Cooperators,* p. 272.

77. Nowak and Highfield are optimistic that human beings will be able to draw on their abilities to cooperate to solve some of the world's most pressing social and ecological challenges.

share their social existence, then we would expect delicate psychological feedback mechanisms to be present to keep the norms agreed by that society intact. In chapter 4, on the evolution of morality, I began to address this idea, and I will take it up again in a discussion of fairness in the following chapter. But for the moment I want to address what human societies have called conscience, as it is presently understood and in relation to its possible evolutionary origins.

Anthropologist Christopher Boehm presents his case for the evolution of conscience drawing on the Darwinian idea of conscience as a moral sense.[78] Boehm believes that Darwin was not able to develop a full theory of conscience because he lacked the data that is now available from a range of disciplines, including primatology, paleoanthropology, cultural anthropology, and cognitive neuroscience.[79] What Darwin *did* notice is that blushing with shame for social misdemeanors was common across different cultures. Boehm argues that conscience is not simply a side effect, but it evolved for specific purposes related to humans' "growing ability to use group punishment to better their own social and subsistence lives and create more socially equalized societies."[80] He defines guilt as an inner anxiety about wrongdoing, and shame as when a past misdeed has become known to others; he prefers to use the word "shame" as it is more common across different cultures and is linked with physiological effects in blushing.[81] Boehm also rejects the idea that other species, such as dogs, can feel shame in the sense of emotional identification with a rule that has been broken. They may look ashamed to us, but that is most likely related to a feeling of discomfort in the face of disapproval, or fear of punishment for breaking a rule, rather than shame as such.[82] Supporting his view is the fact that when a rule is broken by dogs, any delayed punishment has no impact whatsoever on subsequent behavior. One would have anticipated some impact if the dog had internalized the rules and felt shame. The need for normal brain function in the sensitivity of conscience is clear in those

78. Charles Darwin, *The Descent of Man, and Selection in Relation to Sex* (London: Penguin, 2004 [1871]), pp. 71-72.

79. Christopher Boehm, *Moral Origins: The Evolution of Virtue, Altruism, and Shame* (New York: Basic Books, 2012), p. 13.

80. Boehm, *Moral Origins,* p. 15.

81. Boehm, *Moral Origins,* p. 20.

82. Boehm, *Moral Origins,* pp. 21-23. Of course, it is impossible to be certain about the inner workings of other animal minds, as raised in the last chapter, but I tend to agree with Boehm that caution is needed in attributing shame to other species.

who have suffered brain damage, or in psychopaths who apparently lack any sense of shame or moral conscience in a way that seems to be psychologically untreatable.[83] Boehm argues that a moral conscience has evolved not just to deter immoral behavior, but for reasons of evolutionary fitness in order to allow individuals to make strategic decisions about how much of that behavior is displayed before others. He believes, then, that conscience "can often make us into ambivalent conformists."[84] Furthermore, "Our consciences not only identify a given alternative as being moral or immoral, but also help us decide what to do about it."[85] The power of internalization expressed by conscience does not make people socially perfect, but acts like a social compass, as well as allowing awareness of social reputation. Boehm also believes there is a pro-social conscience that encourages us to help others, and not just one that helps us avoid doing harm to others.

What might be the prerequisites for moral conscience to develop? Boehm argues that the perspective taking of chimpanzees, that is, the ability to take into account the motive and reactions of others, shows at least a sense of self, which is a prerequisite for the development of more elaborated forms of conscience.[86] He asks the next question, namely, how far back in evolutionary history was there a moral conscience that helped an individual know when his or her behavior was likely to have devastating consequences? His working hypothesis is that conscience evolved in order to deal with the selection pressure of punishment, so that those who had developed sensitive consciences fared better than those who had not. Hence, "as the severity and cost of such punishment escalated, this created a selection pressure that favoured individuals with better personal self control."[87] He is well aware that his theory depends heavily on the idea that punishment was a major force in shaping gene pools in our distant past. He believes that the transition from a dominant hierarchical alpha male society in ancestral Pan to the egalitarian one that would have predominated 45,000 years ago is significant. He argues further that at the start of large-game hunting about a quarter of a million years ago, alpha male behavior would have inhibited sharing, so the only way to deal with such a prob-

83. Robert Hare, *Without Conscience: The Disturbing World of the Psychopaths among Us* (New York: Guildford Press, 1993).

84. Boehm, *Moral Origins,* p. 31.

85. Boehm, *Moral Origins,* p. 31.

86. Boehm, *Moral Origins,* p. 104.

87. Boehm, *Moral Origins,* p. 149.

lem was by force of violence. Those who evolved with more self-control were less likely to face lethal sanctions;[88] subsequently, such punishment applied to those who were cheating through stealing or through hiding meat. On the basis of field research, Boehm argues that individuals living in forager communities who fail to conform to accepted group norms face a range of disciplinary strategies, including rebukes, criticism, ostracism, ridicule, or shaming, and may eventually also face the ultimate threat of banishment exercises or even in a last resort capital punishment.[89] According to Boehm, Robert Trivers's modeling of altruism in terms of reciprocal benefit does not work in the field, and is only likely to apply to long-term marriage partnerships.[90] Richard Alexander's reputation-based model of altruism fares rather better in relation to field research among foragers. More important still, perhaps, is Boehm's recognition that free-rider modeling by George Williams does not allow a straightforward correspondence between genotype and phenotype. In the case of foragers, it is their social behavior that significantly inhibited any expression of tendencies to bully or intimidate, regardless of their biological origin. The speculative nature of Boehm's hypothesis is clear in his admission that it is possible that alpha males had already been dealt with much earlier than his scheme suggests, but he still believes that modification to the basic system would be through rules of punishment.

Boehm presupposes much that Sara Blaffer Hrdy heavily criticizes, namely, that human dispositions lean fundamentally toward egoism and nepotism and that group punishment was one means through which people were persuaded to behave more altruistically and to deter free riders. Group selection is also a possible explanation for pro-social behavior in that more cooperative groups would be at an advantage than those that are less generous, cooperative, and empathetic. While evolutionary biologists originally thought group effects were likely to be too weak to *explain* pro-

88. Boehm, *Moral Origins,* p. 152.

89. Boehm, *Moral Origins,* p. 46.

90. Trivers built on Hamilton's rule that suggested that altruistic cooperation among kin was directly related to kin relatedness. Trivers's dyadic model attempted to provide an explanation based on subsequent reward, so the underlying assumption was that individual human acts are still basically selfish. The fact that this does not apply in the way individual hunters actually relate to their bands is significant, since it suggests that such models are too simplistic. For classic essays, see William D. Hamilton, "The Genetical Evolution of Social Behavior, I and II," *Journal of Theoretical Biology* 7 (1964): 1-52. Robert L. Trivers, "The Evolution of Reciprocal Altruism," *Quarterly Review of Biology* 46 (1971): 35-57.

social tendencies, all agree that it would lead to their promotion. Hrdy's analysis of the importance of alloparenting implies a strong sense of group identity in child rearing. Group selection has, however, been criticized for its vulnerability to free riders taking advantage of the cooperative aspects of the group. Hence, any evolutionary theory that includes the idea of group selection needs to be able to deal with the free-rider problem. As well as a positive fear of punishment, there was a need to absorb and identify with the group rules. Boehm views, then, in a nutshell, the punishment of deviant behavior as having a more ancient origin than the promotion of virtuous behavior. For him, the degree of sociality and generosity in humans came subsequent to the development of conscience.[91] While a *theological* interpretation of the meaning of conscience goes rather deeper than this, the very basic sense of how to act in relation to rules that are perceived as coming from either external authority or internal insight from experience holds true.

An alternative evolutionary model to Boehm's speculation of the origin of conscience in order to deal with violence is the role it could play in the positive promotion of cooperative behavior in relation to group expectations. Close examination of how !Kung bushmen socialize also shows the extent to which shame can be a powerful motivating force not only in keeping alpha male tendencies in check but also in promoting egalitarian social rules. Boehm adds to this the fear of supernatural punishment as a means of reinforcing conscience.[92] While consistent with current evolutionary theory, his mapping of views of God onto an evolutionary paradigm where this is presupposed in neo-Darwinian terms seems somewhat simplistic. In the first place, it presupposes that social, behavioral sanctioning was

91. Boehm, *Moral Origins,* p. 18.

92. Boehm, *Moral Origins,* p. 202. He does not spell out here the relationship between the evolution of supernatural punishment, moral origins, and neo-Darwinian paradigms. The view that religion was subsequent to moral identity is common. Other scholars have developed this idea as a way of devising an explicitly evolutionary purpose for religious belief, understood in terms of a possible evolutionary role for belief in primarily punitive supernatural agency. See, for example, Dominic Johnson, "Why God Is the Best Punisher," *Religion, Brain and Behavior* 1, no. 1 (2012): 77-84. Although this is a reply to criticisms of the supernatural punisher hypothesis, the overall split among evolutionary theorists becomes particularly clear: Are other animals and humans basically selfish and vicious, needing a supernatural punisher to rein in cheaters, or are they cooperative? I tend to side with the latter, while recognizing that tendency for viciousness is also present. Such a split mirrors debates in theological anthropology regarding human nature as either basically corrupt or good.

insufficient to contain deviant behavior. Second, it assumes that complex human social symbolic systems consistently and in their content conform to neo-Darwinian evolutionary dynamics. If, on the other hand, as indicated above, evolution is appreciated in a wider sense to mean *change through active cultural construction and transmission,* rather than being tied to neo-Darwinian explanations, then this implies a much richer account of the evolutionary dynamics of both conscience and cooperation.[93]

Boehm suggests that conscience evolved as a result of selection pressure against greedy and aggressive behavior, in such a way that coincided with social self-inhibition functions in the brain. In other words, there was a gradual internalization of the external rules that led to social cohesion. It seems to me highly likely that the brain has evolved in such a way that it became more capable of complex self-referential function. I am less sure that we can call this capacity for self-reference *conscience,* which seems to me to be open to instruction as much as depending on an innate capacity for that internalization. While I would agree that the very general capacity for embarrassment or feeling shame is likely to be biologically based, this is not the same as a developed conscience, even according to anthropological definitions that react internally to given externally imposed rules and deviations from these rules. We know as much from the education of young children; a sense of shame only arises in relation to knowledge about certain rules and expectations given by the community. Quite apart from the problems associated with assuming an early alpha male–dominant hierarchy, a developed conscience is more likely to appear after language and the capacity for advanced forms of symbolic thinking have developed. Boehm's answer to this time lag is that the gap between the time of big-game hunting a quarter of a million years ago and cultural modernity around 45,000 years ago is sufficient to allow conscience to evolve — about 7,000 to 8,000 generations.[94] But this still seems to be speculating on conscience origins through an assumption that early hominids had the

93. There are, of course, religious issues in attempting to "explain" religious belief through evolutionary means, even in this expanded sense, since religious believers will always reject attempts to "naturalize" belief in God, which, by definition, cannot be so constrained without emptying that belief of its meaning. For the time being, I intend to bracket out this question, as my purpose is more modest, namely, to follow the dynamics of movement in the way evolutionary theories of cooperation are being developed, and seek resonance with alternative theological accounts of human action and cooperation, without reducing one to the other.

94. Boehm, *Moral Origins,* pp. 162-63.

biologically based social need to control their violent tendencies, and only later became more positive.

There are also alternative hypotheses to the evolutionary origins of conscience proposed by Boehm's model of social selection. One is that conscience evolved to encourage naturally selfish children to pay back some of the investment in parents' parenting.[95] Conscience as a means to promote cooperation arises in this case as a result of curbing the conflict between parents and children, rather than from the need to curb the aggressive behavior of selfish alpha males. But what if conscience evolved as a generalized capacity to maintain and *promote* social cohesiveness in the group, so that those who promoted cooperative behaviors would be rewarded by positive feelings and those who resisted cooperation would start to have negative psychological emotional states? As Boehm suggests, the conscience could be viewed as a "social mirror,"[96] instead of as simply there to control aggressive and other antisocial appetites; its primary role is to lead to feelings of shame when good behavior is avoided, or positive feelings when it is promoted. Boehm also views at least one function of religious belief as a supernatural form of sanctioning, supporting a conscience to act in a certain way. Given his propensity to view the origin of conscience in terms of the social sanctioning of aggressive behavior, it is not surprising that he also views beliefs in the supernatural as a way of sanctioning behavior by punitive feedback. God, in this view, reinforces a punitive conscience.[97] While free riders in any social community reflect an ongoing evolutionary puzzle, to pose that God concepts were invented to solve such a problem seems at best tenuous and at worst erroneous. The social exclusion of free riders is just as likely to deal effectively with their lack of cooperation as any internal mechanism that reinforces good behavior by fear of punishment. Part of the problem of such models is that they are highly speculative and difficult to judge with any accuracy; correlative studies between supernatural sanctioning and other forms of sanctions against different deviant behaviors expressed in different foraging societies

95. Boehm, *Moral Origins,* p. 170.

96. Boehm, *Moral Origins,* p. 172. Jonathan Haidt argues that our initial moral reactions are based on emotive responses, rather more than intellectual understanding. See Jonathan Haidt, "The Moral Emotions," in *Handbook of Affective Sciences,* ed. Richard J. Davidson, Klaus R. Scherer, and H. Hill Goldsmith (Oxford: Oxford University Press, 2003), pp. 852-70.

97. Boehm, *Moral Origins,* p. 202.

do not really amount to proof of the origin of conscience or its relationship with a particular form of religious belief.[98]

The way conscience has come to be understood in the humanities reflects its classical origins and the relationship with a much broader sense of consciousness.[99] But the overall idea of conscience used by evolutionary biologists in a very general sense as a kind of moral compass is intact. I have argued that collective conscience needs to be taken seriously as well as individual conscience in the moral life and that this aspect has been downplayed in scholarly discussion of the topic.[100] Collective conscience is more than simply an individual responding to the norms of the group in the manner discussed by Boehm above; it is more about a sense of the group norms as a whole through collective social action. Émile Durkheim was one of the pioneers of the idea of collective conscience and argued that it was the precursor of more developed religious beliefs involving both social "facts" and collective emotion.[101] His concept of collective conscience is, as in Boehm, more about *constraint* on human action according to certain moral rules than as an enabling force.[102] The difficulty, of course, is related

98. Boehm, *Moral Origins,* pp. 202-3.

99. The word "conscious" is derived from the Latin *conscius,* which means both having joint knowledge with the other and being self-conscious, especially in relation to guilt. Closely related is *conscientia,* which means *knowledge with* or shared knowledge. In classic usage, it appears in juridical texts in Cicero meaning knowledge of a witness. The possible Stoic origins of conscience in the New Testament are hotly debated, though Claude Anthony Pierce's influential commentary argues that the Pauline epistles adapted the sense of conscience found in folk wisdom, particularly a self-referential consideration of past acts that are considered to be wrong. See Claude A. Pierce, *Conscience in the New Testament* (London: SCM, 1955), pp. 13-22.

100. Celia Deane-Drummond, "A Case for Collective Conscience: Climategate, COP-15 and Climate Justice," *Studies in Christian Ethics* 24, no. 1 (2011): 1-18.

101. See Émile Durkheim, "The Rules of Sociological Method," in *The Rules of Sociological Method and Selected Texts on Sociology and Its Method,* ed. Steven Lukes, trans. W. D. Halls (Basingstoke: Macmillan, 1982 [2nd ed. 1901]), p. 56. Durkheim believed that collective emotions eventually came to "assume a shape, a tangible form peculiar to them" that was different from the original expressions, hence giving rise to particular customs, legal and moral rules, statistical analyses of social issues such as marriage and suicide expressing "a certain state of the collective mind" (pp. 54-56). While this account of social evolution seems somewhat questionable, the important point to note is that he identified the social significance of collective emotion.

102. Anthony Giddens, *New Rules of Sociological Method* (London: Hutchinson, 1976), p. 108. Giddens also makes the point that (contra Durkheim) actors may approach moral norms in a "utilitarian" fashion, calculating the risks of sanctions in the case of non-

to the problems associated with working out the basis for collective conscience. Is it simply a "common value system" in the way that Anthony Giddens suggests?[103] Or is it rather more than this, a form of "distributed cognition" developed by Edwin Hutchins?[104] Instead of either alternative, I have argued for the concept of collective conscience as a *heuristic tool* in order to highlight that the moral life is more than simply individual responses to group norms.[105] Such a position avoids the more difficult problem: how to test an evolutionary theory of the origins of a sense of collective culpability.

Steven Hitlin has developed a more sophisticated theory of the social psychology of conscience based on the idea of morality framed by "bright lines" that are perceived and should not be crossed, no-go zones that serve as signposts to speed up the decision-making process when a particular decision about how to act must be made.[106] He also uses "bright lights" to describe the ideals aimed at as being desirable for the good life in a way that is motivating toward proactive choices. Bright lines and lights may be based on more emotive responses, such as disgust, or worked out rationally in relation to group norms.[107] Conscience works, according to Hitlin, to both inhibit some actions and promote others, so that he defines it as "an ongoing process whereby our dual-processing aspects of mind code, analyse and emotionally respond to incoming stimuli through the lenses of

---

compliance (p. 109). This "reasonable" approach to moral norms is somewhat different from the more emotive quality in Durkheim's account.

103. Giddens, *New Rules,* p. 98. Labeling collective conscience as merely a common value system claims, it seems to me, rather too little.

104. Distributed cognition is a theory of psychology that was developed by Edwin Hutchins in the 1990s and analyzes the social aspects of the cognitive process. See, for example, Edwin Hutchins, *Cognition in the Wild* (Cambridge: MIT Press, 1994). It seems to me that distributed cognition makes too strong a claim in relation to collective conscience.

105. I developed this idea in relation to the particular case study of climate change, where I reasoned that such a concept is useful to analyze the way social norms are constructed in a group context. See Deane-Drummond, "A Case for Collective Conscience."

106. Steven Hitlin, *Moral Selves, Evil Selves: The Social Psychology of Conscience* (Basingstoke: Palgrave Macmillan, 2008), pp. 18-34.

107. Such a scheme maps onto the idea of "hot" and "cold" cognitive processes, with the former tied more to emotional systems of reasoning, and the latter as more under direct control. The difficulty of such classification is that it tends to simplify automatic responses as all associated with emotions; some automatic responses may show cognitive elements and arise from experience. First-order desires are more automatic and arise from the subconscious, while second-order desires arise from self-conscious deliberation. See Hitlin, *Moral Selves, Evil Selves,* pp. 22-24, for a useful summary.

our Bright Lights and Bright Lines."[108] Hitlin recognizes that some other animals may have limited bright line equivalents, but conscience as he has defined it is unique. "No other species forms long-term plans, makes abstract moral judgments, or is motivated by shame, guilt, and pride."[109] He argues that the range of emotions associated with bright lights and lines is limited by our biology, even if the content of those lines and lights varies enormously from one culture to the next.[110] He adopts those social characteristics judged as universal from the perspective of evolutionary psychology.[111] But their seeming universal presence across societies does not necessarily point to an evolutionary origin of explicit mental modules, even though it is consistent with it. There is, perhaps, some weight in the idea that a sense of moral fairness and reciprocity is innate rather than culturally learned, but calling this a universal moral grammar in a manner akin to Chomsky's theory of universal language suffers from similar drawbacks.[112] Nonetheless, the idea that conscience at least depends on the evolution of more generalized cognitive abilities for emotion and reasoned judgment is convincing. Certainly, as children's cognitive capacities enlarge and become more sophisticated in linguistic terms, their conscience moves from what might be termed a restrictive bright lines perspective to an inclusion of bright lights.[113] Human conscience development, therefore, depends not just on moral norms, but also on linguistic capacities. It also seems reasonable that conscience would have developed in our earliest ancestors in parallel with such cognitive capacities for symbolic thought.[114] The

108. Hitlin, *Moral Selves, Evil Selves,* p. 30.

109. Hitlin, *Moral Selves, Evil Selves,* p. 53.

110. Universal emotions include shame and disgust, as noted above. Hitlin, *Moral Selves, Evil Selves,* p. 54.

111. This list includes status, roles, divisions of labor, speech on special occasions, proper names, language to describe inner states, tools, elementary logic, facial expression, belief that people are partially responsible for their actions, belief that people have inner lives and make plans, sexual attraction, childhood fears, distinguishing in-group from out-group, and the tendency to form religious beliefs. Hitlin, *Moral Selves, Evil Selves,* p. 55.

112. For a discussion of Chomsky, see previous chapter. Hitlin relies for this discussion on the work of Marc Hauser, who, ironically perhaps, has since been disgraced and exposed for fabricating his scientific results. Hitlin, *Moral Selves, Evil Selves,* p. 56. For a report on Hauser's resignation for fabricating his results, see http://www.huffingtonpost.com/2012/09/05/marc-hauser-ex-harvard-pr_n_1859243.html (accessed March 11, 2013).

113. Hitlin, *Moral Selves, Evil Selves,* pp. 60-62.

114. For discussion of the evolution of symbolic thinking and language development, see previous chapter.

classification of human societies according to horizontal relationships with other close individuals, vertical relationships based on social hierarchies, and divinity based on sacredness[115] is helpful in that conscience development is likely to depend on the perceived priority of one form of social structure over the other. A religious perspective, however, would tend to see the dimension of divinity as impacting on the first two dimensions as well, rather than being somehow separated, even if for heuristic reasons it may be useful to separate it. Social conventions are, however, subject to different "rules" than moral conventions, and it is the latter that are under the scrutiny of conscience control.[116] Hitlin is correct, in my view, to point to the variety of often highly conflicting influences that seek to shape conscience in particular ways.

Given the above, it is not surprising that the Roman Catholic tradition has tended to oscillate between giving priority to individual discernment of what conscience requires and the deliberate shaping of that conscience through given norms; in other words, bright lines and bright lights set forth for individual compliance. The Vatican II stress on the freedom of individual conscience and its anxiety about the influence of philosophical relativism and other potentially "polluting" ideals have shifted the discussion to one of conformity to preset moral rules. Compare, for example, the Vatican II statement *Gaudium et Spes* (1965) with *Veritatis Splendor* (1993). In *Gaudium et Spes* (§16), we find a view of conscience as coercive obedience — "In the depths of his conscience, man detects a law which he does not impose upon himself, but which holds him to obedience" — in the same paragraph with a view of conscience as that which reflects inner, heartfelt religious conviction — "Conscience is the most secret core and sanctuary of a man. There he is alone with God, Whose voice echoes in his depths." *Veritatis Spendor,* on the other hand, uses the language of obedience more forcefully, especially conscience operational in conformity with natural law, hence, "Conscience thus formulates *moral obligation* in the light of the natural law: it is the obligation to do what the individual, through the workings of his conscience, *knows* to be a good he is called to do *here and now.* The universality of the law and its obligation are acknowledged, not suppressed, once reason has established the law's application in concrete present circumstances" (§59, emphasis in original).

115. Hitlin mentions this somewhat in passing in his discussion of evolution and the moral brain. Hitlin, *Moral Selves, Evil Selves,* p. 55.

116. Hitlin, *Moral Selves, Evil Selves,* p. 62.

Yet, even in this paragraph there are hints of the view of *Gaudium et Spes* that speaks of the conscience as being in conformity with the "law of God written on the heart," but it is always concerned with application of the natural law to a particular case. This is developed in subsequent paragraphs §60-62, which stress the need for conformity with divine law, and therefore in conformity with moral truth. Hence, we find that "The judgment of conscience does not establish the law; rather it bears witness to the authority of the natural law and of the practical reason with reference to the supreme good, whose attractiveness the human person perceives and whose commandments he accepts" (§60). The stress is therefore toward a view of conscience understood in conformity with externally ratified authority, rather than with individual autonomy.[117] How far such bright lines become assimilated by individuals depends on a previously conceived notion of the moral authority of the ecclesial community. It is clear, however, that the feeling of shame may accompany perceived breaks in the moral code, quite apart from rationally based arguments against a particular official position. In this case, the emotive desire to fit in with group norms conflicts with rational arguments that deny their validity. There are, however, ritual practices, including the sacrament of reconciliation, that aim to deal with feelings of guilt for wrongdoing and such inner conflicts in conscience.

Which should take priority: an inner sense of right action in one's conscience as open before God, or conformity to collective norms? Thomas Aquinas dealt with this issue and generally gave priority to collective good over individual desires. However, important exceptions to this rule come to the surface in his discussion of conscience. He included conscience in his discussion of *intellectual* acts, rather than as a power or a moral sense.[118] For Aquinas conscience is not a moral power or habit, but a reasonable act of judgment for the good or in avoidance of evil, the framework of which is set out in natural law. It is therefore a subjective, individual judgment about what needs to be done, and can be erroneous. An evolutionary view

117. A review of the historical development of an interpretation of conscience in the Roman Catholic tradition is outside the scope of this chapter. Moral theologian Julie Clague is presently critically engaging this aspect; Julie Clague, "Religious Conscience and Political Life: One Hundred Years of Catholic Teachings and Tensions" (public lecture, Yale Divinity School, March 7, 2013).

118. Thomas Aquinas, *Summa Theologiae, Man, Vol. 11 (1a. 75-83),* trans. Timothy Suttor (London: Blackfriars, 1970), qu. 79.13. Thomas believed that conscience could fulfill a range of functions, including to witness, to bind, to incite, and also to accuse, to torment, or to rebuke. In this, he showed both the regulating and the proactive functions of conscience.

of conscience as a moral compass fits in broadly with such a position, but makes no judgment about what it means for conscience to function properly or what a normative sense of good or evil might be. For Thomas, unlike Augustine, an individual's conscience is an intellectual act of ordering knowledge, and it always binds human persons to act or to refrain from action even if it seems to go against the teachings of the church. He held this view because he believed that an act of will against reason is always wrong, so "when his reason proposes something as being God's command slighting the dictate of reason amounts to slighting the law of God."[119] But at the same time, this was qualified by the insistence that a conscience could be ignorant of the relevant facts of the case, or in error, and human beings have an obligation to inform an ignorant conscience and seek to correct an erroneous one.[120] Further, a particular good has to be seen in relation to the common good.[121] Those judgments that are consistent with conscience are the judgments of properly functioning prudence.[122]

Toward an Inclusive Theo-Dramatics

I will now attempt to bring the various threads of my argument together in arguing for an inclusive theo-dramatics as a theological interpretation of evolutionary dynamics of cooperation, especially that viewed through niche construction theory in the light of human decision making as informed by conscience. I am not, however, simply viewing theo-drama as an "epiphenomenon" of niche construction, or merely as an element of symbolic inheritance, though I appreciate that some scholars working with the presupposition of a naturalistic philosophy may be inclined to interpret such a metaphor in this way.[123] However, I suggest that there are striking

119. Thomas Aquinas, *Summa Theologiae, Principles of Morality, Vol. 18 (1a2ae. 18-21),* trans. Thomas Gilby (London: Blackfriars, 1965), qu. 19.5.

120. Aquinas, *ST, Principles of Morality,* 1a2ae, qu. 19.6.

121. See, for example, Aquinas, *ST, Principles of Morality,* 1a2ae, qu. 19.10.

122. I have filled out a discussion of Aquinas's understanding of conscience in Celia Deane-Drummond, "Freedom, Conscience and Virtue: Theological Perspectives on the Ethics of Inherited Genetic Modification," in *Design and Destiny: Jewish and Christian Perspectives on Human Germline Modification,* ed. Ron Cole-Turner (Basingstoke: Macmillan, 2008), pp. 167-200.

123. See, for example, LeRon Shults, "Wising Up: The Evolution of Natural Theology," *Zygon* 47, no. 3 (2012): 542-48. What was striking in his response, however, was a strong adherence to particular models of how to perceive God as a naturally selected extension of

analogies here that help to clarify what theo-drama might mean in a context where evolutionary theory commonly exists in uneasy tension with theological interpretations of the way the world is and how to interpret the human condition in particular. Theologians always need to be careful to be modest in their language about God and recognize that there will always be limits to the human construction of that language as analogous to, but not identical with, God, who is ultimately beyond categorization, so our words about God, drawing from the human experience of the world, are always analogies. In much the same way, even more constructive theological accounts, when compared with narratives arising from science, permit the possibility of analogous relationships. In this respect, I am not arguing for a natural theology as such, so much as I am suggesting that there are broad analogies between the movement envisaged in niche construction and that represented through my particular interpretation of theo-drama. In fact, I would go so far as to suggest that niche construction serves to inform aspects of what that theo-drama is like, for it calls to attention the active agency of creatures, including the more dramatic and specific constructive role of human beings through cultural construction. Theo-drama as envisaged in the contemporary world is therefore dominated by what anthropologists and others have termed the Anthropocene.

In its original conception in the thought of Balthasar, theo-drama was what might be termed an "externalist" theory, one that accepted the natural world, creation, as an external, if dynamic, stage on which human actors took up their various roles in response to and in obedience to God's commands. In this case, the created world is envisaged as bland material for human creativity whose freedom displays itself most profoundly in dynamic response to God. In this view, standard neo-Darwinian evolutionary interpretations of human existence are too reductionist and do not give sufficient weight to human agency and interaction. If, in the light of niche construction theory, we shift to a much more organic view of human creativity and response, then the natural environment is not some blank stage, but itself becomes woven into the fabric of the drama into which human lives are situated. Reciprocity replaces a univocal human agency on a blank, flat stage, so that other agents, some more conscious than others, come more clearly into view in a dynamic, ecologically vibrant theo-drama.

"agency detection," presupposing the standard neo-Darwinian gene-environment evolutionary model that I am challenging here in terms of its scientific adequacy.

The characteristics that are part of the very, very long play of human beings in the world show up in the beginning not so much through erupting dramatic or violent scenes, but more through a slow unfolding of cooperation and expansion of social worlds. Humans are, as it were, gradually and slowing nudged into cooperative acts, expanding their collaborative processes step-by-step through a slowly unfolding drama where the awareness of God may at first only be dimly perceived. While this is certainly no Eden-like paradise, the predomination of cooperation early on in human history prior to much later tendencies for mass violence is, perhaps, significant. While we may balk at practices such as infanticide, have we lost some features of the simplicity of close relationships in our overindividualized and industrialized world? The pattern of human dramatic action is therefore complex and consistent with an anthropological characterization of human evolution expressed as "hyper-cooperation at multiple levels, extensive niche construction, relatively frequent coordinated intergroup violence, symbol use and hyper-complex information transfer, extremely diverse geographic distribution and ecological patterns."[124]

Theo-drama, therefore, as I am interpreting it, does not preclude the possibility of violence, as the script is not so much written in advance as improvised and responsive to a sense of reciprocity between God and human agents. Humanity's understanding of what God requires is also culturally laden and responsive to external, ecological pressures. Therefore, there are many simultaneous scenes in the theo-drama where the agency of other creatures and their inclusion in that drama may or may not be appreciated. I will develop this aspect further in chapter 8, where I argue for a greater appreciation of other animals as being in kinship relationships with human beings and bound up with our evolutionary, social, and cultural worlds.[125] Of course, the awareness of the presence of God, both in all things and as one to whom human creatures can have personal relation, is a key act in the drama, but this awareness was likely to have dawned gradually rather than all at once, in common with other characteristics that make human beings distinct from other creaturely kinds, and indeed distinct from other hominids that coexisted with *Homo sapiens* in prehistory.

But more important for the Christian vision of theo-dramatics is

124. Fuentes, "Cooperation, Conflict and Niche Construction," p. 86.

125. This is also developed in an article in preparation, Agustín Fuentes and Celia Deane-Drummond, "Exploring Boundaries in Human Becoming: An Argument for the Crucial Importance of Multispecies Relationships in Human Evolution Examined through a Community Niche and Theological Lens," *Philosophy, Theology and the Sciences* (2014).

when, very late in the history of *Homo sapiens sapiens,* the Word of God became flesh and lived among us: God takes a place with human beings on the stage. The radical message of the gospel is that this particular act in one mini–theo-drama in human history has a profound impact on all other theo-dramas, both before and since. Such a metaphysical view of the importance of this particular scene in one particular act in human history is bound to seem like a scandal from an evolutionary perspective. Yet, is such a universalist claim for significance so *very* different from the equally culturally laden scientific attachment to the significance of Darwin's understanding of evolution that is thought to be valid across different cultures, whether or not this is recognized as such by those cultures?

If cooperation is the default position for human societies, as sociologists Ernst Fehr and Herbert Gintis' extensive cross-cultural work on a huge range of human societies suggests, then the prevailing human condition is more likely to be cooperative than its opposite.[126] Just as it requires hermeneutical caution when interpreting the early evolution of human practices seen through current conceptual and cultural frameworks, such as those based on particular gender roles and so on, so it also requires hermeneutical caution when interpreting the much more recently inscribed significance of Christian accounts of theo-dramatics as portrayed in the Gospels and other scriptural texts as normative for Christian ethics. Furthermore, while we can appreciate that other primates exist in social worlds, using primates as models for human evolution is not necessarily helpful, given that the earliest common ancestor is unlikely to bear resemblance to such groups. Do other animals, at least in part, act out their theo-drama in a way that is entangled with that of human beings? I suggest that while in the past our histories were closely interwoven with other species, the world as we know it today has been so shaped by human cultures and societies that it is more appropriate to think of our present age as Anthropocene, that is, dominated by human culture. Our evolving social world has reached a level where human beings seem to be the only actors on the stage, but we should take care lest that act completely drown out all other voices in the play. While I am less inclined than some primatologists to believe that there are ethical lessons to be learned from the social lives of other animals, human lives are diminished and indeed dehumanized when cultural aspects are shorn free of associations with other animal kinds and wider ecological contexts.

126. Ernst Fehr and Herbert Gintis, "Human Motivation and Social Cooperation: Experimental and Analytical Foundations," *Annual Review of Sociology* 33 (2007): 43-64.

CHAPTER SEVEN

Human Justice and Animal Fairness

Is there an alternative social discourse to "rights" language for species other than *Homo sapiens* that takes adequate account of the significant place of animals in human lives and *their own* capacity for flourishing? I suggest that there is a different discourse of justice making and fairness that is useful in consideration of what can be described as the active performative dimension of humans in relation to other animals. Building on a critical account of the evolution of morality and animal ethology, I suggest that the meaning of human justice is clarified when considered in relation to its possible origins and expression as fairness in other social communities. Of course, there are many other ways of parsing out different elements of what justice can mean, including resolution in the face of conflict and even retribution when a wrong is committed, but both of these assume certain rules or principles for just action. It is justice in its principled relationship with fairness that is the specific focus of this chapter. The theoretical work of Martha Nussbaum is significant in this respect, for she has developed a capability approach resonant with Aristotelian philosophy that is appropriate for humans and for nonhumans according to their particular telos or goals for flourishing. But is this adequate in the light of theological considerations of justice making? In this chapter, I will explore more fully the patterns of justice as set forth in Aquinas's moral theology, its relationship to natural law and his hints at natural justice in other animals, as well as more controversial contemporary claims that his approach to moral theology and justice should be interpreted as non-Aristotelian. By this I hope to achieve two tasks that I suggest are very closely intertwined, even if distinct. First, how, generally speaking, should a broad theory of social justice be constructed in relationships with other animals, with implications for animal ethics? And second, how might justice making illuminate distinctive characteristics associated with human nature(s)? The nature/culture boundary shows up once more as a fuzzy line of admixed nature/cultures and cultural nature. A discussion of justice as presented in this chapter also reveals in a stark way the virtual impossibility of reasonably separating theological anthropology from theological ethics; each is entangled in and informed by the other.

The Evolution of Fair Play

Building on a discussion of cooperation in chapter 6, we ask, how do we know when someone is cooperating well, that is, playing fair? One prominent way of testing that hypothesis is by generating theoretical games that show either cooperation or defection, either according to simulated games or by asking participants to play games according to certain rules. Fairness, if understood as persistent cooperation according to the rules of a particular game, is more likely to persist if it is there from the start.[1] Many economic models of cooperation assume that self-interest is the prime motivator. But fairness may also be a motivating factor in itself.[2] From an evolutionary biologist's perspective, the question is also why fairness is motivating if it does not always benefit the individual. In other words, why do I risk playing fair if you might cheat? Is it part of the "indirect reciprocity" complex in which an individual's status is related to reputation and associated social and evolutionary benefits? Biologist Richard Alexander, for example, argues that order and justice in human communities are the ultimate outcome of self-interested behavior, where self-interest is defined as genetic interests.[3] If this is applied to fairness, then what looks like self-sacrifice in acting fairly may enhance one's reputation among peers or provide indirect rewards toward relatives.[4] But while this might appear relatively innocuous, Alexander is also prepared to claim that "Gods are in-

1. For a more detailed discussion of game theoretical models in relation to justice, see J. McKenzie Alexander, *The Structural Evolution of Morality* (Cambridge: Cambridge University Press, 2007), p. 148.

2. Robert H. Frank, *Passions with Reason: The Strategic Role of the Emotions* (New York and London: Norton, 1988), p. 163.

3. Richard Alexander does not devote much discussion to justice, but see Richard Alexander, *The Biology of Moral Systems* (New York: De Gruyter, 1987), p. 192.

4. Alexander, *Biology of Moral Systems,* p. 94.

ventions originally developed to extend the notion that some have greater rights than others to design and enforce rules, and that some are more destined to be leaders, others to be followers."[5] From this followed the ideal of a more universal, impartial, just law. As noted in chapter 4, many evolutionary biologists are more inclined than Alexander to stress cooperation as a fundamentally evolved trait, rather than to explain it indirectly through biological notions of self-interest. However, the self-interested paradigm has spread wider than biologists intended in its use in economic theories about justice. Further, attempts to explain religious belief in God as an "invention" prompted by the self-interests of one group in order to promote and enforce particular rules are quite frankly naïve and lack credibility even in terms of scientific discourse.[6]

Rather more promising is the idea that always being fair in dealing with others is a way of signaling a particular commitment to others that does not so much enhance reputation as allow dispositions that encourage future cooperation.[7] Of course, the idea of dispositions toward action chimes with the classic account of the virtues that I will develop further below. More elaborate, but also highly relevant, is the idea of social coordination norms that are accepted in particular cultures usually without much question. Language, discussed in chapter 5, is an example of such

5. Alexander, *Biology of Moral Systems,* p. 207.

6. While the discussion of the evolution of religion is becoming rather more sophisticated, what is of interest here is the way Alexander is using the particular account of belief in God to argue for a particular way of structuring rules for justice making, which he claims led to the idea of universal law. The element worth retaining in this account is that any claim for universality in law needs to take account of different cultural and social contexts, but this can be done by a thorough anthropological investigation.

7. This leads to literature on commitment signaling and its relationship with religious belief that is outside the scope of this paper. If religious belief motivates cooperation, then costly signaling theory provides the basis for understanding that motivation in biological terms. Rather like a gazelle "stotting" in the face of a predator, costly signaling is understood as a display that gives honest communication to the other. Religious commitment is viewed as a way of signaling to others in the same group the readiness to cooperate. It is hard to fake honest signaling, and in this sense it is preferable to evolutionary theories of religion that perceive it as nonadaptive. Of course, evolutionary explanations such as these point to why religious commitment may naturally stabilize in a community, but they do not make any claims about the truth, or otherwise, of such religious beliefs or practices. See, for example, Joseph Bulbulia and Richard Sosis, "Signaling Theory and the Evolution of Religious Cooperation," *Religion* 41, no. 3 (2011): 363-88; Richard Sosis and Eric Bressler, "Co-operation and Commune Longevity: A Test of the Costly Signaling Theory of Religion," *Cross-Cultural Research* 37, no. 2 (2003): 11-39.

a social coordination norm. But how are these norms related specifically to fairness? In this respect, what might be deemed fair in one culture may not be in another, so that in some African societies such as the Maasai, for example, there are patterns of gift exchange according to need, obligation, respect, and restraint, known as the *osotua* norm (or the umbilical cord norm).[8] Other patterns also coexist with this norm, so that the first way that the Maasai react is in terms of tit-for-tat, or reciprocal, arrangements. The *osotua* norm contrasts with the kind of contractual agreement that largely tends to ignore the needs of the other party that is most characteristic of Western societies' understanding of "fairness." The *osotua* or social contract norms are accepted in those societies that presuppose their worth as a social coordination norm or social coordination convention. But such norms are not internalized in individuals; rather, social coordination norms are flexible in that they can change and adapt with new information or external conditions. These social conventions are accepted by a social group noncritically, but their influence can be transferred once other cultures are aware of the basic rules. In a fascinating study, Lee Cronk has shown that the *osotua* norm can influence subsequent patterns of exchange when subjects from Western cultural contexts are exposed to its ideals.[9] A number of different social convention norms could be used in the original African setting, so that telling Maasai that they are playing according to the *osotua* norm also has the result of shifting patterns of exchange.[10] Of course, what is not yet clear is how far such an influence might persist following such exposure to the norm.

The account so far suggests that "fair play" will have different meanings depending on the particular human culture in question and according to the particular social convention norms that are accepted by that society. But is there anything analogous in other animals that might illuminate this

8. *Osotua* as a social coordination norm is characteristic of the Maa language group of pastoralists known as the Maasai and the Samburu and some other neighboring groups distributed in a band running from Lake Turkana in northern Kenya down into the Rift Valley and beyond in Tanzania. The possible origin of this social convention in terms of risk pooling is discussed in C. Athena Aktipis, Lee Cronk, and Rolando de Aguiar, "Risk-Pooling and Herd Survival: An Agent Based Model of a Maasai Gift-Giving System," *Human Ecology* 39 (2011): 131-40.

9. Lee Cronk and Helen Wasielewski, "An Unfamiliar Social Norm Rapidly Produces Framing Effects in an Economic Game," *Journal of Evolutionary Psychology* 6, no. 4 (2008): 283-308.

10. Lee Cronk, "The Influence of Cultural Framing on Play in the Trust Game: A Maasai Example," *Evolution and Human Behavior* 28 (2007): 352-58.

issue further? Particular greeting rituals are known in many social animals that, while not necessarily as complex or as flexible as social convention norms evident in human societies, at least show the tendency for particular socially coordinated behavior.[11] Biologists have paid a great deal of attention to the particular characteristics of social play in other animals, play that also seems to follow particular accepted conventions. Gordon Burghardt's account of the emergence of animal play shows that play is limited to mammals and birds and is often associated with the young.[12] Part of what play does is to hone social skills in the young, as well as other skills associated with predatory, sexual, defensive, and physiological capacities. Significantly, perhaps, play may also encourage innovative new behaviors.

From his detailed and close observation of play behavior in canids, Marc Bekoff goes further than some in arguing that not only do many other animals cooperate, but they also exhibit what he terms "wild justice." More specifically, Bekoff, in collaboration with philosopher Jessica Pierce, suggests that these insights impinge on how we think about human behavior, so that "Human capacities such as empathy and justice and trust are physical processes involving the brain, as well as other bodily systems."[13] The hormone oxytocin, for example, is known to increase human test subjects' ability to trust or to show empathy in a way that appears to be entirely involuntary.[14] Of course, how far oxytocin is actually causative of such behavior, or how far it is associated with other correlative processes that then impact on that behavior, is not entirely clear. But how might the capacity for justice in particular be related to such processes? Clearly, in this scheme, empathy and the ability to show trust could be thought of as

11. William McGrew, *Chimpanzee Material Culture: Implications for Human Evolution* (Cambridge: Cambridge University Press, 1992); Christophe Bosch, *Wild Cultures: A Comparison between Chimpanzee and Human Culture* (Cambridge: Cambridge University Press, 2012).

12. Gordon M. Burghardt, *The Genesis of Animal Play: Testing the Limits* (Cambridge: MIT Press, 2005).

13. Marc Bekoff and Jessica Pierce, *Wild Justice: The Moral Lives of Animals* (Chicago: University of Chicago Press, 2009), p. 32.

14. Paul J. Zak, *The Moral Molecule: The Source of Love and Prosperity* (New York: Dutton, 2012). While Zak has shown convincingly that the hormone oxytocin is clearly an element present in trusting relationships, to claim that this is in any sense the "source" of complex relationships mistakes fluctuating biological markers with origins. Furthermore, if oxytocin generates affiliation with those in the "in group" but hostility toward strangers, then it could even be said to move in a direction diametrically opposite to the one that justice demands.

prerequisites for the inclination to play fair. Bekoff and Pierce's account shows at times justice and fairness wrapped together in one concept, so that a species-specific "sense of justice" is treated in much the same way as a kind of native "fairness," as if the two are more or less indistinguishable.[15]

Yet, justice entails something more than simple fairness, even if it is grounded on it; that is, justice entails a stronger normative approach that is accepted by a particular community rather than a simpler "innate" sense of fairness or social coordination norm referred to above. The crucial question is, then, how are the two related? This becomes clearer in the definition of justice used by Bekoff and Pierce, who define it both philosophically as "a set of expectations about what one deserves and how one ought to be treated" and, importantly, in terms of biological characteristics, a "justice cluster," that include "several behaviors related to fairness, including a desire for equity and a desire for and capacity to share reciprocally."[16] Furthermore, "The cluster also includes various behavioral reactions to injustice, including retribution, indignation, and forgiveness, as well as reactions to justice such as pleasure, gratitude, and trust."[17] The authors admit that the term "justice" is not used commonly in the biological literature, most probably because it implies a clear set of norms and rules that are hard to identify in other species. One reason why the idea of justice has received resistance is because some studies have shown that when chimpanzees are exposed to "ultimatum" games used by economists to study human behavior, they do not seem sensitive to whether the division of goods is "fair" or not.[18] This work could be criticized, however, in that it used the artificial context of captive animals, and assumed the kind of analogy of exchange in relation to a particular human society; as discussed above in relation to the *osotua* norm, fairness in different cultures is perceived differently. In addition, other research does suggest a greater sensitivity by alloprimates to the fair division of goods.[19]

15. Bekoff and Pierce, *Wild Justice,* p. 115.

16. Bekoff and Pierce, *Wild Justice,* p. 113.

17. Bekoff and Pierce, *Wild Justice,* p. 113.

18. Keith Jensen, Josep Call, and Michael Tomasello, "Chimpanzees Are Rational Maximizers in an Ultimatum Game," *Science* 104 (2007): 13046-51.

19. See Frans de Waal, *The Age of Empathy: Nature's Lessons for a Kinder Society* (New York: Broadway, 2010). De Waal's argument is weaker, however, in the rather too ready extrapolation of observations among primate societies to human morality and decision making, as if what is natural could provide clear guidelines as to how to act. Sarah Brosnan, who has worked alongside de Waal, argues that a strong emotive aversion to inequity evolved

Sarah Brosnan has reported negative reactions to what is perceived as an unfair distribution of goods, or "inequity aversion," in primates and a range of other species.[20] Is the observed reaction by alloprimates to goods received by a companion really the result of inequity aversion, or is it simply a reaction arising from a sense of being punished by not receiving the expected goods?[21] It is notoriously difficult to discriminate between these two alternatives when observing primate behavior. The evolutionary advantage of reactions to inequity is postulated to be related to the positive impact on cooperation. It seems doubtful, however, even in a generous reading, that the observations of primate behavior amount to concrete evidence for justice. As Brosnan points out:

> Most of the animal researchers focus on "inequity" or "inequality" rather than speaking of fairness or justice. There are several broad reasons for this. First, the animal paradigms tend to measure individuals' reactions to outcomes which differ from that of a partner, which is best described as inequity or inequality. Although this is an aspect of fairness, even results indicating a sensitivity to the paradigm would indicate sensitivity to unequal outcomes, but not fairness per se. However, many human studies are focused on justice or fairness, which are more loaded terms indicating an interest in both one's own and others' outcomes, as well as presumably some ideal distribution against which current distributions are being compared.[22]

Furthermore, in a fascinating study of dogs, Alexandra Horowitz showed that inequity aversion has its limits, that dogs will prefer owners who give them more rewards over those that treat them fairly.[23] Furthermore, the evolution of fairness is likely to be subject to considerable complexity,

---

alongside cooperative mechanisms. See Sarah Brosnan, "A Hypothesis of the Co-evolution of Cooperation and Reponses to Inequity," *Frontiers in Decision Neuroscience* (April 2011). Available online at: http://www.frontiersin.org/Decision_Neuroscience/10.3389/fnins.2011.00043/abstract (accessed February 23, 2013). These results imply that a sense of fairness is as much a deep-seated response as the need to cooperate.

20. Sarah F. Brosnan, "Introduction to 'Justice in Animals,'" *Social Justice Research* 25 (2012): 109-21.

21. Nichola J. Raihani and Katherine McAuliffe, "Does Inequity Aversion Motivate Punishment? Cleaner Fish as a Model System," *Social Justice Research* 25 (2012): 213-31.

22. Brosnan, "Introduction to 'Justice in Animals,'" p. 114.

23. Alexandra Horowitz, "Fair Is Fine, but More Is Better: Limits to Inequity Aversion in the Domestic Dog," *Social Justice Research* 25 (2012): 195-212.

since among primates the aversion to inequity varied considerably both between species and between individuals, depending on a range of ecological and other conditions.[24]

Further support for an innate sense of fairness comes from a study of very early child development, which shows that even young babies of six months will respond positively to cooperative tendencies in others and negatively to conflict. Kiley Hamlin argues that this points to a kind of social intelligence that is prior to language development.[25] Bekoff believes that similar kinds of social evaluations are found in other animals; however, social play seems to go further than this in requiring participants to understand *and* abide by the rules, so that it is a learned experience where what is acceptable or not becomes clear during the play itself. Hence, "Animals have to continually negotiate agreements about their intentions to play so that cooperation and trust prevail, and they learn to take turns and set up 'handicaps' that make play fair. They also learn to forgive."[26] The rules of engagement are about behavioral limits, such as how hard to bite, limitations of assertion of dominance, and restraint in sexual advances. Fairness is assumed in play and if fairness is not present, play degenerates into fighting. Animal play is also about choice, and those that play need to work out how to neutralize inequalities in social size or rank. If play becomes unfair, animals will react negatively. Fairness here is still, of course, "an individual's specific social expectations and not some universally defined standard of right and wrong."[27] Playing in dogs is accompanied by a well-known "play bow" that signals the intention to play. Dominant wolves show the intention to play by rolling over on their back in a vulnerable gesture, as well as exhibiting other forms of self-handicapping, such as not biting as hard as they could, and so on. Many other social animals show play behavior, including wallabies, rats, and coyotes.

Play occupies a "relaxed field" that is pleasurable and fun but also cognitively demanding.[28] There is a rhythm to play that goes further than

24. Sara A. Price and Sarah F. Brosnan, "To Each according to His Need? Variability in the Responses to Inequity in Non-human Primates," *Social Justice Research* 25 (2012): 140-69.

25. J. Kiley Hamlin et al., "The Mentalistic Basis of Core Social Cognition: Experiments in Preverbal Infants and a Computational Model," *Developmental Science* 16, no. 2 (2013): 209-26.

26. Bekoff and Pierce, *Wild Justice,* p. 116.

27. Bekoff and Pierce, *Wild Justice,* p. 120.

28. Bekoff and Pierce, *Wild Justice,* p. 120.

some kind of formal counting or score keeping, even if there are basic rules that need to be followed and that are specific for the different species involved.[29] There are other characteristics of play that are worth noting in this context: play is done for its own sake, rather than as a means to an end, using features from ordinary life but in a new way, and it is always in a relaxed mode when the main demands of care are taken over by others.[30] Burghardt distinguishes secondary play that meets the need to hone predatory, defensive, or social skills from tertiary play that is more innovative.[31] Those with an extended period of parental care are more likely to develop more elaborate forms of play behavior. This is relevant in making comparisons between human play behavior and that in other animals, since while there are characteristics in common between them, humans are also capable of distinctive forms of symbolic play from the second year onward. Fascinatingly, "Many of the games and much of the informal play among the !Ko and !Kung involve pretending to be various animals and the hunters pursuing them."[32] Ritualized role play, such as pretend weddings, dolls, and the use of other tools for play, goes much further than anything that can be found in other social animals.

Is it reasonable that the kind of rule-bound social play of other animals and their behavior according to particular expectations be named "justice," or should it be more appropriately called "fairness"? Of course, as Bekoff has indicated, if we define justice according to a set of behaviors that includes fairness, then "wild justice" is an appropriate term. But the freight carried by this use of language may be misleading if it implies a deliberate marking off of norms that are deliberately chosen and specified, rather than nonreflective conformity to rules. There are certainly gray lines here, in that acknowledging the possibility of subjectivity in other animals, such as in the hyenas mentioned in the close ethnographic study discussed in chapter 4, is not the same as implying that there is always a deliberate set of rules for a game or "justice requirements" that need to be followed

29. See Dale Peterson, *The Moral Lives of Animals* (New York: Bloomsbury Press, 2011), pp. 213-14.

30. Discussed in Robert Bellah, *Religion in Human Evolution: From the Paleolithic to the Axial Age* (Cambridge: Harvard University Press, Belknap Press, 2011), p. 77. Bellah also believes that play is the foundation for the subsequent development of religious rituals.

31. Primary play is often solitary and is locomotion only, rather than more complex forms found in secondary play processes. See Burghardt, *Genesis of Animal Play,* pp. 83-89.

32. Melvin Konner, *The Evolution of Childhood: Relationships, Emotion, Mind* (Cambridge: Harvard University Press, Belknap Press, 2011), p. 508.

by those involved in order to "play fair." Marcus Baynes-Rock in his interaction with the hyena Willi was encouraged to play according to the rules of the hyena play framework. But when Marcus suddenly left, the "unfair" breaking of trust, as far as Willi was concerned, had wider social repercussions and negative consequences in the social cohesion of the clan and clan interactions with human beings. This reaction was not a deliberative one, but a spontaneous one that was perfectly understandable according to the accepted rules of hyena play. The difference, in other words, is that the particular requirements for *justice making* in human communities are actively sought and crafted as well as being "hidden" by their prior social acceptance in terms of social conventions.

It might be a closer analogy to call the kind of "wild justice" that Bekoff speaks about a *social convention,* especially as such social conventions also exist in the human community and in some cases impinge on what is then deemed just or unjust in that society. Furthermore, it may be that some social conventions in human societies are initially the subject of deliberation but then later become unexamined norms, or even the other way round. "Playing" according to the rules of the game in human societies, if it follows accepted and unexamined social conventions, would then be rather more like the ritualized play of other animals. The element of reasoning, then, in justice making in human societies does, I suggest, mark off a boundary, albeit a leaky one, compared with wild fairness. The institutional and legal structures that are built around justice making in human societies are clearly unique to humans. On the other hand, the desire for justice in human communities reflects emotive reactions to injustice that in their turn reflect that found in other animals and go further than simple deliberation. How far might such research impinge on current theories of social justice?

Martha Nussbaum and *Frontiers of Justice*

Although Martha Nussbaum has identified herself to some extent with the animal rights movement, her discussion of justice for animals other than our own species is interesting as it opens up a way of thinking about what justice means for creaturely kinds. In deciding what might count as in or out in terms of justice making, she draws a line at sentience, the capacity to feel pain. Although she is highly critical of utilitarian approaches to justice, such as that of Peter Singer, which use minimization of total pain and maximization of pleasure as a way of deciding what justice entails, she suggests that "it seems plausible to consider the possession of sentience as a threshold condition for membership in the community of beings who have entitlements based on justice."[33] Here Nussbaum is, of course, asking which creatures deserve to be *recipients* of human justice making, rather than how far are other creatures capable of exhibiting fair or "just" behaviors according to their own social rules. However, in examining what makes for the flourishing of other animals, she is forced to consider the behavior of animals.

One of the difficulties of her approach is that it tends to generalize across such a wide variety of species by drawing the line at sentience. But here Nussbaum, in one sense, follows a pragmatic stance, for we have "enough on our plate" if we consider sentience as the boundary condition. One of the reasons for this "enough" is that Nussbaum attempts to build up a list of what might be basic capacities for flourishing that creatures other than humans might be entitled to inasmuch as the human community is able to influence this in some way. It would be difficult to design such a list for the huge variety of all creaturely forms, or if we did, it would have to take different shapes for different levels of organization. To see how she has approached developing such a list, I will summarize her argument for including animals in human justice making.

The place she starts for all considerations of what justice means is through a critical dialogue with the work of John Rawls's contract theory. While she shares his political liberalism, she criticizes the way contract theory assumes that any relation of justice will be that between those who are rough equals, or at least those who might reasonably be considered on an equal footing. Historically, this position arose as a challenge to existing social hierarchies within a nation-state where some are given in a seemingly arbitrary way greater opportunity and status than others, while problems such as those relating to mental incapacity or other animals are put "on hold."[34] In particular, the purpose of social contract theory is to

33. Martha Nussbaum, *Frontiers of Justice* (Cambridge: Harvard University Press, Belknap Press, 2006), pp. 361-62.

34. Nussbaum, *Frontiers of Justice,* p. 32. Although the relative imbalance between the poorest and richest nations of the world could be considered equally arbitrary compared with the hierarchies of wealth and birth that contract theory attempted to undermine, the latter does not have any way of dealing with more fundamental challenges to the basic economic arrangements necessary in order to address the issue of inequality between nation-states.

foster mutual advantage between equal parties; hence, it resists examining motivations such as altruism and benevolence.

Instead, drawing on Hugo Grotius's natural law approach, she argues that a human creature has both dignity/moral worth and sociability, leading to a desire for peaceful fellowship. For Nussbaum, these are not rooted in metaphysics, but are "freestanding ethical claims out of which one might build a political concept of the person," that is, it gives a guide for shaping basic human entitlements.[35] It is important for Nussbaum that the outcome is flagged up first, that is, sociability and dignity. A minimally just society would be one where human dignity is respected. Sociability, on the other hand, implies that procedural forms of justice sometimes fall short and mutual advantage is not the only reason for acting justly.[36] In order to adapt Grotius's theory for consideration of animal kinds, Nussbaum rejects the sharp separation between animals and humans that Grotius presupposed.

Social contract theories influenced by Immanuel Kant are equally problematic for Nussbaum, since they root dignity in human reasonableness and envisage contracts between equal parties, hence denying that there are obligations of justice to other animals. For Kantian and other such theories, the only possible basis for fair treatment of animals is *indirect* duties rooted in compassion, rather than justice. Kant believed that if we are cruel to animals we are more likely to be cruel to humans, and if we are kind to animals we are more likely to be kind to humans. Hence, for him, appropriate treatment of animals fostered duties of justice toward humans. For Kant, moral rationality is essential for ethical status.[37] For Nussbaum, this is too fragile a basis for kindness to animals.[38] More importantly, for Nussbaum the asymmetry of power relationships between humans and other animals is such that a social contract with them would not be a "real contract" or one for "mutual advantage," and while some

35. Nussbaum, *Frontiers of Justice,* p. 36.

36. For John Rawls, the correct procedure guarantees a good outcome, so that "there is a correct or fair procedure such that the outcome is likewise correct or fair, whatever it is, provided that the procedure has been properly followed." John Rawls, *Theory of Justice* (Cambridge: MIT Press, 1971), p. 86; also cited in Nussbaum, *Frontiers of Justice,* p. 82.

37. Rationality for Kant was self-reflexive and therefore excluded other animal kinds by definition. While it is possible to challenge how far other animals might be thought of as moral, the point is that animals are excluded in this scheme from any consideration of justice, fairness, or morality.

38. Nussbaum, *Frontiers of Justice,* p. 330. References to this work are placed in the following text.

animals may be very independent, they are not equal in power and resources (pp. 334-35).

Instead, her starting point for consideration of justice among other animals is that they, like humans, are entitled to a dignified existence. She offers this as a basis for justice not just by drawing on Grotius, but also by suggesting that this is a common understanding of what justice entails. So for her, "what we typically mean when we call a bad act unjust is that the creature injured by that act has an entitlement not to be treated in that way, and an entitlement of a particularly urgent or basic type" (p. 337). What is lacking in Kant and Rawls is any notion of the agency or subjectivity of other animals, any notion that they might be "a subject, a creature to whom something is due, a creature who is itself an end." While compassion is important in that justice requires its operation, compassion alone is not enough, for "by itself it is too indeterminate to capture our sense of what is wrong with the treatment of animals" (p. 337).

A dignified existence is incompatible with the way other animals are often treated, and, as minimum entitlements, she argues one would expect "adequate opportunities for nutrition and physical activity; freedom from pain, squalor and cruelty; freedom to act in ways that are characteristic of the species . . . , freedom from fear and opportunities for rewarding interactions with other creatures of the same species, and of different species; a chance to enjoy the light and air in tranquility" (p. 326).

This emphasis on dignity for other animals and not just humans diverges from utilitarian views that make judgments about what justice requires on the basis of outcomes. While this might be an improvement compared with Rawlsian procedural views, Nussbaum engages three elements of utilitarianism: (a) consequentialism, (b) sum ranking, and (c) a substantive view of the good. Consequentialism understood as promoting the best consequences offers the fewest problems for Nussbaum, since goods aimed at may be adjusted and most moral theories have consequentialist elements. However, she challenges whether a view that simply aims at consequences is "the right starting point for political justice" (p. 340). In particular, can consequentialism give sufficient priority to basic justice? Sum ranking simply refers to the total aggregate good consequences in people's lives. She believes that this process is unnecessary, and is misleading in that it tends to treat people (or other creatures) as a means; rather, following Kant, persons should be valued in themselves as having ends. The overall good may be thought of as hedonistic, reflecting a surfeit of pleasure over pain, or Peter Singer's "preference utilitarianism" in which good consequences reflect the desires or preferences of those affected. This leads Singer to conclude that killing, for example, is only wrong when the person has a preference to continue living.[39] But it is the overall or substantive view of the good in utilitarian approaches that Nussbaum finds particularly objectionable; she believes that political activity involves making choices about principles that govern the lives of people who may have very different views about the good or religious convictions. If we begin with the idea of respect, this necessarily means for her "not imposing on them some other person's comprehensive view of the good. What we want our political actors to do, in a liberal state, is just to take care of basic justice, and not to be maximizers of overall good. We actively want them not to pursue the maximization of overall good, because we don't want them to be in the business of defining what the good is in a comprehensive way" (Nussbaum, p. 340).

She therefore considers that the central capabilities approach is sufficiently "thin" to not demand a comprehensive view of the good. It is a way of restraining those who would demand more substantial notions of what the good might be, and as a "partial" notion of the good, it theoretically at least allows endorsement by a greater number of people in different cultural settings. To arrive at a list of what might make for a "rich plurality of life activities," she uses for humans a "species norm," but this is not simply read off of what is "natural," as there is an evaluative process in arriving at what this norm might look like. She is also Aristotelian in grounding her understanding of human dignity in animal capacities, where rationality is just one of those capacities, rather than idealized and then set in opposition to animality (p. 159). She also follows Aristotle in naming complex forms of natural life "wonderful and wonder-inspiring," rather than that which brings disgust. This seems to ground her attention to all forms of life. According to this view, humans are political animals, but she goes further than Aristotle by insisting that the dignity of creatures is worth preserving.

She sums up the difference between capability and contractarian views by suggesting that the former "goes beyond the contractarian views in its starting point, a basic wonder at living beings, and a wish for their flourishing, and for a world in which creatures of many types flourish. It goes beyond the intuitive starting point of Utilitarianism because it takes an

39. This shows up in a sharp way the lack of any deontological or principled foundation in Singer's view. For an alternative reading of Singer, see Charles Camosy, *Peter Singer and Christian Ethics* (Cambridge: Cambridge University Press, 2011).

interest not just in pleasure and pain, but in complex forms of life and flourishing. It wants to see each thing flourish as the sort of thing it is" (p. 349).

Accordingly, there is no longer the difficulty encountered in contractarian approaches to other animals that insist that those that make the rules are the same agents as those for whom the rules are made. Here other beings only enter in a derivative way through trusteeship. The capability approach, on the other hand, views different types of dependency and interdependency differently, so that relations of justice do not just exist between free, equal, and independent human beings. If we extend this to other animals, then they are not receiving benefits indirectly, but rather because they are valued subjects and agents of a life that is more than just the means to the ends of others.

The overall list of what entitlements might be appropriate for other animals is even more difficult to assemble than such a list for humans. This is because of the obvious point that animals are not participating directly in drawing up the principles, so "there is much danger in imposing on them a form of life that is not what they would choose"; therefore, we need to aim for enabling or protecting, rather than for a comprehensive set of goods (p. 352). How do we determine what this might entail? Here Nussbaum relies on what she calls "sympathetic imagining," but then uses "theoretical insights about dignity to correct, refine, and extend both judgments and imaginings" (p. 355). She also believes we can have some access to animal lives by "narrative," which seems to mean "literary artistry," rather like reading a novel. Here "Imagining and storytelling remind us in no uncertain terms that animal lives are many and diverse, with multiple activities and ends both within each species and across species" (p. 355). She is specifically concerned with the individual animal, rather than each species as a whole, which she believes is not proper to the consideration of justice. She puts the maintenance of biodiversity in another moral category, such as aesthetic or scientific significance. This seems to be because for her individual flourishing is an important litmus test of just relations.

How are we to adjudicate between different forms of life? Here she parts company with Aristotle, who affirms a natural hierarchical ranking according to levels of complexity. However, using the capability approach, she admits that more complex forms of life have more to lose, so that they suffer more harm than simple forms of life. In effect, for practical purposes this allows for a ranking to creep into her argument. I already alluded to her use of sentience as a threshold for justice making. She admits that this is somewhat inconsistent in her approach. She also admits that species membership is important to the extent that flourishing is constructed around species norms. It is this that gives us a "benchmark" of what opportunities for a flourishing life might look like. For human beings, such a list is evaluative in an ethical sense, that is, it does not simply endorse all natural human powers just because they seem natural to human beings. There is a particular and specific problem, therefore, in judging what this might be for other animals, for there is a real danger of romanticizing nature. Instead, she suggests that respect for nature is not just "leaving nature as it is," but rather, it must allow for "plausible goals." Thus, should we restrict "harm-causing capabilities in animals" (p. 369)? For animals below the threshold of sentience, moral restrictions do not seem to apply. For those above this threshold, Nussbaum has to resort to utilitarianism and argue for the humane killing of rats, for example, that spread disease.

Should the obligations for humans in relation to other animals be framed in negative terms, so that humans have the obligation not to harm other animals, but not support the welfare of all animals? She rejects this on the basis that humans do have obligations to support the flourishing of animal kinds, and our powers need to be exercised through a form of "paternalism that is highly sensitive to the different forms of flourishing that different species pursue" (p. 375). This allows our treatment of domesticated animals at least to become similar to the way children are treated, that is, in such a way that includes some discipline and training rather than being given complete rein to do as they wish. She also resists adopting "natural" means of population control simply on the basis that it is "natural" because human intervention may mean less suffering. Capability is about bringing each creature to a minimum threshold of entitlements, rather than equality as such. She tries to circumvent this question by suggesting that equal dignity across species is metaphysical rather than strictly necessary. Overall, she hopes for an overlapping consensus on how animals are treated. The basic list of entitlements has to be species-specific, but they are entitlements to:

a. Life. This means resistance to killing for sport or for luxury items, and the more "complexly sentient animals for food."
b. Bodily health. This would encourage laws banning cruel treatment of animals.
c. Bodily integrity. This urges against cruel practices such as declawing cats or mutilating pets in other ways, for example. She does, how-

ever, admit to the possibility of castration of male domestic animals, but only on a case-by-case basis.

d. Senses, imagination, and thought. This would reject confinement for animals, and encourage education for some companion animals.
e. Emotions. Here she argues that animals are entitled to lives where their emotions can be expressed.
f. Practical reason, where present, needs to be supported.
g. Affiliation. This implies animals are entitled to opportunities to form attachments.
h. Play, for social animals.
i. Control over environment. Here she suggests that this includes the right for territorial integrity, or for working animals, dignified working conditions.

Beyond *Frontiers of Justice*

There is much of worth in capability theory compared with its utilitarian rivals, and Nussbaum has put forward a theoretical basis for justice that is in my view far more convincing than Singer's preference utilitarianism or Rawls's procedural contractarianism. She successfully avoids Singer's weakened sense of human dignity that is deeply problematic, especially in relation to vulnerable groups. Rawls's approach is rather more successful, but it still fails to offer an adequate basis for global justice, and it is totally ineffective when it comes to consideration of animals. She is also correct to reject the sharp distinction between human and animal kinds in building a theory of justice making that is more inclusive of other species.

However, her views are still culturally bound in the sense that her understanding of justice draws on and presupposes Western liberal politics and their particular accounts of justice. This may of course be an advantage in that small shifts toward greater equity in relation to other animals in a given cultural context are, perhaps, easier if they are resonant with core aspects of those cultural conventions. But she may have failed to recognize this adequately inasmuch as she eschews any universalizing concepts of the good. The intention to be open to diverse understandings of what the good entails, then, disguises a framework in which the good is honed in particular ways, including a broad natural law framework. I suggest that it is rather more preferable to admit to the difficulties of this task and the culturally bound specifications for justice making than to assume that a given framework can be adapted easily to different cultural contexts.

In the second place, she offers an important role for imagination and wonder as the intuitive starting point for her theory. Nussbaum does not suggest where this idea of wonder comes from or what its basis is, other than that it is simply intuition. But if we ask ourselves what might be *behind* this intuition, then metaphysical positions readily come to the surface. In other words, while there may be a naturalistic interpretation of the emergence of the capacity for wonder, it is much harder to explain why the presence of wonder is so strong. While Nussbaum could have used evolutionary theory to account for this, or the facility for cooperation, for that matter, she leaves any such explanation to one side and simply affirms the importance of the imagination, narrative, and wonder as a poetic appreciation of reality that allows insights into the nature of things. This is analogous to the theological appreciation of all creaturely life as wonderful gifts of God's creation. There seems to be in Nussbaum a latent metaphysical position that is an echo of an earlier age when religious beliefs informed an understanding of wonder and awe, as Augustine taught.[40] One of the problems with the capability approach as framed by Nussbaum is, therefore, her pretension that her views are consistent with a total rejection of metaphysics.

Yet, her attachments to not just wonder but to human dignity and the dignity of life rooted in fellowship and natural law are all dim reflections of a much earlier historical period when God was considered the author of all that is. More than simply the basis for wonder and awe, belief in a Creator also served to inform the value of the human person as made in the image of God. While she recognizes the historical precedents of her ideas connected to natural law in the work of Grotius and others, what she fails to see is that such ideas were grounded in an earlier medieval Christian religious tradition as it emerged in the Western world. Alasdair MacIntyre in *After Virtue* argues that the Enlightenment project of justifying morality had to fail as it opened up a sharp discrepancy between moral rules and human nature; all that was left were fragments of a much richer societal basis for moral action.[41] Here we find human nature shorn of its original teleological roots. Nussbaum brings back the idea of teleology through her

40. For further discussion, see Celia Deane-Drummond, *Wonder and Wisdom: Conversations in Science, Spirituality, and Theology* (London: DLT, 2006).

41. Alasdair MacIntyre, *After Virtue* (London: Duckworth, 1981).

Aristotelian concept of flourishing of human beings and a much deeper appreciation of the intrinsic worth of animal kinds. But her richer theoretical understanding of human nature and other animal kinds, filled out through diverse capabilities, and her acknowledgment of the importance of wonder are wedded somewhat uneasily with a secular post-Enlightenment liberal framework of justice making.[42] Yet, while Amartya Sen's free-floating approach may be more consistent in some respects in a liberal democratic framework, inasmuch as it puts such a high value on freedom in particular, it still coheres with and reinforces a post-Enlightenment version of what that freedom entails.[43] It is, therefore, freedom of choice, rather than freedom to express particular virtues in a particular way. Nussbaum is, I believe, similarly drawn to notions of freedom of choice and still stresses individualism in drawing up her list of desirable capabilities.[44]

When it comes to her specific consideration of animals, the capability approach is promising, but it too suffers some drawbacks based on her failure to acknowledge particular influences in drawing up this list. Why, for example, does the list of animal capabilities *have* to mirror that found in the human community? The reason seems to be pragmatic, rather than based on comparative ethology. While humans are animals, it may make more sense to recognize that there are specific issues that are important to human dignity that do not apply to animals and to acknowledge more fully the lines of continuity as well as discontinuity, as outlined in the first section of this chapter. While she makes some attempt to qualify this, her list still sounds too anthropocentric in its concerns. In other words, the theoretical idea of starting with a basic list of capabilities for different spe-

42. In this, Amartya Sen's capability approach to justice is rather more consistent, as he resists coming up with any theoretically specified list of capabilities. Instead, the list of capabilities that are desirable is worked out through democratic processes that are judged correct by the particular society. For him, attaching to a specific list of what these capabilities might be smacks too much of a theory of justice and is not sufficiently grounded in democratic decision making. Amartya Sen, *The Idea of Justice* (London: Penguin, 2009).

43. Of course, while he claims to ground his theory on the reality of global injustice, how such a theory might work, given such varied conceptions of the good across different political societies, is hard to envisage. A minimum requirement seems to be democracy, but this then restricts the jurisdiction of justice making to democratic societies. It can have very little to say about other societies that are unjust. Such a restriction also applies to animals where there are very different views of what animal-human relationships should entail.

44. This is particularly clear in relation to her work on women. Why, for example, might it be fundamentally important for all women in all societies to have sexual relationships?

cies seems a good one, but such a list should be arrived at through a dialogue with those who are most capable of knowing what that flourishing might be like through sympathetic and close contact with those animals. A generalized list is rather too crude.

Other difficulties come to the surface in her discussion in relation to specific instances of what justice might entail for different creatures. She is forced, for example, to resort to sentience as a boundary condition of who might be worthy recipients of justice. The reason seems pragmatic. She is also forced to concede to utilitarian judgments about what to do in cases where there are conflicts of interest in the flourishing of different animal kinds. There seems, in other words, to be no basis in her theory to decide what might or might not take precedence, other than attempting to avoid maximization of harm. This may work in some contexts but not others, as her examples show all too clearly.

I suggest that a theological position grounded in natural law that acknowledges its metaphysical basis in Christian theology is more consistent with the direction of Nussbaum's thought. In shifting to a theocentric basis for animal concern, the temptation toward an inappropriate reading of the lives of other animals through that of human societies is reduced, though not avoided entirely. If justice is perceived through a religious lens, then this maps out what just relations might look like in a human community rooted in relationships with other creaturely kinds that has insight into the past, present, and future, on earth as it is in heaven. It is, therefore, a way of building the norms for a community niche in terms of just relations that take the notion of justice into an idealized realm as a way of showing what just relations should look like in the present.[45] In this sense, the inclusion of God's justice in theoretical and practical considerations of justice making has an advantage in setting moral ideals higher than they would have been had they been based simply on an understanding of the experience of politics. And this is precisely what we find in Aquinas's development of justice.

Justice as Virtue in Justice for Animals

Consideration of justice making in Aquinas might seem to be rather unpromising, given both the monarchial political relationships that he assumed and his assumption of the superior status of human beings relative

45. I discuss community niche and related ideas in chapter 6.

to other species. Aquinas's explicitly ethical position in relation to animals is clearly impoverished. On a number of occasions he seems to treat animals as mere instruments for human use, and in one instance he suggests that humans may use animals "without any injustice," either by killing them or for some other use.[46] But when he considers human rights and the origin of human justice making, he is equally clear about human commonality with animals. It is this aspect of his thought that is worth exploring more fully here, rather than his compromised view on the ethical treatment of animals, which is only consistent with it if the rights due to humans necessarily trump the natural rights of animals on every and all occasions.

The classic idea of justice as virtue is helpful for the human community in deciding what the parameters of justice making might be, and it opens up a different perspective on "wild justice" compared with procedural approaches. The difference between Aquinas's moral theology and that of Aristotle's *Nicomachean Ethics* is not simply one of addition; rather, it is a reframing of these ideas through consideration of moral virtues charged with grace. Aquinas distinguishes between these two through the terms *virtus acquisita* and *virtus infusa*. I will suggest below that the grace-filled moral virtue of justice is a capacity unique to humans, while other animals have the natural tendency to justice as fairness that in human communities is capable of becoming abstract and politically institutionalized.

Aquinas's discussion of right appears in question 57, and his discussion of justice in questions 58, 59, and following. His discussion of justice was elaborated on the lines of justice as virtue as well as broader legal frameworks for justice making. By contrast, his understanding of "natural right" is predominantly an objective one, which holds its force through duties owed to a person as a participant in an objective moral order. But in early medieval thinking, a significant innovation took place in how to think about

46. Thomas Aquinas, *Summa Contra Gentiles*, book 3, qu. 112. Although this text is quoted by animal rights campaigners to castigate Aquinas, "man uses them without any injustice, either by killing them or by employing them in any other way," in the context in which he raises this issue, namely, that it is right to kill other animals, he is refuting the claim that it is a sin to kill animals. He backs up his argument by citing Genesis, where all flesh is given to humankind to eat, and also supports the idea that animal cruelty should be avoided as it can then foster cruelty between people. While it is disappointing that he adopted what seems like a cavalier attitude to animal killing, he at least sought to demonstrate its limits. Thomas Aquinas, *Summa Contra Gentiles*, trans. Vernon J. Bourke, Dominican House of Studies, Priory of the Immaculate Conception. Available online at: http://dhspriory.org/thomas/ContraGentiles3b.htm#112 (accessed January 19, 2013).

human rights, namely, that they could be *subjective* as well as objective.[47] But Jean Porter believes that Aquinas normally preferred to think of law as a body of precepts, *lex,* rather than as a right to an individual claim, *ius.* But her position on Aquinas is qualified, so "Even those who prefer to speak in terms of the *lex naturalis,* including most notably Aquinas, also refer in some contexts to a natural *ius*- in Aquinas' terms, the object of the virtue of justice. None of this is tantamount to a defense of rights as subjective individual powers, but clearly, the trajectory we are considering is moving in that direction."[48] For Porter, "it is telling that he does not have an overall doctrine of subjective rights" given that other scholastics had already begun to develop this theme.[49] But there are indications that he was not unsympathetic to this view, so he develops *ius naturale* in his discussion of justice in the second part of the *Summa* in question 57.3 on whether *ius gentium* is a natural right *(iure naturali),* where he elaborates his discussion of the relation of right and justice in question 57.1. In this case Aquinas is prepared to name "natural right *(ius naturale),*" which he describes as giving back exactly what one has received so "the right *(ius)* and just *(iustum)* is a work that is commensurate with another person according to some sort of fairness *(aequalitatis modum).*"[50] It is fascinating that he here argues that the

47. Jean Porter, "Natural Right, Authority and Power: The Theological Trajectory of Human Rights," *Journal of Law, Philosophy and Culture* 3, no. 1 (2009): 299-314. Porter points out that objective natural rights express our sense of obligation to others but do not justify why those obligations exist or suggest modifications. This more fixed way of interpreting natural rights is in more recent Catholic encyclical documents. But modern legal theorists take natural and human rights to mean "one of the individual's moral properties," so they are subjective, rather than objective, rights. Subjective rights often require for their exercise specific institutions such as courts of law, while objective natural rights are more general universals of justice. She believes that subjective rights are therefore more generative because they provide a warrant for institutions where they can be reinforced (p. 301). Scholastics who identified natural law with the "inner law" of Romans 2:14 found a scriptural basis for the notion of subjective rights (p. 303). The shift from understanding *ius naturale* as not simply natural law in terms of cosmic harmony, but also with the *rational* faculty of individual human subjects, was highly significant. The association of that rational capacity with the image of God served to reinforce this interpretation of natural rights still further (p. 304). See also, Jean Porter, *Ministers of the Law: A Natural Law Theory of Legal Authority* (Grand Rapids: Eerdmans, 2010), pp. 322-30.

48. Porter, "Natural Right," p. 305. Porter is quoting *Summa Theologiae,* 2a2ae, qu. 57.1.

49. Porter, "Natural Right," p. 306.

50. Thomas Aquinas, *Summa Theologiae, Justice, Vol. 37 (2a2ae. 57-62),* trans. Thomas Gilby (London: Blackfriars, 1975), qu. 57.2. "Fairness" could be translated more literally as

first kind of fairness that we can recognize is that "from the very nature of the case, as when somebody gives so much in order to receive as much in return, this is called natural right *(ius natural)*."[51] However, second, by mutual consent a private contract may be drawn up between two parties so that a person agrees to receive some specific commensuration in return, or it may involve public agreement through the workings of the state, in which case it exerts its authority over the whole civic community as a "positive right."[52]

Aquinas believed that other animals were capable of the first kind of fairness but not the second, so "to perceive a fact simply as such and apart from its implications is not only for men but for other animals as well. And so the right *(ius)* that is called natural in the first sense is common to us and to the other animals."[53] The *ius gentium* is shared in the human community because it is connected with consequences that are worked out by human reasoning, a faculty that Aquinas believed other animals lacked. One of the unfortunate outcomes of such reasoning was that it allowed Aquinas to argue that it was expedient for a slave to be ruled by his wiser master; however, he could have been using this to merely illustrate the idea that common agreements are possible through the existing *ius gentium,* while avoiding specifically endorsing its norms. A possible resolution of the ambiguity in interpretation comes in his discussion of different kinds of dominion, in which he describes the way a slave that is used by his lord for the good of the latter is always "punitive to those subjected to it" and so therefore would not be in the state of innocence before the Fall of humanity. But there can be relationships of dominion between free persons that are proper "to the state of innocence," as when someone directs another to the other's good, or the common good.[54] Aquinas held that children and slaves, due to their ownership by their fathers and masters respectively, did not have the same degree of rights or claims to justice, but he went further than some of his contemporaries in still allowing that each "is an object of justice in some manner."[55] Indeed, he seemed to recognize the

---

"equality" in this context, but as it implies proportional response, "fairness" is the better term.

51. Aquinas, *ST, Justice,* 2a2ae, qu. 57.2.

52. Aquinas, *ST, Justice,* 2a2ae, qu. 57.2.

53. Aquinas, *ST, Justice,* 2a2ae, qu. 57.3. I have inserted *ius* to make clear what "right" refers to in the Latin text.

54. Aquinas, *Summa Theologiae, Man Made in God's Image, Vol. 13 (1a. 90-102),* trans. Edmund Hill (London: Blackfriars, 1964), 1a, qu. 96.4.

55. Aquinas, *ST, Justice,* 2a2ae, qu. 57.4.

possibility that there was a great deal of variety in human nature rather than assuming it was fixed, so that "man's nature, however, is variable," and because of that variability it could not be formally relied upon to supply an adequate notion of justice. He uses here an illustration of how it would be wrong to return a weapon to a known criminal.[56] Of course, if Aquinas had a rather more sophisticated understanding of "natural right," he would have known that communities of other social animals also share in reputational assessment, so one who cheats would not be trusted subsequently. An assessment of the consequences of behavior is also possible to some extent in other animals, though not to the same extent as in humans, and certainly not in the sense of designing structures of justice that take account of possible differences in likely courses of action. Fair play in other animals is judged more immediately and in response to immediate rather than longer-term consequences.

As well as objective natural rights, Aquinas envisaged a twofold category of "divine rights," structured as (a) being commanded because they are good or forbidden because they are evil, such as natural law precepts in the Hebrew Bible, or (b) good because they are commanded, or evil because they are forbidden, such as the disciplinary measures of the old law.[57] This shows that to set up a sharp contrast between natural law and divine command was not Aquinas's intention, but rather both are operational simultaneously in a way that echoes his discussion of acquired and infused virtue. As discussed in Aquinas, paternal right, *dikaion patrikon,* and rights of masters over slaves, *dikaion despotikon,* as well as rights within a family group are somewhat of a "period piece" taking their cues from Aristotle. But the idea of a modification of what is due because of *ownership* is relevant to human relationships with animals, since legally speaking this has dominated Western discourse on what is owed other animals.[58] Hence the kind of justice that is owed to animals is not identical to that owed to humans, but if we acknowledge the particular power of humans over animals in ownership, then justice is still due, but it is suitably adjusted. Nonetheless, this only takes us some way toward understanding what justice for animals might entail, since ownership implies that animals can be treated as property, and thereby suffer a loss of respect. Just as historically it

56. Aquinas, *ST, Justice,* 2a2ae, qu. 57.1.

57. Aquinas, *ST, Justice,* 2a2ae, qu. 57.2.

58. See footnote by Thomas Gilby, pp. 12-13, in Aquinas, *ST, Justice,* commentary on qu. 57.4.

proved unsatisfactory for children and slaves, so ownership is certainly not sufficient as a basis for justice for animals. Yet, since there has been a broadening of rights for children over time, so a shift away from viewing animals as property, which is the most common status in law, may be possible, but only if animals are included in a more substantial way in notions of justice.

A shift away from perceiving animals as property is also implied in the setting in which Aquinas places his discussion of justice in his distinction between the natural law and the eternal law, with its orientation toward the common good of the universe rather than to a specific society as such.[59] For Aquinas, "the world is ruled by divine Providence" and "governed by God's mind," "an Eternal Law is proclaimed by God's utterance, since the Divine Word and the Book of Life are eternal." In this Aquinas is expressing the view that both the natural world and the Bible are an expression of the eternal law.[60] The providential care of God for all creatures follows a law of divine justice, and a creature realizes its specific end or purpose by following eternal law. Intelligent creatures take part in Providence, and for Aquinas "they join in and make their own the Eternal Reason through which they have their natural aptitudes for their due activity and purpose. Now this sharing in the Eternal Law by intelligent creatures is what we call 'natural law.' "[61] It is a strong sense of God's providential and eternal law over all things that permits an inclusive approach to creatures, including those that are nonrational. So Aquinas still allows for a sharing in "the Eternal Reason" by all creatures; the difference between intelligent creatures who share in natural law in a reasonable way and nonrational ones is that nonrational creatures do not understand its meaning, and "therefore we do not refer to them as keeping the law except by figure of speech."[62]

But it is the grounding of natural law in biological and preconscious forces of social cohesion that is fascinating inasmuch as this both parts company with a juristic sense of law as order imposed on the natural world and coheres with contemporary discussion of the biological basis for fairness in other animals. As is well known, Aquinas's understanding of natural law that good is sought and evil is avoided is related, in the first instance, to the natural appetite of all life for self-preservation, and in the second instance,

59. Thomas Aquinas, *The Treatise on Law,* ed. R. J. Henle (Notre Dame, Ind.: University of Notre Dame Press, 1993), p. 205.

60. Thomas Aquinas, *Summa Theologiae, Law and Political Theory, Vol. 28 (1a2ae. 90-97),* trans. Thomas Gilby (London: Blackfriars, 1966), qu. 91.1.

61. Aquinas, *ST, Law and Political Theory,* 1a2ae, qu. 91.2.

62. Aquinas, *ST, Law and Political Theory,* 1a2ae, qu. 91.2.

to the natural appetite of all animals for sexual relations and rearing young.[63] Human self-conscious reasonableness then engages with these other appetites, which are common to all life and other animals, by bringing them under its control insofar "as they can be charged with intelligence."[64] While he was probably optimistic that all such tendencies could be brought under the influence of reason, at least he recognized the continuity between tendencies in all creatures and human law making. He also understood that natural law, once it found expression in different laws, had some measure of flexibility, so "Owing to the great variety of human affairs the common principles of natural law do not apply stiffly to every case. One outcome is the diversity of positive laws among different peoples."[65] This is interesting because he recognizes both universality and diversity in the way justice making comes to be expressed in different societies.

Justice for Aquinas has a number of important elements and a variety of meanings. In the first place, the debt that is due in justice is *both* legal *and* moral.[66] The legal demands are fleshed out through concerns of justice as a principal virtue, but the rendering of what is morally due is fleshed out through those virtues that are annexed to justice. The principles of justice are broadly meshed onto the basic first principle of natural law, namely, to do good and to avoid evil. Avoiding evil is allied with the virtue of innocence, but doing good is about the specific quality of relationships with others, including those between friends, associates, and those above and below one's social state, so that piety is due to superiors, including parents, and affection and humanity to inferiors.[67] Religion, as what is due to God, comes into such a context. Justice is not the same as righteousness, but there is a causal relationship between righteousness and justice. For him, it is "a habit according to which a person wills and does aright."[68] But this habit is willed permanently and in all cases. It is not absolute, however,

63. Aquinas, *ST, Law and Political Theory,* 1a2ae, qu. 94.2.

64. Aquinas, *ST, Law and Political Theory,* 1a2ae, qu. 94.2.

65. Aquinas, *ST, Law and Political Theory,* 1a2ae, qu. 95.2.

66. Thomas Aquinas, *Summa Theologiae, Religion and Worship, Vol. 39 (2a2ae. 80-91),* trans. Kevin D. O'Rourke (London: Blackfriars, 1964), qu. 80.1.

67. While Aquinas's hierarchical ordering of society reflects a monarchical arrangement that is somewhat dated today, at least his insistence on the need for affection and humanity would protect those who are subordinates in the social sphere against abuses in a way that is still relevant today.

68. Aquinas, *ST, Justice,* 2a2ae, qu. 58.1. References to *ST, Justice,* 2a2ae have been placed in the following text.

since only God's justice is everlasting in relation to God's eternal will and purpose.

The stress on justice as a capacity of will, rather than emotion, reinforces his view that justice making is rooted in what is reasonable, but that does not mean emotions are not allied to justice making in its execution (qu. 58.2). Aquinas describes justice as a virtue because acting justly is connected to making a person good, which is the aim of moral virtue. Fulfilling one's obligation to justice willingly is what makes justice a virtue, even though it may be an obligation resulting from a command (qu. 58.3). Importantly, he believes that the act of rendering each his due cannot spring from "the emotive appetite," but rather, it is proper to reason and the will (qu. 58.4). Justice directs human action in relation to others, both individually and corporately, but the priority of justice making is that it serves to direct other virtues toward the common good. Therefore, Aquinas is able to give justice priority among the virtues, so that "the acts of all the virtues can belong to justice in that it orders a man to the common good" (qu. 58.6). How do we decide what the common good might be? For Aquinas, this is shaped by the law, so "it is for law to regulate for the common good" (qu. 58.6). This marks the distinction between charity and justice, for charity "is centred on God's goodness as its proper object, is of its essence a special virtue, so general or legal justice, which regards the common good as its proper object, yet remains a special virtue in essence" (qu. 58.7). In the monarchical context of the time, Aquinas believed that general or legal justice resided in the sovereign ruler as a "master art," distributed in a secondary manner to its subjects. All virtues, inasmuch as they are directed to the common good, are in some sense functioning to promote justice.

Generally speaking, Aquinas perceives any kindness toward animals as an act of charity rather than justice. However, given that he includes all animals in the category of natural right, there are occasions where this may imply that the others to which justice is due include agents capable of action (qu. 58.2).[69] However, his understanding of justice as social vir-

69. I am rather less confident than Judith Barad that Aquinas's meaning here necessarily includes animals, especially as in the same discussion he concludes that "Justice requires a diversity of persons, and accordingly it is only of one man towards another" (qu. 58.2). Of course, if the idea of personhood is extended to other animals, then it would be possible, in theory at least, to make such an extension. For further discussion of this point, see Charles Camosy, "Other Animals as Persons? A Roman Catholic Inquiry," in *Animals as Religious Subjects: Transdisciplinary Perspectives,* ed. Celia Deane-Drummond, Rebecca

tue can be extended with rather more confidence today, given the current scientific understanding of animals as active agents with their own intelligence and responsiveness. Yet, it is also clear that in this context animals are not themselves agents of justice, even if justice is due to them. As noted above, they are agents of fairness, so in this sense they exhibit a form of "justice making." As a virtue, justice is directed toward the common good, and animals are incapable of this kind of abstraction. Given this understanding of justice as that legal and moral virtue that makes its holder good and is directed toward the common good, the inclusion of other animals in the specific brief of justice making is dependent on an adjustment of Aquinas's views in a number of respects. Yet, just as most would resist the notion that general justice resides in a sovereign ruler, so a more democratic understanding of general justice can be extended to animals by way of representation. In order for this to make sense, other animals have to be represented in an understanding of the meaning of the common good, even though they are not agents of such justice precisely in this sense. The idea that acting justly toward animals makes the person who acts in such a way good, works within Aquinas's understanding of justice as virtue. Moreover, one might say that it is only possible for humans with their greater level of abstraction and analysis of social relationships to have this inclusive view of justice making for all other creatures compared with the justice that resides in a real, but limited, way in other social animals.

In addition to this general notion of justice directed to the common good, particular justice orders relationships to others. Here Aquinas introduces the notion of domestic justice, as that which is relevant in the household (qu. 58.7). Justice is, however, even in these contexts, about external deeds, even if he follows Augustine in naming the love of God and neighbor as the root of justice, and this is "the common root of our whole bearing towards others" (qu. 58.8). Justice directs the virtues away from

---

Artinian-Kaiser, and David Clough (London: T. & T. Clark/Bloomsbury, 2013), pp. 259-77; Judith Barad, *Aquinas on the Nature and Treatment of Animals* (Cambridge: International Scholars Publications, 1995), p. 152. Barad suggests that Aquinas's premises (presumably in natural right) make it possible to interpret him in this way, while an alternative is that his premises on the low place of other animals in human society would mean a more exclusive interpretation. While "another" could theoretically be another animal as well as a human, a more cautious interpretation is that he held back from this conclusion, given his own presuppositions that were also culturally conditioned about the place of animals in human society. However, a deliberate extension and modification of his thought are not out of keeping with the direction of his analysis of natural right, and this is what I am proposing here.

self to others. Furthermore, while he rejects the idea that the way to decide what justice entails is to rely on feelings of pleasure or pain, he recognizes that feelings are "adjuncts" of justice, like other moral virtues. Getting our emotional stance right in relation to external actions is the task of virtues other than justice, but justice measures right external action, according to which an act of justice is always to render to each his due (qu. 58.11). By due, he means "rendering to another that which is his" (qu. 57.12), or "to render to each his own" (qu. 58.11). Those who could be included in the category of domestic justice are companion species, that is, pets. If the love of God is the motivation for acting justly toward our human neighbors, much the same could be said for informing why we may be inclined to act justly toward other creatures. Yet, since justice as virtue is an act of will, a refrain that Aquinas insists on repeatedly in the *Summa,* then our actions toward our fellow creatures need to depend on more than whether we happen to feel kindly toward them or not, even if that might help motivate just action.

Aquinas counts those vices that act against the common good as having the same character as injustice, though specific acts of injustice are directed against the common good. There is a parallel here in relation to divine justice, for all sin is iniquity, that is, acts against divine justice (qu. 59.1). Injustice, as Aquinas defines it, is deliberate action against the common good that takes the character of a habit of mind (qu. 59.2). Aptness to make judgments in matters of justice comes from the virtue of justice, but it is also linked closely with prudence. So "passing judgment is an act of justice inasmuch as justice is bent on judging aright, but it is an act of prudence inasmuch as prudence pronounces the judgment. As we have seen, synesis, sound judgment, is part of prudence" (qu. 60.1). Charity allows a person to judge according to divine standards, whereas prudence draws on the law. In this way, Aquinas can say, "From his habit of charity the spiritual man has a bent to judge all things aright according to divine standards, and his judgment is pronounced through the Gift of Wisdom, even as the just man pronounces according to juridical standards through the virtue of prudence" (qu. 60.1). Thus, justice for Aquinas has three elements: it is according to the bent of justice, by which he means the common good; it is within the law, that is, it has proper authority; and it is according to prudence, or practical wisdom. When there is a clash between what is legal according to positive law and natural right, Aquinas urges flexibility, so that "laws that are rightly enacted fall short in cases when to observe them would be to offend against natural right. In such cases, judgment should be delivered, not according to the letter of the law, but by recourse to equity, this being the intention of the lawgiver" (qu. 60.5). The parallel that Aquinas sets up between divine standards and the Gift of Wisdom and acting justly according to juridical standards is somewhat dualistic in that it might imply that acting according to divine standards is somehow separate from political decision making in the human community. Yet, if justice is a virtue that can be learned, as well as infused through the grace of the Holy Spirit, then there is some room for overlap between these two realms. Divine standards imply proper treatment of animals according to their status as creaturely beings declared by God to be good. Further, if we view animals as sharing to some extent in natural rights, which Aquinas also seemed to hold, then where positive law clashes with natural rights, it falls short.

The subdivision of particular justice is commutative justice between individuals, and distributive justice between the state and individuals, so that it "apportions proportionately to each his share from the common stock" (qu. 61.1). For Aristotle, if individuals hold more responsibility in the community, then they are entitled to more in the community according to what he called a "geometric mean"; while recognizing that different societies are structured according to different criteria, only democracy stresses liberality. Between individual persons justice is worked out according to an "arithmetic mean" (qu. 61.2). What concerns us in the present context is not so much whether and to what extent social animals imitate even to a partial degree commutative and distributive justice, but how we might use these categories as applied to other animals. If we accept that democracy is better as a basis for ordering society than alternatives based on, for example, aristocracy or wealth, then we have to find some way of including animals in democratic processes of distributive justice. Here what is owed animals needs to go further than being directly related to their respective levels of responsibility in a human community, for their roles are dependent on human actors and only apply to a very narrow class of other animals. It is therefore difficult to extend the notions of distributive justice to animals in a linear way. On the other hand, where animals are positively harmful to human societies, it makes sense not to promote their welfare at the expense of human flourishing where there is a clash of interests.

When Aquinas wrote his treatise on justice, he offered no consideration of the welfare state that considers those poorest members of the human community as worthy of support, on the basis of human dignity, regardless of their extent of responsibility in a given society. In an analogous way, other animals as living agents are owed support on the basis of natural justice, regardless of their respective role in a human community. Natural justice may require some animals to flourish at the expense of others if the good of the community is at stake. In this I part company from Nussbaum, whose concept of flourishing of other animals seems to be more individualistic and based on an anthropocentric reading of animal needs according to parallels in human societies. While this may be relevant for social animals, I have my doubts that this will work for the bulk of animal species. Her notion of fellowship is helpful, but it is in tension with her understanding of the importance of individual creatures.

The question of restitution for Aquinas applies to wrongs done against commutative justice. It is a return of that which is unjustly taken, or as much as possible in order to reestablish a balance (qu. 61.2). The loss incurred may be an infliction of harm by destroying the good of another or a failure to give benefits owed. In the first case, restitution consists of the restoring of benefits; in the second case, it may not be equivalent (qu. 62.5). Given that we have habitually allowed our human societies to flourish at the expense of other animals and even in some cases have acted in ways that have brought about positive harm toward them, there is a clear need to make restitution for these wrongs. How this might be done practically is hard to envisage, but the first step might be to transform the practices of the institutional church as a way of witnessing to an alternative political arrangement with animals. Admittedly, this is not the same as a shift in democratic governance, but the role of civic society is rather more important in contemporary society compared with the medieval social context. Hence, if the church is to have an authentic voice in pressing for alternative policies and political arrangements for animals, it needs to start by putting into practice those civic virtues of justice making as applied to other creatures. Nussbaum argues that her notion of flourishing is compatible with vegetarianism, but then pulls back from such an alternative in the interests of pragmatism, based on utilitarian notions of animal sentience. If we follow Aquinas, on the other hand, naming justice as virtue in solidarity with that natural justice found in animals, then pressing for elimination of cruelty is a core element of natural rights. We could go further and seek the flourishing of animals, though I would be rather more cautious than Nussbaum of naming what this might entail without careful deliberation of the democratic community.

When considering the broad framework in which Aquinas situates his discussion of justice, those moral virtues annexed to justice include religion, piety, and prayer in a way that shows his indebtedness to Augustine rather than Aristotle. But are we entitled to go as far as scholars such as Andrew Pinsent, Eleanore Stump, and William Mattison and suggest that his virtue of justice is thoroughly non-Aristotelian?[70] Certainly, while he tends to define justice more in relation to Aristotelian conceptions, he uses the category of sin in relation to injustice, so "whoever does an injustice sins mortally."[71] Aristotle, by comparison, believed that even those who acted in ignorance could be pardoned. A crucial difference here is that Aquinas believed that those who acted unjustly were going against the "law of God" in a manner that "strikes at charity." But his interpretation of Aristotle is adjusted to his own, so that "Aristotle's phrase is to be understood of ignorance on a matter of fact, which he calls the ignorance of particular circumstances, and which deserves indulgence, not of ignorance on a matter of right, which provides no excuse."[72] The point here is not so much whether his interpretation of Aristotle is correct, but the way he tries to meld his own view with that of Aristotle, even where he is introducing novel elements, such as the relationship between justice and charity, where the latter is always an infused virtue.

I agree with Pinsent that Aquinas's account of justice in 2a2ae.57-122, as much as it includes specifically annexed virtues in association with it, such as religion, prayer, and so on, shows how the orientation of his justice making is different. Aquinas also discusses "injurious words" that are outside the juridical context, which Pinsent notes are not present in *Nicomachean Ethics*. But this could be explained by Aquinas's emphasis on justice as not simply a legal term but also a moral term, as noted above. Hence, is he really replacing Aristotelian justice in the manner Pinsent suggests, or is he enlarging its scope and terms of reference so that it is inclusive of the religious life and its higher moral demands in terms of God's justice? His stress on the seriousness of such demands is reflected in his categorization of those who sin and remain unrepentant in relation to such elements of injustice as deserving entry into hell. While Pinsent is right that such words do not make sense within an Aristotelian context, they make just as much sense if Aquinas is perceived as accepting the validity of Aristotle within the juridical realm, but then radicalizing its demands in a religious

70. Andrew Pinsent, *The Second Person Perspective in Aquinas's Ethics: Virtues and Gifts* (London: Routledge, 2012), p. 74.

71. Aquinas, *ST, Justice,* 2a2ae, qu. 59.4.

72. Aquinas, *ST, Justice,* 2a2ae, qu. 59.4. See especially reply and points following.

context. If the highest goal of charity is friendship with God, then that goal colors other relationships and points to the severity of resisting its claims. This is made clear in the way Aquinas treats friendliness as part of justice.[73] While he admits that Aristotle rejects this claim, he argues against him in suggesting it must be part of justice as it is between persons. But then he draws on Aristotle to say that it should not mean treating friends and strangers in the same way, but acting in courtesy to all. This shows once more that even where there are important divisions between Aristotle and Aquinas, Aquinas's self-understanding of his position reinterprets and reframes Aristotle in a wider context in accordance with God's justice, rather than rejects his position.

One of the reasons why he chooses to try and accommodate Aristotle is that Aquinas believes that human reason is itself capable of expressing virtue, albeit in a limited way. Hence, Aquinas also rejects the idea that moral virtue is a passion or is rooted in the emotions, so for him moral virtue as a principle of movement for the appetite "begins in the reason and terminates in the appetite in so much as the latter is under the influence of reason," while passion, on the other hand, starts in the appetite and ends in the reason.[74] This explains why he sees that in human reason "certain naturally known principles of both theory and practice are naturally present, which are the seeds of intellectual and moral virtues."[75] But the completion of such virtues is not something natural, but learned. Of course, he believed, incorrectly, that "in nature there is a determinism to one course of action," but if we allow for this by acknowledging that the ability to learn adds complexity to the variety possible through natural processes, then this much can be asserted.[76] Furthermore, while insisting on principles of reason as the essence of virtue, he also allowed for what might be termed adjuncts to that reasonable process through inclusion of the passions. Given Aquinas's definition of virtue as a principle of movement for an appetite, we can ask how far what humans perceive as other animal acts of virtue might be included under such terminology. Given that some other animals habitually act in a certain way in their social relationships, their actions could be designated as vice or virtue in this sense. But

73. Thomas Aquinas, *Summa Theologiae, Virtues of Justice in the Human Community, Vol. 41 (2a2ae. 101-122),* trans. T. C. O'Brien (London: Blackfriars, 1971), qu. 114.2.

74. Thomas Aquinas, *Summa Theologiae, Virtue, Vol. 23 (1a2ae. 55-67),* trans. W. D. Hughes (London: Blackfriars, 1968), qu. 59.1.

75. Aquinas, *ST, Virtue,* qu. 63.1.

76. Aquinas, *ST, Virtue,* qu. 63.1.

the principle of movement for their appetites would be non-self-reflexive and only reasonable in a limited sense. Aquinas allows for this in acknowledging that other animals have the ability to exercise a "type of prudence," and in this way admits at least the shimmering possibility of virtue, but certainly not moral virtue as such.[77] This is clarified further by Aquinas's claim in *Disputed Questions on the Virtues,* where he asserts that the virtues are "human" but implies that his qualification is directed to what is below the level of consciousness, so "the capacities that cannot in any way be specifically human, in the sense that the command of reason cannot reach them (e.g., those powers of life that are below the conscious level), cannot possess the virtues."[78] However, he also aligns human virtue with distinctively human acts, and the difference here is that "human beings are in control of their own actions."[79] But virtue consists in the tendency of sensory desire so that it obeys reason easily and readily.

Pinsent's other line of evidence for the divide between Aristotle and Aquinas draws on the infused virtues, particularly the way mortal sin suddenly and dramatically causes all the infused virtues to be lost. He concludes that in such a condition "any remaining dispositions cease to be effective as virtues."[80] Certainly, acquired and infused virtues are different, but infused virtues are directed to behaving "well as fellow citizens with the saints and of the household of God," while acquired virtues are directed to behavior in human affairs.[81] Therefore, it is about infused virtues that Aquinas speaks when he tells of God working in us and without us, following Augustine. Infused virtues are "caused in us by God" but certainly not "without our consent."[82] All the infused virtues, furthermore, are dependent on charity, so that charity is to infused virtues what prudence is to the other moral (acquired) virtues.[83] Hence, for acquired justice to be done, prudence is necessary, but for infused justice to be done, charity is necessary. A loss of charity leads to a forfeit of all the infused moral virtues that are virtues made perfect through God's grace. Furthermore, for Aquinas, charity as

77. See further discussion on prudence in chapter 2.

78. Thomas Aquinas, *Disputed Questions on the Virtues (DQV),* ed. E. M. Atkins and Thomas Williams, trans. E. M. Atkins (Cambridge: Cambridge University Press, 2005), "On the Virtues in General," art. 3, reply.

79. Aquinas, *DQV,* "On the Virtues in General," art. 4, reply.

80. Pinsent, *The Second Person Perspective,* p. 75.

81. Aquinas, *ST, Virtue,* 1a2ae, qu. 63.4.

82. Aquinas, *ST, Virtue,* 1a2ae, qu. 55.4.

83. Aquinas, *ST, Virtue,* 1a2ae, qu. 66.2.

well as justice are aligned to the will rather than to the emotions, since "although these virtues belong to a faculty of desire, unlike temperateness and courage they do not deal with the emotions."[84] Aquinas's claim that infused virtues are perfect in that they "direct a man well to the absolutely ultimate end" shows the limitations of acquired virtues, which are limited in scope "in respect to what is final in some particular field, not in the whole of life."[85]

Pinsent is therefore correct to surmise that infused virtue is the ultimate standard through which human flourishing can be sought. However, it seems to me that acquired justice, in its close association with practical wisdom, still has its place in assisting human societies to work out requirements for justice in the secular realm.[86] Infused justice, with its hallmark of charity, is an ideal for the Christian community and is a witness to the secular world, but it cannot be reasonably understood to apply to the latter. Further, Aquinas did not think of acquired and infused virtues as removed from the need for constant practice, so that in his treatise on law he claims that practice leads to the acquisition of acquired virtue, while practice for infused virtues means one is disposed toward their reception and when "possessed keeps [them] going and growing."[87] Infused and acquired virtues arise in his discussion in parallel with each other in a way that implies the validity of each, even if infused virtues are perfect inasmuch as they are given directly by God, rather than through practice.[88] Furthermore, he reasoned that some may have a virtue "naturally" and others may have it by more practice, or greater rationality, or by a gift of grace.[89] While the latter is supreme, it does not do away with the other virtues or their role. For example, in some ways those who possess the acquired virtues have an advantage in removing opposing tendencies through practice, whereas those who repent and receive charity and grace, along with the dispositions of the other virtues, "still find it difficult to exercise the virtues that they have received as dispositions, because the tendencies resulting from their earlier sinful activity remain with them."[90]

84. Aquinas, *DQV,* "On the Virtues in General," art. 5, reply.

85. Aquinas, *ST, Virtue,* 1a2ae, qu. 65.2.

86. For a discussion of the relationship between justice and prudence in specific cases, see Celia Deane-Drummond, *Genetics and Christian Ethics* (Cambridge: Cambridge University Press, 2006).

87. Aquinas, *ST, Law and Political Theory,* 1a2ae, qu. 92.1.

88. Aquinas, *DQV,* "On Cardinal Virtues," art. 2, reply.

89. Aquinas, *DQV,* "On Cardinal Virtues," Art. 3, reply.

90. Aquinas, *DQV,* "On Cardinal Virtues," Art. 2, reply to objections 2.

Even in discussion of God's justice and God's works, we find "a double due" of what is owed to God and what is owed to the creature.[91] Justice in God observes what Aquinas terms "divine decency" by rendering to God what is owed to God. God's justice is related to Aquinas's perception of God as Creator "in the plan of divine wisdom," so God's justice becomes closely aligned with God's goodness and with truth.[92] But given this strong belief in God as creating in wisdom in accordance with justice, that means that creation itself is in accordance with divine wisdom and goodness, so "the nature of justice is preserved."[93] This strong affirmation of God's justice as visible in the works of creation means that it is bound to be evident in the created, natural world, so that infused justice makes clear the perfection that is latent in the created order from the beginning. Thomas Williams puts this point well when he claims: "The infused cardinal virtues perfect our natural capacities so that we will deal with the concerns in our natural life in a way that is informed by our supernatural destiny."[94]

Finally, what sense might it make to speak of infused justice as far as the civic realm is concerned? If Aquinas has become so thoroughly non-Aristotelian as to dispense with these aspects of his discussion, one would have expected at least some attention to the way infused justice might work in the civic community. There is no evidence for this, in fact, in *Disputed Questions on the Virtues,* where he explicitly claims, contrary to the strong statement that "virtues arise because of grace not because of our actions," that civic virtue is not appropriately related to grace, hence, "Grace is said to be the form of an infused virtue. This is not, however, in the sense that it gives the virtue its type, but rather insofar as the activity of that virtue is somehow informed by grace. That is why it is not appropriate for civic virtue to come about through the infusion of grace."[95] This is particularly important in discussions on what justice requires, for it means that elements of what he has worked out in relation to natural law, for example, in the *Summa,* still hold.

Jean Porter, it seems to me, offers an extremely helpful analysis of this problem in her examination of the relation between nature, grace,

91. Thomas Aquinas, *Summa Theologiae, God's Will and Providence, Vol. 5 (1a. 19-26),* trans. Thomas Gilby (London: Blackfriars, 1966), qu. 21.1.

92. His theological claims depart from Aristotle and supersede them in this respect. See Aquinas, *ST, God's Will and Providence,* 1a, qu. 21.1; 1a, qu. 21.2.

93. Aquinas, *ST, God's Will and Providence,* 1a, qu. 21.4.

94. Thomas Williams, introduction to *DQV,* p. xxviii.

95. Aquinas, *DQV,* "On the Virtues in General," Art. 9, replies to objections, 18.

and the natural law.[96] She contrasts the kind of knowledge possible in the Beatific Vision with that possible through creaturely knowledge and philosophical principles, operating according to "two disparate forms of intellectual and volitional fulfillment."[97] For Aquinas, then, the ordering of grace and that of nature are distinct and operate under different principles, but that does not mean that they should be split, or that the ordering of nature is rendered redundant. For "the infused cardinal virtues cannot be understood except in relation to their acquired counterparts, and both kinds of virtues can be understood only in relation to natural principles: 'grace and virtue imitate the order of nature, which is set up in accordance with divine wisdom' (II-II 31.3)."[98] Porter argues, correctly in my view, that the significance of Aquinas's scheme is that grace and nature are given their respective authority, not in the sense that there is "pure nature," but in the sense that *safeguards* the importance of nature as intelligible on its own terms, so that the distinctiveness of grace safeguards the witness of nature to divine wisdom.[99] The real problem with a radical shift in emphasis from one that is thoroughly Aristotelian to one that is non-Aristotelian is that it neglects this crucial aspect of Aquinas's thought that is a vital ingredient in the argument of this book, namely, that natural, creaturely kinds have their own integrity and contribution to make in relation to divine wisdom.

The context of "nature" provides the illumination through which the language of grace starts to make sense, so "we have reason to believe that God's grace will be continuous with, or at least not a perversion of, God's creative goodness."[100] This means that the acquired virtues are not dispensed with, but become the means through which the infused virtues can be understood. It also means that "nature as reason" informs both the infused and the acquired virtues, even if the two virtues are directed to different ends. Porter takes a further step in claiming that natural law is still needed to inform the infused virtues, providing them with "much of their concrete normative content."[101] At the same time, the infused virtues are transformative in that conceptions of justice, which would not be

96. Jean Porter, *Nature as Reason: A Thomistic Theory of the Natural Law* (Grand Rapids: Eerdmans, 2005), pp. 378-400.

97. Porter, *Nature as Reason,* p. 382.

98. Porter, *Nature as Reason,* p. 386.

99. Porter draws here on J. P. Torrell, "Nature et grace chez Thomas d'Aquin," pp. 198-201. Porter, *Nature as Reason,* p. 387.

100. Porter, *Nature as Reason,* p. 388.

101. Porter, *Nature as Reason,* p. 390.

possible before, come to light. The crucial relation here is that between justice and charity, so that justice informs the obligations of charity, and charity informs the obligations of justice. It is here that Nussbaum's work falls short, for her understanding of capabilities limits itself to an Aristotelian framework that lacks the radical demand that charity requires. On this basis, the demands of justice are moderated through charity. Porter reasons that the normative ideal of charity implies a particular way of viewing the human person as a fellow companion in the love of God.[102] But by extension, even though other creatures could not, as she indicates, be "the subject of a Beatific Vision," the orientation of charity will also redirect what justice requires in relation to other creatures. But equally, as Porter is also concerned to point out, the obligations of charity and religion do not supersede the demands of natural justice.[103]

Some Tentative Conclusions

I have argued in this chapter that while evolutionary accounts of morality have a tendency to put too much emphasis on their explanatory power, they show at least the need to ask questions about the origin and variety of meanings of justice when considered both within other animal communities and in relation to human communities. If justice is considered in relation to the capacity for fairness, then an innate sense of that fairness emerges in the development of very young human babies and in the way other animals play. It is clear that fair play in such cases is according to certain rules, but it is doubtful that it is self-conscious or the result of deliberation. At the same time, nondeliberative social conventions are common in different human societies. Most theories of justice are deliberative inasmuch as they are based on well-articulated philosophical principles, but they are also nondeliberative inasmuch as they absorb a presupposed aspect of the culture in which such reasoning is worked out. Martha Nussbaum's theory of justice, influenced by a combination of John Rawls's conception of fairness and Aristotelian accounts of flourishing, is more accommodating to the lives of other animals in that it sets out to extend ways of conceiving their flourishing alongside that of human

102. Porter, *Nature as Reason,* p. 393.

103. Aquinas, *ST, Virtues of Justice,* 2a2ae, qu. 104.6. See Porter, *Nature as Reason,* p. 395.

lives according to given capabilities most characteristic of their species. But her drawing up of this list of capabilities shows itself to be shaped by prior conceptions of what constitutes a good life, both for humans and for other animals. It therefore carries elements of the universalizing tendency that Nussbaum eschews. At the same time, in an attempt to avoid specification, metaphysical elements are smuggled into the discussion, but in a way wherein some of the richness emerging from a more detailed, thicker appropriation of a given tradition is lost. I then make an argument for going back to Aquinas's account of justice making, inasmuch as it brings in theological elements that are missing from Nussbaum's account and is also rooted in an understanding of nature as reasonable and human nature as rational animals.

The Aristotelian elements in Aquinas's account give a suitably biologically grounded basis for human justice making that draws on the lives of humans as rational animals. He achieves this both in his understanding of the way justice as virtue functions and in his understanding of the natural law. When comparing his view with evolutionary models of religion and morality, it is clear that even the latest theories, such as those based on an analysis of costly signaling or the release of hormones like oxytocin in trust games, are related to an explanation of trusting relationships within a group, rather than toward an out-group. Inasmuch as justice is a virtue of the will rather than emotions, implying a self-conscious and deliberate aim to do good to the other, this plants justice as virtue firmly in the deliberative action of human societies. However, that does not mean that other animals even in Aquinas's scheme are outside the influence of justice, for eternal law works providentially on all of creation. In a sense, without justice as reason that Aquinas believed was needed to curb their base "lusts and brutalities," humans become the very worst of all animals, but with the perfection of virtue, humans potentially become capable of even greater good.[104] Natural law, therefore, works with justice as virtue in order to frame human justice making in its various contexts. Inasmuch as there are different meanings of justice in Aquinas's account, so justice as virtue has both legal and moral elements. It is one of the cardinal virtues, and as an acquired virtue it is regulated by the stipulations of prudence, or practical wisdom. In other words, justice is not possible without prudence.

But Aquinas's account is more complicated than this again, in that it includes other virtues in alignment with justice that seem to go beyond

104. Aquinas, *ST, Law and Political Theory,* 1a2ae, qu. 95.1.

what one might expect if it just applied to the social and political community. For example, justice is both acquired through practice and infused, and piety as gift is aligned with justice. Infused justice is given by the grace of God to an individual who is suitably open to receiving that virtue, but it is never dissociated from the infused virtue of charity. The inclusion of charity with justice is important as it provides the motivation needed for a just life. The dazzling array of moral perfections associated with infused virtues, including justice, has led some to question how far Aquinas's thought has parted company from Aristotelian accounts of virtue and justice.

But if his account is severed from Aristotle, this also undercuts the biological grounding of his thought that is so imperative in natural law. There is, of course, a contrast between a life possible under the jurisdiction of acquired virtue and positive law, and that potentially realizable through perfected and infused virtues. The orientation toward perfection does not evacuate or empty out the importance of what might be termed natural and acquired virtues. Rather, one can only be understood in relation to the other. Aquinas realized ahead of his time that human beings could only really be understood by making sympathetic comparisons with other creatures. We find, on the one hand, the life of other animals and, on the other, the perfected life according to the Beatific Vision. Human lives, muddled as they are, fall somewhere in between. He was not as consistent in his ethics as his ontology implied, so the treatment of other animals needs to be adjusted according to an appreciation of the common and shared life that other animals are capable of attaining. It would be stretching the point here to argue for interjustice relationships. However, we can, it seems to me, press for a deeper appreciation of what fairness might mean to other animal communities. Therefore, the conception of fairness that informs justice-making needs to be worked out in association with a rich understanding of our human community interlaced with other animal communities and kinds. Space does not permit an examination of what this might mean in more detailed, practical terms.[105] What this might mean in terms of developing more specific relationships of love, friendship, and kinship is developed in the chapter that follows.

105. This chapter lays a foundation, or perhaps a prolegomenon, for animal ethics, but that has to await further development.

CHAPTER EIGHT

Tracing Common Ground: The Drama of Kinship

Concrete familial bonds are nurtured, in the first instance, through intimate relationships, and this is true of all social species. The tie to kin is indeed so strong that a specific evolutionary theory of altruism known as *kin selection* tries to quantify familial relationships according to respective closeness to family members by matching the degree of altruism with genetic closeness.[1] But this is a very narrow definition of kinship tied specifically to genetic markers. To make sense of the very different kinds of loving relationships in human and other highly social species, and beyond that to include close interspecies relationships, the definition of what that closeness entails needs to be opened up to include a greater variety of forms: *philia, eros, agape,* as well as altruism. I could add here more general virtues such as kindness and compassion that help fill out how those different forms of intimacy might find specific expression in given examples. This kaleidoscope portrait of loving regard starts to tease out a much broader meaning of "kin" than that defined by kin selection in a way that opens up far beyond familial relationships within the human community.

I will argue in this chapter that even kinship is still insufficient for a theological interpretation of how humans connect with other animals, even if it provides a good starting point. Traditional theological language, such as the image of God, may be useful but only if suitably qualified. In the first place, the biologically situated nature of all creaturely lives needs to be recognized as grounded in ecologically bounded yet fluid relationships, in

1. Kin selection has also been termed inclusive fitness, and a landmark article on this topic was first published by W. D. Hamilton, "The Genetical Evolution of Social Behaviour I," *Journal of Theoretical Biology* 7 (1964): 1-16.

which social and ecological processes not only provide feedback in terms of restraining the evolved possibilities that can emerge in a community, but are also actively shaped by animal agency through niche construction in the way I have already outlined in chapter 6. At the same time, social species show complex forms of cultural expression that, properly understood, cannot be separated from natural dynamics in what Donna Haraway terms "natureculture."[2]

In this chapter, I will consolidate the basic concept discussed in chapter 6 that the language of *theo-drama* captures the dynamic yet directed sense in which human and other creaturely lives display agency and are interconnected in evolutionary and theological terms. A web of life is a popular symbol for many ecotheologians, but it gives the impression of being too static: creatures are envisaged as merely bound together in interrelationships.[3] In evolutionary terms, the dynamic relationships between human beings and other kinds are frequently mixed in terms of how far other animals are welcomed, rejected, or even used and abused by different human communities and in present-day cultures. But while violence is integral to the interrelationships between species, as well as within human species, it is not necessarily primary; that is, cooperation, rather than conflict, is arguably deeper in evolutionary terms. Anthropologist Tim Ingold's stress on the importance of entering into the space in which human beings have shown creativity and movement is perhaps a further secularized analogy of what I perceive in theological terms as the role of theo-drama that supplements the concept of niche construction that I have discussed previously. Hence, rather than attempting to describe the world as it is made in a static way, "we join with things in the very processes of their formation and dissolution."[4] Furthermore, like Ingold, I suggest that human creativity lies not so much in stark novelty as in the "capacity to bring forth" in a way that is content to draw on and use preexisting models. In theological terms, the methodology of drawing secular thought into a dialectical relationship with theology is inspired by the thought of Aquinas. Finally, theo-drama, like the redrawing of anthropology that Ingold seeks, is content to improvise and be flexible and responsive, in this case, to evolutionary insights about the human condition. But a theological re-

2. Donna Haraway, *The Companion Species Manifesto: Dogs, People, and Significant Others* (Chicago: Prickly Paradigm, 2003).

3. See, for example, Ruth Page, *God and the Web of Creation* (London: SCM, 2009).

4. Tim Ingold, introduction to *Redrawing Anthropology: Materials, Movements, Lines*, ed. Tim Ingold (Farnham: Ashgate, 2011), pp. 1-20, here 2.

sponse to such mixed human relationships makes sense in terms of the basic categories of creation and redemption.

An eschatology for justice making according to the common good for the individual and the community as a whole is the goal of that theo-drama, summed up in the Hebrew concept of *shalom;* however, inasmuch as it is eschatological, such peaceful coexistence cannot be anticipated except as a foretaste of a future hope of what is to come. Yet, in the dynamics of such drama we see the specifically human response to God's call, an energizing grace that is capable of being aware of the presence of the Holy Spirit. In this respect, the specific virtue of practical wisdom points the way forward in refining what it means to be human, but now in the light of practical issues of ecological and creaturely ethics. These, then, are the raw materials that inform the basic ingredients of this chapter. I will attempt to show how a map for theological ethics that is grounded in a suitably qualified theological anthropology can emerge from reflection on the liminal space between humans and other creaturely kinds. Spelling out what that map might imply in practical terms must of necessity be left to a further volume on theological ethics of sustainability, or more accurately perhaps, flourishing.

Evolving Biological Love: The Nature of Altruism and the Animal Connection

Altruism is perhaps one of the areas in which there has been a significant amount of scientific research stemming to a large extent from an internal problem within Darwin's account of natural selection. The problem is this: If, as standard interpretations of Darwin suggest, there is a basic biological tendency toward conservation of one's own genes, expressed through the concept of "selfishness," how is it that caring for others has ever arisen in evolutionary history? Biologist Jeffrey Schloss puts the problem starkly: "If the struggle for existence is the engine of natural selection and survival of the fittest is the direction of travel, then those organisms that sacrifice their biological well-being for the good of another will be kicked off the train."[5]

5. Jeffrey Schloss, "Emerging Accounts of Altruism: 'Love Creation's Final Law?'" in *Altruism and Altruistic Love: Science, Philosophy, and Religion in Dialogue,* ed. Stephen G. Post, Lynn G. Underwood, and William B. Hurlbut (New York: Oxford University Press, 2002), pp. 212-42, here 214.

Theoretical considerations that altruism was impossible seemed to run counter to observations of natural history across a wide range of species, where sacrificial traits appeared in, for example, the way mixed flocks of birds warn other species of danger; or where vulnerable young are cared for, even when that caring is across different species; or the case of sterile castes of social insects; as well as numerous examples from observations of primate behavior.

Evolutionary biologists have proposed two theories to account for altruistic behavior: inclusive fitness, or kin selection, and reciprocal altruism. Inclusive fitness postulates that sacrificial altruistic behavior will be favored by natural selection as long as the overall cost to the individual is less than the gain to recipients multiplied by the genetic closeness to that individual.[6] Reciprocal altruism, on the other hand, as the name suggests, postulates that self-sacrificing behavior will be favored by natural selection as long as there is sufficient likelihood that the recipient will promote the fitness of the giver in some way by compensatory acts.[7] In both cases, the argument is that reproductive self-interest wins through, even if the individual is not conscious of acting "selfishly." If the benefit is through kin selection, or what we could loosely term "nepotism," then conscious motivation may be entirely unselfish, but if the benefit is through reciprocal altruism, or what we could loosely term "favoritism," then conscious motivation can be either selfish or unselfish. Some sociobiologists have used these ideas to try and explain behavior in human societies, and they even have made the somewhat extreme claim that *all* cooperative behavior in human communities can be explained according to such theories.[8] For kin selection and reciprocal altruism, both the overall goal of cooperation and the process itself seem to be imbibed with selfishness, whether or not this is consciously recognized. Michael Ghiselin dismisses the idea that there can ever be genuine altruism from a biological perspective, thus he claims, notoriously, "Scratch an 'altruist,' and watch a 'hypocrite' bleed." What passes for cooperation turns out to be a mixture of opportunism and exploitation.[9]

6. As proposed by Hamilton, "The Genetical Evolution of Social Behavior I."

7. First proposed by Robert L. Trivers, "The Evolution of Reciprocal Altruism," *Quarterly Review of Biology* 46 (1971): 35-57.

8. For example, see E. O. Wilson, *On Human Nature* (Cambridge: Harvard University Press, 1978), p. 157, and Richard D. Alexander, *The Biology of Moral Systems* (New York: De Gruyter, 1987), p. 195.

9. Michael T. Ghiselin, *The Economy of Nature and the Evolution of Sex* (Berkeley: University of California Press, 1974), p. 247.

More recently E. O. Wilson, like David Sloan Wilson, has tended to favor what he terms multilevel selection, in which competition between groups allows for natural selection working at the level of the group.[10] In E. O. Wilson's newer approach, individual selection still favors selfish instincts, while group selection favors individual intragroup altruism. He concludes: "Individual selection is responsible for much of what we call sin, while group selection is responsible for the greater part of virtue."[11] According to this model, natural selection still works to promote selfishness, but once it is operationally transferred to the group level, the possibility of intragroup altruism between individuals in that group emerges. Reliance on group selection to account for altruism brings its own dilemmas, however, not least because many biologists doubt if selection at the group level is strictly necessary in order to explain altruism. Furthermore, E. O. Wilson seems to presume an attachment of group selection to gene frequency in a way that is not borne out by concrete evidence, so "Group selection is differential longevity and lifetime fertility of those genes that prescribe traits of interaction among members of the group, having arisen during competition with other groups."[12] He also believes that there was some crossover between the two levels of selection, so that on occasion inventive forms of selfish behavior benefited the group as a whole, and sometimes the group rewarded productive individuals with privilege and status. But he is rigid in his belief that "an iron rule exists in genetic social evolution," namely, that "selfish individuals beat altruistic individuals" and "groups of altruists beat groups of selfish individuals."[13]

Wilson's proposal that individuals are linked together through a network that impacts on their survival and reproductive capacity qualifies kinship relationships so that they become less important in evolutionary terms. He therefore opposes inclusive fitness theory as the key to evo-

10. Multilevel selection can be distinguished from conventionalist approaches to group and individual selection in that in the former individual selection is in relation to a specific group, while in the latter individual selection is in relation to the total metapopulation as a whole. A classic account of group selection is in Elliott Sober and David Sloan Wilson, *Unto Others: The Evolution and Psychology of Unselfish Behavior* (Cambridge: Harvard University Press, 1998). For a more recent discussion of theoretical aspects, see Elliott Sober, *Did Darwin Write the Origin Backwards? Philosophical Essays on Darwin's Theory* (New York: Prometheus Books, 2011), pp. 162-77.

11. E. O. Wilson, *The Social Conquest of Earth* (New York: Liveright Publishing/Norton, 2012), p. 241.

12. Wilson, *Social Conquest of Earth,* p. 242.

13. Wilson, *Social Conquest of Earth,* p. 243.

lutionary dynamics; instead, "what counts is the hereditary propensity to form the myriad alliances, favors and exchanges of information and betrayals that make up daily life in the network."[14] That does not mean, of course, that groups are not extremely important in evolutionary terms, but an alternative to Wilson's thesis is one raised at the start of this book, namely, that evolution has not just one genetic dimension, following what he believes is the "iron law" of natural selection, but different dimensions. It seems to me that by narrowing explanatory theories to neo-Darwinian accounts of genetic selection acting at either the individual or the group level, Wilson distorts proper consideration of other evolutionary trajectories.

While the idea that human nature is inherently at its most basic level self-interested might possibly appeal to some theological traditions, such a cynical view undercuts the possibility of any genuine self-sacrificing behavior. But critics of this view are not confined to the religious or philosophical community. Other biologists have objected to the unhelpful rhetoric that may be used, namely, the conflation between "selfish" reproductive outcomes and "selfish" motivations.[15] Furthermore, the assumption that altruism is constricted to other kin, or only those who can benefit the reproductive success of the giver in some way, does not bear close scrutiny. That this is the case for human beings capable of disinterested altruism, who could never be construed in terms of reproductive gain for the individual, is self-evident and casts grave doubt on the merits of strident forms of sociobiological approaches to human behavior. One argument might be to dismiss sociobiology as insufficient in that by largely confining its analysis or, perhaps more accurately, *reducing* epistemological significance to the biological, evolutionary level, it fails to take sufficient account of cultural levels of analysis that are more complex and are related to biological nature in contested ways. Genes, especially in the work of authors such as Richard Dawkins, seem to have teleological significance for all life-forms, thus constricting the overall direction of movement of different living organisms in specific ways.[16]

14. Wilson, *Social Conquest of Earth,* p. 243.

15. Jeffrey Schloss, "Sociobiological Explanations of Altruistic Ethics: Necessary, Sufficient or Irrelevant to the Human Moral Quest?" in *Investigating the Biological Foundations of Human Morality,* ed. James Hurd (New York: Edwin Mellen Press, 1996), pp. 107-45; David Sloan Wilson, "On the Relationship between Evolutionary and Psychological Definitions of Altruism and Selfishness," *Biology and Philosophy* 7, no. 1 (1992): 61-68.

16. This has persisted in his thought, so that in the thirtieth anniversary edition of *The*

E. O. Wilson notoriously described culture as constrained on a "genetic leash," even while admitting that altruistic acts are shaped by that culture. How far and to what extent human behavior is constrained by biological factors is still heavily contested even among biologists, with the most conservative being accused of genetic determinism.[17] Added to this, among sociobiologists there is often a supercilious or one might say arrogant attachment to a naïve objectivism that is universally positivistic in tone, as if there were no alternatives. Jeffrey Schloss describes this as a problem of inappropriate universal, objective knowledge, characterized only as self-evident when viewed through the metaphor of a visitation from outer space.[18] I prefer to see more strident and positivistic forms of evolutionary Darwinism as a way of presenting scientific material as a grand narrative.[19] Both criticisms raise a similar objection, namely, an unwarranted belief in the absolute truth of particular biological claims, not all of which are adequately substantiated.

Such an explanation of genuine altruism as a side effect of group benefits is left with the problem of what to do with those individuals who cheat. It comes, therefore, as no surprise that such cheaters would be brought into line by punitive methods. Biologists have, however, attempted to solve some of the theoretical problems within reciprocal altruism by creating mathematical models that envisage the behavior of those who defect in offering reciprocity, or cheat, following an initial expression of altruism. If this behavior is conscious, then cheating might be detectable through involuntary cues. However, the argument goes that if it relies on self-deception, then the disguise would be complete. While altruism may

Selfish Gene, the closing sentences are as follows: "But the individual body, so familiar to us on our planet, did not have to exist. The only kind of entity that has to exist in order for life to arise, anywhere in the universe, is the immortal replicator." Richard Dawkins, *The Selfish Gene* (Oxford: Oxford University Press, 2006), p. 266.

17. Jeffrey Schloss believes that there are no theories of "hard determinism" in discussions of the character and extent of altruism, but among biologists there are debates about the relative constraining force of genes. So such biologists are still Darwinians who adhere to what Schloss calls a "soft determinism" characterized by E. O. Wilson, Richard D. Alexander, and Michael Ruse through to the theories of Susan Blackmore and Henry Plotkin, where the genetic leash is in effect broken. He places Francisco Ayala in an intermediate position. See Jeffrey Schloss, "Introduction to Part III," in *Altruism and Altruistic Love,* pp. 145-50, here 146-47.

18. Schloss, "Emerging Accounts of Altruism," p. 219.

19. See discussion in Celia Deane-Drummond, *Christ and Evolution: Wonder and Wisdom* (Minneapolis: Fortress, 2009), pp. 10-24.

be self-deceived in some instances, to universalize this approach and claim that all such instances are self-deceiving is unreasonable.[20]

One way around the problem is to suggest that those instances of what might be termed "genuine" altruism are basically nonadaptive, that is, to admit that they are present but only in a "temporary" sense, for natural selection works over extremely long time periods. The practice of laying eggs in the nest of a different species, for example, could be viewed as a way of manipulating parental instincts of the host species. Alternatively, on a longer timescale one might argue that the earliest humans had different selection pressures, so the genetic makeup does not match well to current environments. Of course, proving that such a process has occurred is extraordinarily difficult, given the historical gap envisaged, and much of the evidence used can be challenged on scientific grounds.[21] Francisco Ayala envisages a rather different nonadaptive biological account of altruism, arguing that it is a pleiotropic effect in which a single gene leads to different phenotypes and thus nurtures kin and nonkin, where only the latter are not adaptive.[22] While this and other nonadaptive models have the merit of not shoehorning altruism into a narrowly conceived self-interested paradigm, they seem somewhat defeatist and push altruism to the margins of biological explanation.

There is, however, a further, rather broader line of defense for biologists, and that is to challenge the underlying merits of the rhetoric of selfishness as such. According to this view, rather than understanding cooperation and altruism as added subsequently as a "veneer" to a basically selfish nature, we should understand cooperation as *basic* to biological nature as such, even in the simplest of organisms. In other words, instead of "selfishness" rhetoric, we need "cooperation" rhetoric. Primatologist Frans de Waal has argued for this position from his pioneering observations of chimpanzees and bonobos.[23] Such an approach fits in more readily with

20. Jerome Kagan, "Morality, Reason and Love," in *Altruism and Altruistic Love,* pp. 40-50.

21. I discuss this point earlier in this monograph and also briefly in Deane-Drummond, *Christ and Evolution,* pp. 77-78.

22. Francisco Ayala, "The Difference of Being Human: Ethical Behavior as an Evolutionary Byproduct," in *Biology, Ethics, and the Origins of Life,* ed. Holmes Rolston III (Boston: Jones and Bartlett, 1995), pp. 113-36.

23. Frans de Waal, "Morally Evolved: Primate Social Instincts, Human Morality, and the Rise and Fall of 'Veneer Theory,'" in Frans de Waal, *Primates and Philosophers,* ed. Stephen Macedo and Josiah Ober (Princeton: Princeton University Press, 2006), pp. 1-80.

those biologists who argue that altruism is mediated through categories other than direct reciprocity. In this case, the payoff following altruistic acts is envisaged as indirectly mediated either through enhancing the reputation of the individual, for example, or through enhancing psychological well-being by promoting a sense of connectivity. But altruism is still perceived in this view as tied in some sense to biological categories. The study of primates and other social species is significant in that it permits the study of cultures that have some analogy with human cultures, and therefore provides means through which the tension between natural and cultural factors might be envisaged. Research on altruism raises the difficulty of envisaging how and in what sense cultural factors influence and impinge on behaviors that may have a physiological or biological basis. Although de Waal, correctly in my view, objects to veneer theories, as a biologist he still envisages cooperative behavior as basically adaptive, that is, evolved in such a way that it is consistent with natural selection.

The evolutionary history of hominids sheds some light on the possible origins of other-regarding emotions and interspecies relationships. Debates among anthropologists regarding the evolution of compassion are worth considering, as is the evolution of tool use; both compassion and tool use arguably had a profound impact on the shape of social relationships. Penny Spikins and her colleagues have argued that there were important developmental stages in the appearance of compassion in hominid species.[24] The topic has not been discussed widely in the literature for the obvious reason that it is impossible to have certain knowledge about how humans felt toward one another when there are no tangible written or other records. Compassion is one of a suite of important sociomoral emotions that include empathy, shame, and remorse; all of these help regulate the behavior of the individual in relation to others in the group. Compassion, as Spikins has defined it, is not simply an emotion appropriate to another's emotion, that is, empathy, but it is also a motivation to help. When compassion is the motivation for actions in social animals, including, for example, caring for infants, looking after or helping injured pets, or even punishing cheats, such actions are accompanied by hormonal shifts in the level of oxytocin in the brain that is accompanied by feelings of well-being.

Primatologists such as Frans de Waal appear to reserve the term

24. Penny A. Spikins, H. E. Rutherford, and A. P. Needham, "From Homininity to Humanity: Compassion from the Earliest Archaics to Modern Humans," *Time and Mind: The Journal of Archaeology, Consciousness and Culture* 3, no. 3 (2010): 303-26.

"compassion" for hominid societies, while allowing for empathy and what he terms "directed altruism" among primates.[25] However, if we allow for Spikins's broader, more inclusive definition of compassion that does not necessarily depend on premeditated assistance, then some form of "compassion" and certainly acts of "directed altruism" can be found in dolphins, elephants, and higher primates.[26] But she recognizes a critical difference between other primates and modern humans, namely, that compassion in species other than humans is always fleeting and nondeliberate. In humans, compassionate acts, such as caring for the elderly, include ones that are deliberate and long term, so that the emotive force of compassion is regulated by a reasoned approach. Human compassion is also very diverse and can be extended out toward comparative strangers, those not necessarily in kinship relationship with us, and other species, as well as objects such as gardens or photographs and concepts such as justice, peace, or liberty. Spikins does not mention religious belief, but the ability to commit oneself to God or religious artifacts would also fall in a similar category in terms of motivation for loving action. Compassionate motivations may also be suppressed in some "tough" social environments. According to this view, the capacity for compassionate motivation could at times be disadvantageous in that it could lead to exploitation. Hence, predominantly selfish behavior follows in those contexts where compassion is suppressed.

Spikins argues that evidence for care for the chronically infirm or elderly in very early hominid societies points to a very early origin of compassion in the genus *Homo.* A well-established example is a female *Homo ergaster* from about 1.5 million years ago (mya).[27] The symptoms that show up in bone remains suggest an excess intake of vitamin A leading to hypervitaminosis A, which leads to a reduction in bone density and coarse bone growths, but in the living hominid other symptoms would have included

25. Frans de Waal, "Putting the Altruism Back into Altruism: The Evolution of Empathy," *Annual Review of Psychology* 59 (2008): 279-300. A shorter summary of his position can also be found in Frans de Waal, "The Evolution of Empathy," in *The Compassionate Instinct: The Science of Human Goodness,* ed. Dacher Keltner, Jason Marsh, and Jeremy Adam Smith (New York: Norton, 2010), pp. 16-25. Perhaps surprisingly, this book does not discuss human compassion toward other animals.

26. Her separation of the motivating force of acts of compassion in other animals from "instinctive behavior" is perhaps hard to justify given how little we really know about other animal minds. See Spikins, Rutherford, and Needham, "From Homininity to Humanity," p. 306.

27. David W. Cameron and Colin P. Groves, *Bones, Stones, and Molecules* (San Diego: Elsevier, 2004).

nausea, headaches, blurred vision, lethargy, loss of muscular coordination, and impaired consciousness, all developing over weeks and months. Evidence for such a disease in her skeleton could only have appeared after a long time, thus providing concrete evidence that she was looked after by others. Another example comes from finds in Dmanisi in Georgia where a hominin that lived 1.77 mya lost virtually all its teeth before death, and so would probably have been dependent on others for support. A little later, among the Neanderthals, an old man of between thirty-five and fifty was found at the Shanidar I site, dating from about 80,000 years ago. He had suffered multiple fractures including a brain injury, but the majority of these injuries occurred in adolescence. Other evidence shows care extended to a middle Pleistocene infant suffering from craniosynostosis who had cranial deformities and who remarkably lived until age five. Of course, what is not clear is how widespread such a practice might have been. But compassion to those with severe disabilities, including acromesomelic dysplasia in early Upper Paleolithic modern humans, illustrates the extension of compassion to those born with severe disabilities.

Spikins associates caregiving with the motivation to take risks on behalf of others, a strategy that would be very important in hunting mammals and competing with predators for carcasses. The work of Pat Shipman and other anthropologists who show markings associated with stone toolmaking on animal bones dated from about 2.6 mya provided an important breakthrough in hominin evolution. The cut marks on animal bones caused by stone tools could be distinguished from the teeth marks of other predators, and thus provided convincing evidence for their invention and use in processing animal carcasses.[28] Examination of traces of debris on the tools themselves from later sites (1.5 mya) gives some evidence for their use on animal carcasses, but also, subsequently, on soft plants such as reeds and wood. What is remarkable is that cut marks in animal bones from the Olduvai site dating some 2.6 mya show that a wide range of predators were subject to tool marks, from very small animals, such as hedgehogs, to middle-sized antelopes and larger giraffes and elephants.[29] Shipman

28. Pat Shipman, *The Animal Connection: A New Perspective on What Makes Us Human* (New York: Norton, 2011), pp. 40-44.

29. This is unusual in that it represents the whole range of species characteristic of the fossil record of that period, while other carnivores such as spotted hyenas or lions, for example, limit themselves to prey somewhat larger than themselves when hunting in groups. Furthermore, cut marks on bones of animals show that the large antelope was the preferred prey of the earliest hominids, over and above the normal predator-prey relationship among

argues that the shift from a largely herbivorous diet to an omnivorous one meant that humans had to pay more attention to other animals, including close observation of their habits.[30] This was not the case for other carnivores who approached prey on the basis of their relative weight. Shipman also believes that the incentive for geographic expansion was based on the search for more food sources, and this is what happened in the expansion of *Homo habilis* and *Homo erectus* about 2.3 mya and 1.9 mya respectively. Furthermore, intraspecific competition for carcasses among carnivores meant that early hominids could be threatened by other species ready to attack in order to get at an attractive carcass. Out of the eleven carnivores consisting of lions, leopards, cheetahs, striped hyenas, brown hyenas, spotted hyenas, long-legged hyenas, a form of wolf, two species of saber-toothed cat, and a false saber-toothed cat, eight outweighed hominids. Between 2.7 and 1.7 mya hominids increased in size to about 120 pounds, so bringing a selective advantage over carnivore competitors. About 2 mya bone tools started to be used. Either way, the close observation of other animals was a huge evolutionary advantage for early hominids, and their survival depended on it.

Shipman argues that it was the very ancient and natural attraction humans had to observe animals that eventually allowed the first domestication to take place, namely, that of the wolf into a domestic dog, *Canis familiaris,* the friendly dog. Dog skulls found in the Goyet Cave in Belgium date from about 32,000 years ago, that is, much earlier than formal domestication of plants and animals in the Neolithic period between 12,000 and 10,000 years ago, when goats, sheep, pigs, and cattle were domesticated.[31] The first dogs were probably used to help find or track prey and to protect territory. But, as Shipman points out, the process of domesticating a wolf predator is very different from herding herbivores such as wild sheep or goats.[32] Another explanation is that the wolves themselves took the initiative by living in proximity to human villages and settlements and so gained the benefits of eating food scraps from human village life. Either or both possibilities seem likely. But the important messages that come from this research are that the process of domestication is gradual, that it happened more than once in different geographical locations, and that it is based on

carnivores. Their ability to do this was related to the ability to make stone tools, including tools as ammunition in hunting. See Shipman, *The Animal Connection,* pp. 48-54.

30. Shipman, *The Animal Connection,* p. 61.

31. Shipman, *The Animal Connection,* pp. 207-17.

32. Shipman, *The Animal Connection,* pp. 224-25.

an understanding of animal behavior, so "Those humans who observed more keenly, learned more quickly how to quiet a frightened or anxious animal, and figured out how to keep it alive and docile were rewarded with a new kind of tool: an animal that would do the bidding of humans or at least cooperate with them."[33]

Recognition of domestication in prehistory is notoriously difficult, but there are clues that point to such a practice. Dogs were rarely depicted in prehistoric art, which more often portrayed images of prey or predators, such as woolly mammoths, lions, bears, and rhinos. One reason might be that dogs were put in the human family category as cooperators in the hunt, so, like humans, they were rarely depicted in such art.[34] The accumulation of specific animal bones with archaeological remains is not necessarily conclusive either, as it could indicate specific hunting practices. More accurate is evidence for domestication from the explicit slaughter of animals before the onset of winter, and that can be discerned from the age and sex distribution of animal bones at archaeological sites. In the Botai archaeological site in Kazakhstan, researchers have found evidence from analyses of molar wear and chemical changes in the soil in areas marked off by corrals for the domestication of horses, dated to 3700-3100 B.C.[35] Shipman notes the challenge that comes with the domestication of horses, so that in common with all those who are experienced in horsemanship, there is a need for sensitivity and clear communication and respectful relationships, sharing in the movement of another species. Shipman argues, convincingly in my view, that domestication arose not so much because of a deliberate decision to manage food sources efficiently, but initially because of a universal human affective impulse to take in and manage wild animals. It was the secondary benefits from domestication, including milk, wool, protection, and power, that encouraged further domestication, rather than demand for the primary products of meat, hide, and bone.

The archaeological evidence, then, on the relationship between humans and other animals shows clearly the evolutionary entanglement between them. Domestication is a way that humans have managed the evolutionary trajectory of wild species to their tame counterparts in ways that are useful and productive for both parties. Furthermore, the process shows

33. Shipman, *The Animal Connection,* p. 225.

34. Shipman, *The Animal Connection,* pp. 227-28.

35. Shipman, *The Animal Connection,* pp. 236-43. Sandra Olsen and her team conducted this research, and their later discovery of traces of degraded fats from horse milk on remains of potsherds silenced even the most ardent critics.

an ambiguity in human/other animal relationships. On the one hand, there is a natural tendency of humans to identify with other animals and, in some cases, incorporate them into the human family. On the other hand, there is a tendency to view them as tools for humans' use. Given the millennia over which such attitudes have appeared, it is hardly surprising that both attitudes are prevalent in contemporary societies. But Shipman has not analyzed sufficiently the different attitudes between humans and other animals that are characteristic of hunter-gatherer societies and those most characteristic of domestication.

According to Ingold, hunter-gatherers do not view the prey they hunt as being overcome by violence; rather, they understand their activity as being at one with their environment, and even the kill in this sense is perceived to be nonviolent. The deep involvement with their environment means that there is no separation between people and nature in a hunter-gatherer society, so "caring for an environment is like caring for people: it requires a deep, personal and affectionate involvement, an involvement not just of mind or body but of one's entire, undivided being."[36] From the perspective of hunter-gatherers, when an animal is killed it is taken to be in an amicable and friendly relationship with humans by giving its permission and being willing to be sacrificed. There is an economy here of trust and of mutual sharing where other life-giving agencies nurture human life in a way that seems quite alien to a Western mind that views hunting of other animals as an exertion of power and dominance. Once domestication took place, however, the relationships with other animals changed, so that for pastoralists it was founded not on a principle of trust but on domination.[37] This is an important departure from Shipman, who views the place of animals in human societies as an extension of human tool use. Shipman also distinguishes domination that exists between people from domestication of animals that he considers is more like human manipulation of objects. Instead, Ingold believes that early pastoralists perceived other animals in their care as endowed with powers of sentience and autonomy that had to be overcome through domestication.[38] He believes that it was only with the onset of industrialized agriculture much later that other animals came to be thought of as objects for human use and abuse. So, the trust that

36. Tim Ingold, *The Perception of the Environment: Essays on Livelihood, Dwelling, and Skill* (London: Routledge, 2011), p. 69.

37. Ingold, *Perception of the Environment,* p. 72.

38. Ingold, *Perception of the Environment,* p. 74.

was characteristic of early hunter-gatherer societies toward other animals provided the opportunity for domestication of some animals, but then over time those relationships shifted to those of domination rather than of trust and mutual autonomy.

Theological Perspectives on Love

So far, I have attempted to map out different biological and anthropological accounts of other-regarding tendencies where evolutionary scientists have continually struggled to account for unselfish behaviors in humans in their community and in wider relationships with their environment, as well as account for empathy existing in other social species. I have shown that not all scientists envisage human nature at its deepest root as selfish, even in a qualified, so-called "nonmoral" sense according to conservation of genes. An alternative position stressing the primacy of cooperation is gaining ascendancy. This debate has some parallels with the contrast between those theological and philosophical traditions that stress the depth of human depravity and sin and those that stress human goodness. The difference, though, is that even theologians who are most convinced that humanity is basically sinful refuse to admit to an overall teleology of selfishness as the means through which life flourishes. Furthermore, in many cases the guiding paradigm of genic natural selection seems to dominate to such an extent that other modes of explanation of altruism are pushed to the margins in a form of epistemological reductionism. What is needed, therefore, are ways of thinking through what it means to be human, and to love in particular, that are conscious of the riches of cultural traditions and, in the context of the present work, theological traditions in particular, while at the same time being aware of biological debates about altruism. Anthropological studies open up the possibility of a more nuanced account of the history of close evolutionary relationships with other animals. But theology as an articulation of religious experience in human communities has emerged in the context of centuries of human experience of loving regard in relationship to others, including God. Just as other animals should not be perceived as objects subject to human use in evolutionary history, except in modern industrialized societies, but as agents in their own right, so human relationships with God are situated in such a way as to stress both human autonomy and dependence. A relationship with God is always, however, drawing on analogies of the experience of relationships in human societies.

Agape is perhaps that form of love most characteristically associated with theological reflection. Contemporary discussion of *agape* often takes its bearings from the work of Anders Nygren, who regarded *agape* as God's unconditional, spontaneous, sacrificial love that is indifferent to the worth of the one who receives, is directed toward sinners, is opposed to self-love, and initiates relationships with creatures.[39] Nygren, however, has overstated the case for *agape* in its exclusiveness, both in the way he opposes *agape* to self-love and *eros,* and in narrowing it to sacrificial forms rather than allowing for reciprocal categories.[40] Thomas Jay Oord points to the variety of biblical interpretations of *agape* that convey a much wider set of meanings, so that it is not always unconditional, as in 2 Corinthians 9:7; opposed to self-love, as in Ephesians 5:28; or even self-sacrificial. In places *agape* is used in Scripture in a way that seems to convey notions of *philia* (friendship) or even *eros* (desire), as in Luke 7:5, John 3:19, 2 Timothy 4:8, Hebrews 1:9, and Revelation 12:11.[41] The sheer variety of meanings in Scripture has spawned a range of different interpretations of *agape,* from narrow definitions that equate *agape* with altruism and other-regard, through to broader, more expansive definitions that stress the direction of movement toward goodness. Oord argues that a definition of *agape,* to be useful, needs to distinguish itself from *philia* and *eros,* so he resists more expansive definitions. Reducing *agape* to selfless altruism is problematic for Oord in that it does not seem to allow for the possibility of self-affirmation.[42] He also rejects suggestions that *agape* is uniquely characterized by the particular way in which God loves the world, as this seems to exclude the possibility that humans can show *agape.* He suggests, instead, that *agape* should promote the attainment of well-being, so he arrives at a definition of *agape* as an "intentional sympathetic response to promote overall well-being when confronted by that which generates ill-being."[43]

39. Anders Nygren, *Agape and Eros,* trans. Philip Watson (New York: Harper and Row, 1957 [1930]).

40. A full discussion of these critical engagements is outside the scope of this chapter, but see Thomas Jay Oord, *Defining Love: A Philosophical, Scientific, and Theological Engagement* (Grand Rapids: Brazos, 2010), p. 34.

41. James Moffat, *Love in the New Testament* (London: Hodder and Stoughton, 1929), pp. 51-56.

42. This reference to self-affirmation in the context of discussion about altruism is ironical, perhaps, in view of the way altruism is commonly interpreted according to a selfishness paradigm in the biological literature, as discussed above.

43. Oord, *Defining Love,* p. 43.

Yet, we might ask here if Oord has successfully met the challenge he sets for himself of distinguishing *agape* from *philia* and *eros,* for a sympathetic response implies *philia* and intentions imply *eros,* while all loves coalesce in the possibility of promoting well-being. The difference, perhaps, is that *philia* and *eros* may at times have negative as well as positive outcomes. It seems to me, therefore, that, rather like biblical usage, *agape* is a more generalized version of love that makes more sense if it deliberately allows for the possibility of other forms of love to be qualified within it. Hence, *philia* may have destructive tendencies, but when guided by *agape* it can lead to an overall love that is open rather than closed. Confining the application of *agape* to sinners and to the human community in the traditional sense is also deeply problematic, in that it does not take sufficient account of the possibility of love offered to or received from other animals, or even other objects, as mentioned in the anthropological study earlier. While Oord's definition of *agape* could in theory be interpreted in a more inclusive sense, he fails to criticize those who are more anthropocentric in their definitions.[44] Oord recognizes that *agape* is unique in its response to what he terms ill-being, so that it offers love in the face of enmity, hostility, and evil in a way that goes beyond anything that might seem remotely possible through *philia* and *eros.* While this distinction in some ways makes good sense, I am more inclined to think that forms of *eros* and *philia* are still present, even when *agape* responds to ill-being; it is just these forms that are disciplined in a particular way whereby desires and attachments are directed toward an eschatological end.

The discussion above points to a question that has been hotly debated in theological circles, that is, the place of *eros* in an overall mapping of what it means to express Christian love. *Eros,* in the classical sense, means desire for that which is considered worthwhile or good, which may be inanimate or animate; in popular usage, it is more often than not associated with sexual attraction. But to be counted as an aspect of genuine love, *eros* aims to affirm what is valuable and good while being constrained by the need to promote overall flourishing.[45] The *eros* hovering in the background of love

44. Oord lists sixteen different definitions of *agape* by theologians, most of which are either theocentric or anthropocentric. Oord, *Defining Love,* pp. 37-38.

45. Oord defines *eros* in a similar way, except that he uses the term "well-being." I prefer to use the term "flourishing," as it implies a rather more expansive interpretation of flourishing in communities, whereas "well-being" is more often than not associated with statistical measurements of human development. In this, I am close to Oord's intentions. See Oord, *Defining Love,* p. 47.

as *agape,* then, can be thought of as directed toward valuation of an ultimate end as the object of desire so as to promote overall flourishing, even in the face of immediate difficulties, setbacks, and hostilities. Indeed, in a second sense, the capacity to look beyond an individual creature's hostility and affirm the creature's goodness in spite of behavior that suggests the contrary, that is, to exercise *agape,* may only be possible if *eros* is present in some way. While Oord describes this as "mixed love," if *agape* is envisaged in an inclusive manner, then it seems always to be bound up in some way with other love forms, including *eros.* If *eros* is removed from an understanding of how God loves, we have arrived at a portrait of God who loves clinically rather than passionately. There is also a sense in which the biblical account implies that God shows preferential love for humans compared with other creatures, even if God cares for all creatures. However, such examples of God apparently favoring human welfare in the name of human "worth" are just as likely to be an aspect of the sense in which God expresses *philia,* or friendship love, as they are to be expressing differences in intrinsic worth or goodness.[46] In either sense, understanding God's love as totally undifferentiated jars with the Judeo-Christian tradition. What is more problematic is identifying God's love with sensual lust, which is one reason why usage of the term *eros* may have been avoided in the New Testament.[47]

Augustine is often criticized because he links love with desire, so that charity *(caritas)* is desire for God's sake, and cupidity *(cupiditas)* is desire for its own sake in other creatures or in oneself. This might imply that love is related to desire for God and to a corresponding devaluation of the natural order; texts such as his *Teaching Christianity* seem to suggest this, rather than affirming that order and finding practical expression for love in doing good.[48] Yet, such readings of Augustine set aside other aspects of his

46. Oord claims that the following texts suggest God values humans more than sheep or birds: Matthew 6:26; 10:31; 12:12; Luke 12:7; 12:24. He does not specify why such valuation is different. Thomas Oord, *The Nature of Love: A Theology* (St. Louis: Chalice Press, 2010), p. 45.

47. Moffat, *Love in the New Testament,* p. 35. One of the reasons why the theology of Hans Urs von Balthasar continues to be controversial is not just that he has aligned sexuality with his vision of God's love as expressed in the sacraments, but also that his portrayal of that sexuality seems to be a negative one, displaying the dominance of man over woman in sexual relationships. How far this is deliberate misogyny according to some feminist scholars is debatable, and evidence is at best highly speculative. For further discussion, see Deane-Drummond, *Christ and Evolution,* pp. 247-50.

48. This is the largely negative position on Augustine taken by Oord; see *The Nature of Love,* pp. 58-61.

thought that stress the expansive goodness of creation, human creativity, and responsibility, as in *De Trinitate.*[49] In *Teaching Christianity* Augustine seems to be reacting to an inordinate love of material things that then distracts humans from love of God. He therefore refuses to deny properly ordered love in response to the perceived goodness in the natural world. It may be that a remnant of his Manichean phase creeps into aspects of his work when he speaks about "using" other creatures, but once we see his thought filtered through that of Thomas Aquinas, it is clear that the love of humans for other creatures stems from an acknowledgment of the basic and intrinsic goodness of all creation. Jame Schaefer puts this succinctly when, commenting on the way Aquinas portrays the goodness of creation as that which elicits a response in humans, she states, "Love for their goodness should direct human actions toward preserving the good that creatures have (their existence and their natures) and receiving the good that they do not have (whatever they need to sustain their existence)."[50] In other words, this is desire that is directed and channeled in a particular way, namely, as that which echoes the love of God, although for Aquinas only the latter has the capacity to love in a way that infuses goodness into those beings that God freely creates.[51]

For Aquinas, the three types of love, namely, natural, sensitive, and rational love, are united analogically through a principle of motion.[52] He recognizes at least the possibility of love as a sensitive appetite in all animals, including humans, in a way that seems remarkably modern. Robert Milner is therefore correct to see passionate, sensitive love as being included in rational love, rather than separated off from it. Furthermore, the

49. "The earth is good by the height of its mountains, the moderate elevation of its hills, and the evenness of its fields; and good is the farm that is pleasant and fertile; and good is the house that is arranged throughout in symmetrical proportions and is spacious and bright; and good are the animals, animate bodies; and good is the mild and salubrious air; and good is the food that is pleasant and conducive to health . . . and good is the soul of a friend with sweetness of concord and the fidelity of love; and good is the just man." Augustine, *The Trinity,* trans. Stephen McKenna (Washington, D.C.: Catholic University of America Press, 1963), 8.3.4, p. 247.

50. Jame Schaefer, *Theological Foundations for Environmental Ethics: Reconstructing Patristic and Medieval Concepts* (Washington, D.C.: Georgetown University Press, 2009), p. 259.

51. Thomas Aquinas, *Summa Theologiae, God's Will and Providence, Vol. 5 (1a. 19-26),* trans. Thomas Gilby. London: Blackfriars, 1966), 1a, qu. 20.2.

52. Robert Milner, *Thomas Aquinas on the Passions* (Cambridge: Cambridge University Press, 2009), p. 118.

love of God is in some sense better elicited through the more passive action of *amor sensitivus* than through reason alone. It is the passions, which we share with other animals, then, that draw us more fully to God, even if the rational act of the will is also involved. Milner concludes that for Thomas, "The power of God to draw creatures to himself by sensible means exceeds the power of human reason."[53] *Caritas* and *dilectio,* on the other hand, are motions of the will. He also distinguishes the love characteristic of friendship from that of concupiscence.[54] The latter is characteristic of other animals, where love is related to a particular need or desire. But the love of friendship is love for the other in and of itself. Of course, Aquinas did not have the knowledge of current ethology. Research in that field has shown that associations between highly social animals seem to be preference based, rather than simply according to concupiscence, but as in other investigations of animal minds, it is notoriously hard to prove underlying motivations for particular actions. Furthermore, the full ideal of friendship to which Aquinas points, namely, a form of love that is capable of loving others for themselves in a manner akin to love of self, is not likely to be possible for other animals, given their cognitive capacities.

Aquinas also links the more rational love of charity with the form of love known as friendship, or *philia,* in naming charity as human friendship with God.[55] More important, perhaps, for this discussion, Aquinas argues that true justice and chastity are only possible where charity is present.[56] This shows that far from being detached from concrete expressions of right action, charity is intimately associated with them, so "there can be no true justice or true chastity if the due reference to the end by means of charity is lacking, however rightly disposed one may be about other things."[57] This links eschatological expectation, as expressed in charity, with present reality, so, he suggests, "the glory of heaven, far from supplanting nature, brings it to perfection. Now the order of charity, which we have outlined, has its origin in nature, and since all things naturally love themselves more than others, it follows that this order of charity

53. Milner, *Thomas Aquinas,* p. 122.

54. Milner, *Thomas Aquinas,* p. 123.

55. Thomas Aquinas, *Summa Theologiae, Charity, Vol. 34 (2a2ae. 23-33),* trans. R. J. Batton (London: Blackfriars, 1975), 2a2ae, qu. 23.4: "charity is a friendship between man and God." This differs from an Aristotelian understanding of friendship as that which is confined to the human community.

56. Aquinas, *ST, Charity,* 2a2ae, qu. 23.7.

57. Aquinas, *ST, Charity,* 2a2ae, qu. 23.7.

will remain in heaven."[58] He also adds in the same article (qu. 26.13) that "a man must love himself more than others, and all the more the greater his charity," hence self-love is affirmed rather than denied where charity means friendship with God. The Hebrew idea of *hesed* that puts emphasis on the faithful love of God in covenant relationship also implies the possibility of friendship with God. What both Aquinas and Augustine insisted upon was a grounding motivation for love in nearness to God, in the first instance, that then flows out to include other human beings and other creatures. It is, in other words, a love that is infused by divine grace.

But friendship for Aquinas presupposes the ability not only to love oneself, but also to perceive another as an individual subject; hence, the person who loves her friend wills the friend's good and not her own, though not necessarily more than her own good.[59] The closest friendships will therefore be with those who are considered other selves who share the same basic capacities and interests in flourishing. In this sense, another's good becomes part of our own good. In biological terms, this ability to recognize depth of connection is sometimes called a form of "deep engagement,"[60] but it certainly cannot be reduced to this as an explanation of its origin. Furthermore, a deeper appreciation of Aquinas's understanding of human friendship with God as *caritas* promotes loving others as God loves, so inviting greater openness and hospitality to others. In this way, even strangers become included in a circle of friendship. Aquinas, in his less well-known *Commentary on the Sentences of Peter Lombard,* also considers the possibility that we might exercise charity toward other creatures, even those that are irrational, because we know that in them there is some likeness to God.[61] Countering

58. Aquinas, *ST, Charity,* 2a2ae, qu. 26.13.

59. Thomas Aquinas, *Summa Theologiae, Love and Desire, Vol. 19 (1a2ae. 22-30),* trans. Eric D'Arcy (London: Blackfriars, 1967), 1a2ae, qu. 28.3.

60. This is suggested in John Tooby and Leda Cosmides, "Friendship and the Banker's Paradox: Other Pathways to the Evolution of Adaptations for Altruism," in *Proceedings of the British Academy: Vol. 88; Evolution of Social Behavior Patterns in Primates and Man,* ed. W. G. Runciman, John M. Smith, and R. I. M. Dunbar (Oxford: Oxford University Press, 1996), pp. 119-43. Schloss believes that the move to describe a form of love in biological terms as deep engagement is welcome, since it goes beyond selfishness rhetoric, and shows that reciprocity is not inevitable within an evolutionary explanation. Schloss, "Emerging Accounts of Altruism," pp. 226-27.

61. Thomas Aquinas, *On Love and Charity: Readings from the Commentary on the Sentences of Peter Lombard,* trans. Peter A. Kwasniewski, Thomas Bolin, and Joseph Bolin (Washington, D.C.: Catholic University of America Press, 2008), Part III, Distinction 28, Art. 2, pp. 186-88.

such a view, he cites Augustine, who claims that charity is always confined to those who belong to a society referred to God, and Aristotle, who denied that benevolence could ever exist in relation to irrational things. In the end, he sides with Augustine in denying the possibility of full friendship with irrational things on the basis that "they do not share a human life with us, as regards existence or the activities of life."[62] But he does qualify this by suggesting that other animals could be loved through the agency of charity and through their association with human beings. But given that he is wrong about the extent to which other animals are entangled with human lives and are subjects of a life, his argument against friendship with them as subjects breaks down, at least in part. Furthermore, he denies that the trace of divine likeness found in other animals in any sense resembles the likeness destined for humans transformed through grace, so the likeness in other animals "does not suffice for this."[63] But that is to presume what the life of glory is like, and so cannot readily be sustained. In *qualifying* the tight restrictive charitable relationships found in Augustine and Aristotle, he took at least the first step in the right direction.

Another reason why friendship is an important ingredient in an understanding of what love entails is that it serves to shift the agenda from freedom, understood as individual free choice, to fidelity. While Paul Waddell's discussion of friendship puts this more sharply and suggests that the moral life should shift from choice and sincerity to transformation and adherence to a given moral order, I consider that it is on the ground of friendship rooted in charity that choices can be made in a way that leads to appropriate authentic transformation, and the shape of that moral order is subject to the restraints of divine law but is not fixed in advance.[64] But Waddell is on the right track when he suggests that "friendship born from

62. Aquinas, *On Love and Charity,* Part III, Distinction 28, Art. 2, response, p. 187.

63. Aquinas, *On Love and Charity,* Part III, Distinction 28, Art. 2, replies to objections, 3, p. 188. Aquinas admitted that while humans are in the same genus as other animals, it is in bodily powers that humans are similar, but for him the possession of an immaterial soul meant humans were closer to angels than other animals; Art. 3, replies to objections, 4, p. 189.

64. By "divine law," I am following Aquinas and mean the Ten Commandments, which forms the backdrop of the moral life in the Judeo-Christian tradition. Paul Waddell, *Friendship and the Moral Life* (Notre Dame, Ind.: University of Notre Dame Press, 1989), pp. 16-17. For Aquinas, the first principle of natural law to do good and avoid evil is unalterable; Thomas Aquinas, *Summa Theologiae, Law and Political Theory, Vol. 28 (1a2ae. 90-97),* trans. Thomas Gilby (London: Blackfriars, 1966), 1a2ae, qu. 94.5, while those secondary precepts that are oriented toward what "nature teaches all animals" and "all life" toward self-preservation (qu. 94.2) can be changed.

and seeking the kingdom may be exactly the kind of love which enables us ultimately to be friends of the world. In that case, we do not leave preferential love behind, we extend its domain."[65] Of course, the crucial aspect here is that friendship is directed in a certain way toward a good end; and in this sense, as for *eros,* friendship needs to be accommodated within the constraints of the more universal love of *agape.* While it is common to view *philia* as being in tension with *agape,* I suggest that once *philia* is transformed through engagement with *agape,* it moves from an exclusive to an inclusive, yet directed, focus. The character of *some* preferential love is still there, in its character as *philia,* but it is open rather than closed. Love, which is so generalized that it shows none of the qualities of *philia,* lacks a certain dynamism and depth; the danger, of course, like *eros,* is that this particular expression of energy can work against what might be termed genuine love that seeks to build up the common life.

If we now consider the manifold ways in which what used to be thought of as the exclusive province of humans is shared with other animals, then the possibility of a limited or restricted form of genuine friendship with other animal subjects becomes real rather than illusory. This is not going to be exactly the same as friendship with cospecifics, but inasmuch as other animals share our familial lives, some measure of friendship is possible. But just as it is very difficult to fully empathize with another human being, there will always be a sense in which our lack of imaginative empathy is bound to fail, since while we can try hard to imagine what it might be like to be a bat or a dog, such a desire is not reciprocated in a way that is necessary for the full flowering of friendship, and this brings us back to our own sense of human distinctiveness. Agustín Fuentes expresses this well when he suggests "paradoxically, the very sympathetic imagination that allows us to engage in 'bat-beingness' is what prevents us from ever truly knowing what it is to be a bat, because we have this trait that they lack."[66] At the same time, the possibility that humans can engage with other animals that have the capacity to participate in personal relationships, and therefore can be termed "persons," opens up the possibility of interspecies friendship.[67] Humans and other animals share the

65. Waddell, *Friendship,* p. 73.

66. Agustín Fuentes, "The Humanity of Animals and the Animality of Humans: A View from Biological Anthropology Inspired by J. M. Coetzee's *Elizabeth Costello,*" *American Anthropologist* 108 (2006): 124-32, here 125.

67. Charles Camosy believes that it is essential to link image bearing with the possibility of personhood, and so implies that my own reticence to include other animals as

capacity to show not only complex social interactions, but also social traditions that share common ground with human cultures.[68] Furthermore, as I have argued repeatedly in this book, human and other animal societies have coevolved and are entangled with one another at multiple levels to a greater and lesser extent, becoming drawn into human societies through association or domestication. This, I suggest, deepens the possibility of commitment to these highly social animal subjects in a way that is difficult to imagine for creatures lacking such capacity. Nonetheless, ecological flourishing in general, and the land in particular, is included in the possible objects of human love and attention. The difference perhaps relates to a greater sense of subjectivity in other animals that is lacking in relation to the land, even if earlier hunter-gatherer societies probably failed to make such distinctions. However, those other creatures that lack subjectivity still deserve our neighborly kindness and respect. This is where animal rights writers such as Tom Regan fall short, for he uses the concept of "subject of a life" to restrict his moral position, and remains in tension with environmental ethicists' emphasis on the land as a biotic community.[69] For even though some ecotheologians write as if the natural world as a whole can be envisaged as acting like a subject, illustrated in poetic terms through Franciscan language such as mother earth or brother sun, in practice such commitment seems to be a communal response to attachment to memories in a given place, rather than an experience of direct interpersonal relationships. Ellen Davis's convincing argument that the biblical tradition, especially the Hebrew Bible, is basically agrarian also implies that the Israelites' respectful attitude to the land is bound up with their strong sense of faithfulness to Yahweh.[70]

---

bearers of the divine image automatically excludes them from the category of the personal. While he claims to base his association of personhood with image bearing on a reading of Thomas Aquinas, I resist such an association, as recognition of agency is not the same as recognition of a particular form of agency, namely, divine image bearing. See discussion in Charles Camosy, "Other Animals as Persons? A Roman Catholic Inquiry," in *Animals as Religious Subjects: Transdisciplinary Perspectives,* ed. Celia Deane-Drummond, Rebecca Artinian-Kaiser, and David Clough (London: T. & T. Clark/Bloomsbury, 2013), pp. 259-77.

68. See, for example, William C. McGrew, "Culture in Non-human Primates?" *Annual Review of Anthropology* 27 (1998): 301-28.

69. Tom Regan, *The Case for Animal Rights* (Los Angeles: University of California Press, 1983).

70. Ellen Davis, *Scripture, Culture, and Agriculture: An Agrarian Reading of the Bible* (Cambridge: Cambridge University Press, 2009).

Bearing God's Image

Throughout this book I have explored different facets of what has traditionally been thought of as exclusive characteristics of human beings, or more accurately perhaps, following Ingold, Western cultural characteristics of the human condition. Some of these characteristics in traditional Christian thought have been mapped onto what it means to be made in the image of God, as a way of identifying special traits that mark out human beings in a particular way compared with the rest of the created order. I have argued that in each case what used to be thought of as a uniquely human characteristic has now come under fire, inasmuch as the difference between humans and other animal kinds is one of degree. Reason, freedom, morality, and language — all have their counterparts in those animals who have relevant cognitive and social capacities. Social traditions are also present in nonhuman primates and in some other animals, and it is appropriate therefore to call these cultural developments, because they seem to be passed on by social facilitation rather than through direct genetic or physiological development. Can the limited degree to which other animals share what could be termed structural aspects of behavior compared with humans be used as a basis of separation? I suggest that this move is faulty because it assumes that human beings are paradigmatic, and then other animals are measured in comparative terms. There is another problem with this view, and that is, how can humans ever really tell what other animals are like? The more cynical view that we are always reading into animal behavior what we find in human cultures and societies is not all that convincing, for even though forms of communication, for example, are different in other animal societies, using the particular human capacity for imaginative empathy allows us to discover aspects of that animal society that would be impossible if we assumed the opposite view, namely, that animals just react according to some sort of preprogramming. But while the language of uniqueness might seem problematic, the language of distinctiveness certainly is not, and the evolutionary history of hominids shows in a clear way that a particular subspecies of a particular species, namely, *Homo sapiens sapiens,* had particular capacities and skills growing in their communities that allowed them to be distinctively successful. Like other species, human beings are able to carve out their particular worlds in particular ways, constructing their own niche that then feeds back into their evolutionary development. But this implies the importance not just of ontology, but also of function and activity, and this trend has also come to the surface in theological discussions of human nature.

Hence, understanding humans as made in the divine image has not just been characterized through ontological characteristics of reason, freedom, and so on. Another approach draws on the specific *task* named in the Genesis text, to have dominion over the earth. The way this has been approached in our most recent cultural history shows not so much dominion as domination, where the human capacity to manipulate both its own nature and that of other animals through its uses of technology and forms of industrial agriculture has escalated to an extent that was unprecedented even half a century ago. This opens up a boundary between the natural and the artificial, but now this is superimposed on other animal subjects. A reexamination of the Christian tradition shows that, just as in longer trajectories of evolutionary history, other animals are present with humans in ways that show them both as symbols of human culture and as real creatures sharing in concrete human history. Justice for animals forces us back to consider what expressing justice as virtue might mean, for, according to this active view of image bearing, our self-understanding of who we are cannot be separated from what we do. In other words, our theological anthropology cannot be separated from our theological ethics; the two act together in dynamic interrelationship, a hermeneutical circle in which our acts inform who we become, and vice versa.

Therefore, in considering what it means to be made in the image of God, ontological characteristics need to be married with, rather than separated from, the particular vocation of human beings and directed toward that end. For example, it is no use knowing that humans excel and are distinctive in their capacity for freedom compared with other animals, unless that freedom is then directed toward a particular task, namely, one that coheres with building up righteousness and the coming kingdom of God. Again, it is no good knowing that human reason is highly distinctive, emerging from a particularly well developed cerebral cortex in *Homo sapiens,* unless that reason is directed in a certain way that is in tune with humans' particular capacity to show love and affection. Human language should be used to build up rather than tear down relationships with others, including those others that are not humans. Our moral life is shaped by the different characteristics of human beings working in concert for a good end. As I indicated above, love needs to be the primary virtue that serves all other virtues, and in this I agree with Thomas Aquinas, who stated that charity is the mother of all virtues.[71] The possibility of the opposite path toward evil is always knocking at the door of human being and becoming, but once the focus of human attention is on the ultimate good to be attained, or what Aquinas called charity understood as friendship with God, the likelihood of error is somewhat diminished but never eradicated. Humanity understood as made in the image of God may be marred but not lost. Human beings are also not left alone, since Jesus Christ as God incarnate has given humanity a particular way of expressing the image of God, since he was not just the image of God, but also the manifestation of God.[72] The orientation of human beings as made in the image of God is therefore directed toward *imago Christi,* becoming like Jesus Christ. Inasmuch as the incarnation affirms material reality as such, the task for human beings becomes one that similarly affirms creaturely life.[73]

But where does this place other creatures in particular in relation to the divine image bearing of humans? Do they also share in some sense in divine image bearing? Traditional mapping of humans as superior to other creatures in bearing God's image is unfortunate, to say the least. Aquinas, for example, was quite ready to admit that all creatures showed forth "a likeness of the Trinity by way of trace, in that there is something in all of them that has to be taken back to the divine Person as its cause."[74] He also suggested that not only creatures, but the "entire universe, in all its parts, is ordained towards God as its end, insomuch as it imitates, as it were, and shows forth the Divine goodness, to the glory of God."[75] But within his scheme there is a hierarchical ordering of things, so that "less nobler"

71. Aquinas, *ST, Charity,* 2a2ae, qu. 23.8. For a discussion of love and other emotions in Aquinas, see, for example, Milner, *Thomas Aquinas,* and for his discussion on love, see pp. 111-39.

72. I have developed the idea of *imago Christi* as important for a theological anthropology in Deane-Drummond, *Christ and Evolution,* pp. 279-87.

73. I remain unconvinced by arguments that name the incarnation of Christ as coming in the flesh, or even as Lamb of God, as pointing to the special or preferential significance of *mammals* for God, apart from their ritual and symbolic place; rather, Christ's coming affirms all creaturely and material existence. See, for example, David Grumett, "Christ the Lamb of God and the Christian Doctrine of God" (presentation to "Animals and Religion Consultation, Thinking Animals: Re-thinking Theology; Abrahamic and Indigenous Traditions," American Academy of Religion Conference, Atlanta, October 30, 2010).

74. Thomas Aquinas, *Summa Theologiae, Creation, Variety, and Evil, Vol. 8 (1a. 44-49),* trans. Thomas Gilby (London: Blackfriars, 1967), 1a, qu. 45.7.

75. Thomas Aquinas, *Summa Theologiae, Cosmogony, Vol. 10 (1a. 65-74),* trans. William A. Wallace (London: Blackfriars, 1967), 1a, qu. 65.2.

creatures exist for the sake of the "nobler," with human beings at the top of the pinnacle. This version of image bearing is therefore somewhat troubling in its exclusivity because it might seem to encourage an instrumental attitude to other creatures.

But other aspects of his thought point to a more moderate view. For example, where he specifically addresses the idea of whether image bearing could be found in "nonrational creatures" and urges that "only intelligent creatures are properly speaking after God's image," at the same time, the natural world *also* reflects God's likeness. In this way, "in intensity and concentration a better likeness of the divine perfection is to be found in the intelligent creation, which has a capacity for the highest good."[76] The *extent* of likeness to God is related to existence, being alive, and finally intelligence. Yet, is this distinction between image and likeness sufficient, given that it seems to create too big a gap between humans, which he believed (incorrectly) were the only "reasonable" creatures, and all other creaturely kinds? Or does the renewed insight into the comparative intelligence of alloprimates, that is, all primates other than humans, suggest that primates at least share in some facets of the divine image? Furthermore, in making charity the goal of human existence, the elevation of human reasoning is qualified by the priority Aquinas gives to God's wisdom.[77]

I have had reason to critique an overconcentration on intelligence as being the most important factor in defining image bearing. On the other hand, if we follow both Augustine and Aquinas in naming God's firstborn Son as the perfect image of God in the truest sense in comparison to human beings who bear the image as in an "alien nature,"[78] this does not mean that specific human intelligence has to be highlighted as a means of adjudicating who bears that image, for this view implies that image bearing is received or possibly *imprinted* as a gift of God's grace. Indeed, once Aquinas goes on to consider if God's image is restricted to the human mind, he allows for the possibility of the image of the Trinity appearing as "a trace" in bodily aspects of humanity, as well as in other creatures. For him, love exercised through human will and "a word procession" exercised through human intelligence allow for "an image of the uncreated Trinity by a sort of portraiture in kind." Other creatures do not, for him, show forth "a word

76. Thomas Aquinas, *Summa Theologiae, Man Made in God's Image, Vol. 13 (1a. 90-102),* trans. Edmund Hill (London: Blackfriars, 1964), 1a, qu. 93.2.

77. For Aquinas, charity is ruled "by the wisdom of God," and so "it goes beyond reason." Aquinas, *ST, Charity,* 2a2ae, qu. 24.1.

78. Aquinas, *ST, Man Made in God's Image,* 1a, qu. 93.1.

procession" or "love," even though they show a "trace."[79] These hints mean that further aspects of Aquinas's thinking may possibly be rescued if we apply his discussion of image bearing in relation to men and women to humanity and particular animals.

In discussing the difference between men and women, Aquinas names three stages in image bearing. The first stage is a natural aptitude for understanding or loving God as an activity of mind. The second stage is where there is a settled habit of mind that shows love and knowledge of God, but this is still imperfect, and conformity is by the grace of God working in human beings. The third stage of image bearing is one where knowledge and love of God are perfect, but the image shows forth the glory of God. The first stage is found in all people, the second stage is found in the just, and the third only in the blessed. For Aquinas, the second and third stages are only found in men and not women; he uses 1 Corinthians 11:7 to support his argument that women are for the glory of men. Of course, including women in the first tier of image bearing was a step in the right direction, given the enormous prejudice against women at the time. Yet, even this more muted distinction between men and women seems somewhat irrational, especially as numerous examples of women saints must have been known to Aquinas in a way that would have undermined his argument. However, it seems reasonable to suggest that the potential for receiving knowledge and love of God is likely to be more perfect in human beings than in other animals, even alloprimates. An unanswered question is how and in what sense the grace of God could be said to explicitly work in human beings compared with other creaturely kinds.[80] But with the emphasis put on the action of God and the capacity to receive God's grace, the possibility of at least a weak form of image bearing existing in some other animal kinds is not ruled out. A distinction is made between human beings and other creatures, but this distinction cannot be used as a basis for their instrumental use. Rather, true image bearing is about what we *receive* given our particular capacities and how we respond to that grace in particular reasoned acts of love and responsibility.

Aquinas was quite ready to use the language of divine likeness as applied to other animals, as noted above. The disadvantage of applying

79. Aquinas, *ST, Man Made in God's Image,* 1a, qu. 93.6.

80. Such a question presupposes a more developed account of pneumatology, which is outside the scope of this book.

language of image bearing to other animals is that they will inevitably be viewed as falling short in relation to humans, even if this could be viewed as a possible ethical advantage of including them in the same religious category as humankind.[81] The language of likeness, on the other hand, need not be so divisive if one notes that Aquinas understands this term in two senses. Likeness is used in a general sense to apply to the whole of the created order reflecting the Trinity. However, a deeper likeness to God comes through the work of God's grace in perfecting humankind. Hence, naming animals as being in the likeness of God should not be viewed as a way of diminishing their worth over and against the category of image bearing. Furthermore, likeness language allows for a greater variety for these kinds, so other animals bear the likeness of God in their own way. If, as I have suggested here, image bearing is as much about a particular performance in a theo-drama as ontology, then other animals in the likeness of God enter into that performance as participants in a shared relationship with human beings and are bound up with them. The difference between other animals and humans is that only the latter are capable of an awareness of their active role in their performance and in this sense are capable of using their minds to adapt to new possible futures. Inasmuch as other animals are not yet perfect, they are still capable of being transformed into a more perfected divine likeness, but this is through the work of grace in eschatological hope rather than in an expectation for present reality.

In considering image bearing, therefore, we need to be aware not just of human virtues, but more precisely how human beings are related to God. "Anthropomorphism" is a word more commonly used to describe appropriation of human categories in order to think about God, and it is the kinship titles that are the most intimate, even though their figurative potency is now lost because of centuries of familiarity.[82] Janet Soskice has made a case for recovering kinship titles as applied to God and that these titles name a particular way of envisaging God as being our kind, our kin, so "holding before us the vision of love." This bears on and opens up an eschatological anthropology such that "our constant becoming is our way

81. I have taken this aspect up in Celia Deane-Drummond, "In God's Image and Likeness: From Reason to Revelation in Humans and Other Animals," in *Image of God, Image of Humanity? Perspectives on Theological Anthropology for the 21st Century,* ed. Lieven Boeve, Yves De Maeseneer, and Ellen Van Stichel (New York: Fordham University Press, 2014).

82. Janet Soskice, *The Kindness of God: Metaphor, Gender, and Religious Language* (Oxford: Oxford University Press, 2007), pp. 1-3.

of being children of God."[83] But her apparent preference for image bearing meaning "mystery" because God is "mystery"[84] is in tension with her insistence on the more practical, concrete kinship metaphors that describe God. While there is something mysterious or even awesome about the claim that human beings are made in the image of God, if this dominates human perception it may lead to a detachment from other creatures and from the concrete, ethical tasks that are bracketed into a biblical understanding of what image bearing entails. In fact, Soskice goes on to criticize portraying the divine image in christological language because it might imply a lack of image bearing as related to women's maternal and other capacities.[85] Yet, it seems to me that such christological language points less to the specific capacities of Christ as a human *male* than to the pattern of faithful relating to God in carrying out his specific *mission.* It is the specific God-given responsive obedience of humanity as men or women that is shaped through understanding what it is to image God in Christ, rather than Jesus' gendered biological nature as such. The ability to connect with divine vocation is unique to individual persons and at the same time part of the overall drama of salvation history. This seems to be the direction hinted at in Soskice's account, for by drawing on Schleiermacher she points to the importance of the arrival of Eve in the Genesis text. Eve is different from and yet like Adam; it was only after Eve had arrived that Adam became capable of hearing the voice of God and carrying out his mission. But has the almost familiar encounter of difference between men and women lulled us into a false sense of human security? I suggest that once we allow ourselves to be exposed to the possibility of human encounter with *other creatures,* then this sharpens up once again the more specific role of human beings in the overall theo-drama; in other words, in encountering other animals we become more human.

83. Soskice, *The Kindness of God,* p. 6. Soskice, in her discussion of theological anthropology, follows tradition in confining image bearing to humanity, but, oddly, she seems to justify this on the basis that nothing in creation should be venerated as divine. However, image bearing does not mean that humans are divine either, nor is the choice necessarily so stark as that between a pagan view of a divine cosmos and a Christian one where image bearing is traditionally constricted to human beings (p. 37).

84. Soskice, *The Kindness of God,* p. 39. "Some Orthodox theologians suggest, to my mind convincingly, that to say 'man is in the image of God' is to say that 'man is mystery' because God is mystery" (p. 39).

85. She draws on Catholic social teaching in making these remarks, especially *Gaudium et Spes.* Soskice, *The Kindness of God,* pp. 47-48.

Bearing God's Wisdom

I have hinted above that human beings and other creatures share in a theo-dramatic history with God, one that is orchestrated by the presence of the grace of the Holy Spirit but showed forth in its most strident clarity through the particular drama of the life, death, and resurrection of Jesus Christ. By pointing to the dramatic nature of his life and passion, other subjects, including other animals, are drawn into that dramatic history. In other words, we do not just rely on the Genesis account to offer us a statement on what it is to be human, but find this filled out through the particular manner in which Christ is portrayed on earth as recipient in a dramatic encounter of creaturely and divine freedom. Behind this free action is the divine energy of love that permeates and fills the creation and points to its fulfillment. Theo-drama is, then, a theological way of reading history in an eschatological key that eschews the reductionism of an epic or grand narrative, and points to particular occasions and particular events. Each stage in the long drama of evolutionary history forms a scene that is a moment in an overall act where the script has yet to be written in detail, even if the overall shape is well known, but only becomes clear to humans in retrospect.[86] I suggest that a hermeneutic of theo-drama encourages a greater sense of human agency compared with grand narrative accounts, in that it points to the significance of individual human acts and decisions in a way that tends to be lost when a narrative is viewed as an inevitable marching of events. Those individual acts cannot be separated from the communities in which they take place, thus bringing into alignment the evolutionary concept of niche construction and theo-dramatics. Of course, there will still be some narrative elements in theo-drama as in any good play, but the specific circumstances that arise and the contingencies built into history will have particular poignancy. The possibility of religious intimacy is present as well, going deeper into the concept of kinship, so this intimacy finds expression in lyric accounts of the spousal closeness between God and human beings in the mystical writings of authors such as the twelfth-century Cistercian monk Bernard of Clairvaux.[87]

86. I have filled out the significance of theo-drama for interpreting evolutionary history in *Christ and Evolution,* where I draw heavily, but critically, on the writings of Hans Urs von Balthasar. Although aspects of his thought are problematic, his account is one of the richest contemporary expositions of the concept of theo-drama available. See Deane-Drummond, *Christ and Evolution.*

87. Bernard of Clairvaux, *On Loving God,* Christian Classics Ethereal Library. Avail-

Yet, in this view God is not so much a subject like other subjects, even though God can be thought of in a metaphorical sense as personal, but rather the presence of God makes itself known in the dynamic interaction of the players in the drama.

How far is the idea that other animal kinds might be included in a theo-drama even remotely imaginable? I suggest that this is actually more realistic than it appears at first sight, for anthropologists are beginning to realize that the boundaries between considering animals as either wild or domesticated, as discussed above, are not just becoming more blurred in evolutionary terms, but are also breaking down in studies of contemporary cultures, offering the possibility that other animals will come to share in human social lives in ways that have deep implications for both societies. The question becomes: Can trust between humans and other animals be restored where relationships have consistently developed into habits of domination? This is illustrated in the work of anthropologists who are beginning to show ever-greater entanglements of social and structural ecologies.[88] If we have arrived at the epoch of the Anthropocene, in which humans are major agents of global change on earth,[89] then it becomes all the more important to understand the relationships between humans and other animals. A transdisciplinary anthropology known as ethnoprimatology is starting to emerge that includes other primates and places humans and other primates in the same shared, entangled ecological, and social, space.[90] Here

---

able online at: http://www.ccel.org/ccel/bernard/loving_god.titlepage.html (accessed April 4, 2013).

88. "Social ecology" is concerned with social networks even across species, including history, political economy, and culture, while "structural ecology" is that which is associated with biotic landscapes and physical environments where people and other animals live. Agustín Fuentes, "Naturalcultural Encounters in Bali: Monkeys, Temples, Tourists and Ethnoprimatology," *Cultural Anthropology* 25, no. 4 (2010): 600-624, here 600. See also Agustín Fuentes, "Social Minds and Social Selves: Redefining the Human-Alloprimate Interface," in *The Politics of Species: Reshaping Our Relationships with Other Animals,* ed. Raymond Corby and Annette Lanjouw (Cambridge: Cambridge University Press, 2014), 179-88. I am grateful to Agustín Fuentes for giving me access to this chapter at the proof stage before final publication.

89. For a social commentary, see Bronislaw Szerszynski, "The End of the End of Nature: The Anthropocene and the Fate of the Human," *Oxford Literary Review* 34, no. 2 (2012): 165-84. He comments on the paradox of the Anthropocene, where humanity will be recorded in geological time but in the same moment wiped out, so "The Anthropocene strata will thus be both laid down and built up, and both instituted and abolished, in the same gesture" (p. 181).

90. Fuentes, "Naturalcultural Encounters in Bali," p. 601.

the prefix "ethno-" marks the specifically anthropogenic social, economic, and political histories that are woven into a discussion of primate societies. Ethnoprimatology accepts that the natural world is constructed and constructive, rather than presuming scientific objectivity or pristine "wild" nature. Furthermore, primates appear in their symbolic form, as in cultural anthropology, as well as through scientific observations of behavior, as in primatology.[91] Here we arrive at the idea of a niche that is both fundamental in expressing basic requirements and realized in how this is met in the presence of others. In this way, "Humans and alloprimates can be important partners in the construction of social and ecological niches."[92] While a traditional paradigm uses the tool of "fitness" according to adaptation to a given environment, this approach offers instead a discernment of processes, patterns, and relationships within shared niches and mutual ecologies.

In a fascinating study of the long-tailed macaques living in the temple forest complex at Padangtegal, Bali, Agustín Fuentes remarks that unlike other studies of human-monkey interfaces that discuss shared use of space or resource conflict, "these naturecultural contact zones are instead characterized by subtle behavioral and ecological interactions against the backdrop of the longue durée of human histories and paleohistories."[93] This counters a more common view that "this interface is one of conflict and competition."[94] He argues that in this context there is neither strict competition nor purely reciprocal association between humans and alloprimates. Rather, "the interface between species constructs mutual ecologies that structure their relationships. In these zones there is an entanglement of economies, bodies, and daily practice that leads to the construction and coproduction of niches."[95] In the temple complexes, resident monkey groups are participants in ritual practice.[96] For the Balinese, "all actors in

91. Fuentes argues, convincingly in my view, that critics of this approach attempt to shoehorn such studies into traditional models of primate research, but he suggests that "it is impossible to deny that the majority of primate populations now interact regularly and consistently with humans." Fuentes, "Naturalcultural Encounters in Bali," p. 603.

92. Fuentes, "Naturalcultural Encounters in Bali," p. 604.

93. Fuentes, "Naturalcultural Encounters in Bali," p. 606.

94. Fuentes, "Social Minds," p. 182.

95. Fuentes, "Naturalcultural Encounters in Bali," p. 607.

96. They are viewed in diverse ways by the Balinese, either as just part of the environment, as a nuisance, or as emissaries of spiritual-natural forces. Fuentes, "Naturalcultural Encounters in Bali," p. 608. Space does not permit a full discussion of attitudes here, but macaques seem largely able to anticipate when they are permitted to feast on the food offerings from their experience of human contact.

this scenario are part of a natural ecology."[97] On a biological scale, human alteration of the landscape has shaped the population genetics of the macaques in particular ways, where gene flow is channeled down specific riverine corridors created by the Balinese agricultural system.[98] The point here is that there is an interlacing of human and macaque histories so that their environments are constructed on particular lines, shaped by particular decisions made in human societies. Fuentes concludes, "We should move past the notion of definitive discrete distinctions in favor of fluid and reciprocating interfaces that change over time creating spaces, bodies and niches of relevance to our understanding of human animal and the other animal experiences."[99]

By contrast with macaques, Fuentes concludes that "Based on what we know about the ape-human interface, the future of the great apes, gorillas, chimpanzees, and orangutans is extremely bleak. The basic pattern is a negative one for the apes."[100] Their need for a large geographical area for their habitat and diverse fruit in their diet, as well as their very slow and easily disrupted reproductive cycles, makes them particularly vulnerable to extensive habitat alteration. Taboos against hunting chimpanzees and gorillas among some central African indigenous peoples are weakening. They are also a target of bushmeat hunting in Africa and the pet trade in Asia, and their body parts are harvested for their supposed therapeutic benefits in some cultures. The loss of ape habitats due to forest clearance, which amounts to humanly induced niche *destruction* for the apes rather than construction, along with increasing human populations in areas where humans and apes have coexisted, leads to expanded conflict with apes along with rapidly shrinking numbers. But the sheer vulnerability of these ape populations brings to the surface once more the possibility of extending human affiliation beyond their own kind, so, as Fuentes points out, "a distinctive evolutionary discontinuity is that humans can cast this physiological, social and symbolic bonding 'net' beyond biological kin, beyond reciprocal exchange arrangements, beyond mating investment, and, in particular, even beyond our species (with dogs, horses, even other primates) . . .

97. Balinese do not generally distinguish between material and nonmaterial agents, so the natural and supernatural worlds and niches coexist, simultaneously and equally. Fuentes, "Naturalcultural Encounters," p. 608.

98. Fuentes, "Naturalcultural Encounters," p. 609.

99. Fuentes, "Naturalcultural Encounters," p. 618.

100. Fuentes, "Social Minds," p. 183.

incorporating other species into our network of caring and sharing, our 'kin' writ large."[101]

Given this fluid and dynamic context, how might we envisage the particular role of humanity in such exchanges? Where does, in other words, our particular responsibility as humans lie? I suggest that in order to draw on such fluid boundaries in a creative way that looks not just to immediate benefits, but to what might be broadly termed "the common good" understood in the widest sense in ecological terms and in relation to future generations, the exercise of wisdom or practical reason in shaping what love might mean in given scenes of the theo-drama is crucial. It is like the lens through which the energy of love needs to flow in order for the drama of salvation to come to fruition. While the possibility of turning aside from that wisdom is always there, due to human weakness, myopia, or even evil, improvisation plays a part, in that the script is not fixed from the beginning, other than being orientated toward a good end (Rom. 8:28). Just as God as Creator acted to create the world in love, but also through wisdom,[102] so human beings as God's image bearers are also called to act in love, with compassion and through wisdom.

Such a tradition of equating the way God works in the world with God's wisdom is very ancient and is particularly evident in the writings of the medieval Franciscan Saint Bonaventure. Bonaventure believed that the eschatological goal of peace could be achieved by contemplation through a ladder of Christian wisdom, but this wisdom was always acutely aware of its dependence on divine grace.[103] While his ladder of ascent to God might give the impression of leaving creaturely things behind, the movement from considering creatures, to considering self, to considering God is a recognized pattern in the spiritual life. Bonaventure stresses continuously the importance of God's grace in enlightening human wisdom, even when considering creaturely things, for "no one arrives at wisdom except through

101. Fuentes, "Social Minds," p. 186. The more explicit issues of how humans are to act, that is, ethical questions, cannot be developed fully in this monograph. I am presupposing the good of protecting ape populations for theological reasons, rather than developing detailed ethical arguments from the perspective of theological ethics.

102. I recognize that this statement presupposes a particular account of God's creative activity in the world, as a Creator who acts in love and through wisdom. I have argued for this position in earlier work; see Celia Deane-Drummond, *Creation through Wisdom: Theology and the New Biology* (Edinburgh: T. & T. Clark, 2000, 2003).

103. Bonaventure, *The Journey of the Mind to God*, ed. Stephen F. Brown, trans. Philotheus Boehner (Indianapolis: Hackett, 1993), prologue, p. 2.

grace, justice and knowledge."[104] He also argues that there are different ways of seeing material things and arriving at insight into the way God's power, wisdom, and goodness "shine forth in created things" by scientific observation, by faith, and by reasonable contemplation.[105] For Bonaventure, "every creature is by its very nature a figure and likeness of the eternal Wisdom . . . any creature which He chose to institute for the purpose of signifying . . . which not only has the character of sign in the ordinary sense of the term, but also the character of sacrament as well."[106] But the most exalted sense of the presence of the wisdom of God comes when Bonaventure contemplates the human mind, so "our mind like the house of God is inhabited by Divine Wisdom, it is made a daughter, a spouse, a friend of God; it is made a member, a sister, a co-heir of Christ the Head, it is made a temple of the Holy Spirit, faith laying the foundation, hope building it up, and sanctity of soul and body dedicating it to God."[107] Significantly, he adjusts a prayer to the Ephesians so that our goal is to know the breadth, height, and depth of the wisdom of God. In the final contemplation, the intellect ceases to be active and the mind and all its affections "pass over" completely in loving adoration; it is a mystical experience that is a wisdom received by the Holy Spirit.[108] He names this as a mystical passing out of this world that is experienced as a form of death. Yet, there are problems with such a tradition because it leaves behind material forms on the ladder of ascent, for it serves to separate human wisdom from that of other creatures in naming only humans as capable of such ecstatic heights.

An important difference to stress in this analogous relationship between the wisdom of creature and Creator is that God as Creator creates the very stuff of life whereas humans are only able to change what is created. Once humans believe that they can re-create themselves, the temptation to be like gods lurks at the door. Our action through wisdom is colored by recognition of those species who are our kin and who are capable of active agency as fellow players in an overall drama of salvation.[109] The special kinship of alloprimates needs to be acknowledged; they share creaturely life with humans in a particularly intimate way and not only sur-

104. Bonaventure, *Journey*, I, §8.

105. Bonaventure, *Journey*, I, §§11-13.

106. Bonaventure, *Journey*, II, §12.

107. Bonaventure, *Journey*, IV, §8.

108. Bonaventure, *Journey*, VII, §4.

109. How far other primate species are capable of something approaching human wisdom has not, as far as I am aware, been the topic of active research.

prise us by their similarity and uniqueness, but open up new perspectives on what it means to be human. We are surprised by such observations in a manner similar to how we are often surprised by our own kin, such as members of our own family and particularly our children. Frans de Waal has hinted that the cooperation present in alloprimates gives lessons for human society.[110] While this implies a naturalism that is somewhat problematic, recognition of the interlacing of interspecific societies throws up particular questions for human societies.

Shalom: The Goal of Flourishing

Given this intermeshing and interlacing of human and other creaturely kinds, difficult decisions still need to be made by human beings in setting priorities for particular acts of conservation or intervention. By viewing the problems not just as isolated incidents but as part of a wider pattern of ecological preservation, niche construction, and ongoing evolutionary change, humans have the capacity to consider not just intersubjective relationships but also wider impacts on the tapestry of complex interactions between species. Yet making these decisions when confronted by such complexity will dwarf any sense of our own intelligence, for the wider we range in looking at ecological issues, the harder it is to predict in any accurate way the precise consequences of human actions. Even if we are living in an epoch of Anthropocene, where human domination of the natural world has huge impacts, the precise impact of human activity is often only dimly apparent at the time when actions are taking place.

There are, of course, exceptions to this level of uncertainty in defining the consequence of human acts where it is plainly obvious what given actions might lead to in terms of the suffering or destruction of human cultures and societies and those of other species and animal kinds. It may be one of the reasons why the animal rights movement has such a vociferous following, since it is obvious that many of the ways in which we continue to keep other animal kinds in quite appalling conditions in "factory farms" border on criminality as well as plain immorality. Such observations show the inhuman face of humanity, who has turned away from its fellow sub-

110. The subtitle of his book suggests this, but the book itself is rather more cautious in its conclusions. Frans de Waal, *The Age of Empathy: Nature's Lessons for a Kinder Society* (London: Souvenir Press, 2009).

jects and narcissistically concentrated on its own material gain or pleasure. The wisdom of the liminal in which we find ourselves, hovering on that liminal space between humans and other animals and between humans and our own constructed selves, is a wisdom that cries out in the dark space of unknowing that is opened up in such encounters. It is unknowing in the sense of opening up the depth to which human depravity can sink, but it is also unknowing in that it challenges us to think more about our human actions and reactions in such encounters. It borders on a mystical knowing that is unknowing, but now we find such mysterious encounter in ordinary concrete exchanges of daily life, including those occasions that allow us to encounter specific other creatures, rather than in mysticism arising perhaps through the deliberate experience of extreme asceticism. Yet, those earlier contemplative mystics touched on something important in recommending restraint in insatiable human desire or self-love misdirected inward rather than outward toward others in friendship. Ironically, perhaps, those early saints who were most deprived of human social contact found that other animals became their closest intimates; even if we allow for the hagiographic style of writing, the close companionship with other animals is self-evident.[111]

It is, perhaps, the exercise of the virtues that helps us know how to act in the theo-drama in building up a world that shows traces or hints of *shalom,* or right relationships with God and with every other creature.[112] While ecotheologians may believe that *shalom* is possible on earth, I am less convinced that it is ever likely to be attainable, given the present conditions of instability, strife, biodiversity loss, political and domestic violence, climate change, and so on. Further, evolutionary science, *qua* science, admits of no moral intention, even if it is decidedly value-laden once its philosophical and cultural presuppositions are exposed. Theology can be rather more explicit in this sense, so imaging our way into such a vision can be fruitful in encouraging a particular portrait of human being and becom-

111. Schaefer, *Theological Foundations,* pp. 150-64.

112. *Shalom* is a term used by writers such as Nicholas Wolterstorff, *Until Justice and Peace Embrace* (Grand Rapids: Eerdmans, 1983), pp. 69-70; Robert Wenberg, *God, Humans, and Animals: An Invitation to Enlarge Our Moral Universe* (Grand Rapids: Eerdmans, 2003); Jürgen Moltmann, "The Ecological Crisis: Peace with Nature?" *Scottish Journal of Religious Studies* 9 (1988): 5-18. Moltmann often prefers to use the term "Sabbath," as in *God in Creation* (London: SCM, 1985), pp. 5-7. I am using the term *shalom* in this context to put more emphasis on creaturely flourishing as such, rather than on the holiness of time that "Sabbath" implies.

ing, just as Bonaventure imagined a world of perfect peace in beginning his meditation on the journey of the mind to God. *Shalom* is a Hebrew term, and represents not just an absence of hostility, but enjoyment in relationships. This has some analogy with the idea of Sabbath, but now it is directed to future hope. This implies delight in the natural world and in relationships with other animals, as well as concern for their welfare. *Shalom* is the general vocation and destination of humanity in relationship to other creaturely kinds, but it is an eschatological goal to be sought by keeping this vision in mind. The vision of a peaceable kingdom, epitomized in Isaiah 65:25, "The wolf and the lamb will feed together, and the lion will eat straw like the ox," or Isaiah 11:6, "The wolf will live with the lamb, the leopard will lie down with the goat, the calf and the lion and the yearling together," represents peace where there had once been enmity. Yet, other animals are not just here for symbolic reasons; there is a real sense in which the coming kingdom will not include the destructive predatory relationships between other animals that we have come to accept in the name of noninterference. I am not, however, suggesting that we *should* interfere in the name of promoting peaceful relations, or that this image of *shalom* gives us a blueprint for how to act now, but that we need to bear in mind that an eschatological goal includes the transformation of other creatures as well as the transformation of humanity. We are caught up *together* in a common society that we can hope will be transformed for the greater glory of God. That glory is certainly humanity fully alive, but it is a life enriched by an interlaced past, present, and future with other animals in all their marvelous diversity.

Bibliography

Akins, Chana K., and Thomas R. Zentall. "Imitation in Japanese Quail: The Role of Reinforcement of Demonstrator Responding." *Psychonomic Bulletin and Review* 5, no. 4 (1998): 694-97.

Aktipis, C. Athena, Lee Cronk, and Rolando de Aguiar. "Risk-Pooling and Herd Survival: An Agent Based Model of a Maasai Gift-Giving System." *Human Ecology* 39 (2011): 131-40.

Alexander, J. McKenzie. *The Structural Evolution of Morality.* Cambridge: Cambridge University Press, 2007.

Alexander, Richard D. *The Biology of Moral Systems.* New York: De Gruyter, 1987.

Anderson, John R., Daniel Bothell, Michael D. Byrne, Scott Douglass, Christian Lebiere, and Yulin Qin. "An Integrated Theory of the Mind." *Psychological Review* 111 (2004): 1036-60.

Aquinas, Thomas. *Commentary on Aristotle's "De Anima."* Translated by Robert Pasnau. New Haven: Yale University Press, 1999.

———. *Commentary on Aristotle's "Metaphysics."* Translated by Richard J. Blackwell, Richard J. Spath, and W. Edmund Thirlkel. Notre Dame, Ind.: Dumb Ox Books, 1995.

———. *Disputed Questions on the Virtues.* Edited by E. M. Atkins and Thomas Williams. Translated by E. M. Atkins. Cambridge: Cambridge University Press, 2005.

———. *On Love and Charity: Readings from the Commentary on the Sentences of Peter Lombard.* Translated by Peter A. Kwasniewski, Thomas Bolin, and Joseph Bolin. Washington, D.C.: Catholic University of America Press, 2008.

———. *On Truth.* Vol. 1. Translated by Robert Mulligan. Chicago: Regnery, 1952.

———. *On Truth.* Vol. 3. Translated by Robert Mulligan. Chicago: Regnery, 1954.

———. *Summa Contra Gentiles.* Translated by Vernon J. Bourke. Dominican House of Studies, Priory of the Immaculate Conception. Online: http://dhspriory.org/thomas/ContraGentiles3b.htm#112 (accessed January 19, 2013).

———. *Summa Theologiae, Charity, Vol. 34 (2a2ae. 23-33).* Translated by R. J. Batton. London: Blackfriars, 1975.
———. *Summa Theologiae, Christian Theology, Vol. 1 (1a. 1).* Translated by Thomas Gilby. London: Blackfriars, 1964.
———. *Summa Theologiae, Consequences of Charity, Vol. 35 (2a2ae. 34-46).* Translated by Thomas R. Heath. London: Blackfriars, 1972.
———. *Summa Theologiae, Consequences of Faith, Vol. 32 (2a2ae. 8-16).* Translated by Thomas Gilby. London: Blackfriars, 1975.
———. *Summa Theologiae, Cosmogony, Vol. 10 (1a. 65-74).* Translated by William A. Wallace. London: Blackfriars, 1967.
———. *Summa Theologiae, Creation, Variety, and Evil, Vol. 8 (1a. 44-49).* Translated by Thomas Gilby. London: Blackfriars, 1967.
———. *Summa Theologiae, Divine Government, Vol. 14 (1a. 103-109).* Translated by T. C. O'Brien. London: Blackfriars, 1975.
———. *Summa Theologiae, Father, Son, and Holy Ghost, Vol. 7 (1a. 33-43).* Translated by T. C. O'Brien. London: Blackfriars, 1965.
———. *Summa Theologiae, Fear and Anger, Vol. 21 (1a2ae. 40-48).* Translated by John Patrick Reid. London: Blackfriars, 1964.
———. *Summa Theologiae, The Gifts of the Spirit, Vol. 24 (1a2ae. 68-70).* Translated by Edward D. O'Connor. London: Blackfriars, 1974.
———. *Summa Theologiae, God's Will and Providence, Vol. 5 (1a. 19-26).* Translated by Thomas Gilby. London: Blackfriars, 1966.
———. *Summa Theologiae, The Gospel of Grace, Vol. 30 (1a2ae. 106-114).* Translated by Cornelius Ernst. London: Blackfriars, 1972.
———. *Summa Theologiae, Justice, Vol. 37 (2a2ae. 57-62).* Translated by Thomas Gilby. London: Blackfriars, 1975.
———. *Summa Theologiae, Law and Political Theory, Vol. 28 (1a2ae. 90-97).* Translated by Thomas Gilby. London: Blackfriars, 1966.
———. *Summa Theologiae, Love and Desire, Vol. 19 (1a2ae. 22-30).* Translated by Eric D'Arcy. London: Blackfriars, 1967.
———. *Summa Theologiae, Man, Vol. 11 (1a. 75-83).* Translated by Timothy Suttor. London: Blackfriars, 1970.
———. *Summa Theologiae, Man Made in God's Image, Vol. 13 (1a. 90-102).* Translated by Edmund Hill. London: Blackfriars, 1964.
———. *Summa Theologiae, Parts of Temperance/Well Tempered Passion, Vol. 44 (2a2ae. 155-170).* Translated by Thomas Gilby. London: Blackfriars, 1964.
———. *Summa Theologiae, Principles of Morality, Vol. 18 (1a2ae. 18-21).* Translated by Thomas Gilby (London: Blackfriars, 1965).
———. *Summa Theologiae, Prudence, Vol. 36 (2a2ae. 47-56).* Translated by Thomas Gilby. London: Blackfriars, 1973.
———. *Summa Theologiae, Psychology of Human Acts, Vol. 17 (1a2ae. 6-17).* Translated by Thomas Gilby. London: Blackfriars, 1970.

———. *Summa Theologiae, Purpose and Happiness, Vol. 16 (1a2ae. 1-5).* Translated by Thomas Gilby. London: Blackfriars, 1969.

———. *Summa Theologiae, Religion and Worship, Vol. 39 (2a2ae. 80-91).* Translated by Kevin D. O'Rourke. London: Blackfriars, 1964.

———. *Summa Theologiae, Sin, Vol. 25 (1a2ae. 71-80).* Translated by John Fearon. London: Blackfriars, 1969.

———. *Summa Theologiae, Virtue, Vol. 23 (1a2ae. 55-67).* Translated by W. D. Hughes. London: Blackfriars, 1968.

———. *Summa Theologiae, Virtues of Justice in the Human Community, Vol. 41 (2a2ae. 101-122).* Translated by T. C. O'Brien. London: Blackfriars, 1971.

———. *The Summa Theologica.* Benziger Bros. ed., 1947. Translated by Fathers of the English Dominican Province. Complete work online: http://dhspriory.org/thomas/summa/index.html (different sections were accessed at intervals from June 2009 to May 2013).

———. *The Treatise on Law.* Edited by R. J. Henle. Notre Dame, Ind.: University of Notre Dame Press, 1993.

Ashley, J. Matthew. "Reading the Universe Theologically: The Contribution of a Biblical Narrative Imagination." *Theological Studies* 71, no. 4 (2010): 870-902.

Atran, Scott. *In Gods We Trust: The Evolutionary Landscape of Religion.* New York: Oxford University Press, 2004.

Augustine. *The Trinity.* Translated by Stephen McKenna. Washington, D.C.: Catholic University of America Press, 1963.

Ayala, Francisco. "The Difference of Being Human: Ethical Behavior as an Evolutionary Byproduct." In *Biology, Ethics, and the Origins of Life,* edited by Holmes Rolston III, pp. 113-36. Boston: Jones and Bartlett, 1995.

Balcombe, Jonathan. *Second Nature: The Inner Lives of Animals.* New York: Palgrave Macmillan, 2010.

Balthasar, Hans Urs von. *First Glance at Adrienne von Speyr.* Translated by Antje Lawry and Sergia Englund. San Francisco: Ignatius, 1968.

———. *The Glory of the Lord: A Theological Aesthetics.* Vol. 5, *Realm of Metaphysics in the Modern Age.* Edited by Brian McNeil and John Riches. Translated by Oliver Davies, Andrew Louth, Brian McNeil, John Saward, and Rowan Williams. Edinburgh: T. & T. Clark; San Francisco: Ignatius, 1991.

———. *The Glory of the Lord: A Theological Aesthetics.* Vol. 6, *Theology: The Old Covenant.* Translated by Brian McNeil and Erasmo Leiva-Merikakis. Edinburgh: T. & T. Clark; San Francisco: Ignatius, 1991.

———. *The Glory of the Lord: A Theological Aesthetics.* Vol. 7, *Theology: The New Covenant.* Translated by Brian McNeil. Edinburgh: T. & T. Clark; San Francisco: Ignatius, 1989.

———. *Man in History.* London: Sheed and Ward, 1968.

———. *Theo-Drama: Theological Dramatic Theory.* Vol. 1, *Prolegomena.* Translated by George Harrison. San Francisco: Ignatius, 1988.

———. *Theo-Drama: Theological Dramatic Theory.* Vol. 2, *The Dramatis Personae: Man in God.* Translated by George Harrison. San Francisco: Ignatius, 1990.

———. *Theo-Drama: Theological Dramatic Theory.* Vol. 3, *The Dramatis Personae: The Person in Christ.* Translated by George Harrison. San Francisco: Ignatius, 1992.

———. *Theo-Drama: Theological Dramatic Theory.* Vol. 4, *The Action.* Translated by George Harrison. San Francisco: Ignatius, 1994.

———. *Theo-Drama: Theological Dramatic Theory.* Vol. 5, *The Last Act.* Translated by George Harrison. San Francisco: Ignatius, 1998.

———. *A Theological Anthropology.* Eugene, Ore.: Wipf and Stock, 2010 (1967).

Barad, Judith. *Aquinas on the Nature and Treatment of Animals.* San Francisco: International Scholars Publications, 1995.

Barnard, Alan. *Genesis of Symbolic Thought.* Cambridge: Cambridge University Press, 2012.

Barrett, Justin. "The Naturalness of Religion and the Unnaturalness of Theology." In *Is Religion Natural?* edited by Dirk Evers, Michael Fuller, Antje Jackelen, and Taede A. Smedes, pp. 3-23. London: T. & T. Clark/Continuum, 2012.

———. *Why Would Anyone Believe in God?* Lanham, Md.: Alta Mira Press, 2004.

Bateson, Patrick, and Peter Gluckman. *Plasticity, Robustness, Development, and Evolution.* Cambridge: Cambridge University Press, 2011.

Baynes-Rock, Marcus. "Hyenas Like Us: Social Relations with an Urban Carnivore in Harar, Ethiopia." Ph.D. diss., Department of Anthropology, Macquarie University, Australia, 2012.

———. "Life and Death in the Multispecies Commons." *Social Science Information* (2013).

———. "Local Tolerance of Hyena Attacks in East Hararge Region, Ethiopia." *Anthrozoös* (2013).

Bechara, Antoine. "The Role of Emotion in Decision-Making: Evidence from Neurological Patients with Orbitofrontal Damage." *Brain and Cognition* 55 (2004): 30-40.

Bechara, Antoine, Hanna Damasio, and Antonio Demasio. "Emotion, Decision-Making and the Orbitofrontal Cortex." *Cerebral Cortex* 10, no. 3 (2000): 295-307.

Bekoff, Marc. *Animal Passions and Beastly Virtues: Reflections on Redecorating Nature.* Philadelphia: Temple University Press, 2006.

———. *The Emotional Lives of Animals.* Novato, Calif.: New World Library, 2007.

Bekoff, Marc, and Dale Jamieson. *Readings in Animal Cognition.* Cambridge: MIT Press, 1995.

Bekoff, Marc, and Jessica Pierce. *Wild Justice: The Moral Lives of Animals.* Chicago: University of Chicago Press, 2009.

Bellah, Robert. *Religion in Human Evolution: From the Paleolithic to the Axial Age.* Cambridge: Harvard University Press, Belknap Press, 2011.

Benzoni, Francisco. *Ecological Ethics and the Human Soul: Aquinas, Whitehead, and the Metaphysics of Value.* Notre Dame, Ind.: University of Notre Dame Press, 2007.

Berkman, John. "Towards a Thomistic Theology of Animality." In *Creaturely Theology: On God, Humans, and Other Animals,* edited by Celia Deane-Drummond and David Clough, pp. 21-40. London: SCM, 2009.

Bernard of Clairvaux. *On Loving God.* Christian Classics Ethereal Library. Online: http://www.ccel.org/ccel/bernard/loving_god.titlepage.html (accessed April 4, 2013).

Bhaskar, Roy. *A Realist Theory of Science.* London: Verso, 1997.

Biggar, Nigel. "Evolutionary Biology, 'Enlightened' Anthropological Narratives, and Social Morality: A View from Christian Ethics." *Studies in Christian Ethics* 26, no. 2 (2013): 152-57.

Bloom, Paul. "Religion, Morality, Evolution." *Annual Review of Psychology* 63 (2012): 179-99.

Boehm, Christopher. *Moral Origins: The Evolution of Virtue, Altruism, and Shame.* New York: Basic Books, 2012.

Boeve, Lieven, Yves De Maeseneer, and Ellen Van Stichel, eds. *Image of God, Image of Man? Perspectives on Theological Anthropology for the 21st Century.* New York: Fordham University Press, 2013.

Bonaventure, *The Journey of the Mind to God.* Edited by Stephen F. Brown. Translated by Philotheus Boehner. Indianapolis: Hackett, 1993.

Bosch, Christophe. *Wild Cultures: A Comparison between Chimpanzee and Human Culture.* Cambridge: Cambridge University Press, 2012.

Boyer, Pascal. *Religion Explained: The Evolutionary Origins of Religious Thought.* New York: Basic Books, 2002.

Broom, Donald. *The Evolution of Morality and Religion.* Cambridge: Cambridge University Press, 2003.

Brosnan, Sarah. "A Hypothesis of the Co-evolution of Cooperation and Reponses to Inequity." *Frontiers in Decision Neuroscience* (April 2011). Online: http://www.frontiersin.org/Decision_Neuroscience/10.3389/fnins.2011.00043/abstract (accessed February 23, 2013).

———. "Introduction to 'Justice in Animals.'" *Social Justice Research* 25 (2012): 109-21.

Brown, William. *The Seven Pillars of Creation: The Bible, Science, and the Ecology of Wonder.* Oxford: Oxford University Press, 2010.

Bulbulia, Joseph, and Richard Sosis. "Signaling Theory and the Evolution of Religious Cooperation." *Religion* 41, no. 3 (2011): 363-88.

Burghardt, Gordon M. *The Genesis of Animal Play: Testing the Limits.* Cambridge: MIT Press, 2005.

Byrne, Richard. "Culture in Great Apes: Using Intricate Complexity in Feeding Skills to Trace the Evolutionary Origin of Human Technical Prowess." In

Social Intelligence: From Brain to Culture, edited by Nathan Emery, Nicola Clayton, and Chris Firth, pp. 147-60. Oxford: Oxford University Press, 2008.

Cameron, David W., and Colin P. Groves. *Bones, Stones, and Molecules.* San Diego: Elsevier, 2004.

Camosy, Charles. "Other Animals as Persons? A Roman Catholic Inquiry." In *Animals as Religious Subjects: Transdisciplinary Perspectives,* edited by Celia Deane-Drummond, Rebecca Artinian-Kaiser, and David Clough, pp. 259-77. London: T. & T. Clark/Bloomsbury, 2013.

———. *Peter Singer and Christian Ethics.* Cambridge: Cambridge University Press, 2011.

Candea, Matei. " 'I Fell in Love with Carlos the Meerkat': Engagement and Detachment in Human-Animal Relations." *American Ethnologist* 37, no. 2 (2010): 241-58.

Chalmers, David. *Philosophy of Mind: Classical and Contemporary Readings.* New York: Oxford University Press, 2002.

Clague, Julie. "Religious Conscience and Political Life: One Hundred Years of Catholic Teachings and Tensions." Public lecture, Yale Divinity School, March 7, 2013.

Clark, Stephen. "Enlarging the Community: Companion Animals." In *Introducing Applied Ethics,* edited by Brenda Almond, pp. 318-30. Oxford: Blackwell, 1996.

Clayton, Nicola S., and Nathan J. Emery. "Canny Corvids and Political Primates: A Case for Convergent Evolution in Intelligence." In *The Deep Structure of Biology: Is Convergence Sufficiently Ubiquitous to Give a Directional Signal?* edited by Simon Conway Morris, pp. 128-42. Conshohocken, Pa.: Templeton Foundation Press, 2008.

Clayton, Philip, and Jeffrey Schloss, eds. *Evolution and Ethics: Human Morality in Biological and Religious Perspectives.* Grand Rapids: Eerdmans, 2004.

Clough, David. "All God's Creatures: Reading Genesis on Human and Non Human Animals." In *Reading Genesis after Darwin,* edited by Stephen C. Barton and David Wilkinson, pp. 145-62. Oxford: Oxford University Press, 2009.

———. "Not a Not-Animal: The Vocation to Be a Human Animal Creature." *Studies in Christian Ethics* 26, no. 1 (2013): 4-17.

———. *On Animals: Systematic Theology.* London: T. & T. Clark/Continuum, 2012.

———. "Putting Animals in Their Place: On the Theological Classification of Animals." In *Animals as Religious Subjects: Transdisciplinary Perspectives,* edited by Celia Deane-Drummond, Rebecca Artinian-Kaiser, and David Clough, pp. 209-24. London: Bloomsbury/T. & T. Clark, 2013.

Coakley, Sarah. "Evolution, Cooperation and Ethics: Some Methodological and Philosophical Hurdles." *Studies in Christian Ethics* 26, no. 2 (2013): 135-39.

———. "Sacrifice Regained: Evolution, Cooperation, and God." Gifford Lectures. University of Aberdeen, Scotland, April 17–May 3, 2012. Online: http://www.abdn.ac.uk/gifford/about/ (accessed March 18, 2013).

———. *Sacrifice Regained: Reconsidering the Rationality of Religious Belief.* Inaugural lecture, October 13, 2009. Cambridge: Cambridge University Press, 2012.

Cohen, Simon Baron. *The Essential Difference: Male and Female Brains and the Truth about Autism.* New York: Basic Books, 2004.

Conradie, Ernst, ed. *Creation and Salvation.* Vol. 2, *A Companion on Recent Theological Movements.* Berlin: LIT Verlag, 2012.

Conway Morris, Simon. *Life's Solution: Inevitable Humans in a Lonely Universe.* Cambridge: Cambridge University Press, 2003.

Creager, Angela, and William Chester Jordan, eds. *The Animal-Human Boundary.* Rochester, N.Y.: University of Rochester Press, 2002.

Cronk, Lee. "The Influence of Cultural Framing on Play in the Trust Game: A Maasai Example." *Evolution and Human Behavior* 28 (2007): 352-58.

Cronk, Lee, and Helen Wasielewski. "An Unfamiliar Social Norm Rapidly Produces Framing Effects in an Economic Game." *Journal of Evolutionary Psychology* 6, no. 4 (2008): 283-308.

Cunningham, Conor. *Darwin's Pious Idea: Why the Ultra-Darwinists and Creationists Both Get It Wrong.* Grand Rapids: Eerdmans, 2010.

Dally, Joanna M., Nathan J. Emery, and Nicola S. Clayton. "Cache Protection Strategies by Western Scrub-Jays *(Aphelocoma californica):* Hiding Food in the Shade." *Proceedings of the Royal Society B* 271 (2004): 5387-90.

———. "Food-Caching Western Scrub-Jays Keep Track of Who Was Watching When." *Science* 312 (2006): 1662-66.

Damasio, Antonio R. "The Somatic Marker Hypothesis and the Possible Functions of the Prefrontal Cortex." *Philosophical Transactions of the Royal Society B* 351, no. 1346 (1996): 1413-20.

Darwin, Charles. *The Descent of Man, and Selection in Relation to Sex.* London: Penguin, 2004 (1871).

Davidson, Donald. *Subjective, Intersubjective, Objective.* Oxford: Oxford University Press, 2001.

Davis, Ellen. *Scripture, Culture, and Agriculture: An Agrarian Reading of the Bible.* Cambridge: Cambridge University Press, 2009.

Dawkins, Richard. *The God Delusion.* London: Houghton Mifflin, 2006.

———. *The Selfish Gene.* Oxford: Oxford University Press, 2006.

Deacon, Terence W. *The Symbolic Species: The Co-evolution of Language and the Brain.* New York and London: Norton, 1997.

Deane-Drummond, Celia. "Are Animals Moral? Taking Soundings through Vice, Virtue, Imago Dei and Conscience." In *Creaturely Theology: On God, Humans, and Other Animals,* edited by Celia Deane-Drummond and David Clough, pp. 190-210. London: SCM, 2009.

———. "The Breadth of Glory: A Trinitarian Eschatology for the Earth through Critical Engagement with Hans Urs von Balthasar." *International Journal of Systematic Theology* 12, no. 1 (2010): 46-64.

———. "A Case for Collective Conscience: Climategate, COP-15 and Climate Justice." *Studies in Christian Ethics* 24, no. 1 (2011): 1-18.

———. *Christ and Evolution: Wonder and Wisdom.* Minneapolis: Fortress, 2009.

———. "Creation." In *Cambridge Companion to Feminist Theology,* edited by Susan Parsons, pp. 190-207. Cambridge: Cambridge University Press, 2002.

———. *Creation through Wisdom: Theology and the New Biology.* Edinburgh: T. & T. Clark, 2000.

———. "Degrees of Freedom: Humans as Primates in Dialogue with Hans Urs von Balthsar." In *Beyond Human: From Animality to Transhumanism,* edited by Charlie Blake, Claire Molloy, and Steven Shakespeare, pp. 180-200. London: Continuum, 2012.

———. "Freedom, Conscience and Virtue: Theological Perspectives on the Ethics of Inherited Genetic Modification." In *Design and Destiny: Jewish and Christian Perspectives on Human Germline Modification,* edited by Ron Cole-Turner, pp. 167-200. Basingstoke: Macmillan, 2008.

———. *Genetics and Christian Ethics.* Cambridge: Cambridge University Press, 2006.

———. "God's Image and Likeness in Humans and Other Animals: Performative Soul-Making and Graced Nature." *Zygon* 47 no. 4 (2012): 934-48.

———. "In God's Image and Likeness: From Reason to Revelation in Humans and Other Animals." in *Questioning the Human? Perspectives on Theological Anthropology for the 21st Century,* edited by Lieven Boeve, Yves De Maeseneer, and Ellen Van Stichel. New York: Fordham University Press, 2014.

———. "Plumbing the Depths: A Recovery of Natural Law and Natural Wisdom in the Context of Debates about Evolutionary Purpose." *Zygon* 42, no. 4 (2007): 981-98.

———. *Re-imaging the Image of God, Goshen Lectures, 2012.* Kitchener, Ontario, Canada: Pandora Press, 2014.

———. "Taking Leave of the Animal? The Theological and Ethical Implications of Transhuman Projects." In *Transhumanism and Transcendence: Christian Hope in an Age of Technological Enhancement,* edited by Ron Cole-Turner, pp. 115-30. Washington, D.C.: Georgetown University Press, 2012.

———. *Wonder and Wisdom: Conversations in Science, Spirituality, and Theology.* London: DLT, 2006.

———, ed. *Brave New World: Theology, Ethics, and the Human Genome.* London: T. & T. Clark, 2003.

Deane-Drummond, Celia, and David Clough, eds. *Creaturely Theology: On God, Humans, and Other Animals.* London: SCM, 2009.

Deane-Drummond, Celia, Rebecca Artinian-Kaiser, and David Clough, eds. *Animals as Religious Subjects: Transdisciplinary Perspectives.* London: T. & T. Clark/Bloomsbury, 2013.

Derrida, Jacques. *The Animal That Therefore I Am.* Edited by Marie-Louise Mallet. Translated by David Wills. New York: Fordham University Press, 2008.

Dixson, Alan F. *Primate Sexuality: Comparative Studies of the Prosimians, Monkeys, Apes, and Human Beings.* 2nd ed. Oxford: Oxford University Press, 2013.

Downes, William. *Language and Religion.* Cambridge: Cambridge University Press, 2011.

Dunbar, Robin. "The Social Brain Hypothesis." *Evolutionary Anthropology* 6 (1998): 178-90.

Dupré, John. *Humans and Other Animals.* Oxford: Oxford University Press, 2002.

———. "On Human Nature." *Human Affairs* 2 (2003): 109-22.

Durkheim, Émile. "The Rules of Sociological Method." In *The Rules of Sociological Method and Selected Texts on Sociology and Its Method,* edited by Steven Lukes, translated by W. D. Halls. Basingstoke: Macmillan, 1892 (2nd ed. 1901).

Edmunds, Matt. *A Theological Diagnosis: A New Direction on Genetic Therapy, "Disability," and the Ethics of Healing.* London: Jessica Kingsley, 2011.

Edwards, Denis. *How God Acts: Creation, Redemption, and Special Divine Action.* Minneapolis: Fortress, 2010.

———. *Jesus and the Cosmos.* Mahwah, N.J.: Paulist, 1991.

Enard, Wolfgang, Molly Przeworski, Simon E. Fisher, Cecilia S. L. Lai, Victor Wiebe, Takashi Kitan, Anthony P. Monaco, and Svante Pääbo. "Molecular Evolution of FOXP2, a Gene Involved in Speech and Language." *Nature* 418 (August 22, 2002): 869-72.

Falk, Dean. *Finding Our Tongues: Mothers, Infants, and the Origins of Language.* New York: Perseus Book Group/Basic Books, 2009.

———. "Prelinguistic Evolution in Early Hominins: Whence Motherese?" *Behavioural and Brain Sciences* 27 (2004): 491-541.

Fehr, Ernst, and Herbert Gintis. "Human Motivation and Social Cooperation: Experimental and Analytical Foundations." *Annual Review of Sociology* 33 (2007): 43-64.

Fergusson, David. *Faith and Its Critics: A Conversation.* Oxford: Oxford University Press, 2009.

Fitch, W. Tecumseh. "Comparative Vocal Production and the Evolution of Speech: Re-interpreting the Descent of the Larynx." In *The Transition to Language,* edited by Alison Wray, pp. 21-45. Oxford: Oxford University Press, 2010.

Frank, Robert H. *Passions with Reason: The Strategic Role of the Emotions.* New York and London: Norton, 1988.

Frayer, David. "Cranial Base Flattening in Europe: Neanderthals and More Recent

Homo sapiens." *American Journal of Physical Anthropology,* suppl. 14 (1992): 77.

Fuentes, Agustín. "Blurring the Biological and Social in Human Becomings." In *Biosocial Becomings: Integrating Social and Biological Anthropology,* edited by Tim Ingold and Gisli Palsson, pp. 42-58. Cambridge: Cambridge University Press, 2013.

———. "The Community Niche as Focal Context in Assessing Pleistocene Human Evolution." *Current Anthropology,* in preparation.

———. "Cooperation, Conflict and Niche Construction in the Genus *Homo*." In *War, Peace, and Human Nature: The Convergence of Cultural and Evolutionary Views,* edited by Douglas P. Fry, pp. 78-94. Oxford: Oxford University Press, 2013.

———. "Ethnoprimatology and the Anthropology of the Human-Primate Interface." *Annual Review of Anthropology* 41 (2012): 101-17.

———. "The Humanity of Animals and the Animality of Humans: A View from Biological Anthropology Inspired by J. M. Coetzee's *Elizabeth Costello*." *American Anthropologist* 108, no. 1 (2006): 124-32.

———. "Naturecultural Encounters in Bali: Monkeys, Temples, Tourists and Ethnoprimatology." *Cultural Anthropology* 25, no. 4 (2010): 600-624.

———. *Race, Monogamy, and Other Lies They Told You: Busting Myths about Human Nature.* Berkeley: University of California Press, 2012.

———. "Social Minds and Social Selves: Redefining the Human-Alloprimate Interface." In *The Politics of Species: Reshaping Our Relationships with Other Animals,* edited by Raymond Corby and Annette Lanjouw, pp. 179-88. Cambridge: Cambridge University Press, 2014.

Fuentes, Agustín, and Celia Deane-Drummond. "Exploring Boundaries in Human Becoming: An Argument for the Crucial Importance of Multispecies Relationships in Human Evolution Examined through a Community Niche and Theological Lens." *Philosophy, Theology and the Sciences* (2014).

Fuentes, Agustín, Matthew Wyczalkowski, and Katherine C. MacKinnon. "Niche Construction through Cooperation: A Non-linear Dynamics Contribution to Modeling Facets of the Evolutionary History in the Genus *Homo*." *Current Anthropology* 51 (2010): 435-44.

Galef, Bennett G. "Culture in Animals?" In *The Question of Animal Culture,* edited by Kevin N. Laland and Bennett G. Galef, pp. 222-46. Cambridge: Harvard University Press, 2009.

Ghiselin, Michael T. *The Economy of Nature and the Evolution of Sex.* Berkeley: University of California Press, 1974.

Giddens, Anthony. *New Rules of Sociological Method.* London: Hutchinson, 1976.

Gong, Tao, and Lan Shuai. "Modeling the Co-evolution of Joint Attention and Language." *Proceedings of the Royal Society B* 279, no. 1747 (2012): 4643-51.

Gould, Stephen Jay. *The Structure of Evolutionary Theory.* Cambridge: Harvard University Press, Belknap Press, 2002.

Green, Joel. "Humanity — Created, Restored, Transformed, Embodied." In *Rethinking Human Nature: A Multidisciplinary Approach,* edited by Malcolm Jeeves, pp. 271-94. Grand Rapids: Eerdmans, 2011.

Grodzinski, Uri, and Nicola S. Clayton. "Problems Faced by Food-Caching Corvids and the Evolution of Cognitive Solutions." *Philosophical Transactions of the Royal Society B* 365 (2010): 977-87.

Grumett, David. "Christ the Lamb of God and the Christian Doctrine of God." Presentation to "Animals and Religion Consultation, Thinking Animals: Re-thinking Theology; Abrahamic and Indigenous Traditions," American Academy of Religion Conference, Atlanta, October 30, 2010.

———. *Teilhard de Chardin: Theology, Humanity, and Cosmos.* Leuven: Peeters, 2005.

Haidt, Jonathan. "The Moral Emotions." In *Handbook of Affective Sciences,* edited by Richard J. Davidson, Klaus R. Scherer, and H. Hill Goldsmith, pp. 852-70. Oxford: Oxford University Press, 2003.

Hall, Pamela. *Narrative and the Natural Law.* Notre Dame, Ind.: University of Notre Dame Press, 1994.

Hamilton, W. D. "The Genetical Evolution of Social Behavior, I and II." *Journal of Theoretical Biology* 7 (1964): 1-52.

Haraway, Donna. *The Companion Species Manifesto: Dogs, People, and Significant Others.* Chicago: Prickly Paradigm, 2003.

———. *When Species Meet.* Minneapolis: University of Minnesota Press, 2008.

Hare, Robert. *Without Conscience: The Disturbing World of the Psychopaths among Us.* New York: Guildford Press, 1993.

Harrison, Victoria. *The Apologetic Value of Human Holiness: Von Balthasar's Christocentric Philosophical Anthropology.* Dordrecht: Kluwer Academic, 2000.

Hart, Donna, and Robert W. Sussman. *Man the Hunted: Primates, Predators, and Human Evolution.* Boulder, Colo.: Westview Press, 2008.

Haught, John. *God after Darwin: A Theology of Evolution.* Boulder, Colo.: Westview Press, 2007.

Herman, Louis M., Douglas G. Richards, and James P. Wolz. "Comprehension of Sentences by Bottlenosed Dolphins." *Cognition* 16 (1984): 129-219.

Hewlett, Barry. "Human Relations Area Files." In *Diverse Contexts of Human Infancy.* Englewood Cliffs, N.J.: Prentice-Hall, 1989.

Hill, Peggy S. M. *Vibrational Communication in Animals.* Cambridge: Harvard University Press, 2008.

Hitlin, Steven. *Moral Selves, Evil Selves: The Social Psychology of Conscience.* Basingstoke: Palgrave Macmillan, 2008.

Hockings, Kimberley J., and Tatyana Humle. "Best Practice Guidelines for the

Prevention and Mitigation of Conflict between Humans and Great Apes." Gland, Switzerland: IUCN/SCC Primate Spec. Group, 2009.

Horowitz, Alexandra. "Fair Is Fine, but More Is Better: Limits to Inequity Aversion in the Domestic Dog." *Social Justice Research* 25 (2012): 195-212.

Hrdy, Sarah Blaffer. *Mother Nature: A History of Mothers, Infants, and Natural Selection.* New York: Pantheon Books, 1999.

———. *Mothers and Others: The Evolutionary Origins of Mutual Understanding.* Cambridge: Harvard University Press, Belknap Press, 2009.

Hutchins, Edwin. *Cognition in the Wild.* Cambridge: MIT Press, 1994.

Huyssteen, J. Wentzel van. *Alone in the World? Human Uniqueness in Science and Theology.* Grand Rapids: Eerdmans, 2006.

Ingold, Tim. "Humanity and Animality." In *Companion Encyclopedia of Anthropology,* edited by Tim Ingold, pp. 14-32. London: Routledge, 1994.

———. Introduction to *ReDrawing Anthropology: Materials, Movements, Lines,* edited by Tim Ingold, pp. 1-20. Farnham: Ashgate, 2011.

———. Introduction to *What Is an Animal?* edited by Tim Ingold, pp. 1-16. London: Routledge, 1994.

———. *The Perception of the Environment: Essays on Livelihood, Dwelling, and Skill.* London: Routledge, 2011.

———. "The Wedge and the Knot: Hammering and Stitching the Face of Nature." In *Nature, Space, and the Sacred: Transdisciplinary Perspectives,* edited by Sigurd Bergmann, Peter Manley Scott, Maria Jansdotter Samuelson, and Heinrich Bedford-Strohm, pp. 147-62. Farnham: Ashgate, 2009.

Itakura, Shoji. "Gaze Following and Joint Visual Attention in Nonhuman Animals." *Japanese Psychological Research* 46, no. 3 (2004): 216-26.

Jablonka, Eva, and Marion Lamb. *Evolution in Four Dimensions: Genetic, Epigenetic, Behavioral, and Symbolic Variation in the History of Life.* Cambridge: MIT Press, 2005.

Jeeves, Malcolm. "The Emergence of Human Distinctiveness: The Story from Neuropsychology and Evolutionary Psychology." In *Re-thinking Human Nature: A Multidisciplinary Approach,* edited by Malcolm Jeeves, pp. 176-205. Grand Rapids: Eerdmans, 2011.

———, ed. *Re-thinking Human Nature: A Multidisciplinary Approach.* Grand Rapids: Eerdmans, 2011.

Jensen, Keith, Josep Call, and Michael Tomasello. "Chimpanzees Are Rational Maximizers in an Ultimatum Game." *Science* 104 (2007): 13046-51.

Johnson, Dominic. *Payback: God's Punishment and the Evolution of Cooperation.* Oxford: Oxford University Press, 2013.

———. "Why God Is the Best Punisher." *Religion, Brain and Behavior* 1, no. 1 (2011): 77-84.

Jonas, Hans. *The Phenomenon of Life: Towards a Philosophical Biology.* Evanston, Ill.: Northwestern University Press, 2001 (1966).

Jong, Jonathan, and Aku Visala. "Three Quests for Human Nature: Some Philosophical Reflections." *Philosophy, Theology and the Sciences,* in preparation.

Joyce, Richard. *The Evolution of Morality.* Cambridge: MIT Press, 2006.

Kagan, Jerome. "Morality, Reason and Love." In *Altruism and Altruistic Love: Science, Philosophy, and Religion in Dialogue,* edited by Stephen G. Post, Lynn G. Underwood, and William B. Hurlbut, pp. 40-50. New York: Oxford University Press, 2002.

Kane, Robert. *The Oxford Handbook of Free Will.* 2nd ed. Oxford: Oxford University Press, 2011.

Kelsey, David. *Eccentric Existence: A Theological Anthropology.* Vol. 1. Louisville: Westminster John Knox, 2009.

———. *Eccentric Existence: A Theological Anthropology.* Vol. 2. Louisville: Westminster John Knox, 2009.

Kendal, Jeremy, Jamshid J. Tehrani, and F. John Odling-Smee. "Human Niche Construction in Interdisciplinary Focus." *Philosophical Transactions of the Royal Society B* 366 (2011): 785-92.

Kenny, Anthony. *What I Believe.* London: Continuum, 2007.

Kilby, Karen. *Balthasar: A (Very) Critical Introduction.* Grand Rapids: Eerdmans, 2012.

Kirksey, S. Eban, and Stephan Helmreich. "The Emergence of Multispecies Ethnography." *Cultural Anthropology* 25, no. 4 (2010): 545-76.

Knight, John, ed. *Animals in Person: Cultural Perspectives on Human-Animal Interactions.* New York: Berg, 2005.

Konner, Melvin. *The Evolution of Childhood: Relationships, Emotion, Mind.* Cambridge: Harvard University Press, Belknap Press, 2011.

Korsgaard, Christine. "Morality and the Distinctiveness of Human Action." In *Primates and Philosophers: How Morality Evolved,* edited by Frans de Waal, pp. 110-12. Princeton: Princeton University Press, 2009.

Laland, Kevin, and Gillian Brown. *Sense and Nonsense: Evolutionary Perspectives on Human Behavior.* Oxford: Oxford University Press, 2011.

Laland, Kevin N., F. John Odling-Smee, and Marc W. Feldman. "Cultural Niche Construction and Human Evolution." *Behavioral Brain Sciences* 23 (2000): 131-75.

Lash, Nicholas. *The Beginning and End of Religion.* Cambridge: Cambridge University Press, 1996.

Lemos, John. *Common Sense Darwinism: Evolution, Morality, and the Human Condition.* Chicago: Open Court, 2008.

Lieberman, Philip. *The Unpredictable Species: What Makes Human Beings Unique.* Princeton: Princeton University Press, 2013.

Linzey, Andrew. *Why Animal Suffering Matters: Philosophy, Theology, and Practical Ethics.* Oxford: Oxford University Press, 2009.

Losinger, Anton. *The Anthropological Turn: The Human Orientation of the Theology of Karl Rahner.* New York: Fordham University Press, 2000.

MacIntyre, Alasdair. *After Virtue.* London: Duckworth, 1981.

———. *Dependent Rational Animals: Why Human Beings Need the Virtues.* Chicago: Open Court, 1999.

———. *Three Rival Versions of Moral Inquiry.* Notre Dame, Ind.: University of Notre Dame Press, 1990.

Magnus, Albertus. *On Animals: A Medieval Summa Zoologica.* Vol. 1. Translated by Kenneth F. Kitchell and Irven Michael Resnick. Baltimore: Johns Hopkins University Press, 1999.

———. *On Animals: A Medieval Summa Zoologica.* Vol. 2. Translated by Kenneth F. Kitchell and Irven Michael Resnick. Baltimore: Johns Hopkins University Press, 1999.

Matsuzawa, Tetsuro, Masaki Tomonaga, and Masayuki Tanaka, eds. *Cognitive Development in Chimpanzees.* Tokyo: Springer-Verlag, 2006.

Mattison, William III. "Can Christians Possess the Acquired Virtues?" *Theological Studies* 72 (2011): 558-85.

McCabe, Herbert. "Animals and Us." In *The Good Life: Ethics and the Pursuit of Happiness,* pp. 95-114. London: Continuum, 2005.

———. *The Good Life: Ethics and the Pursuit of Happiness.* London: Continuum, 2005.

McCowan, Brenda, and Diana Reiss. "The Fallacy of 'Signature Whistles' in Bottlenose Dolphins: A Comparative Perspective of 'Signature Information' in Animal Vocalizations." *Animal Behaviour* 62 (2001): 1151-62.

McFadyen, Alistair. *The Call to Personhood.* Cambridge: Cambridge University Press, 1990.

McGregor, Peter. Introduction to *Animal Communication Networks,* edited by Peter McGregor, pp. 1-6. Cambridge: Cambridge University Press, 2005.

McGrew, William. *Chimpanzee Material Culture: Implications for Human Evolution.* Cambridge: Cambridge University Press, 1992.

———. "Culture in Non-human Primates?" *Annual Review of Anthropology* 27 (1998): 301-28.

Mercado, Eduardo, III. "Mapping Individual Variations in Learning Capacity." *International Journal of Comparative Psychology* 24 (2011): 4-35.

Meynard, Thierry, ed. *Teilhard and the Future of Humanity.* New York: Fordham University Press, 2006.

Midgley, Mary. *Beast and Man: The Roots of Human Nature.* 2nd ed. London: Routledge, 1995; original 1978.

———. *The Ethical Primate: Humans, Freedom, and Morality.* London: Routledge, 2004.

Milner, Robert. *Thomas Aquinas on the Passions.* Cambridge: Cambridge University Press, 2009.

Milton, Kay. "Anthropomorphism or Egomorphism: The Perception of Non-human Persons by Human Ones." In *Animals in Person: Cultural Perspectives on Human-Animal Interactions,* edited by John Knight, pp. 255-71. New York: Berg, 2005.

Mirkes, Renée. "Aquinas on the Unity of Perfect Moral Virtue." *American Catholic Philosophical Quarterly* 71, no. 4 (1998): 589-605.

Mithen, Stephen. *The Singing Neanderthals: The Origins of Music, Language, Mind, and Body.* London: Orion/Phoenix, 2005.

Moffat, James. *Love in the New Testament.* London: Hodder and Stoughton, 1929.

Moltmann, Jürgen. "The Ecological Crisis: Peace with Nature?" *Scottish Journal of Religious Studies* 9 (1988): 5-18.

Mongrain, Kevin. *The Systematic Thought of Hans Urs von Balthasar: An Irenaean Retrieval.* New York: Herder and Herder, 2002.

Munz, Peter. *Beyond Wittgenstein's Poker: New Light on Popper and Wittgenstein.* Farnham: Ashgate, 2004.

Murray, Michael. "Scientific Explanations of Religion and the Justification of Religious Belief." In *The Believing Primate: Scientific, Philosophical, and Theological Reflections on the Origin of Religion,* edited by Jeffrey Schloss and Michael J. Murray, pp. 168-78. Oxford: Oxford University Press, 2009.

Neville, Robert Cummings. *The Truth of Broken Symbols.* Albany: State University of New York Press, 1996.

Nguyen, Nam H., Emily D. Klein, and Thomas R. Zentall. "Imitation of a Two Action Sequence by Pigeons." *Psychonomic Bulletin and Review* 12, no. 3 (2005): 514-18.

Nichols, Aidan. *No Bloodless Myth: A Guide through Balthasar's Dramatics.* Edinburgh: T. & T. Clark, 2000.

Noble, William, and Iain Davidson. *Human Evolution, Language, and Mind: A Psychological and Archaeological Enquiry.* Cambridge: Cambridge University Press, 1996.

Noske, Barbara. "The Animal Question in Anthropology: A Commentary." *Society and Animals* 1, no. 2 (1993): 185-90.

Nowak, Martin, Corina Tarnita, and Edward O. Wilson. "The Evolution of Eusociality." *Nature* 466 (2010): 1057-62.

Nowak, Martin, with Roger Highfield. *Super Cooperators: Altruism, Evolution, and Why We Need Each Other to Succeed.* New York: Free Press, 2011.

Nowak, Martin, and Sarah Coakley. *Evolution, Games, and God: The Principle of Cooperation.* Cambridge: Harvard University Press, 2013.

Nuccetelli, Susana, and Gary Seay. *Ethical Naturalism: Current Debates.* Cambridge: Cambridge University Press, 2012.

Nussbaum, Martha. *Frontiers of Justice.* Cambridge: Harvard University Press, Belknap Press, 2006.

Nygren, Anders. *Agape and Eros.* Translated by Philip Watson. New York: Harper and Row, 1957 (1930).

Oakes, Edward T. *Pattern of Redemption: The Theology of Hans Urs von Balthasar.* New York: Continuum, 1994.

Odling-Smee, F. John. "Niche Inheritance." In *Evolution: The Extended Synthesis,* edited by Massimo Pigliucci and Gerd B. Muller, pp. 175-207. Cambridge: MIT Press, 2010.

Oord, Thomas Jay. *Defining Love: A Philosophical, Scientific, and Theological Engagement.* Grand Rapids: Brazos, 2010.

———. *The Nature of Love: A Theology.* St. Louis: Chalice Press, 2010.

Page, Ruth. *God and the Web of Creation.* London: SCM, 2009.

Pagola, José. *Jesus: A Historical Approximation.* Miami: Convivium Press, 2012.

Pannenberg, Wolfhart. *Anthropology in Theological Perspective.* Translated by Matthew J. O'Connell. Philadelphia: Westminster, 1985.

Pasnau, Robert. *Thomas Aquinas on Human Nature: A Philosophical Study of "Summa Theologiae."* Cambridge: Cambridge University Press, 2001.

Pearce, John M. *Animal Learning and Cognition.* New York: Psychology Press, 2008.

Penn, Derek C., and Daniel J. Povinelli. "On the Lack of Evidence That Non-human Animals Possess Anything Remotely Resembling a 'Theory of Mind.'" *Philosophical Transactions of the Royal Society B* 362 (2007): 731-44.

———. "On the Lack of Evidence That Non-human Animals Possess Anything Remotely Resembling a 'Theory of Mind.'" In *Social Intelligence: From Brain to Culture,* edited by Nathan Emery, Nicola Clayton, and Chris Firth, pp. 393-414. Oxford: Oxford University Press, 2008.

Penn, Derek C., K. J. Holyoak, and Daniel J. Povinelli. "Darwin's Mistake: Explaining the Discontinuity between Human and Nonhuman Minds." *Behavioral and Brain Sciences* 31 (2008): 109-78.

Pepperberg, Irene. *Alex and Me: How a Scientist and a Parrot Discovered a Hidden World of Animal Intelligence and Formed a Deep Bond in the Process.* New York: Harper Perennial, 2009.

Peters, Ted. *Playing God: Genetic Determinism and Human Freedom.* New York: Routledge, 1997.

Peterson, Dale. *The Moral Lives of Animals.* New York: Bloomsbury Press, 2011.

Piattelli-Palmarini, Massimo, and Juan Uriagereka. "A Geneticist's Dream, a Linguist's Nightmare: The Case of FOXP2." In *The Biolinguistic Enterprise: New Perspectives on the Evolution and Nature of Human Language Faculty,* edited by Anna Maria Di Sciullo and Cedric Boeckx, pp. 100-125. Oxford: Oxford University Press, 2011.

Pierce, Claude A. *Conscience in the New Testament.* London: SCM, 1955.

Pinsent, Andrew. *The Second Person Perspective in Aquinas Ethics: Virtues and Gifts.* London: Routledge, 2012.

Plantinga, Alvin. "Games Scientists Play." In *The Believing Primate,* edited by Jeffrey Schloss and Michael J. Murray, pp. 139-67. Oxford: Oxford University Press, 2009.

Polkinghorne, John. *Science and Providence.* London: SPCK, 1989.

Porter, Jean. *Ministers of the Law: A Natural Law Theory of Legal Authority.* Grand Rapids: Eerdmans, 2010.

———. *Natural and Divine Law: Reclaiming the Tradition for Christian Ethics.* Grand Rapids: Eerdmans, 1999.

———. "The Natural Law and the Normative Significance of Nature." *Studies in Christian Ethics* 26, no. 2 (2013): 166-73.

———. "Natural Right, Authority and Power: The Theological Trajectory of Human Rights." *Journal of Law, Philosophy and Culture* 3, no. 1 (2009): 299-314.

———. *Nature as Reason: A Thomistic Theory of the Natural Law.* Grand Rapids: Eerdmans, 2005.

Price, Sara A., and Sarah F. Brosnan. "To Each according to His Need? Variability in the Responses to Inequity in Non-human Primates." *Social Justice Research* 25 (2012): 140-69.

Prinz, Jesse. *Beyond Human Nature: How Culture and Experience Shape the Human Mind.* London and New York: Norton, 2012.

Quash, Ben. *Theology and the Drama of History.* Cambridge: Cambridge University Press, 2005.

Rahner, Karl. *Hominisation: The Evolutionary Origin of Man as a Theological Problem.* Translated by W. T. O'Hara. New York: Herder and Herder, 1965 (1958).

———. "Man (Anthropology): Theological." In *Sacramentum Mundi III,* edited by Karl Rahner, pp. 365-70. New York: Herder and Herder, 1969.

———. "Man (Anthropology) III. Theological." In *Encyclopedia of Theology: A Concise Sacramentum Mundi,* edited by Karl Rahner, pp. 887-93. London: Burns and Oates, 1975.

———. *Theological Investigations.* Vol. 17, *Jesus, Man, and the Church.* Translated by Margaret Kohl. New York: Crossroad, 1981.

Raihani, Nichola J., and Katherine McAuliffe. "Does Inequity Aversion Motivate Punishment? Cleaner Fish as a Model System." *Social Justice Research* 25 (2012): 213-31.

Rawls, John. *Theory of Justice.* Cambridge: MIT Press, 1971.

Regan, Tom. *The Case for Animal Rights.* Los Angeles: University of California Press, 1983.

Reynhout, Kenneth. *Interdisciplinary Interpretation: Paul Ricoeur and the Hermeneutics of Theology and Science.* Lanham, Md.: Lexington Books/Rowman and Littlefield, 2013.

Robinson, Andrew. *God and the World of Signs: Trinity, Evolution, and the Metaphysical Semiotics of C. S. Peirce.* Leiden: Brill, 2012.

Rogers, Eugene. *Sexuality and the Christian Body: Their Way into the Triune God.* Oxford: Wiley/Blackwell, 1999.

———. *Thomas Aquinas and Karl Barth: Sacred Doctrine and the Natural Knowledge of God.* Notre Dame, Ind.: University of Notre Dame Press, 1999.

Rose, Deborah Bird. "Introduction: Writing in the Anthropocene." *Australian Humanities Review* 49 (2009): 87.

Röska-Hardy, Louise. "Introduction — Issues and Themes in Comparative Studies: Language, Cognition and Culture." In *Learning from Animals: Examining the Nature of Human Uniqueness,* edited by Louise S. Röska-Hardy and Eva M. Neumann-Held, pp. 1-12. Hove, U.K., and New York: Psychology Press, 2009.

Rossano, Matt J. *Supernatural Selection: How Religion Evolved.* New York: Oxford University Press, 2010.

Ruse, Michael. *The Philosophy of Human Evolution.* Cambridge: Cambridge University Press, 2012.

Russell, Robert John. *Time in Eternity: Pannenberg, Physics, and Eschatology in Creative Mutual Interaction.* Notre Dame, Ind.: University of Notre Dame Press, 2012.

Sarot, Marcel. "Christian Faith, Free Will and Neuroscience." Paper delivered to the European Society for Philosophy of Religion, Soesterberg, the Netherlands, September 1, 2012. Published in *Ars Disputandi,* in press.

Schaefer, Jame. *Theological Foundations for Environmental Ethics: Reconstructing Patristic and Medieval Concepts.* Washington, D.C: Georgetown University Press, 2009.

Schloss, Jeffrey. "Darwinian Explanations of Morality: Accounting for the Normal but Not the Normative." *Zygon* (2013).

———. "Emerging Accounts of Altruism: 'Love Creation's Final Law?'" In *Altruism and Altruistic Love: Science, Philosophy, and Religion in Dialogue,* edited by Stephen G. Post, Lynn G. Underwood, and William B. Hurlbut, pp. 212-42. New York: Oxford University Press, 2002.

———. "Introduction to Part III." In *Altruism and Altruistic Love: Science, Philosophy, and Religion in Dialogue,* edited by Stephen G. Post, Lynn G. Underwood, and William B. Hurlbut, pp. 145-50. New York: Oxford University Press, 2002.

———. "Sociobiological Explanations of Altruistic Ethics: Necessary, Sufficient or Irrelevant to the Human Moral Quest?" In *Investigating the Biological Foundations of Human Morality,* edited by James Hurd, pp. 107-45. New York: Edwin Mellen Press, 1996.

Schloss, Jeffrey, and Michael Murray. "How Might Evolution Lead to Hell?" *Religion, Brain and Behavior* 1, no. 1 (2011): 93-99.

———, eds. *The Believing Primate: Scientific, Philosophical, and Theological Reflections on the Origin of Religion.* Oxford: Oxford University Press, 2009.

Sen, Amartya. *The Idea of Justice.* London: Penguin, 2009.

Shea, John. "*Homo sapiens* Is as *Homo sapiens* Was: Behavioral Variability versus 'Behavioral Modernity' in Palaeolithic Archaeology." *Current Anthropology* 52 (2011): 1-35.

Shettleworth, Sara. *Cognition, Evolution, and Behaviour.* 2nd ed. Oxford: Oxford University Press, 2010.

Shipman, Pat. *The Animal Connection: A New Perspective on What Makes Us Human.* New York: Norton, 2011.

Shults, LeRon. "Wising Up: The Evolution of Natural Theology." *Zygon* 47, no. 3 (2012): 542-48.

Silk, Joan B. "Who Are More Helpful, Humans or Chimpanzees?" *Science* 311 (2007): 1248-49.

Smith, Christian. *Moral, Believing Animals.* Oxford: Oxford University Press, 2003.

———. *What Is a Person? Re-thinking Humanity, Social Life, and the Moral Good from the Person Up.* Chicago: University of Chicago Press, 2010.

Sober, Elliott. *Did Darwin Write the Origin Backwards? Philosophical Essays on Darwin's Theory.* New York: Prometheus Books, 2011.

Sober, Elliott, and David Sloan Wilson. *Unto Others: The Evolution and Psychology of Unselfish Behavior.* Cambridge: Harvard University Press, 1998.

Sosis, Richard, and Eric Bressler. "Co-operation and Commune Longevity: A Test of the Costly Signaling Theory of Religion." *Cross-Cultural Research* 37, no. 2 (2003): 11-39.

Soskice, Janet. "Imago Dei and Sexual Difference: Towards an Eschatological Anthropology." In *Rethinking Human Nature: A Multidisciplinary Approach,* edited by Malcolm Jeeves, pp. 295-306. Grand Rapids: Eerdmans, 2011.

———. *The Kindness of God: Metaphor, Gender, and Religious Language.* Oxford: Oxford University Press, 2007.

Speck, Josef. *Karl Rahners Theologische Anthropologie. Eine Einführung.* Munich: Køsel, 1967.

Spikins, Penny A., H. E. Rutherford, and A. P. Needham. "From Homininity to Humanity: Compassion from the Earliest Archaics to Modern Humans." *Time and Mind: The Journal of Archaeology, Consciousness and Culture* 3, no. 3 (2010): 303-26.

Stenmark, Mikael. "Is There a Human Nature?" *Zygon* 47, no. 4 (2012): 890-902.

Sterelny, Kim. *The Evolved Apprentice: How Evolution Made Humans Unique.* Cambridge: MIT Press, 2012.

Steward, Helen. "Animal Agency." *Inquiry* 52, no. 3 (2009): 217-31.

Stewart-Williams, Steve. *Darwin, God, and the Meaning of Life: How Evolutionary Theory Undermines Everything You Thought You Knew.* Cambridge: Cambridge University Press, 2010.

Strum, Shirley. "Darwin's Monkey: Why Baboons Can't Become Human." *Yearbook of Physical Anthropology* 149 (2012): 3-23.

Stulp, Gert, Nathan J. Emery, Simon Verhulst, and Nicola Clayton. "Western Scrub-Jays Conceal Auditory Information When Competitors Can Hear but Cannot See." *Biology Letters* 5 (2009): 583-85.

Stump, Eleanore. "The Non-Aristotelian Character of Aquinas Ethics: Aquinas on the Passions." *Faith and Philosophy* 28, no. 1 (2011): 29-43.

Sussman, Robert W., and C. Robert Cloninger, eds. *Origins of Altruism and Cooperation.* New York: Springer-Verlag, 2011.

Szerszynski, Bronislaw. "The End of the End of Nature: The Anthropocene and the Fate of the Human." *Oxford Literary Review* 34, no. 2 (2012): 165-84.

Tattersall, Ian. *Masters of the Planet: The Search for Our Human Origins.* New York: Palgrave Macmillan, 2012.

———. "A Possible Context for the Emergence of Human Cognitive and Linguistic Abilities." *Euresis* 4 (2013): 31-39.

Taylor, Charles. *Human Agency and Language: Philosophical Papers.* Cambridge: Cambridge University Press, 1985.

Teilhard de Chardin, Pierre. *The Human Phenomenon.* Translated by Sarah Appleton-Weber. Brighton: Sussex Academic Press, 1999 (1955).

———. *Man's Place in Nature: The Human Zoological Group.* Translated by René Hague. New York: Harper and Row, 1966 (1956).

Timpe, Kevin. "Why Christians Might Be Libertarians: A Response to Lynne Rudder Baker." *Philosophia Christi* 6, no. 2 (2004): 279-88.

Tinbergen, Niko. "On Aims and Methods of Ethology." *Zeitschrift für Tierpsychologie* 20 (1963): 410-33.

Tomasello, Michael. *Constructing a Language: A Usage Based Theory of Language Acquisition.* Cambridge: Harvard University Press, 2005.

———. *Why We Cooperate.* Cambridge: MIT Press, 2009.

Tomasello, Michael, and Josep Call. *Primate Cognition.* Oxford: Oxford University Press, 1997.

Tomasello, Michael, Malinda Carpenter, Josep Call, Tanya Behne, and Henrike Moll. "Understanding and Sharing Intentions: The Origins of Social Cognition." *Behavioral and Brain Sciences* 28 (2005): 675-735.

Tooby, John, and Leda Cosmides. "Friendship and the Banker's Paradox: Other Pathways to the Evolution of Adaptations for Altruism." In *Proceedings of the British Academy: Vol. 88; Evolution of Social Behavior Patterns in Primates and Man,* edited by W. G. Runciman, John M. Smith, and R. I. M. Dunbar, pp. 119-43. Oxford: Oxford University Press, 1996.

Tracy, Thomas. "Evolution, Divine Action and the Problem of Evil." In *Evolutionary and Molecular Biology: Scientific Perspectives on Divine Action,* edited by Robert John Russell, William R. Stoeger, and Francisco J. Ayala, pp. 511-30. Vatican City: Vatican Observatory; Berkeley, Calif.: Center for Theology and the Natural Sciences, 1998.

Trivers, Robert L. "The Evolution of Reciprocal Altruism." *Quarterly Review of Biology* 46 (1971): 35-57.

Tyack, Peter L. "Development and Social Functions of Signature Whistles in Bottlenose Dolphins *Tursiops truncates.*" *Bioacoustics* 8, no. 1-2 (1997): 21-46.

Vaart, Elske van der, Rineke Verbrugge, and Charlotte K. Hemelrijk. "Corvid Recaching without 'Theory of Mind': A Model." *PloS ONE* 7, no. 3 (2012).

Vass, George. *The Mystery of Man and the Foundations of a Theological System.* London: Sheed and Ward, 1985.

Vauclair, Jacques. "Categorisation and Conceptual Behaviour in Nonhuman Primates." In *The Cognitive Animal: Empirical and Theoretical Perspectives on Animal Cognition,* edited by Marc Bekoff, Colin Allen, and Gordon M. Burghardt, pp. 239-45. Cambridge: MIT Press, 2002.

Velde, Rudi te. "*Natura In Seipsa Recurva Est:* Duns Scotus and Aquinas on the Relationship between Nature and Will." In *John Duns Scotus,* edited by E. P. Bos, pp. 155-70. Amsterdam: Rodopi, 1988.

Verplaetse, Jan, Jelle de Schrijver, Sven Vanneste, and Johan Braeckman, eds. *The Moral Brain: Essays on the Evolutionary and Neuroscientific Aspects of Morality.* Dordrecht: Springer, 2009.

Vidal, Fernando. "Human Persons and Human Brains: A Historical Perspective within the Christian Tradition." In *Rethinking Human Nature: A Multidisciplinary Approach,* edited by Malcolm Jeeves, pp. 30-60. Grand Rapids: Eerdmans, 2011.

Visala, Aku. "Theism, Compatibilism and Neurodeterminism: A Response to Marcel Sarot." Paper delivered to the European Society for Philosophy of Religion, Soesterberg, the Netherlands, September 1, 2012. *Ars Disputandi,* in press.

Waal, Frans de. *The Age of Empathy: Nature's Lessons for a Kinder Society.* London: Souvenir Press, 2009.

———. *Chimpanzee Politics.* Baltimore: Johns Hopkins University Press, 1997.

———. "The Evolution of Empathy." In *The Compassionate Instinct: The Science of Human Goodness,* edited by Dacher Keltner, Jason Marsh, and Jeremy Adam Smith, pp. 16-25. New York: Norton, 2010.

———. *Good Natured: The Origins of Right and Wrong in Humans and Other Animals.* Cambridge: Harvard University Press, 1996.

———. "Morally Evolved: Primate Social Instincts, Human Morality, and the Rise and Fall of 'Veneer Theory.'" In Frans de Waal, *Primates and Philosophers,* edited by Stephen Macedo and Josiah Ober, pp. 1-80. Princeton: Princeton University Press, 2006.

———. "Putting the Altruism Back into Altruism: The Evolution of Empathy." *Annual Review of Psychology* 59 (2008): 279-300.

Waddell, Paul. *Friendship and the Moral Life.* Notre Dame, Ind.: University of Notre Dame Press, 1989.

Wade, Nicholas. *The Faith Instinct: How Religion Evolved and Why It Endures.* New York: Penguin Press, 2009.

Wegner, Daniel M. "Précis of 'The Illusion of Conscious Will.'" *Behavioral and Brain Sciences* 27, no. 5 (2004): 2-45.

Wells, Spencer. *Pandora's Seed: Why the Hunter-Gatherer Holds the Key to Our Survival.* London: Penguin Books, 2011.

Wenberg, Robert. *God, Humans, and Animals: An Invitation to Enlarge Our Moral Universe.* Grand Rapids: Eerdmans, 2003.

Wildman, Wesley J. *Science and Religious Anthropology: A Spiritually Evocative Naturalist Interpretation of Human Life.* Farnham: Ashgate, 2009.

Williams, Bernard. *Moral Luck.* Cambridge: Cambridge University Press, 1981.

Williams, Rowan. "Balthasar and Rahner." In *The Analogy of Beauty: The Theology of Hans Urs von Balthasar,* edited by John Riches, pp. 11-34. Edinburgh: T. & T. Clark, 1986.

Wilson, Andrew, and Sabrina Golonka. "Embodied Cognition Is Not What You Think It Is." *Frontiers in Psychology* 4 (2013): 1-13.

Wilson, David Sloan. "Clash of Paradigms." 2012. Online: http://www.thisviewoflife.com/index.php/magazine/articles/clash-of-paradigms (accessed March 18, 2013).

———. "On the Relationship between Evolutionary and Psychological Definitions of Altruism and Selfishness." *Biology and Philosophy* 7, no. 1 (1992): 61-68.

———. "Religion and Spirituality in the Context of Everyday Life." Public lecture, Center of Theological Inquiry and Center for the Study of Religion, Princeton University, October 4, 2012.

Wilson, E. O. *On Human Nature.* Cambridge: Harvard University Press, 1978.

———. *The Social Conquest of Earth.* New York: Liveright Publishing/Norton, 2012.

Wolterstorff, Nicholas. *Until Justice and Peace Embrace.* Grand Rapids: Eerdmans, 1983.

Wood, Bernard. "Reconstructing Human Evolution: Achievements, Challenges, and Opportunities." *Proceedings of the National Academy of Sciences USA* 107 (2010): 8902-9.

Wood, Matthew. *Vitalism: The History of Herbalism, Homeopathy, and Flower Essences.* 2nd ed. Berkeley, Calif.: North Atlantic Books, 2000.

Wray, Alison. "Introduction: Conceptualizing Transition in an Evolving Field." In *The Transition to Language,* edited by Alison Wray, pp. 1-18. Oxford: Oxford University Press, 2010.

Wynne, Clive D. L. *Animal Cognition: The Mental Lives of Animals.* Basingstoke: Palgrave Macmillan, 2001.

Zak, Paul J. *The Moral Molecule: The Source of Love and Prosperity.* New York: Dutton, 2012.

Zilhao, Joao. "The Emergence of Language, Art and Symbolic Thinking." In *Homo symbolicus: The Dawn of Language, Imagination, and Spirituality,* edited by Christopher N. Henshilwood and Francesco D'Errico, pp. 111-31. Amsterdam: John Benjamins, 2011.

Zizioulas, John. *The Eucharistic Communion and the World.* London: T. & T. Clark, 2011.

———. "Preserving God's Creation." *King's Theological Review* 12, no. 1 (1990): 1-6.

Index